EP Exam Review

3rd Edition

Volume 2 of 2

Paul Haas, M.D.

April Felton
Scot Felton
Wes Todd

Over the past 20 years, the treatment for complex cardiac arrhythmias has evolved from primary medical therapy to more frequent, invasive, and definitive therapies with ablations. As such, the number of ablations performed has increased substantially. Electrophysiology, once a niche field, has become a well-established specialty throughout hospitals around the world. There is now a tremendous need for lab staff, industry personnel, and physicians trained in the intricacies of electrophysiology. Unfortunately, there are very few formal educational opportunities for trainees. Education is frequently done "on the fly" by more experienced lab members, industry members, and practicing electrophysiologists. This is inadequate. This text is designed to be broad—appropriate for EP lab staff, individuals studying for the RCES and IBHRE exams, industry personnel, and new fellows.

Paul Haas, M.D.

EP Essentials LLC

EP Exam Review

Table of Contents

EP Essentials LLC

Volume 1:

Volume 2:

EP Essentials LLC

Chapter 11
3D Mapping

EP Essentials LLC

3D Map Interpretation

1. From this 3D map match each numbered structure to its name.
   a. **Mitral Orifice**
   b. **LA Appendage**
   c. **Transseptal Catheter**
   d. **Right Inferior Pulmonary Vein**
   e. **Common Left Pulmonary Vein**
   f. **Right Superior Pulmonary Vein**

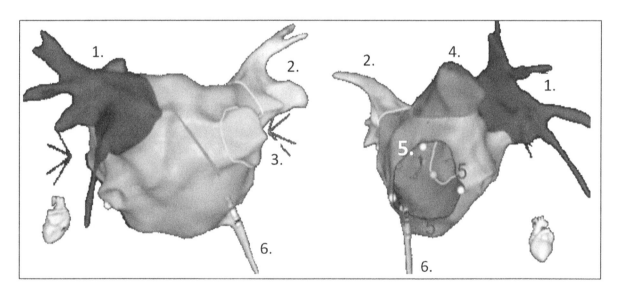

CORRECTLY MATCHED ANSWERS ARE:
1. e. Common Left Pulmonary Vein
2. f. Right Superior Pulmonary Vein
3. d. Right Inferior Pulmonary Vein
4. b. LA Appendage
5. a. Mitral Orifice
6. c. Transseptal Catheter

This shows the two left pulmonary veins (darkest color/blue) joined in one large common antrum. Right image is LAO and left image is a left posterior view.

2. From this 3D map match each numbered structure to its name.
   a. TV
   b. SVC
   c. RAA
   d. RA
   e. Distal CS
   f. LV branch of CS
   g. IVC
   h. CS (Main Body)
   i. Middle Cardiac Vein

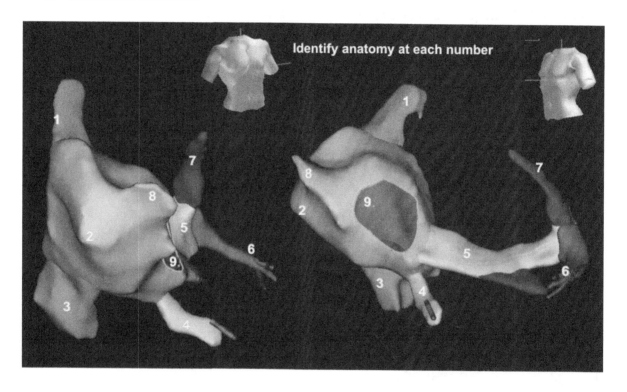

CORRECTLY MATCHED ANSWERS ARE:
   1. b. SVC
   2. d. RA
   3. g. IVC
   4. I. Middle Cardiac Vein (arising from inferior RA)
   5. h. CS Main Body
   6. f. LV branches of CS
   7. e. Distal CS
   8. c. RAA
   9. a. TV

3. This patient returned three years after successful PVI of all four pulmonary veins. He did well until last month when AF recurred. This CARTO image resulted after a curative wide area cardiac ablation (WACA). Match the numbered locations on the CARTO image with their name.

    a. **Focal ablation in LSPV**
    b. **WACA of antrum to RPVs**
    c. **RIPV**
    d. **Transseptal puncture area**
    e. **Right phrenic nerve**
    f. **RSPV**
    g. **LSPV**
    h. **LIPV**
    i. **LAA**

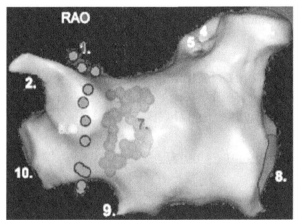 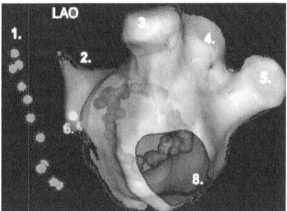

CORRECTLY MATCHED ANSWERS ARE:
1. e. Phrenic
2. f. RSPV
3. i. LAA
4. g. LSPV
5. h. LIPV
6. Focal ablation in RSPV
8. Mitral Valve
9. WACA around RPVs

The LAO view best shows the correct alignment. This shows one of the many possible anomalies in RA anatomy - cardiac vein arising from RA instead of normal CS origin. From EP Digest " Implantation of Dual Chamber Intracardiac Defibrillator"

4. What "normal" tissue setting may be used on a 3D anatomic RV voltage map?
  a. 0.5 mV
  b. 1.5 mV
  c. 4.0 mV
  d. 6.5 mV

ANSWER: b. 1.5 mV. CARTO 3D system uses red for the lowest voltages, while Abbott 3D mapping system uses gray for scar tissue. This is important in post-MI VT, because most reentry sites are bounded by scar tissue.

Using Ensite system (Abbott), "The color display for depicting normal and abnormal voltage myocardium ranged from "red" standing for "electroanatomical scar tissue" (amplitude <0.5 mV) to "purple" representing "electroanatomical normal tissue" (amplitude =1.5 mV). Intermediate colors represent the "electroanatomical border zone" (signal amplitudes between 0.5 and 1.5 mV). JACC, 3-D "Electromechanical Voltage Mapping..." Volume 51, Issue 7, February 2008 >

Using CARTO (Biosense Webster), a three-dimensional electroanatomic voltage map was created of the left ventricular endocardium. Voltage 1.5 mV was classified as normal. Gray point tags indicate sites of catheter contact, but local electrogram (EGM) <0.25 mV, with no pacing capture, consistent with dense scar. See: http://www.innovationsincrm.com/cardiac-rhythm-management/2011/February/51-ventricular-tachycardia-substrate-voltage-map

5. Match the cardiac chamber to its 3D electroanatomic map image (older CARTO image).
  a.   RA
  b.   LA
  c.   RV
  d.   LV

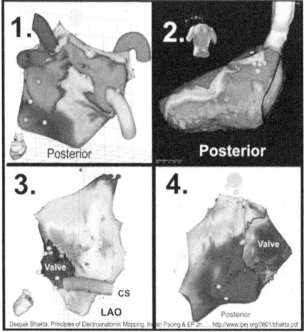

CORRECTLY MATCHED ANSWERS ARE:
1. b. LA - Note 4 PVs
2. d. LV - Note LV apex, AO, MV
3. a. RA - Note CS tube & TV opening
4. c. RV - Note Tricuspid valve the right

Watch for the hole in the shell which will be a valve you can look through to see the opposite wall. Note the tricuspid valve in #3 and #4. CARTO makes the vessels into tubes as shown. In #3 RA, note the CS arising from the area of the tricuspid valve. The little face or heart picture indicates the view. EnSite image at #2 shows the LV apex to the left and mitral valve on the right. LV is football shaped. Unfortunately, the colors don't show up in these images.

6. 3-D anatomic reconstruction is useful in cardiac ablation. Match the name of the mapping system to its primary principle of operation:

a. CARTO (BWI)	**1. Phased array ultrasound**
b. ENSITE (Abbott)	**2. Basket mapping catheter**
c. ICE	**3. Electrical impedance 3D mapping**
d. Rhythmia (Boston)	**4. Magnetic field 3D mapping**

MATCHED ANSWERS:
a. CARTO: 4. Magnetic field 3-D mapping
b. EnSite (Abbott): 3. Electrical Impedance 3-D mapping. Newer Ensite X incorporates magnetics as well but utilized differently than Carto.
c. ICE: 1. Phased array Ultrasound
d. Rhythmia (Boston): 2. Basket mapping catheter

All these systems measure the locations of the cardiac
shell and catheters in an X, Y & Z coordinate system, like GPS mapping.

CARTO: "Magnetic electroanatomic mapping system (CARTO, Biosense-Webster Inc, Diamond Bar, CA) is based on the principle that a coil placed in the magnetic field will generate an electrical current.... In the electrophysiology laboratory, the magnetic field is generated by a unit mounted under the patient table (5 x 10-6 to 5 x 10-5 Tesla) which creates the mapping space around the patient's chest. The locator pad has three [to six] coils (patches), each of which generates a magnetic field which decays as a function of distance from that coil (patch). The sensor within the catheter measures the strength of the magnetic field which determines its distance from each coil.... This mapping system uses proprietary deflectable catheters.... CARTO-Merge® Module facilitates [integration of] ... segmented CT or MRI images... Similarly, the CARTOSound™ Image Integration Module [can] incorporate the electroanatomic map to a map derived from intracardiac echocardiography (ICE)...."

"Ensite (Abbott) The fundamental principle .... is an impedance-based measure, which is dependent on the voltage gradient that exists across tissue when a current is applied through the surface electrodes. This mapping system is based on localization of multiple electrodes using an electrical field generated by three pairs of surface electrodes placed on the patient's body along three orthogonal axes. The patches emit a low-current, high-frequency electrical field (5.7 kHz signal) across the chest using different frequencies for the x, y, and z axes. The conventional catheters are localized by measuring the electrical potential or field strength received by them.... The system also has the capability to import and integrate three-dimensional CT or MRI images to facilitate anatomically based ablation procedures." See: Kabra, "Recent Trends in Imaging for Atrial Fibrillation Ablation, " Indian Pacing Electrophysiology. J. 2010;10(5):215-227 and Deepak Bhakta, Principles of Electroanatomic Mapping, Indian Pacing & EP Jn., ... http ://www.ipej.org/0801/bhakta.pdf

ICE: "Intracardiac ultrasound provides a useful imaging tool for continuous direct visualization of all the chambers of the heart as well as the pulmonary veins during catheter ablation of atrial fibrillation.... One of the main uses of the ICE imaging includes facilitation of transseptal puncture by guiding the needle to the membranous part of the fossa ovalis." ICE is used on PVI ablations to help guide the catheters, cut down on fluoro time, and check for effusions. It is especially useful for lead extractions since you may tear the heart and cause an effusion.

RPM: "Real-time Position Management (RPM) system (Boston Scientific) combines full EP recording functionality with advanced mapping, navigation, and catheter visualization. For this system, two reference catheters and one mapping-ablation catheter are used. This 3-D mapping system uses ultrasound ranging techniques to determine the position of a mapping-ablation catheter compared to the two reference catheters. One reference catheter is positioned in the CS and the other in the RV apex. The mapping-ablation catheter is a 7 Fr, 4-mm tip bidirectional steerable catheter. The reference catheters have a 6 Fr fixed curve distal shaft. The shaft of the CS reference catheter has nine 1-mm ring electrodes and one 2-mm tip electrode (interelectrode distance, 1 mm), whereas the RV reference and ablation catheters contain three 1-mm ring electrodes and one 4-mm tip electrode (interelectrode distance, 1 mm)" See: Issa, chapter on Imaging

7. In 3D anatomical imaging of ventricular scar, a substrate map color-coded may be overlayed on a 3-D LV shell image. What is a substrate map?
   a. **Map of local activation - earliest in red**
   b. **Map of peak-to-peak voltages sampled on endocardial surface**
   c. **Isochronal map depicting all the points with an activation time within a specific range**
   d. **Propagation map of electrical activation waves spreading as a continuous animated loop**

ANSWER: b. Map of peak-to-peak voltages sampled on endocardial surface, sometimes called a voltage or scar map. "In addition to facilitating activation mapping, the CARTO system provides location mapping features capable of recording sites of anatomic relevance, areas of low endocardial voltage representing scar, and areas of ablation. Structures such as the bundle of His can be tagged to prevent inadvertent energy delivery resulting in conduction impairment when ablating tachycardias originating in this region. Vessels such as the CS and PVs may also be marked to supply spatial orientation to assist

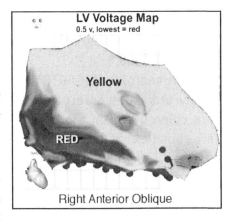

LV Voltage Map
0.5 v, lowest = red
Yellow
RED
Right Anterior Oblique

mapping efforts. Scar mapping can also be achieved by tracing the endocardial surface and recording the amplitude of local potentials. As with endocardial activation, a voltage scale may be arbitrarily chosen to display only the areas of lowest voltage amplitude, to distinguish between areas of scar, dense scar, and relatively normal tissue." Deepak Bhakta, Principles of Electroanatomic Mapping, Indian Pacing & EP Jn., ...
http://www.ipej.org/0801/bhakta.pdf

8. In 3D voltage mapping of patients with history of heart attack, LV scar is usually colored:
   a. Grey/red
   b. Blue/purple
   c. Green/yellow
   d. Orange/yellow

ANSWER: a. Grey/red. Issa says, "The voltage map displays the peak-to-peak amplitude of the electrogram sampled at each site. This value is color-coded and superimposed on the anatomical model, with red as the lowest amplitude and orange, yellow, green, blue, and purple indicating progressively higher amplitudes. The gain on the 3-D color display allows the user to concentrate on a narrow or wide range of potentials. By diminishing the color scale, as might be required to see a fascicular potential or diastolic depolarization during reentry, larger amplitude signals will be eliminated. To visualize the broad spectrum of potentials, present during a tachycardia cycle, the scale would be opened to include an array of colors representing a spectrum of voltages. Local electrogram voltage mapping during sinus, paced, or any other rhythm can help define anatomically correct regions of no voltage (presumed scars or electrical scars), low voltage, and normal voltage, although the true range of normal is often difficult to

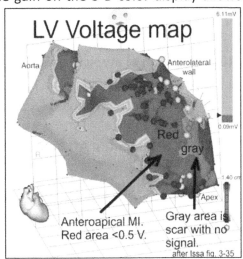

LV Voltage map
6.11mV
Aorta
Anterolateral wall
0.09mV
Red
gray
1.40 cm
Apex
Anteroapical MI.
Red area <0.5 V.
Gray area is scar with no signal.
after Issa fig. 3-35

define, especially with bipolar recordings, and different criteria have been used. Myocardial scars are seen as low voltage, and their delineation can help in understanding the location of the arrhythmia."

"Electroanatomical (CARTO) voltage map of the left ventricle in a patient with ventricular tachycardia after anteroapical myocardial infarction. ...all sites with voltage less than 0.5 mV are colored red on the map, and those with voltage more than 0.6 mV are purple, with interpolation of color for intermediate amplitudes. Usually, the gray area denotes no detectable signal (scar). Red circles denote ablation sites." Areas of infarction are clear and may create borders for reentry. See: Issa, chapter on "Electroanatomical Mapping"

9. 3D isochronal maps show lines or colors:
    a. **Of equal voltage at a specific time in the CL**
    b. **Of wave front progression from an irritable focus**
    c. **Of wave front progression from a reentry exit point**
    d. **Occurring at the same time compared to a reference EGM**

ANSWER: d. Occurring at the same time compared to a reference EGM. Isochrones (same time) are lines that connect points of equal activation time, like in the image the 35 ms isochrone is where the depolarization wave is located 35 ms after the reference, here the beginning of P wave (see reference box). Isochronal maps are the common means of depicting an activation pattern. They are sometimes annotated with arrows to indicate the major propagation paths or colored moving from red (0) through blue. This diagram shows CS pacing of the LA as the activation passes up the LA and across the septum to the RA. If this were a color map, the black (CS=0 time) would be red and move through orange, yellow, green, and blue.

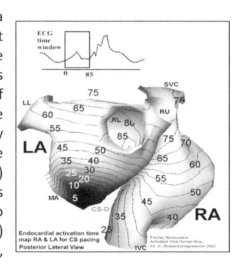

10. What form of atypical atrial flutter is shown in this CARTO isochronal map?
    a. **CW peritricuspid AFL**
    b. **CCW peritricuspid AFL**
    c. **CW perimitral AFL**
    d. **CCW perimitral AFL**

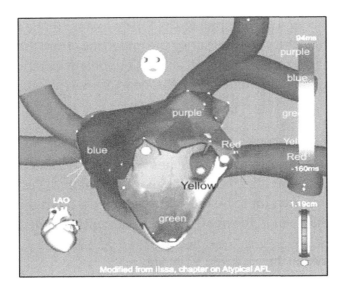

ANSWER: c. CW perimitral AFL around the Mitral annulus (perimitral). This is an LAO view of the LA and PVs, looking through the mitral valve. Since activation proceeds down the LA free wall (red-yellow-green) around the mitral annulus and up the septal wall (blue/purple) it is clockwise perimitral AFL.

11. The main goal of activation mapping of macro reentrant tachycardias (e.g., AFL) is to:
   a. **Identify of the critical isthmus in diastole**
   b. **Determine the direction of the reentry loop**
   c. **Reconstruct the 3-D geometry of the chamber**
   d. **Determine reentry by resetting and entrainment of the tachycardia**

ANSWER: a. Identification of the critical isthmus in diastole. Issa says, "The main goal of activation mapping of macro reentrant tachycardias (e.g., post-MI VT, scar related VT) is identification of the isthmus critical for the macro reentrant circuit [in AFL this is normally the cavotricuspid isthmus] .... Therefore, the goal of activation mapping during macro reentry is finding the site(s) with continuous activity spanning diastole or with an isolated mid-diastolic potential." See: Issa, chapter on Isthmus Dependent AFL

12. The Abbott Ensite contact mapping system utilizes:
   a. **A nitinol expandable basket**
   b. **Electrical impedance mapping**
   c. **Magnetic electroanatomic mapping**
   d. **A balloon mounted multielectrode array**

ANSWER: b. Electrical impedance mapping. The EnSite system made by Abbott creates a 3D model of a chamber in the heart by measuring the impedance from the catheter tip to various skin electrodes. CT images can be imported and built upon. An electrical signal is transmitted between the patches, and catheters within the heart sense the strength of the signal and build the 3D model.

Mapping can be performed with any mapping or ablation catheter. As the physician sweeps the catheter inside the heart chamber it outlines the structures and relays the signals to a computer system which generates the 3D model of the chamber. Resulting images can be colored modified by the operator to be useful. The 3D model helps the physician guide the ablation catheter to the point in the heart where treatment is needed. See: abbott.com

13. This structure is circled in the displayed 3D image.
   a.   **Right Superior Pulmonary Vein**
   b.   **Left Superior Pulmonary Vein**
   c.   **Left Atrial Appendage**
   d.   **Superior Vena Cava**

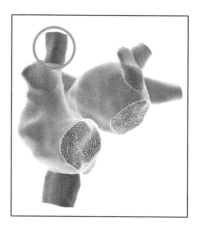

ANSWER: d. Superior Vena Cava. This image is in LAO, notice how the view is through the AV valves (tricuspid & mitral). LAO is helpful is discerning the right vs. left side of the heart.

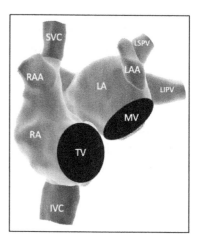

14. This is the area/wall of the left atrium displayed in the 3D map.
   a. Posterior
   b. Anterior
   c. Lateral
   d. Septal

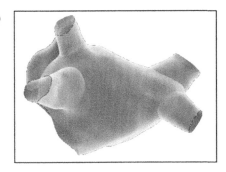

ANSWER: a. Posterior. This is the posterior wall of the left atrium. The left atrium is the most posterior chamber of the heart and pulmonary veins are located on the posterior aspect of the LA. The LAA, on the other hand, is on the anterior aspect of the left atrium.

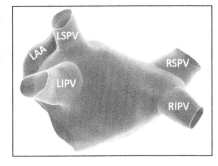

15. What type of map is displayed in the image?
   a. Reentrant RV VT
   b. Reentrant LV VT
   c. Focal RV VT
   d. Focal LV VT

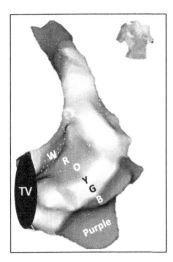

ANSWER: c. Focal RV VT. This is a focal rhythm as the activation on the LAT map travels outward from the earliest (white) location to the latest (purple). Notice the location of the tricuspid valve, this is the clue that it is a map of the RVOT. The complete RV model down to the RV apex was not created since it was not the area of interest. Image modified from: https://ars.els-cdn.com/content/image/1-s2.0-S0972629217302504-gr2.jpg

16. **What is the rhythm observed in the following 3D map?**
    a. **Typical Counterclockwise AFL**
    b. **Typical Clockwise AFL**
    c. **Atrial Tachycardia**
    d. **Sinus Rhythm**

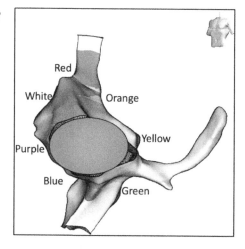

ANSWER: a. Typical Clockwise AFL. With all current mapping systems, white or red identifies the earliest area of activation and purple the latest. This is an LAO view of the right atrium. The circle cut out in the center represents the tricuspid valve. In this image, you may view the wave of activation from white, red, orange, yellow, green, blue, and purple in a clockwise rotation around the valve.

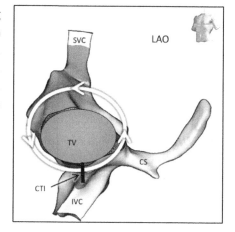

17. **Where is the most likely ablation target for the following rhythm?**
    a. **Sinus Node Modification**
    b. **Cavotricuspid Isthmus**
    c. **Septal Wall**
    d. **SVC to IVC**

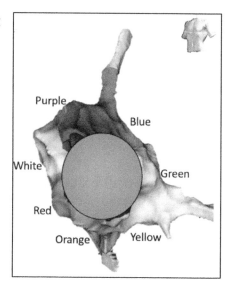

ANSWER: b. Cavotricuspid Isthmus or CTI. This is the area from the tricuspid valve to the IVC which are both nonconductive areas. To terminate an atrial flutter, a line of block must be drawn from a nonconductive area to another nonconductive area. The CTI is the target to terminate the typical counterclockwise AFL displayed in the 3D image. In this image the wave of depolarization travels from white, red, orange, yellow, green, blue, and purple in the counterclockwise direction around the tricuspid valve in this LAO view. In typical atrial flutter, this is the ablation target no matter if the circuit is traveling in the clockwise or counterclockwise direction if the critical isthmus is the CTI.

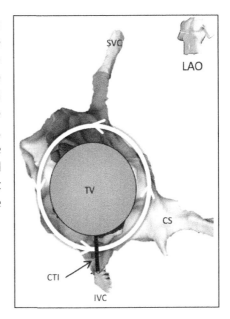

18. The following Rhythmia 3D images represent these map types.
- a. A. Substrate, B. Score
- b. A. Substrate, B. LAT
- c. A. LAT, B. Substrate
- d. A. LAT, B. Score

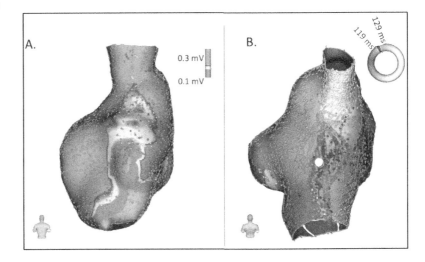

ANSWER. b. A. Substrate, B. LAT. Rhythmia is the 3D mapping system by Boston Scientific. In example A, the scale is in mV. Therefore, this is a voltage or substrate map. This type of map measures the voltage of the tissue to demonstrate healthy vs. diseased tissue or identify any other areas of low voltage such as the IVC which is nonconductive tissue. The scale here is from 0.1 to 0.3 mV, but this scale dependent on the chamber being mapped as well as adjusted dynamically to help identify channels within the low voltage area for example. Example in B is a LAT or local activation time map. This timing map helps to identify sites of early activation as well as signal propagation.

19. This example is a PA view of the right atrium. What is the most likely diagnosis?
- a. Atrial Flutter around a previous transseptal puncture site
- b. Left Atrial Flutter with passive RA activation
- c. Inappropriate Sinus Tachycardia
- d. Typical Clockwise AFL
- e. Incisional RA Flutter

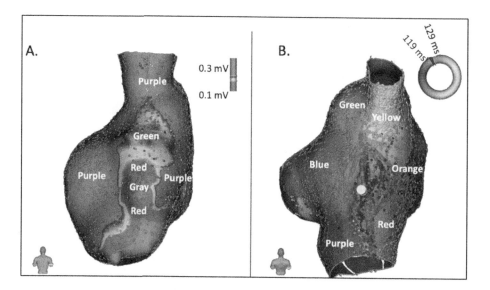

ANSWER: e. Incisional RA Flutter. In this PA view of the RA, significant scaring is observed (A) at the areas of gray and red, correlating with tissue of approximately 0.1 mV or below. This is an area of an incisional scar from prior cardiac surgery. In the LAT map (B), activation is observed traveling around this area of scar from red, orange, yellow, green, blue, and purple. It is a reentrant circuit; therefore, the wavefront continues again in this pattern.

- The circuit is not seen looping around the septal wall, but is on the posterior RA, ruling out AFL around a previous transseptal access site.
- The entire circuit is accounted from within the RA; therefore, option b (LA Flutter) may be ruled out.
- Inappropriate sinus tachycardia would be observed with a focal map appearance in which the earliest site is at the location of the sinus node and becomes progressively later, unlike this reentrant map.
- Typical AFL travels around the TV and is dependent on conduction through the CTI which is not the case in this example. The CTI is not an active participant of the rhythm.

20. **Which cardiac chamber is displayed in example #1?**
    a. **Right Atrium**
    b. **Left Atrium**
    c. **Right Ventricle**
    d. **Left Ventricle**

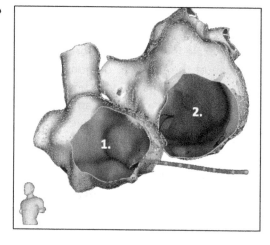

ANSWER: a. Right Atrium. This map image displays the right and left ventricle in an LAO view. In LAO, the view is looking through the AV valves. This view is helpful in deciphering the right vs. left side of the heart.

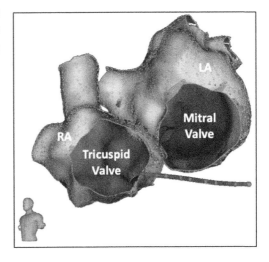

21. **Match the label with the correct cardiac structure.**
    a. **IVC**
    b. **SVC**
    c. **LIPV**
    d. **RIPV**
    e. **LSPV**
    f. **RSPV**
    g. **Posterior LA**
    h. **Posterior RA**

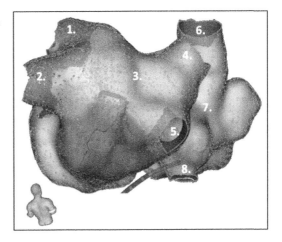

ANSWERS: This is a posterior view of the right and left atria.
    1. e
    2. c
    3. g
    4. f
    5. d
    6. b
    7. h
    8. a

22. **The following image demonstrates two different views of the RA LAT map during atrial flutter. What observation may be made?**
    a. **Flutter circuit is around the Crista Terminalis**
    b. **The flutter is not dependent on the RA**
    c. **Entire circuit is within the RA**
    d. **Flutter is CTI dependent**

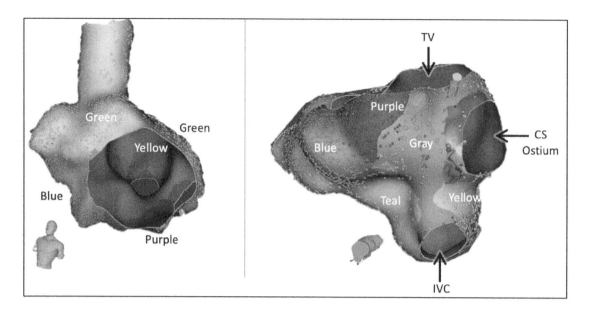

ANSWER: b. The flutter is not dependent on the RA. Recall, the color schematic for an LAT map is from white/red (depending on mapping system) to purple. Here, the early activation of the circuit is not represented; there is no red or orange. The only yellow that is observed is on the posterior septal aspect of the RA. Gray in the map represents an area of scar. This patient has had a previous CTI ablation as seen by the large area of scar from the TV to the IVC (CTI line) in the image on the right.

23. In the previous question, what would be the next possible suggestions for the physician? (Select two)
   a. Perform entrainment from the distal CS
   b. Perform 3D LAT mapping of the LA
   c. Begin an SVC-to-IVC ablation line
   d. "Touch-up" the CTI ablation line
   e. Cardiovert the patient

ANSWER: a & b. To prove this is a left-sided flutter the physician may entrain the tachycardia from various places in the heart to see if it is part of the AFL circuit. Entrainment is often performed in the distal CS, proximal CS, CTI, and/or lateral RA wall and the results are compared. Some physicians do not want to potentially terminate the rhythm with entrainment and with the LAT maps of the RA in this example, they may move directly to 3D mapping of the left atrium. See: EP Essentials, *Understanding EP*, chapter on atrial flutter entrainment.

24. What is the rhythm displayed in the following 3D map?
   a. **Typical Counterclockwise AFL**
   b. **Left Atrial Tachycardia**
   c. **Sinus Rhythm**
   d. **AVRT**

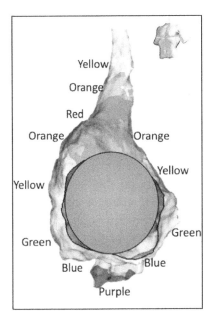

ANSWER: c. Sinus Rhythm. This sinus map was created by the Ensite system by Abbott. The very earliest site of activation (white) is not observed in this LAO view but would be more visible from the RAO perspective. The early (red) activation is observed at the location of the SVC/lateral RA junction. This is the area of the sinus node. This is a map of a focal rhythm unlike the reentrant atrial flutter rhythms observed previously. Notice how the impulse spreads out from the site of activation until purple is observed at the base of the RA. This is much like dropping a pebble in the water and watching the waves expand outward from the earliest site.

25. What rhythm is observed in the following LAT maps?
   a. **Typical AFL**
   b. **Mitral Valve AFL**
   c. **LA scar-related flutter**
   d. **RA scar-related flutter**

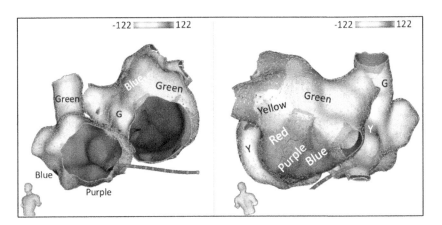

ANSWER: c. LA scar-related flutter. This image displays both the RA and the LA. The entire flutter circuit is observed on the posterior wall of the LA; notice all colors from red to purple are represented in order. There is a small island of scar (gray) in the center of the circuit.

26. In the previous example, where would RF ablation be performed?
   a. CTI
   b. SVC to IVC
   c. MV to LIPV
   d. LIPV to RIPV

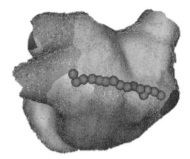

ANSWER: d. LIPV to RIPV. To successfully ablate atrial flutter, a complete line of block must be created from one nonconductive area to another which would prohibit use of the critical isthmus. For example, an ablation line from the mitral valve to the LIPV is from one nonconductive area to another within the LA, but the rhythm is not dependent on that part of the atria therefore will be ineffective. Notice the ablation lesions in the example from the LIPV to the RIPV. The circuit is no longer able to travel around the island of scar.

27. A patient with paroxysmal AF presented to the EP lab in sinus rhythm. Tachycardia was induced and is displayed in the following LAT map images. What is the most likely trigger of this patient's atrial fibrillation?
   a. Firing from the RSPV
   b. Firing from the LSPV
   c. Roof dependent AFL
   d. Mitral annular AFL
   e. Posterior wall rotors

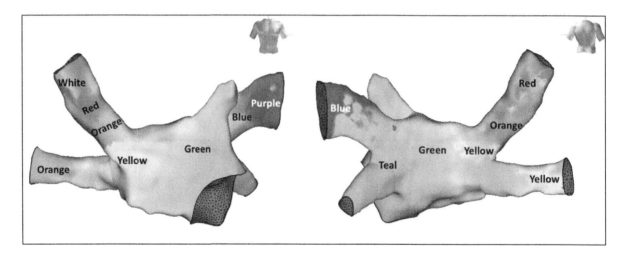

ANSWER: a. Firing from within the RSPV. This rhythm presented with a 2:1 (A:V) atrial tachycardia. Ablation of the earliest activation site at the anterior aspect of the RSPV terminated the rhythm. Firing from within the pulmonary veins is one of the triggers for atrial fibrillation.

28. The following LAT map was created after an ablation line was created from the LIPV to the RIPV for LA flutter. What is observed?
   a.   Further ablation needed from LSPV to RSPV
   b.   Successful line of block
   c.   Leak near the LIPV
   d.   AFL continues

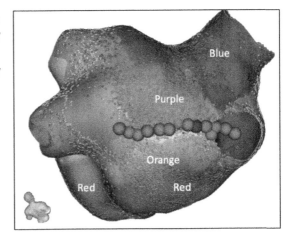

ANSWER: b. Successful line of block. The earliest activation is seen near the location of the distal CS (pacing site). It then spreads in both directions (orange), but it is unable to pass through the ablation line. The color immediately after the ablation line is purple… color may not travel from orange to purple it must first display yellow, green, and blue. The impulse wavefront traveled around the anterior wall until reaching the ablation line on the posterior wall.

29. This LAT map displays the activation pattern with CS pacing after a CTI ablation was performed for typical AFL. What is observed?
   a.   Lateral-to-Medial Block
   b.   Medial-to-Lateral Block
   c.   Bidirectional Block
   d.   Incomplete Block

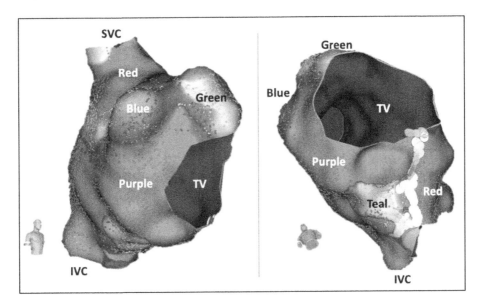

ANSWER: d. Incomplete Block. In this example there is a gap in which signal is still able to travel across the CTI. This gap is located on the IVC aspect and further ablation is required. Just because an ablation line was performed and AFL was terminated, it does not mean that the procedure is complete.

30. This 3D image is an LAT map of atrial activation within coronary sinus (PA view) during RV pacing. Which of the following <u>two</u> descriptions best match the activation pattern?
   a.   Accessory pathway activation pattern
   b.   AV nodal activation pattern
   c.   Concentric activation
   d.   Eccentric activation
   e.   No retrograde conduction

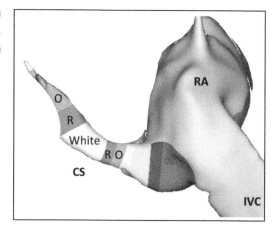

ANSWER: a & d. The earliest atrial activation is displayed mid CS. During normal conduction, there is only one route from the ventricle to the atrium and that is via the AV node. This normal activation would display the earliest atrial signal on the His channels followed by proximal to distal CS. Here, the earliest activation is mid CS, which would display eccentric activation. This map also displays bracketing of the accessory pathway. Notice how the activation is later either side of the early (white) activation. This bracketing assists in identifying the accessory pathway location. Detailed mapping will next be performed within the left atrium on the posterior mitral valve annulus.

31. What is depicted by the arrow in the 3D mapping image.
   a.   Anterior Wall
   b.   Inferior Wall
   c.   Lateral Wall
   d.   Septal Wall

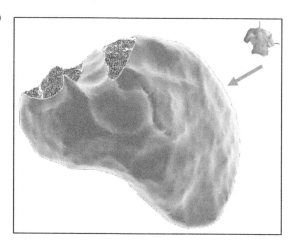

ANSWER: a. Anterior Wall. This is a model of the LV, notice the mitral and aortic valve cutouts. This view is looking at the septal wall with the lateral wall not shown. While collecting this geometry, the mapping personnel would also collect substrate and timing data, which is not displayed in this image. See: EP Essentials *"Understanding EP: A Comprehensive Guide"* section on VT.

32. The successful area of ablation is circled in the 3D mapping image # 10. What rhythm was most likely ablated?

a. AVNRT
b. AVRT
c. Atrial Tachycardia
d. Atrial Flutter

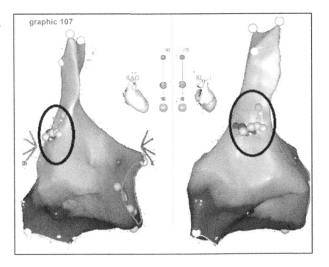

ANSWER: c. Atrial tachycardia firing from the crista terminalis area. This area is close to the sinus node, but differential mapping of the Sinus rhythm and pacing techniques (not displayed), showed that this was an Atrial tachycardia and was not confused with any Sinus tachycardia. Even in a black and white picture, it should be clear on the area mapped. In the RAO view (left image), remember the atrium is to the left and the ventricle to the right. This makes the valve area cut out the tricuspid valve. The cutout below is the IVC and above is the SVC. The crista terminalis runs along the lateral aspect of the atrium.

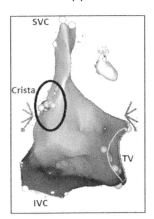

Huang says, "Focal ATs usually occur along the crista terminalis in the right atrium and near the pulmonary veins in the left atrium. Less frequently, they arise from the coronary sinus, the coronary sinus ostium, the parahisian region, the appendages, or, rarely, along the tricuspid or mitral annulus." See: Catheter Ablation of Cardiac Arrhythmias by Huang and Wood's chapter on Ablation of Focal Atrial Tachycardias.

33. What type of ablation is being performed in the 3D mapping image #111 displayed?

a. PVI
b. AVNRT
c. Atrial Flutter
d. Accessory Pathway

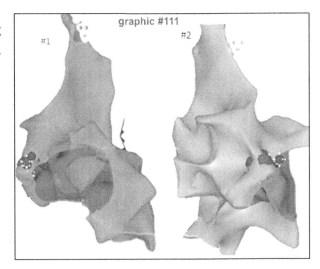

ANSWER: d. Accessory Pathway.

34. Which view is displayed in #1?
   a. **AP**
   b. **PA**
   c. **RAO**
   d. **LAO**

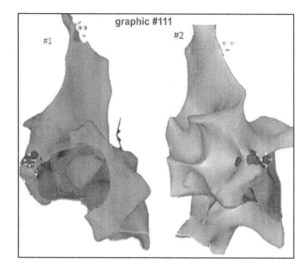

ANSWER: d. LAO. This ablation is being performed on the right atrium on the lateral aspect of the Tricuspid valve (slightly Anterior). Notice the valve cutout and the cutout on the top and bottom of the structure. This is the Tricuspid valve, SVC, and IVC which are all on the right atrial side. View #1 is LAO and #2 is the RAO projection. Remember that in LAO, you are looking down the Mitral and Tricuspid valve annulus or down the barrel of the LV. LAO will show what is right sided vs. left sided. To take it one step further, you can tell what is lateral or medial. RAO will help you see what is atrial vs. ventricular. Also, from RAO you can tell what is anterior vs. posterior.

- PVI (pulmonary vein isolation) is performed during atrial fibrillation ablations. This is performed in the left atrium (pulmonary veins) not the RA.
- Atrial flutter would have a line of block created in the CTI (cavotricuspid isthmus). In other words, a line of block is made in typical atrial flutter from the tricuspid valve all the way back to the IVC. This ablation is a focal area not a line of block.
- AVNRT ablations are in the location of the slow pathway which would be located more on the septal vs. the lateral side of the atrium.

This is a focal ablation on the lateral aspect of the tricuspid valve, so most likely an AP ablation. Accessory pathways are located along the valve annulus connecting the atrium to the ventricle such as shown here. Although atrial tachycardia may fire from anywhere in the atrium, this is an unlikely location.

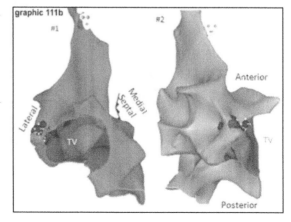

35. Which of the following mapping strategies is utilized to identify the arrhythmogenic substrate responsible for tachycardia?
   a. **LAT Map – Local Activation Time**
   b. **Reentrant Map**
   c. **Voltage Map**
   d. **Pace-Map**

ANSWER: c. Voltage Map. A voltage map is another term often used for a substrate map in which the voltage of the myocardium is acquired. This image is of the left ventricle after substrate mapping during sinus rhythm. The areas of gray demonstrate scar tissue whereas purple represents healthy tissue with this system (Abbott Precision) with CARTO, red is the color that they use to signify scar/low voltage. The other colors represent the values in between. Myocardial tissue with a voltage of >1.5 mV is healthy and below 0.5 in the ventricle or 0.3 in the atrium is diseased or scar. It is best to dynamically adjust the low voltage setting even to as low as 0.1 to find potential channels within the low voltage areas.

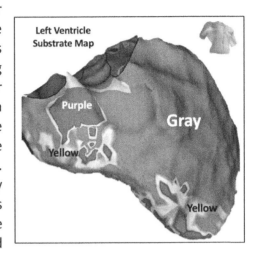

36. When obtaining a detailed 3D map, this may <u>increase</u> the mapping time.
   a. **Multielectrode Catheters**
   b. **Point-by-Point Mapping**
   c. **High-Density Catheters**
   d. **Automapping**

ANSWER: b. Point-by-Point Contact Mapping. During point-by-point mapping, the mapping personnel will analyze each point (acquired signal). This individual will decide if the point reflects that of the tachycardia and where to annotate, or mark, the signal. The point (signal) may be annotated at the earliest onsite, peak signal, or latest activation, or other defined characteristics. When utilizing automapping, the mapping system will automatically acquire points and annotate the signals to a set specification. Depending on the type of rhythm, the specification for point acquisition may be adjusted. This will increase the number of points acquired along with consistent annotation.

37. Which of the following is/are associated with the use of 3D mapping? (Select all that apply)
   a. Decrease in x-ray exposure
   b. Increased procedural time
   c. Visualization of wavefront propagation
   d. Visualization of the tissue health

ANSWERS: a, c, & d. The use of 3D mapping will aid in <u>decreasing</u> the procedural time as well as the amount of x-ray utilized. In some cases, a physician may perform an ablation with zero fluoro usage. With newer mapping software, automapping software, and the use of high-density mapping catheters and advanced ablation catheters, procedural times have decreased ever further. After acquiring activation timing data, the system may play a propagation map demonstrating the course of the tachycardia (or mapped rhythm) through the tissue. Tissue health is visualized in the essence of tissue voltage. Healthy tissue will have a higher voltage and areas of scar will display minimal to no signal and fractionated signals.

38. The main goal of activation mapping of macro reentrant tachycardias (e.g., AFL) is:
   a. Determining reentry by resetting and entraining the tachycardia
   b. Reconstruct the 3D geometry of the chamber
   c. Determining the direction of the reentry loop
   d. Identification of the critical isthmus

ANSWER: d. Identification of the critical isthmus. "The main goal of activation mapping of macro reentrant tachycardias (e.g., post-MI VT, scar related VT) is identification of the isthmus critical for the macro reentrant circuit [normally this is the cavotricuspid isthmus]. Therefore, the goal of activation mapping during macro reentry is finding the site(s) with continuous activity spanning diastole or with an isolated mid-diastolic potential."
See: Issa, chapter on Isthmus Dependent AFL.

39. A substrate map is often utilized to assess the _____.
   a. Reentrant circuit
   b. Voltage of the tissue
   c. Pacing morphology map
   d. Activation of the tachycardia

ANSWER: b. Voltage of the tissue. Substrate maps are commonly utilized in the LA during PVI (pulmonary vein isolation) for AF. This will access the tissue health with higher voltages representing healthier tissue and lower voltages being more diseased or scar. This method is also commonly utilized in VT ablations to demarcate areas of scar. There are other uses for substrate maps as well such as identifying a low voltage bridge for slow pathway ablations and even to help identify and "healthier" channels within an area of scar that map participate in a reentrant tachycardia (atypical AFL / ischemic VT).

Chapter 12
Therapy

EP Essentials LLC

Terminology:

RF ablation:
- Most common type of ablation therapy
- Creates a discrete homogeneous lesion
- Cell death occurs at 50°C

Cryo Ablation:
- Therapy that uses the removal of heat from tissue
- It restores normal electrical conduction by freezing the cardiac tissue or pathways that interfere with the normal distribution of the heart's electrical impulses.
- Uses liquid nitrous oxide (N2O)
- Catheter cools to -75°C (cryocatheter – different with cryoballoon). The catheter will adhere to the tissue, so it will not slide along the wall like RF. Creates an ice ball.

RF Ablation:

1. Match the ablation method below to the type of SVT for which it is best suited.
1. **Irrigated RF or 8 mm RF catheter**
2. **4 mm RF catheter**
3. **Cryoballoon**
4. **Cryocatheter**

a. **AVNRT slow path ablation**
b. **Pulmonary vein isolation for AF**
c. **AFL cavotricuspid isthmus ablation**
d. **Accessory pathway near AV node**

CORRECTLY MATCHED ANSWERS ARE:

1. Irrigated or 8 mm RF catheter: c. AFL cavotricuspid isthmus (CTI) ablations require large, deep lesions
2. 4 mm RF catheter: a. AVNRT slow path ablation near AV node requires shallow, precise lesions to prevent AV block
3. Cryoballoon: b. Pulmonary Vein Isolation for AF
4. Cryocatheter: d. Accessory pathway near AV node (or AVNRT in young patients)

Although ablation is done upon a physician's preference and most AF ablation procedures are still performed with irrigated RF catheters, the Cryoballoon is designed specifically for this task. Most still use RF for AVNRT, although some prefer the cryo-catheter for younger patients for safety reasons.

Zipes say, "Another potential area where cryoablation offers great promise is in the ablation of accessory pathways either located in a paraseptal location near the native conduction system or in an anatomic location, such as within the coronary sinus, where the application of RF energy could lead to unwanted collateral damage.... Especially for smaller and younger pediatric patients, the development of the CCA (CryoCath) techniques has enhanced the safety of catheter ablation, particularly when the ablation target tissues are around the septum, atrioventricular (AV) node and His bundle, and coronary sinus and possibly in areas where the coronary artery is vulnerable. The CCA is appealing because safety is enhanced by the longer time to produce a smaller scar, thus allowing the surgeon more time to observe for, and limit the potential area of, undesired effects."

"Cooled tip catheters are preferred for long linear ablations (in the RA or LA), complex atrial arrhythmias (AFL or AF), targets resistant to previous conventional ablation (focal tachycardias or BTs), and specific areas with low local blood flow, including the coronary sinus (CS), particularly CS aneurysms. Clinical trials have found irrigated tip catheters to be more effective than and as safe as conventional catheters for AFL ablation, facilitating the rapid achievement of bidirectional isthmus block. Irrigated tip catheters also were found to be safe and effective in eliminating BT conduction resistant to conventional catheters, irrespective of the location, and they have been successfully used for PV isolation for treatment of AF. Irrigated tip catheters also offer an advantage over conventional RF catheters in the case of some post–myocardial infarction (MI) VTs, facilitating creation of larger and deeper lesions which can help eliminate intramyocardial or subepicardial reentrant pathways necessary for VT circuit." See Issa, chapter on Ablation Energy Sources

2. During RF ablation, what mode of heating is responsible for increasing the temperature of the ablation electrode and the closest 1-2 mm of tissue?
   a. **Inductive heating**
   b. **Convective heating**
   c. **Conductive heating**
   d. **Resistive heating**

ANSWER: d. Resistive heating is limited to a small volume of tissue in close contact with the electrode. The RF energy dissipates almost as soon as it leaves the electrode tip. Heat is produced wherever the resistance is greatest: the electrode tip and indifferent electrode. That is why indifferent electrodes are large, have a conductive jelly and are placed close to the heart (back). Some labs even use two indifferent electrodes on long ablation cases to spread out the indifferent electrode heat dissipation, and this is required for 8 mm catheters.

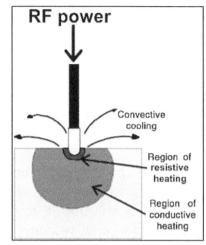

Issa says, "During alternating current flow, charged carriers in tissue (ions) attempt to follow the changes in the direction of the alternating current, thus converting electromagnetic (current) energy into molecular mechanical energy or heat. This type of electric current-mediated heating is known as ohmic (resistive) heating." See: Issa, chapter on Ablation Energy Sources

3. During RF ablation, what type of heating increases the temperature of the deeper tissue 2-5 mm beneath the electrode?
  a. **Inductive heating**
  b. **Convective heating**
  c. **Conductive heating**
  d. **Resistive heating**

ANSWER: c. Conductive heating. Deep conduction is by heat transfer from the close ohmic region to adjacent deeper myocardial tissue. Convective heating (or cooling) occurs when the blood carries away heat from the electrode by convection, just like smoke is carried away by convection in the wind. Resistive or Ohmic heating occurs due to direct RF application in the first 2mm of tissue.

Issa says, "The remainder of tissue heating occurs because of heat conduction from this rim to the surrounding tissues. On initiation of fixed-level energy application, the temperature at the electrode-tissue interface rises monoexponentially to reach steady state within a few seconds (= 7 to 10 seconds), and the steady state is usually maintained between 80° and 90°C. However, whereas resistive heating starts immediately with the delivery of RF current, conduction of heat to deeper tissue sites is relatively slow and requires 1 to 2 minutes to equilibrate (thermal equilibrium) .... Therefore, RF ablation requires at least 30 to 60 seconds to create full-grown lesions." See: Issa, chapter on Ablation Energy Sources

4. Using an irrigated RF ablation catheter, how much power will be lost to passing blood if only half of the electrode is in contact with cardiac tissue?
   a. **More than half of the power will be lost**
   b. **Less than half of the power will be lost**
   c. **Half of the power will be lost**
   d. **No power loss**

ANSWER: a. More than half of the power will be lost into the blood because blood has lower impedance and will thus conduct more electric current.
See: Issa, chapter on Ablation Energy Sources

5. What fluid is used to perfuse irrigated ablation catheters?
   a. **Room temperature heparinized saline**
   b. **Ice cold heparinized saline**
   c. **Room temperature saline**
   d. **Ice cold D5W**

ANSWER: a. Room temperature heparinized saline. "Most electrophysiologists use this type of single point catheter today. Irrigated catheters have tiny holes at the tip that spread cooled water, usually a saline solution, to the ablation area. In this way, the electrophysiologist can deliver high levels of radiofrequency energy while moderating the temperature where the catheter connects with heart tissue." See: StopAfib.org

6. Compared to plain RF ablation, irrigated tip catheters have the advantage that they can maintain lower tip temperature with: (Select two best answers)
   a. **More accurate temperature regulation**
   b. **Higher power delivery to cardiac tissue**
   c. **Higher tissue interface temperature**
   d. **Less char and thrombus formation**
   e. **Less pain**

ANSWERS: d. Less char and thrombus formation and b. Higher power delivery to cardiac tissue. Compared to plain RF ablation, irrigated tip lesions are deeper with a narrow neck around the electrode.

Issa says, "Cooled tip catheters have several advantages. First, they allow the desired power to be delivered independent of local blood flow, which results in increased lesion size. Second, they reduce the temperature of the ablation electrode as well as the temperature at the tissue interface, especially with the open irrigation system, which helps spare the endocardium and reduce the risk of clots and charring. Third, when compared with standard 8-mm tip ablation catheters, a 3.5- to 4-mm

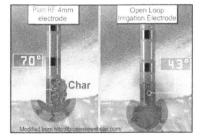

irrigated electrode offers higher mapping accuracy while providing comparable ablation lesion size. There is a significant discrepancy between monitored electrode temperature and tissue temperature during cooled RF ablation. With high irrigation flow rates, catheter tip temperature is not representative of tissue temperature and therefore feedback cannot be used to guide power output." See: Issa, chapter on Ablation Energy Sources

7. During typical AFL ablation it is best to use _____ RF catheters to prevent _____.
   a. **Cooled, Pulmonary Embolism**
   b. **Cooled, nerve and esophageal damage**
   c. **8-mm tip, stroke, or TIA**
   d. **8-mm tip, nerve, or esophageal damage**
   e. **4-mm tip, AV block**

ANSWER: a. Cooled, Pulmonary Embolism. Cooled or irrigated RF catheters help prevent char and embolism, but not deep tissue damage. They tend to make deeper burns than non-irrigated ablation catheters and thus are more likely to cause nerve or esophageal damage in the LA.

"Heat generated by radiofrequency energy can cause blood around the ablated area to clot (thrombus formation). If a clot were to dislodge from the [left side of the] heart, a stroke could occur. To decrease the chance that this might happen, irrigated radiofrequency energy catheters were developed. Irrigated catheters have tiny holes at the tip that spread cooled water, usually a saline solution, to the ablation area. In this way, the electrophysiologist can deliver high levels of radiofrequency energy while moderating the temperature where the catheter connects with heart tissue." See: StopAfib.org

8. Thirty seconds of a successful 7F, 4 mm RF catheter ablation typically causes:
   a. **Lesions at a distance from 3-4 mm deep, but not on surface**
   b. **Large lesions 8-10 mm wide and approximately 6mm deep**
   c. **Transmural lesions 2-3 mm wide**
   d. **Small lesions, 2-3 mm deep**

ANSWER: d. Small lesions 2-3 mm deep. RF energy produces little stimulation of the nerve. It can be used in titrated amounts and produces small (4-5 mm and approximately 3 mm deep) homogeneous lesions which are not arrhythmogenic. Irrigated tip ablation lesions are deeper than dry/non-irrigated RF lesions.

Issa says, "In a typical 7 F catheter (2.2 mm in diameter) with a 4-mm ablation electrode tip, the resulting lesion is 5 to 6 mm in diameter and 2 to 3 mm deep. Larger-electrode or saline-irrigated catheters result in bigger lesions." Using cooled open irrigated catheters deepens and enlarges the burn lesions. See: Issa, chapter on, "Ablation Energy Sources" & //www.palmettohealth.org/heartbody_links.cfm?id=3946

9. The main mechanism of RF ablation is:
   a. Ionizing radiation damage to affected cells (somatic damage)
   b. Mechanical cell wall disruption (barotrauma)
   c. Destruction of cell nuclei (apoptosis)
   d. Tissue heating

ANSWER: d. Tissue heating (burning). Wilber says, "The mechanism of ablation from RF sources is tissue heating. Electric current passing through a resistive medium such as myocardium generates heat in the region near the source where current density is the highest. Thermal conductive heating accounts for the bulk of lesion formation." See: Catheter Ablation of Cardiac Arrhythmias: Basic Concepts and Clinical: edited by David J. Wilber, et. al.

10. With standard saline closed irrigated tip ablation catheters, to avoid endocardial burning and char formation when more than 30 Watts are being delivered:
   a. Monitor for tip temperature rise
   b. Increase flow to 15-30 ml/min
   c. Monitor for impedance rise
   d. Reduce flow to <10 ml/min

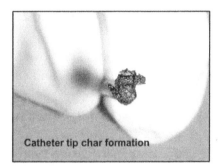
Catheter tip char formation

ANSWER: b. Increase flow to 15-30 ml/min. Issa says, "There is significant discrepancy between monitored electrode temperature and tissue temperature during cooled RF ablation. .... With high irrigation flow rates, catheter tip temperature is not representative of tissue temperature and therefore feedback cannot be used to guide power output."

"The flow rate of the irrigation determines the degree of cooling.... With the internally irrigated ablation system, the approved flow rate is fixed at 36 mL/min and is not presently manipulated. With the externally irrigated ablation system, an irrigation flow rate of 10 to 17 mL/min during RF application (2 to 3 ml/min during all other times) may be selected in a power-controlled mode with a delivered power of up to 30 W. The irrigation flow rate should be increased to 20 to 30 ml/min when more than 30 W are delivered to avoid excessive heat development at the superficial tissue layers." These flow rates are company specific. Some irrigation systems maintain a constant flow rate regardless of the power level. See: Issa, chapter on "Ablation Energy Sources"

11. What type of pump is usually used with cooled or open irrigated ablation catheters?
   a. Gravity drip (IV system)
   b. Peristaltic (roller)
   c. Impeller (helical)
   d. Centrifugal (fan)

ANSWER: b. Peristaltic (roller). Several rollers are attached to a rotor to compress a flexible tube. As the rotor holding the rollers turns, it wrings or strips the saline through the flexible tube. This process is called peristalsis and is used in many biological systems such as the gastrointestinal tract. See: Biosensewebser.com

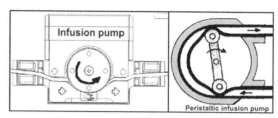

12. When ablation comes on with open irrigated tip catheters the irrigation pump:
   a. **Maintains a constant infusion rate of 13-30 ml/min**
   b. **Maintains a constant infusion rate of 5-10 ml/min**
   c. **Increases flow from 2ml/min to 8-30 ml/min**
   d. **Increases flow from 2ml/min to 4-8 ml/min**

ANSWER: c. Increases flow from 2ml/min to 8-30 ml/min. The exact amount may vary between manufactures and catheters.

13. With irrigated ablation systems, all infusion pumps contain alarms for an open door and:
   a. **Leak in irrigation system detection**
   b. **Electrical ground fault detection**
   c. **In-line bubble detection**
   d. **In-line blood detection**

ANSWER: c. In-line bubble detection. Both Biosense Webster and Abbott pumps contain in-line bubble detectors, as bubbles infused into the left heart could lead to a TIA or stroke. The Abbott pump has additional error detection for: speed error, electrical error, and obstructed flow. See: Biosensewebster.com and abbott.com

14. In the EP lab coagulum refers to:
   a. **Mixture of coagulated fibrin & erythrocytes**
   b. **Clot on a diagnostic electrode or sheath**
   c. **Denatured protein from boiled blood**
   d. **Charred muscle on the catheter tip**

ANSWER: c. Denatured protein from boiled blood. Wilber says, "As long as tissue temperatures do not exceed 100° C, ablation proceeds unimpeded. If the electrode tissue interface temperature reaches this threshold, however, blood at the surface begins to boil. This produces an adherent collection of denature blood proteins that is referred to as coagulum. The Coagulum accumulates on the electrode surface, resulting in less electrode surface area being available for conduction and the local power density increases.

Increasing power density results in more heating, more conduction, and progressively less available conducting electrode surface area. Within a second, most of the electrode is covered with coagulum, and a sudden rapid rise in electrical impedance ensues, preventing effective RF delivery from that point forward. It is then necessary to remove the electrode from the patient and scrape the coagulum from the electrode before resuming ablation. In the worst case, coagulum can embolize from the catheter tip, leading to adverse consequences if ablation is being carried out in the left atrium or ventricle...As the temperature approaches and then exceeds 100 ° C, a sudden rise in electrical impedance is observed." See: Catheter Ablation of Cardiac Arrhythmias: Basic Concepts and Clinical ... edited by David J. Wilber, et. al.

15. This is the most used energy source for cardiac ablation.
   a. **DC**
   b. **RF**
   c. **Cryo**
   d. **Laser**

ANSWER: b. RF energy. RF, or radiofrequency energy, is the most utilized energy source today. RF energy continues to evolve with irrigated and force sensing catheters. This energy source may be utilized to treat all types of rhythms from SVT to VT.

16. Which of the following are complications or limitations of RF ablation?
   (Select all that apply)
   a. **Damage to adjacent structures**
   b. **Transmural lesions**
   c. **Coagulation**
   d. **Steam Pop**

ANSWERS: a, c, and d. The goal of RF ablation is to create a transmural lesion.
"Application of RF energy to tissues results in thermal ablation through resistive heating of the tissue with subsequent heat conduction to deeper tissue layers. Successful ablation lesion creation relies on a multitude of factors, contact force, power, impendence, temperature, duration. The proximity of the posterior atrial wall to the esophagus makes it a potential site of thermal injury. Thermal injury can cause ulceration formation or the creation of an atrial-esophageal fistula – a devastating consequence that is often fatal. Further concerns include collateral injury to phrenic nerve as well as the vagus nerve and its branches. Coagulation and tissue necrosis induced by thermal energy in RF is associated with a risk of thrombus formation." See: Sugrue, A., et al (2018). Irreversible electroporation for the treatment of cardiac arrhythmias.

17. During RF cardiac ablation what usually creates the most successful lesions.
   a. **Temperature drop >10 degrees**
   b. **Temperature rise >10 degrees**
   c. **Impendence drop >10 ohms**
   d. **Impedance rise >10 ohms**

ANSWER: c. Impendence drop >10 ohms. "Impedance decrease during RF ablation is a specific marker of local tissue heating, and therefore can be used as a real-time indicator of lesion creation. Local impedance changes occur during RF ablation as the tissue temperature rises, resulting in increased ion mobility within the tissue being heated, and therefore a decrease in impedance to current flow." See: Chinitz, et al, Impedance-guided RF Ablation: 2017

18. These two are true about using half normal saline during cardiac ablation (select two):
   a. **Contact force no longer factors in size**
   b. **Increase risk of steam pops**
   c. **Decrease in tissue heating**
   d. **Deeper ablation lesion**

Answer: b & d. The use of half normal saline with an irrigated ablation catheter may create larger ablation lesions but with a higher risk of causing a steam pop.

"Standard externally irrigated RFA is performed using normal saline (NS) with a concentration of 0.9% (9 grams per liter) sodium chloride. We previously demonstrated that externally irrigated ablation using a lower ionic concentration and charge density can create larger and deeper lesions...Half-normal saline (HNS) ablation created larger lesions than NS ablation, and lesions created using 5% dextrose in water (D5W) were significantly larger than either HNS or NS lesions. We hypothesized that the lower charge density of HNS and D5W decreased loss of RFA through dispersion to a lower impedance environment surrounding the catheter, thereby allowing for more effective RF current delivered to myocardial tissue."

In this example, endocardial ablations were delivered at 30 W for 30 s with the same amount of contact force and irrigation flow rate.

See: Nguyen, et al, RF Ablation Using an Open Irrigated Electrode Cooled with Half-NaCl. JACC: 2017

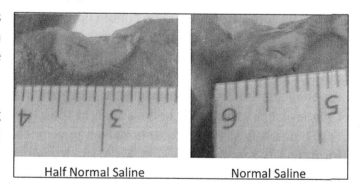

Half Normal Saline   Normal Saline

19. RF ablations of either accessory pathways or AV node are typically done with a 4 mm tip catheter using approximately:
  a. **30 Watts at 80-90° C**
  b. **5 Watts at 80-90° C**
  c. **30 Watts at 60° C**
  d. **5 Watts at 60° C**

ANSWER: c. 30 Watts at 60° C. Murgatroyd says, "A power of 30 W delivered to a 4 mm tip catheter typically creates a lesion approximately 4-5 mm in diameter and depth, which is adequate...If heat dissipation by blood flowing past the tip is low (in venous structures for example), very high surface temperatures may be reached causing potentially dangerous gas formation and charring at the electrode interface. The limiting factor is the temperature at which impedance rises. For this reason, most ablation systems now use an electronic mechanism that automatically adjusts output to achieve a desired temperature. A typical setting might be 60° C, ...if the system prevents the tissue interface from reaching 100° C, gas formation and charring will be avoided." See: Murgatroyd, chapter on "Conventional Energy"

20. During an RF ablation, most destruction (burning) of myocardial tissue is due to:
  a. **Electrical disruption of sodium/ potassium pump**
  b. **Resistive heating from direct electrode contact**
  c. **Electrical disruption of mitochondrial DNA**
  d. **Conduction of heat into tissue**

ANSWER: d. Conduction of heat into tissue. Issa says, "Only a thin rim of tissue in immediate contact with the RF electrode is directly heated (within the first 2 mm of depth from the electrode). The rest of the heating occurs because of heat conduction from this rim to the surrounding tissue...deep tissue temperatures continue to rise for several seconds after interruption of RF delivery (the so-called thermal latency phenomenon). Therefore, RF ablation requires at least 30 to 60 seconds to create full lesions.... The range of tissue temperatures used for RF ablation is 50° to 90° C."
See: Issa, chapter on "Ablation Energy Sources"

21. You are using a saline irrigated tip ablation catheter at 35 Watts. To avoid endocardial burning and char formation it is most important to:
  a. **Monitor for tip temperature rise**
  b. **Monitor for impedance rise**
  c. **Increase flow rate**
  d. **Reduce flow rate**

ANSWER: c. Increase flow rate. Issa says, "There is a significant discrepancy between monitored electrode temperature and tissue temperature during cooled RF ablation. .... With high irrigation flow rates, catheter tip temperature is not representative of tissue temperature and therefore feedback cannot be used to guide power output."

"Saline-irrigated catheters cause peak tissue heating several millimeters from the electrode-tissue interface. Because maximum tissue heating does not occur at the electrode-tissue interface, the value of temperature and impedance monitoring is limited with this type of catheter [irrigated tip]. Therefore, it has been challenging to monitor lesion formation and optimize power delivery during cooled RF ablation."

"The flow rate of the irrigation determines the degree of cooling. Faster flow rates would allow greater power application without impedance rises, increase the difference between tissue and electrode temperature, and thereby potentially increase the risk of steam pops if temperature is used to guide ablation. With the internally irrigated ablation system, the approved flow rate is fixed at 36 mL/min and is not presently manipulated. With the externally irrigated ablation system, an irrigation flow rate of 10 to 17 mL/min during RF application (and 2 to 3 mL/min during all other times) may be selected in a power-controlled mode with a delivered power of up to 30 W. The irrigation flow rate should be increased to 20 to 30 mL/min when more than 30 W are delivered to avoid excessive heat development at the superficial tissue layers." Newer irrigated tip catheters are being developed that allow increased power with less saline flow. See: Issa, chapter on "Ablation Energy Sources"

22. When delivering RF ablation energy, what is referred to as a pop?
  a. **Steam formation at catheter tip**
  b. **Coagulum formation at catheter tip**
  c. **Micro bubble formation, seen on echo**
  d. **Short circuit between RF generator and catheter tip**

ANSWER: a. Steam formation at catheter tip. Issa says, "Higher power can be used with convective cooling, but higher power can cause superheating within the tissue (with subendocardial tissue temperatures exceeding 100°C), which can result in boiling of any liquids under the electrode. Consequently, evaporation and rapid steam expansion can occur intramurally, and a gas bubble can develop in the tissue under the electrode. Continuous application of RF energy causes the bubble to expand and its pressure to increase, which can lead to eruption of the gas bubble (causing a popping sound) through the path with the least mechanical resistance, leaving behind a gaping hole (the so-called pop lesion). This is often toward the heat-damaged endocardial surface (crater formation) or, more rarely, across the myocardial wall (myocardial rupture). This is often associated with sudden impedance rise and catheter dislodgment and can cause significant tissue damage."
See: Issa, chapter on "Ablation Energy Sources"

23. The chief factor opposing RF ablation heating of myocardium is:
  a. **Heat loss to circulating blood**
  b. **Inadequate electrode contact**
  c. **Too large a tip electrode**
  d. **Coagulum build up**

ANSWER: a. Heat loss to circulating blood. We want the tip to be cool and the RF energy to do the work of heating and ablating. That is why irrigated ablation catheters were developed. "The dominant factor opposing effective heating of myocardium is convective heat loss into the circulating blood pool.... The concept of convective cooling can explain why there are few coronary complications with conventional RF ablation. Coronary arteries function as a heat sink.... A low catheter tip temperature can be caused by a high level of convective cooling, allowing a higher amount of power to be delivered to the tissue and yielding large lesions. This is best illustrated with active cooling of the ablation electrode using irrigation during RF energy delivery; the tip temperature is usually below 40° which allows the application of high-power output for longer durations." See Issa, chapter on "Ablation Energy Sources"

24. After 30 seconds of ablation with a non-irrigated RF catheter, the tissue temperature 1 mm below the catheter tip is typically _____ than the ablation console temperature reading.
   a. 12°C cooler
   b. 21°C cooler
   c. 12°C warmer
   d. 42°C warmer

ANSWER: d. 42° warmer. Issa says, "Whereas tissue heating is the target of power delivery, the blood pool is the most attractive route for RF current because blood is a better conductor and has significantly lower impedance than tissue, and because the contact between electrode and blood will often be better than with tissue. Therefore, with normal electrode-tissue contact, much more power will generally be delivered to blood than to cardiac tissue."

"The electrode temperature rise is an indirect process—the ablation electrode is not heated by RF energy, but it heats up because it happens to touch heated tissue. Consequently, the catheter tip temperature is always lower than, or ideally equal to, the superficial tissue temperature. Conventional electrode catheters with temperature monitoring only report the temperature [of the tip] and it is likely that the measured temperature underestimates the peak tissue temperature; it can be significantly lower than the tissue temperature. With a sensor placed approximately 1 mm beneath a 4-mm electrode, the temperature within the tissue is on average 42° ± 6°C higher than at the electrode tip after 30 seconds of RF delivery, with a preset target temperature of 70°C." See: Issa, chapter on "Ablation Energy Sources"

25. During RF ablation what is the minimum temperature the tissue needs to be heated to, so that a significant lesion is created?
   a. 50° C
   b. 60° C
   c. 70° C
   d. 80° C

ANSWER: a. 50° C. Issa says, "The range of tissue temperatures used for RF ablation is 50° to 90°C. Within this range, smooth desiccation of tissue can be expected. If the temperature is less than 50°C, no or only minimal tissue necrosis results.... Once the peak tissue temperature

exceeds the threshold of 100°C, boiling of the plasma at the electrode-tissue interface can ensue. When boiling occurs, denatured serum proteins and charred tissue form a thin film that adhere to the electrode, forming an electrically insulating coagulum, which is accompanied by a sudden increase in electrical impedance preventing further current flow into the tissue and further heating." Some physicians like you verbally read out the temperature during ablation to assure it never goes below 50.
See: Issa, chapter on "Ablation Energy Sources"

26. During ablation when the impedance rises suddenly you should?
   a. **Turn down the power level**
   b. **Stop ablating and inform the doctor**
   c. **Keep ablating and inform the doctor**
   d. **Keep ablating. This is expected and normal**

ANSWER: b. Stop ablating and inform the doctor. The catheter is not in contact with the tissue and may be forming "char" or "coagulum". Issa says, "Typically, the impedance associated with firm catheter contact (before tissue heating has occurred) is 90 to 120 ohms. When catheter contact is poor, the initial impedance is 20% to 50% less, because of the lower resistivity of blood. Moreover, larger electrodes have larger contact area and, consequently, lower impedance."

"The impedance drop during RF ablation is mainly because of a reversible phenomenon, such as tissue temperature rise, rather than an irreversible change in tissues secondary to ablation of myocardial tissue. Therefore, impedance provides a useful qualitative assessment of tissue heating; however, it does not correlate well with lesion size. A 5- to 10-Ohm reduction in impedance is usually observed in clinically successful RF applications, correlates with a tissue temperature of 55° to 60°C, and is rarely associated with coagulum formation. Larger decrements in impedance are noted when a coagulum formation is imminent. Once a coagulum is formed, an abrupt rise in impedance to more than 250 ohm is usually observed."
See: Issa, chapter on "Ablation Energy Sources"

27. You are monitoring the ablation parameters during RF ablation with power levels of 15 watts. Maximum catheter temperature may vary depending on the type of ablation catheter. All the following are considered excessive temperatures and increases the likelihood of a steam pop EXCEPT: (Which one is acceptable?)
   a. **>35° in internally irrigated RF**
   b. **>42° in externally irrigated RF catheter**
   c. **>55° using 4 mm ablation catheter**
   d. **>65° using 8 mm ablation catheter**

ANSWER: a. >35° in irrigated RF is OK. Huang & Wood recommendation for irrigated RF power titration is, "Watch for electrode-tip temperature to increase to 37 to 40° C. If the tip temperature rises above 42° C, decrease power or reposition catheter to reduce risk for steam pop. If temperature remains above 40° C despite power <20 W, the ablation catheter tip is wedged in tissue. Consider repositioning catheter or increasing irrigation flow rate." For conventional 8 mm RF catheters the limit is 55° and for 4 mm RF catheters 65°C. See: Huang & Wood, chapter on Guiding Lesion Formation during RF Energy Application

28. You are monitoring the X-ray & ICE monitors during an irrigated RF ablation for AF when you see a sudden shower of small reflections in the LA. This suggests:
   a. **Boiling at electrode-tissue interface**
   b. **Development of intracardiac shunt**
   c. **Coagulum or clot embolization**
   d. **Sheath flushing with contrast**

ANSWER: a. Boiling at electrode-tissue interface. Microbubbles from boiling are easily seen on ICE and occur when the surface temperature exceeds 100°C: too hot. Microbubble formation correlates with surface temperature and not tissue temperature. A microbubble shower may be an indication of coagulum formation or an impending "steam pop."

29. During an irrigated RF ablation you note a continuing rise in catheter impedance as you decrease the power to <20 W. The tip temperature has risen to over 42° C. The most common cause of this is:
   a. **Catheter wedging in a crevice or small vein**
   b. **Catheter slippage with poor tissue contact**
   c. **Local tissue damage with necrosis**
   d. **Excessive coolant flow rate**

ANSWER: a. Catheter wedging in a crevice or small vein. Huang & Wood recommendation for irrigated RF power titration is, "If temperature remains above 40° C. Despite power <20 W, the ablation catheter tip is wedged in tissue. Consider repositioning catheter or increasing irrigation flow rate. If the problem persists, check the integrity of cooling system... In general, electrode temperatures of less than 40° to 45° and impedance drops of 5 to 10 ohms are sought. See: Huang & Wood, chapter on Guiding Lesion Formation during RF Energy Application

30. Some labs monitor the esophageal temperature during PVI. Keeping the temperature _____ is most important when ablating the area of the ____:
   a. **<37.0° C (or <1° above baseline), Posterior LA**
   b. **<38.5° C (or <2° above baseline), Posterior LA**
   c. **<37.0° C (or <1° above baseline), Triangle of Koch**
   d. **<38.5° C (or <2° above baseline), Triangle of Koch**

ANSWER: b. <38.5° C (or 2° Above baseline), Posterior LA. Singh says, "delivering high-power RF applications on the LA posterior wall between left and right PVs might deeply damage the esophagus, precipitating LA fistula formation.... The esophagus is close to the ostia of the PVs and lies only a short distance from the LA wall.... delivering high-power RF applications on the

LA posterior wall between left and right PVs might deeply damage the esophagus, precipitating LA fistula formation."

"The use of 3D mapping systems that allow the integration of CT scans or MR images of LA, PVs, and esophagus, provides a new high-definition visualization tool that permits a rapid understanding of complex cardiac anatomical relationships. The location of the esophagus can also be tagged by the electroanatomical system (CARTO, Ensite, Rhythmia).

A nasogastric tube is inserted into the esophagus. The mapping catheter is coated with lubricant and passed down the nasogastric tube under fluoroscopy guidance."
"Power on the posterior wall was limited to 25 watts and terminated when the temperature increased 2°C from baseline. Using this strategy, no patients had esophageal thermal injury on follow-up endoscopy. Taken together, these studies suggest that with careful esophageal temperature monitoring, and interrupting RF with an increase of 2°C, the risk of esophageal injury and AEF will be low. See: "Strategies to Prevent Esophageal Injury During Catheter Ablation of Atrial Fibrillation", MOSSAAB,
http://www.innovationsincrm.com/cardiac-rhythm-management/2012/April/261-strategies-prevent-esophageal-injury

"Although limiting RF power titration and ablation duration in response to esophageal temperature 38.5°C does not eliminate AF ablation-associated esophageal injury, these data suggest that it may be associated with reduced esophageal injury." See: Singh, "Esophageal Injury and Temperature Monitoring During Atrial Fibrillation Ablation "
http://circep.ahajournals.org/content/1/3/162.full.pdf

31. You bring a non-pacemaker dependent patient with a DDD pacer to the EP lab for an ablation. To avoid accidental reprogramming of the PPM, before applying RF ablation it is safest to:
   a. RF ablation is safe around active PPMs
   b. Reprogram the PPM to VOO at a rate lower than the intrinsic
   c. Reprogram the PPM to VOO at a rate higher than the intrinsic
   d. Reprogram the PPM to OOO or VVI at a rate lower than the intrinsic
   e. Reprogram the PPM to OOO or VVI at a rate higher than the intrinsic

ANSWER: d. Reprogram the PPM to OOO or VVI at a rate lower than the intrinsic rate. You wouldn't want it faster than the intrinsic rate, as it would always fire, interfering with your EP study. You want it turned off (OOO) or at least only on minimally when the rate drops below a critical bradycardia level.

"RF catheter ablation: If the patient is not dependent, the pacemaker can be programmed to OOO or VVI at a lower rate than the intrinsic heart rate. If the patient is dependent, the PM should be programmed to VOO mode and a temporary PM wire should be in place as back-up. Reinterrogation of the PM after the procedure is essential and integrity of the pacing circuit should be evaluated."

"In conclusion, implanted pacemakers frequently exhibit transient, unpredictable responses to RF energy application. Although all pacemaker functions were restored post ablation, some devices had to be reset manually. The anomalies observed during the RF application argue for the simultaneous use of an external pacemaker in pacing-dependent patients. The three [of 38] devices in the untoggled backup mode had to be reprogrammed to obtain normal operations."

See: "Effects of RF catheter ablation on patients with permanent pacemakers. J. Interv. Card. EP," http://www.ncbi.nlm.nih.gov/pubmed/9869976://www.palmettohealth.org

32. In preparing an atrial tachycardia patient for RF ablation, you view this RAO fluoro image that shows:

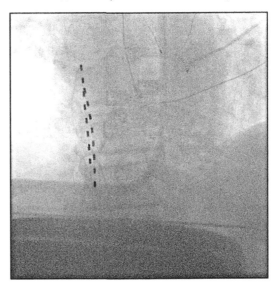

   a. **Esophageal temperature probe**
   b. **Spinal stimulator electrodes**
   c. **Implantable defibrillator**
   d. **Lumbar fusion plates**

ANSWER: b. Spinal stimulator electrodes shown implanted in the epidural space. These stimulators are like pacemakers but intended to alleviate back pain and refractory ischemic pain. The impulses from these stimulators can interfere with EGM sensing and RF ablation and should be turned off during an EP procedure. Worse, being so close to the heart and next to the spinal cord, they can conduct RF energy causing the leads to heat up resulting in spinal cord injury. This may pose a contraindication to intracardiac RF ablation. Submitted by Brent Lawhorn, CEPS, EP Lab, Medical University of South Carolina.

33. In AF or AFL it may be necessary to ablate within the distal CS. It is safest to ablate only along the inner surface of the CS because of possible damage to the:
   a. **Circumflex Coronary Artery**
   b. **Right Coronary Artery**
   c. **Left Atrial Appendage**
   d. **Vein of Marshall**

ANSWER: a. Circumflex Coronary Artery. The Circumflex runs in the left AV groove alongside the CS. Ablation in the CS runs the risk of burning through to the adjacent circumflex coronary artery resulting in MI or tamponade.

Issa says, "The CS might provide both the substrate and ectopic triggers for persistent AF.... Ablation within the CS is performed with the ablation catheter positioned in the distal CS (approximately 4 o'clock in the left anterior oblique projection) and gradually dragged proximally to the CS ostium, with the catheter tip deflected toward the LA to minimize the risk of circumflex coronary artery injury. Power is limited to 25 W and the irrigation rate is adjusted manually to achieve temperatures between 40 and 45° C, with the

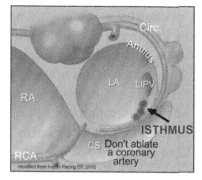

highest irrigation flow rates required for ablation in the distal CS (up to 60 mL/min)."
See: Issa, chapter on "Atrial Substrate Ablation in Atrial Fibrillation"

34. The increase in tissue temperature during RF ablation is a result of _____ at the catheter/tissue interface.
   a. Electromagnetic Heating
   b. Convention Heating
   c. Conductive Heating
   d. Resistive Heating

ANSWER: d. Resistive Heating. "Tissue heating with RF energy is a result of resistive heating at the interface between the catheter and the tissue. This heating is a direct function of the current density at the catheter ablation electrode on to the myocardial interface extending a few millimeters into the tissue." See: Avitall, Cryotherapy of cardiac arrhythmia: From basics to the bedside. Heart Rhythm 2015.

35. Resistive heating increases the tissue's _____ energy by increasing the molecular movement.
   a. Potential
   b. Electrical
   c. Chemical
   d. Kinetic

ANSWER: d. Kinetic. Kinetic energy is motion, potential energy is stored energy, electrical energy results from the flow of electric charge, chemical energy is stored in the bonds of atoms and molecules. "Resistive heating increases the tissue's kinetic energy by virtue of increasing molecular movement."
See: Avitall, Cryotherapy of cardiac arrhythmia: From basics to the bedside. Heart Rhythm 2015.

Contact Force Ablation:

1. What is contact force in ablation catheters?
   a. Catheter tip resistance through tortuosity
   b. Catheter tip-to-blood pool contact
   c. Catheter shaft-to-sheath contact
   d. Catheter tip-to-tissue contact

ANSWER: d. Catheter tip-to-tissue contact. Contact force is the measurable feedback that will tell the operator if their catheter tip is indeed touching the myocardium. During ablation, the operator is looking to create a transmural lesion when possible. If a catheter is close to the tissue, but not touching, there may still be a large signal observed. However, the ablation performed will not create an effective lesion. See: EP Essentials Blog Post about contact force. www.ep-essentials.com/blog/

2. Ablation catheter contact force is measured in _____.
   a. Kilograms
   b. Newtons
   c. Pounds
   d. Grams

ANSWER: d. Grams. Contact force is measured in grams. The catheter utilized in the TOCCATA study (TactiCath by Abbott) has a resolution and sensitivity of about 1 g.
See: Reddy, et al. The relationship between contact force and clinical outcome during radiofrequency catheter ablation of atrial fibrillation in the TOCCATA study. Heart Rhythm, Vol 9, No 11. 2012

3. Which of the following technologies may be utilized to determine the contact force of the ablation catheter? (Select all that apply)
   a. Catheter Tip Impedance
   b. Light Interferometry
   c. Precision Spring
   d. Laser Beam

ANSWER: b & c. The SMARTTOUCH catheter by Biosense Webster utilizes a spring mechanism to obtain contact force. The TactiCath and TactiFlex by Abbott is based on light interferometry which can compute both magnitude and orientation of contact force. Laser is a type of energy delivery (not widely utilized) for ablation therapy. Catheter tip impedance may be monitored to observe an impedance drop of ≥ 10%, signaling successful lesion creation.
See: EP Essentials Blog Post about contact force. www.ep-essentials.com/blog/

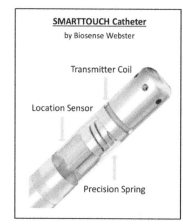
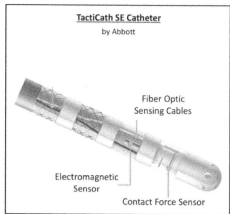

4. Which of the following would be the ideal contact force to create a successful RF lesion?
   a. 5-10 g
   b. > 50 g
   c. 10-20 g
   d. 1-5 g

ANSWER: c. 20 g. A high contact force, such as answer b., may lead to cardiac perforation. According to the TOCCATA study which identified the relationship between contact force (CF) and clinical outcomes during RF (radiofrequency) ablation of atrial fibrillation, an average CF during ablation of < 10 g resulted in an AF recurrence rate of 100%. However, the recurrence rate dropped to 47% (or 53% success rate) when the average CF during ablation was between 10 and 20 g. The rate of success increased to 80% when the average CF during ablation was >20 g. See: Reddy, et al. The relationship between contact force and clinical outcome during radiofrequency catheter ablation of atrial fibrillation in the TOCCATA study. Heart Rhythm, Vol 9, No 11. 2012

5. Which of the following may be helpful to increase the ablation catheter contact force?
   a. Utilization of a support "buddy" wire
   b. Decrease irrigation rate
   c. Increase irrigation rate
   d. Long steerable sheath

ANSWER: d. Long steerable sheath. Changing the irrigation rate may affect the lesion size but will not change the amount of catheter tip-to-tissue contact. To increase catheter contact, the operator may manipulate the catheter utilizing the steerable curve(s). In addition, a long steerable sheath may be utilized. This will aid in supporting the catheter to help increase the contact force. Utilizing the steerable curve of the sheath will support the catheter in the various areas of the heart.
See: EP Essentials – Understanding EP: A Comprehensive Guide. The section on Sheaths and Catheters.

6. Which is true of all contact force catheters on the market? (Select all that apply)
   a. **Radiofrequency Energy**
   b. **Steerable Catheter**
   c. **Irrigated Catheter**
   d. **Laser Energy**
   e. **Cryo Energy**

ANSWER: a, b, c. At the time of this publication, the available contact force sensing catheters are irrigated, steerable, and deliver RF energy.
See: EP Essentials Blog Post "Is it worth the hype" about contact force. www.ep-essentials.com/blog/

7. If contact force is observed under 10 g, how can the operator increase the lesion efficacy? (Select all that apply)
   a. **Utilize a long support sheath to increase contact**
   b. **Disable force sensing**
   c. **Increase RF duration**
   d. **Increase impedance**
   e. **Increase RF power**

ANSWER: a, c, e. An average CF during ablation of <10 g resulted in an AF recurrence rate of 100% during the TOCCATA study. To compensate for the low contact force the operator may increase the RF power and/or duration. Utilizing a supportive steerable sheath may help increase the catheter tip-to-tissue contact.
See: EP Essentials Blog Post "Is it worth the hype" about contact force. www.ep-essentials.com/blog/

Cryoablation:

1. What is used as the refrigerant in cryoablation?
   a. **Compressed CO2 gas**
   b. **Nitrous oxide gas**
   c. **Liquid Nitrogen**
   d. **Liquid Helium**

ANSWER: b. Nitrous oxide gas. Medtronic says, "During a cardiac ablation procedure, pressurized liquid nitrous oxide (N2O) is delivered from a tank in the CryoConsole. The liquid refrigerant travels in an ultra-fine tube through the coaxial shaft of the cryoablation catheter to the tip of the catheter. The liquid refrigerant vaporizes as it is sprayed into the tip. As it vaporizes, it absorbs heat from the surrounding tissue, thereby cooling and freezing the target tissue. The warmed refrigerant is vacuumed back to the CryoConsole through a large lumen within the shaft of the catheter and coaxial umbilical. The CryoConsole discharges the vapor into the hospital scavenging system." See: Medtronic product literature

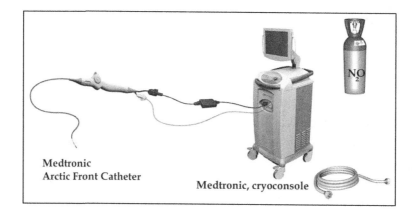

Medtronic
Arctic Front Catheter

Medtronic, cryoconsole

2. The cryoablation balloon for PVI is inflated with:
  a. **N2O (Nitrous Oxide), which is different than regular cryoablation systems**
  b. **NO (Nitric Oxide), which is different than regular cryoablation systems**
  c. **N2O (Nitrous Oxide), the same as regular cryoablation**
  d. **NO (Nitric Oxide), the same as regular cryoablation**

ANSWER c. N2O (Nitrous Oxide), the same as regular cryoablation. N2O is nitrous oxide, the refrigerant liquid, that when injected into the balloon vaporizes and makes the Cryoballoon cold. It is also known as laughing gas. NO (not used here) is nitric oxide, the chemical liberated in vascular endothelium that is a powerful vasodilator with a short half-life in the blood. Viagra, nitroglycerine, and amyl nitrite work by generating nitric oxide in blood vessels. Cath lab studies may also administer NO gas to patients testing for reversible pulmonary vascular resistance.

3. The Cryoballoon (Arctic Front) has two balloons, one inside the other. The inner balloon is _____the outer balloon_____.
  a. **Inflated with N2O, senses any leak in inner balloon**
  b. **Inflated with N2O, prevents tearing of endothelium on premature pullback**
  c. **Inflated with N2O, is inflated with diluted contrast**
  d. **Inflated with diluted contrast, is inflated with N2O**
  e. **Prevents tearing of endothelium on premature pullback, is inflated with N2O**

ANSWER: a. Inflated with N2O, senses any leak in inner balloon. There are two balloons for safety. Should a leak develop there is a sensor in the outer balloon to send an alarm and deflate. It is a rather rigid plastic to stand up to freezing. It is not a soft compliant balloon like a Swan (right-heart catheterization).

4. How should you prepare the Cryoballoon prior to use?
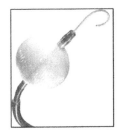
   a. **Never pull the balloon sheath off the catheter**
   b. **Pull the balloon sheath off the tip of the catheter**
   c. **Immerse it in saline and inflate with air, looking for leaks**
   d. **Immerse it in liquid N2O and inflate with air, looking for leaks**

ANSWER: a. Never pull the balloon sheath off the catheter. It should be pulled back onto the catheter shaft, not off the catheter tip, because it may be impossible to get it back on without damage to the balloon. Prior to insertion place the balloon in saline flush and dislodge any adherent bubbles.

5. The main precaution while the Cryoballoon is inflated during a PVI cryoablation is:
   a. **Never advance the catheter, it may rupture the balloon**
   b. **Never pull back on the catheter, as it may rupture the balloon**
   c. **Never advance the catheter, as it may damage adherent tissue**
   d. **Never pull back on the catheter, as it may damage adherent tissue**

ANSWER: d. Never pull back on the catheter, as it may damage adherent tissue.
Medtronic says, "Cryo-adhesion: Do not pull on the catheter, sheath, umbilical cables, or console while the catheter is frozen to the tissue, as this may lead to tissue injury." This is the same effect as licking a frozen railroad track. If you pull the frozen tongue off before it thaws, you will tear the adherent tissue. See: Medtronic.com, ARCTIC FRONT®, 2AF232, 2AF282 Cardiac CryoAblation Catheter Technical Manual.

6. The Arctic Front Cryoballoon requires a _____ ID sheath,
   a. **9 F**
   b. **10 F**
   c. **11 F**
   d. **12 F**

ANSWER: d. 12 F. The FlexCath steerable and deflectable sheath is approved for the Medtronic Cryocatheter. Its specifications are: Inner diameter: 12 F, Outer diameter: 15 F, Usable length: 65 cm, Total length: 81 cm, Radiopaque marker: 5 mm proximal to sheath tip. See: Medtronic Product Specs.

7. What ablation method is least painful?
   a. **Irrigated RF**
   b. **Microwave**
   c. **Cryoablation**
   d. **Pulsed field ablation**

ANSWER: c. Cryoablation. "Less discomfort–Cryoablation results in little or no discomfort or pain during the procedure. It shows greater stability and minimization of risk to damaging critical structures–as cold temperatures are applied; Cryocatheters stick to the tissue they touch, much like a tongue on cold metal. This is an advantage because ablation is performed in a beating heart where there is constant movement. This helps prevent accidental damage to critical structures nearby."

"Cryoablation allows for tissue to be slightly frozen to test whether it is responsible for causing an arrhythmia. Heat-based therapies don't allow that—once the tissue is burned, it stays burned. By contrast, cryoablation allows the electrophysiologist to re-warm frozen tissue (that is not responsible for the arrhythmia) and restore its normal electrical function. It minimizes the risk of perforation. Because it preserves tissue integrity, there is minimal risk of perforation with cryoablation." However, you cannot continue cryoablation much beyond 30 seconds before permanent damage occurs. When the cryo. is turned off early, the body will slowly rewarm the ablated area and make it viable again. See: http://Palmettohealth .org

8. When using cryoablation in AVNRT, if AV block develops:
   a. **Junctional rhythm is likely to result**
   b. **Complete AV Block is likely to result**
   c. **2nd degree AV Block is likely to result**
   d. **AV Block is often reversible by thawing the region**

ANSWER: d. AV Block is often reversible by thawing the region. Issa says, "Cryomapping" is designed to verify that ablation at the chosen site will have the desired effect and to reassure the absence of complications (i.e., to localize electric pathways to be destroyed or spared). This is generally performed using various pacing protocols that can be performed during cryomapping (or ice mapping) at -30°C. At this temperature, the lesion is reversible (for up to 60 seconds), and the catheter is stuck to the adjacent frozen tissue because of the presence of an ice ball that includes the tip of the catheter (Cryoadherence). This permit programmed electrical stimulation to test the functionality of a potential ablation target during ongoing ablation and prior to permanent destruction; it also allows ablation being performed during tachycardia without the risk of catheter dislodgment on termination of the tachycardia." See: Issa, chapter on Ablation Energy Sources

9. In cryoablation, formation of an ice ball at the catheter tip and adherence to the myocardium is indicated when:
   a. **Catheter temperature suddenly drops**
   b. **Distal electrodes show electrical noise**
   c. **Premature beats or junctional rhythms develop**
   d. **ST elevation or T wave inversion develops on closest ECG leads**

ANSWER: b. Distal electrodes show electrical noise. Issa says, "Formation of an ice ball at the catheter tip and adherence to the underlying myocardium are signaled by the appearance of electrical noise recorded from the ablation catheter's distal bipole. Once an ice ball is formed, programmed stimulation is repeated to verify achievement of the desired effect. If cryomapping does not yield the desired result within 20 to 30 seconds or results in unintended effect (e.g., AV conduction delay or block), cryomapping is interrupted, allowing the catheter to thaw, and become dislodged from the tissue; after a few seconds, the catheter may be moved to a different site and cryomapping repeated." See: Issa, chapter on Ablation Energy Sources

Huang & Wood say, "When temperatures reach -20° C and colder, electrical noise appears on the distal electrode pair, with loss of the local electrogram signal due to ice ball formation." See: Huang & Wood, chapter on Catheter Cryoablation

10. During a PVI procedure, the cryoballoon (Arctic Front) should be inflated using the _____ in the _____.
   a. **Hand injection syringe: PV then pulled back to the PV ostium**
   b. **Hand injection syringe; LA then advanced into the PV ostium**
   c. **CryoConsole start button; PV then pulled back to the PV ostium**
   d. **CryoConsole start button; LA then advanced into the PV ostium**

ANSWER: d. CryoConsole start button; LA then advanced into the PV ostium. The Medtronic manual says: "Pulmonary vein narrowing or stenosis – Catheter ablation procedures inside or near pulmonary veins may induce pulmonary vein narrowing and/or stenosis. Do not ablate in the tubular portion of the pulmonary vein. Do not inflate the balloon while the catheter is positioned inside a pulmonary vein. Always inflate the balloon in the atrium and then position it at the pulmonary vein ostium." Inflating the balloon in the pulmonary vein may result in vascular injury." See: Medtronic, ARCTIC FRONT®, 2AF232, 2AF282 Technical Manual.

11. How and when should the cryoballoon (Arctic Front) be deflated?
   a. **Physician pulls back on the inflation syringe only when balloon temp is < 0° C.**
   b. **Physician inflation syringe only when balloon temperature is > 20° C.**
   c. **Technician presses the STOP button. The console waits until the temp is < 0° C then deflates automatically.**
   d. **Technician presses the STOP button. The console waits until the balloon temperature is > 20° C then deflates automatically.**

ANSWER: d. Technician presses the CryoConsole STOP button. The console waits until the balloon temperature is above 20° C then deflates automatically. When you hit the stop button, the balloon waits to deflate until the temperature rises to 20°. (Don't hit "stop" twice as it will rapidly deflate and may tear the vein to which it is frozen). See: Medtronic, ARCTIC FRONT®, 2AF232, 2AF282 Cardiac Cryoablation Catheter Technical Manual.

12. What is a typical inflation time for the cryoballoon (Arctic Front) in a PVI procedure?
   a. **30 seconds**
   b. **1-2 minutes**
   c. **3-4 minutes**
   d. **5-6 minutes**

ANSWER: c. 3-4 minutes. Medtronic says, "On average, PVI is typically achieved after two to three, 4-minute applications of energy per vein. A circular mapping catheter is then used to confirm pulmonary vein isolation." Newer balloons may only need three minutes of inflation to ablate the circular lesion. Since the balloon is rigid and does not conform to irregular shapes it takes several attempts to get a good ablation. With the newer balloon, these freeze times will vary with physician preference, the seal, and time to isolation.
See: https://wwwp.medtronic.com Arctic Front simulation PVI Complications

13. Prior to cryoablation, how can you tell if the inflated cryoballoon (Arctic Front) is properly positioned? Select four best answers below.
   a. **Balloon pressure should increase.**
   b. **It is in the tubular portion of the PV.**
   c. **The distal contrast injection remains in the PV.**
   d. **The distal pressure rises from the LA to PA level.**
   e. **The inflated balloon should be round - not oval.**
   f. **The motion of balloon on fluoroscopy should stop bouncing.**
   g. **The ICE color Doppler may be used to identify leaks around balloon**

ANSWERS: c. d. e. g. When you do a small hand contrast injection, it should occlude the PV with a tight seal, so contrast remains in the PV. d. A PV wedge pressure shows you have occluded the PV and should rise to PA pressure. This is like a pulmonary capillary wedge with a Swan-Ganz, but instead of looking downstream the catheter looks upstream to the PA. e. The balloon is rigid and could damage the tubular portion of the PV. It should be inflated in the LA to its spherical shape and then inserted into the antrum. Many labs use ICE Doppler to search for jets (leaks) around the inflated balloon. See: Medtronic.com

14. Cryoablation of the slow pathway in AVNRT usually results in:
   a. **An ice ball**
   b. **Junctional Tachycardia**
   c. **More thrombus than RF ablation**
   d. **More long-term success than RF ablation**

ANSWER: a. An ice ball, or cryoadherence. Issa says, "Formation of an ice ball at the catheter tip and adherence to the underlying myocardium are signaled by the appearance of electrical noise recorded from the ablation catheter's distal bipole.... During cryoablation of the slow pathway, no junctional rhythm is observed. Thus, other parameters must be used to validate the potential effectiveness of the ablation site. In fact, the absence of junctional rhythm can be advantageous because it allows the maintenance of NSR during ablation and enables monitoring of the PR interval throughout the procedure.... Furthermore, once the catheter tip temperature is reduced below 0°C, progressive ice formation at the catheter tip causes adherence to the adjacent tissue (cryoadherence), which maintains stable catheter contact at the site of ablation and minimizes the risk of catheter dislodgment during changing cardiac rhythm.... The acute and long-term success rates of cryoablation are slightly less than those with RF ablation (85% to 90%)." If junctional rhythm begins, you should pace slightly faster to watch for PR interval lengthening.

ICE Ball

See: Issa, chapter on AVNRT

15. You are performing a cryoablation on a patient with AVNRT. After 20 seconds of the energy application, complete AV block develops. You should stop ablation and expect:
   a. **Junctional rhythm**
   b. **Permanent complete heart block**
   c. **To switch to a pacemaker implant**
   d. **Reversal of AV Block with thawing**

ANSWER: d. Reversal of AV Block with thawing. Issa says, "Cryomapping is designed to verify that ablation at the chosen site will have the desired effect and to reassure the absence of complications (i.e., to localize electric pathways to be destroyed or spared). This is performed using various pacing protocols that can be performed during cryomapping (or ice mapping) at -30°C. At this temperature, the lesion is reversible (for up to 60 seconds), and the catheter is stuck to the adjacent frozen tissue because of the presence of an ice ball that includes the tip of the catheter (cryoadherence). These permits programmed electrical stimulation to assess the functionality of a potential ablation target during ongoing ablation and prior to permanent destruction; it also allows ablation being performed during tachycardia without the risk of catheter dislodgment on termination of the tachycardia."
See: Issa, chapter on Ablation Energy Sources

16. Which of the following best describes the mechanism of cryoablation?
   a. **Cooling of the tissue**
   b. **Conductive heating**
   c. **Resistive heating**
   d. **Removal of heat**

ANSWER: d. Removal of heat. "Cryo technologies remove heat from tissues, lowering molecular movement and stored kinetic energy, which results in tissue cooling and ice formation. Blood flow and surrounding body tissues return heat to the deficit area, a potential obstacle during ablation of a highly perfused organ such as the heart."
See: Avitall, Cryotherapy of cardiac arrhythmia: From basics to the bedside. Heart Rhythm 2015.

17. Which of the following describes the ablation catheter selected for a PVI ablation utilizing cryo technology?
   a. **Contact force catheter**
   b. **Irrigated catheter**
   c. **Balloon catheter**
   d. **4 mm catheter**

ANSWER: c. Balloon catheter. "Cryocatheters come in two distinct types: traditional tip ablation catheters used for focal ablation and balloon used for PV isolation. Focal cryocatheters can have 4-, 6-, and 8-mm tips and have three additional proximal ring electrodes allowing for recording signals… The cryoballoon catheter features an inflatable balloon that acts as the expansion chamber as the liquid nitrous oxide converts to gas. Rapid and intense cooling leads to ice formation of the tissues in contact with the balloon. It has internal thermocouples to monitor temperature within the balloon."
See: Avitall, Cryotherapy of cardiac arrhythmia: From basics to the bedside. Heart Rhythm 2015.

18. Which of the following ablation catheters would be selected for ablation of an anteroseptal accessory pathway?
   a. **4 mm cryocatheter**
   b. **6 mm cryocatheter**
   c. **8 mm cryocatheter**
   d. **Cryoballoon**

ANSWER: a. 4 mm cryocatheter. Many physicians will still use RF ablation for an anteroseptal pathway, but if choosing cryotherapy, the most appropriate selection is the 4mm cryocatheter. Anteroseptal pathways are located near the bundle of His, ablation of the His would lead to complete heart block. The 4 mm cryocatheter is selected to form a more discrete lesion due to this proximity. It is often utilized over RF energy due to the slight reversibility if therapy is stopped in time. A 6 mm cryocatheter may be utilized for AVNRT, 8mm for areas further from the AV node, and the cryoballoon for pulmonary vein isolation.
See: Avitall, Cryotherapy of cardiac arrhythmia: From basics to the bedside. Heart Rhythm 2015.

19. Which of the following improvements were made on the 2nd generation of the cryoballoon? (Select two)

    a. Four times the number of refrigerant ports
    b. Twice the number of refrigerant ports
    c. Refrigerant ports moved proximally
    d. Refrigerant ports moved distally
    e. Direct tissue visualization
    f. Addition of contact force
    g. Addition of irrigation

ANSWER: b & d. "Compared to the first generation, the second generation has twice the number of refrigerant spray ports, which were moved distally to produce a more homogeneous cooling effect on the distal hemisphere of the balloon. Because of improved clinical outcomes in acute and long-term clinical studies, an exclusive use of the second-generation balloons is recommended." See: Avitall, Cryotherapy of cardiac arrhythmia: From basics to the bedside. Heart Rhythm 2015.

21. The mechanism responsible for inducing freezing capitalizes on this phenomenon.

    a. Parasympathetic effect
    b. Sympathetic effect
    c. β-agonists
    d. J-T effect

ANSWER: d. J-T effect. "At the most basic level, the J-T effect is the change in temperature of an expanding gas. For the J-T effect to occur, a specific set of parameters must be maintained. Liquefied gas is kept under constant pressure and insulated to prevent heat and energy exchange with the surrounding environment. This gas is passed under constant pressure from a small vessel (such as tubing or catheter stem) into an expansion chamber. In the expansion chamber the liquefied gas converts to gas, resulting in absorption of heat to produce tissue cooling and freezing." See: Avitall, Cryotherapy of cardiac arrhythmia: From basics to the bedside. Heart Rhythm 2015.

22. Different cell types respond differently to freezing, most cells die at _____ °C.

    a. 0
    b. -5
    c. -15
    d. -20

ANSWER: d. -20°C. "The majority of cells tolerate freezing temperatures between 0°C and -15°C for short periods. Because of the solute concentration levels present in cells, freezing does not typically occur until cells reach temperatures <5°C. When temperatures reach -20°C, most cells die. The duration of freeze time necessary for cellular death is proportional to freezing temperature, with lower temperatures requiring shorter duration of freezing.

Temperatures reaching < -50°C are always lethal, regardless of duration...research suggests that water permeability of cellular membranes controls freezing rate."
See: Avitall, Cryotherapy of cardiac arrhythmia: From basics to the bedside. Heart Rhythm 2015.

23. Which of the following may be observed with cryoablation for pulmonary vein isolation? (Select all that apply)
   a. **Atrial Esophageal Fistula**
   b. **Phrenic Nerve Palsy**
   c. **Hemoptysis**
   d. **PV Stenosis**

ANSWER. All the above. "Cryoablation within the PVs could extend into the parenchyma of the lungs and cause hemoptysis. Temperature <55°C is sufficient to induce cellular death. The proportion of ice at the PV may be large enough to engulf lung tissues, causing small vessels to rupture, which results in hemoptysis. Avoiding placement of the cryoballoon deep within the PV and limiting the freeze time if the temperatures are <50°C will minimize the injury. Oversizing the PV ostial diameter by using an appropriately sized balloon will ensure that the balloon does not migrate into the PV." See: Avitall, Cryotherapy of cardiac arrhythmia 2015.

24. Cell _____ results from extracellular and intracellular ice formation during cryoablation.
   a. **Hyperhydration**
   b. **Hyponatremia**
   c. **Hypernatremia**
   d. **Dehydration**

ANSWER: d. Dehydration. "Extracellular and intracellular ice formation results in dehydration as water crystallizes. Slow ice formation (<1.67°C/min) results in extracellular ice crystals that expel salt, thereby increasing ion concentration in the extracellular space. This osmotic gradient will shift intracellular fluid to the extracellular space, dehydrating the cell and increasing the intracellular concentration of solutes to lethal levels." See: Avitall, Cryotherapy of cardiac arrhythmia: From basics to the bedside. Heart Rhythm 2015.

25. Which of the following will give the best cryoablation lesion? (Select 4)
   a. **Rest period between freezes**
   b. **Long freeze time at -10°C**
   c. **Single ablation lesions**
   d. **Repeated cycles**
   e. **High thaw rate**
   f. **Low thaw rate**
   g. **-50°C reached**
   h. **-80°C reached**

ANSWERS: a, d, f, g. "Repeated cycles help ensure complete ablation. Repeating the freeze/thaw cycle has shown to extend lesion boundaries with each successive ablation, resulting in faster cooling and colder absolute temperatures. With subsequent freeze/thaw cycles, more cells lyse, greater microcirculatory failure occurs (reducing perfusion), and more fluid builds up. These factors improve the success of consecutive freezes.

As the tissue slowly thaws, it is subject to prolonged dehydration, solute effects, and ice recrystallization. Low thaw rates are preferable to high rates. Frostbite is commonly treated using fast defrosting, and studies have shown that quickly thawing cells has a preservative effect. During the procedure, the optimal thawing temperature allows the natural body heat and blood flow to thaw tissues.

The limited data suggest improved outcomes with rest periods during cryoablation. Ablated tissues allowed to restore temporarily in a state of hemostasis. During this period, a greater break down of microcirculatory systems occurs and additional fluid builds up (hemorrhaging, lysed cells, and static blood)."
See: Avitall, Cryotherapy of cardiac arrhythmia: From basics to the bedside. Heart Rhythm 2015.

26. After cryoablation is performed, how long does it take before the lesion is fully formed?
   a. 1 week
   b. 3 weeks
   c. 6 weeks
   d. 12 weeks

ANSWER: b. 3 weeks. "At 3 weeks the lesion is fully formed. At 6 weeks, lesions are dense with collagen, fat deposition, and surrounded by a periphery of small blood vessels. The lesion site fills with differentiated fibroblasts, creating a moderate degree of fibrosis. After 12 weeks, the lesion is fibrotic and has no signs of hemorrhage, inflammation, or necrosis."

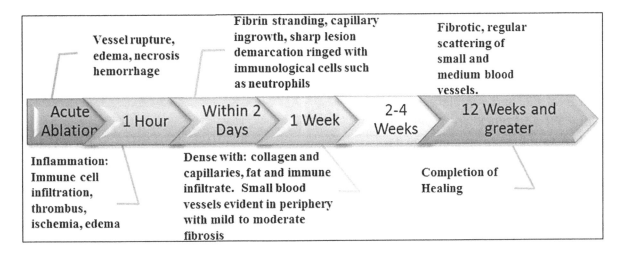

See: Avitall, Cryotherapy of cardiac arrhythmia: From basics to the bedside. Heart Rhythm 2015.

27. Esophageal fistula formation is possible with cryoablation if the esophageal temperature _____.
   a. Decreases by 1°C
   b. Decreases by 3°C
   c. Increases to 38°C
   d. Increases 3°C above baseline

ANSWER: b. Decreases by 3°C. "Clinical research has shown that compared with RF ablation, cryoablation carries a lower risk of fistula formation and is less severe if it occurs. However, if the luminal esophageal temperature decreased by only 3.1ºC from ambient temperature (second to ablation procedures in the inferior veins), fistula formation was possible. Although fistula formation is less common with cryoenergy, it remains as difficult to detect as with RF. The healing process begins 1–4 days after ablation with re-epithelialization followed by fibroblast infiltration and mild to moderate fibrosis. During this period, any esophageal ulceration is at its most vulnerable, and physical (hard food) or chemical (gastric acid) stress may exacerbate the injury, leading to rupture. After 28 days, the wound appears histologically normal." See: Avitall, Cryotherapy of cardiac arrhythmia: From basics to the bedside. Heart Rhythm 2015.

28. In cryomapping, formation of an ice ball at the catheter tip and adherence to the myocardium occurs when:
   a. Catheter temperature suddenly drops
   b. Distal electrodes show electrical noise
   c. Premature beats or junctional rhythms develop
   d. ST elevation or T wave inversion develops on closest surface leads

ANSWER: b. Distal electrodes show electrical noise - noted in the Cryo. mapping catheter shown. This diagram #2 shows the electrical noise caused by the ice ball as well as lengthening PR interval #2, and AV block at #3. The long PR and block are reversed soon after stopping the cryo energy #4.

Note the temperature was only -25°, so the ablation process can be reversed by warming.

Issa says, "Formation of an ice ball at the catheter tip and adherence to the

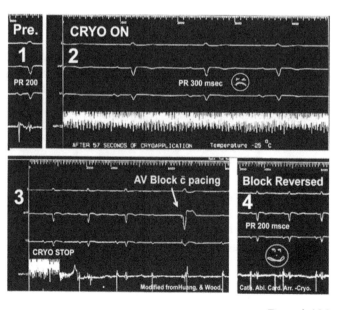

underlying myocardium are signaled by the appearance of electrical noise recorded from the ablation catheter's distal bipole. Once an ice ball is formed, programmed stimulation is repeated to verify achievement of the desired effect. If cryomapping does not yield the desired result within 20 to 30 seconds or results in unintended effect (e.g., AV conduction delay or block), cryomapping is interrupted, allowing the catheter to thaw, and become dislodged from the tissue; after a few seconds, the catheter may be moved to a different site and cryomapping repeated." See: Issa, chapter on Ablation Energy Sources

29. What ablation method is initially temporary, and the injury is usually reversible. This allows you to assess and confirm an ablation site before destroying it. This is especially useful to prevent AV block when ablating the AVN slow pathway. This type of test ablation is termed:
  a. **Temporizing ablation**
  b. **Entrainment mapping**
  c. **Energy titration**
  d. **Cryomapping**

ANSWER: d. Cryomapping. Medtronic says, "Freezor can create temperatures at its tip as low as -75° C inside a beating heart. It offers a site-testing capability – which involves a technique called cryomapping – which may aid physicians to avoid unwanted electrophysiological effects on AV node conduction. In Cryomapping mode, the Cryoablation system temporarily chills conducting tissue in the target area, creating a reversible electrical effect. This allows for precise site testing and confirmation prior to proceeding with definitive ablation. This is helpful when performing AVNRT procedures."

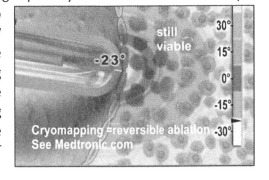

See: Medtronic.com

"As the temperature decreases during cryoablation, the electrical properties of the affected tissue gradually decrease. This gradual effect on the heart tissue permits the physician to observe changes in electrical properties of the affected tissue gradually. Stopping cryoablation will usually result in recovery of the heart tissues properties in these outermost regions. This property usually permits the physician to regulate the size of the region of heart tissue more precisely. When applied to particularly sensitive regions of the heart such as the AV node. This property of catheter cryoablation may significantly decrease the risk of unintentional damage to the AV node, reducing the risk of the need for a permanent pacemaker during catheter ablation in this region." http://stanfordhospital.org

"Freezing to an intermediate temperature of -30° C will result in reversible injury to the tissue "temporarily" eliminating cardiac conduction. This allows for "cryomapping" in order to avoid potentially serious complications such as inadvertent creation of heart block...."
See: Steinberg, chapter on "EP Equipment"

30. Match the ablation energy to the description or mechanism of action.
   1. Laser
   2. Radiofrequency
   3. Cryothermal
   4. Microwave
   5. Electroporation (Pulsed Field Ablation)

   a. Electric fields are applied to increase cell permeability leading to apoptosis
   b. Lowering the molecular movement and stored kinetic energy of the tissue to remove heat
   c. The source of heat comes from electromagnetic radiation
   d. The current flows through the tissue causing the ions to move back and forth resulting in localized frictional heat surrounding the electrode
   e. Produces a vibrational excited state in molecules and can be delivered in a continuous or pulse mode to create tissue heating and lesion formation

ANSWERS: 1. e, 2. d, 3. b, 4. c, 5. a
Laser: Produces a vibrational excited state in molecules and can be delivered in a continuous or pulse mode to create tissue heating and lesion formation
Radiofrequency: The current flows through the tissue causing the ions to move back and forth resulting in localized frictional heat surrounding the electrode
Cryothermal: Lowering the molecular movement and stored kinetic energy of the tissue to remove heat
Microwave: The source of heat comes from electromagnetic radiation
Electroporation (Pulsed Field Ablation): Electric fields are applied to increase cell permeability leading to apoptosis

AV Node Ablation:

1. A patient with an EF of 40% has had two PVI ablation procedures returns with symptomatic persistent AF. His rapid AF is poorly controlled with medications. You expect the treatment to be:
   a. AV Node ablation and VVI pacemaker
   b. AV Node ablation and DDD pacemaker
   c. Modified Maze procedure and VVI pacemaker
   d. Modified Maze procedure and DDD pacemaker

ANSWER: a. AV Node ablation and VVI pacemaker. Braunwald says, "Radiofrequency catheter ablation ... is a useful strategy in patients who are symptomatic from AF because of a rapid ventricular rate that cannot be adequately controlled pharmacologically as a result of either inefficacy of or intolerance to rate-control drugs and who either are not good candidates for ablation of the AF or already have undergone an unsuccessful attempt at catheter ablation of the AF. Because of the better success rate with catheter ablation of paroxysmal AF than of persistent AF, AV node ablation is more often performed in patients with persistent than with paroxysmal AF."

"In patients with persistent AF, a ventricular pacemaker is implanted, and a dual-chamber pacemaker is appropriate if the AF is paroxysmal. Most patients have a good clinical outcome with right ventricular pacing; but in patients with left ventricular dysfunction, biventricular pacing for cardiac resynchronization therapy is appropriate. In patients with an ischemic or nonischemic cardiomyopathy and an ejection fraction =30% to 35%, an ICD may be appropriate for primary prevention of sudden death. However, a simple pacemaker without the ICD often is adequate for patients with a borderline ejection fraction (30% to 35%) and a rapid ventricular rate because the ejection fraction is likely to improve to >35% after the ventricular rate has been controlled by AV node ablation." See: Braunwald, chapter on "AF: Nonpharmacologic management"

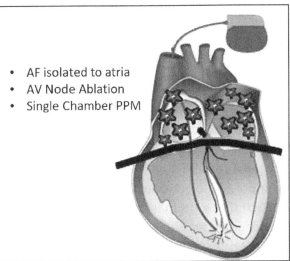

- AF isolated to atria
- AV Node Ablation
- Single Chamber PPM

2. Where should you place the ablation catheter to do an AV node ablation on the above patient in persistent AF?
   a. Ablate at the site of maximum His amplitude in both RA and LV (if needed)
   b. From the RA, identify the His then pull back the ablation catheter
   c. From the RA, identify the His then advance the ablation catheter
   d. From the LV, ablate at the site of maximum His amplitude beneath the aortic valve

ANSWER: b. From the RA, identify the His then pull back the ablation catheter.
Ellenbogen says, "Ideally the ablation is guided by mapping proximal His bundle recordings. The catheter is positioned to record the maximum His potential. Although it is often tempting to ablate at the site of maximal His recording, ablation at this site often produces right bundle branch block only. The catheter is withdrawn toward the atrium to record an A/V ratio of 1: or 12:2 and a small His electrogram, usually less than 0.15 mV in amplitude. The catheter tip may need to be deflected slightly inferiorly to follow the course of the AV conduction system.... The failure to record the His often predicts failure to AV junctional ablation on the right side. Cardioversion to sinus rhythm may allow better demonstration of the His potential.... Successful ablation sites usually produce accelerated junctional rhythm within 5 seconds and complete AV nodal block within 30 seconds." See: Ellenbogen chapter AV Junction Ablation and Modification for Heart Rate Control of Atrial Fibrillation.

3. What is the most important thing to do before AV node ablation procedure a patient in persistent AF?
   a. **Place a DDD pacemaker and set to DDI mode with rate 60-70**
   b. **Place an RV demand pacemaker with rate 40-50 bpm**
   c. **Use rate control drugs and cardiovert**
   d. **Do a TTE to assure no clots are present**

ANSWER: b. Place an RV demand pacemaker with rate 40-50 bpm. This will kick in as soon as the AV node is destroyed and idioventricular bradycardia starts. Atrial pacing or DDD is not appropriate since the patient will continue in AF after AVN ablation. If the PPI is not implanted before ablation, place a temporary RV pacer so you can support the patient after ablation. Do a TEE not a TTE to rule out LA thrombus. Note the ECG showing the backup pacer taking over and firing at a slow rate after AV node ablation.

Ellenbogen says, "Before AV junction ablation is performed, appropriate ventricular backup pacing must be ensured. This can be achieved by either placing a temporary electrode catheter at the RV apex or implanting a permanent pacemaker before the ablation procedure. By implanting the device weeks before the ablation procedure, the problems associated with post implantation pacemaker system malfunction are avoided.... The pacemaker should be set to VVI or VOO mode at 40-50 bpm before ablation." See: Ellenbogen, chapter on AV Node Ablation

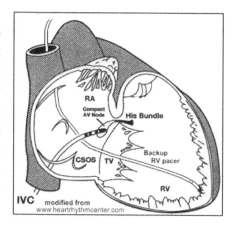

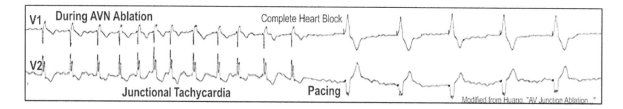

4. A 78-year-old patient with paroxysmal atrial fibrillation with rapid ventricular conduction, comes into your EP lab for an AV node ablation. The patient has an underlying sinus rate of 30 bpm. His pacemaker is programmed to DDD 60 bpm that is currently pacing as shown. What is the best method to identify CHB during AV node ablation?
   a. **Set the device to VVI 40**
   b. **Set the device to VOO 40**
   c. **Give Isuprel while ablating**
   d. **Increase rate & extend the device PR interval**

ANSWER: d. Increase rate and extend the device PR interval. All the answers may be performed during an AV node ablation; however, d. is the best answer for this patient.

INCORRECT ANSWERS ARE:

- Not a or b: If the underlying HR were higher than 40 this would be acceptable, as the atrial rate would be faster than the slowly paced ventricle in CHB.
- Not c: If the patient did not have an atrial lead this would be an excellent way to increase the patient's heart rate and watch for complete heart block. Typically, this is done with the ventricular rate set VVI 40. However, since we have an atrial lead, it makes more sense to pace the atrium at a faster rate. If we do this in combination with extending the PR interval the patient's innate conduction system will track the atrial rate. Once CHB is achieved, you should see atrial pacing and associated ventricular paced beats.
- It is more physiologic to pace DDD. If they have P waves, then they may track with their own sinus rate. The idea is to keep the atrial contribution. Typically, after AVN ablation for the first month or so the patient is paced at a faster rate, like low-rate limit of 80. This is thought to prevent torsades. However, if the patient is chronic AF, then he would have a single chamber VVI device. Typically, after AVN ablation for the first month or so the patient is paced at a faster rate, like low-rate limit of 80. This is thought to prevent torsades.

5. This EGM is recorded on an 86-year-old patient with a dual chamber ppm. This patient has paroxysmal atrial fibrillation with RVR (rapid ventricular response). Which ablation catheter location is the best site for AVN ablation?
   a. Site 1
   b. Site 2

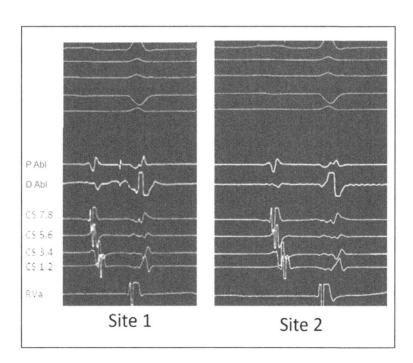

ANSWER: a. Site 1. Notice the sharp His deflection in between the atrial and ventricular deflections on Site 1. This is just distal to the AV node at the His bundle. Ablation at this location would result in CHB. Even though the His itself is very well insulated and difficult to ablate. The Ablation catheter needs to be withdrawn slightly for best results. The best location would show a smaller His on the proximal ablation channel and larger on the distal ablation channel (tip).

6. Which EGM shows the best location for an AV node ablation on this patient with persistent atrial fibrillation with RVR (rapid ventricular response)?
   a. **Site 1**
   b. **Site 2**

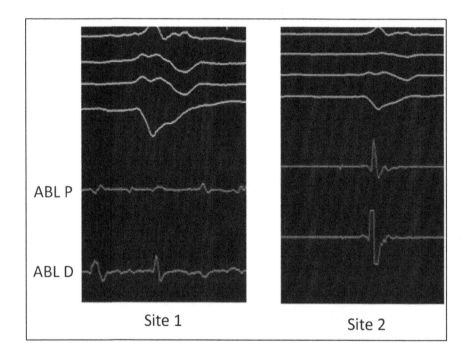

ANSWER: a. Site 1 is best for AV node ablation. It may be quite challenging trying to locate a His signal for an AV node ablation in a patient currently in atrial fibrillation. In atrial fibrillation the His is mixed in with all the extra atrial deflections from the fibrillation; however, the HV interval is relatively fixed. Therefore, look for a small, sharp deflection preceding every QRS complex. The EGM in Site 2 shows a nice sharp deflection on the ablation catheter preceding the QRS; however, this is not the His deflection. This is the right bundle branch signal which looks like a His deflection. Notice that there are no atrial signals on the ablation catheter. The catheter is too far into the ventricle. If the physician is having difficulties locating the His potential, he may advance to the ventricle, find the right bundle branch potential, and pull the catheter back until an atrial, His, and ventricular signal is observed.

7. In an AV node ablation, when the catheter is properly positioned on the AV node, what rhythm usually begins within seconds after beginning ablation?
   a. First degree AV block followed by 2nd degree AV block
   b. Second degree type II AB block followed by complete AV block
   c. Atrial tachycardia followed by 2nd degree AV block
   d. Accelerated junctional rhythm followed by complete AV block

ANSWER: d. Accelerated junctional rhythm followed by complete AV block. Ellenbogen says, "successful ablation sites usually produce accelerated junctional rhythm within five seconds and complete AV nodal block within 30 seconds." See: Ellenbogen chapter AV junction ablation and modification.

8. Parents want their child to have the SAFEST ablation to preserve the AV conduction. What ablation method is perceived to be the best for a young person with AVNRT?
   a. Non-irrigated RF
   b. Cryoablation
   c. Microwave
   d. Irrigated RF

ANSWER: b. Cryoablation. When ablating near the AV node there is always risk of creating AV block. If you do, with cryo- you have a window of opportunity to rewarm and rejuvenate the tissue. The AV block is temporary if you stop cryo-ablation as soon as you see dropped V waves. This is especially important for children with a life of activity ahead of them. Many EP labs use cryoablation on all children.

Papagiannis says, "even AV block occurring during cryoablation is reversible during the early phase of application. This fact has made cryoablation the preferred modality in many pediatric electrophysiology laboratories...." Because the cryoablation catheter "sticks" to the tissue, it makes it better for small active hearts since the ablation catheter won't move around as much as an RF ablation catheter.

"Although the arrhythmia recurrence rate is higher than that of RF ablation, cryoablation offers several advantages, such as greater safety regarding the AV conduction system and the coronary arterial circulation, which are of paramount importance in young patients with smaller and growing hearts. During preprocedural discussion and informed consent, most of the parents of our patients prefer the higher risk of recurrence to the small but existent risk of AV block and damage to the coronary arteries."
See: Papagiannis, Cryoablation Versus Radiofrequency Ablation, for Atrioventricular Nodal Reentrant Tachycardia in Children: Long-Term Results, Hellenic J Cardiol 2010; 51: 122-126

9. Your patient has coronary artery disease, persistent AF, dilated LA, and hypertension. He is scheduled for CABG surgery. What therapy would be given to provide freedom from AF without antiarrhythmic drugs?
   a. Coronary artery surgery with cardiac sympathetic nerve removal
   b. Minimally invasive surgical ablation (modified MAZE)
   c. AV node ablation with DDD pacemaker implant
   d. Pulmonary vein isolation with cryoballoon
   e. Pulmonary vein Isolation with RF

ANSWER: b. Minimally invasive surgical ablation (modified MAZE). Braunwald states: "In a population of patients with AF, with a dilated LA and hypertension, or a failed prior AF catheter ablation, minimally invasive surgical ablation is superior to catheter ablation to achieve freedom of left atria arrhythmia without anti-arrhythmic drugs during a follow-up of 12 months. Surgical ablation was, however, associated with a greater risk of adverse events, particularly those related to the procedure.... Pulmonary vein isolation often is sufficient to eliminate paroxysmal AF but rarely is sufficient for persistent AF."

"A large variety of surgical ablation tools have been developed to simplify the classic Cox maze procedure. These tools allow the surgeon to substitute an ablation line for a surgical incision. Several different types of energy have been used for surgical ablation: radiofrequency energy, cryoenergy, microwave, laser, and high-intensity focused ultrasound. The tool that most consistently produces transmural ablation lines is a clamp device intended to isolate the pulmonary veins by use of bipolar radiofrequency energy"

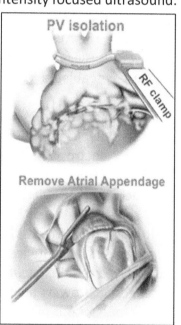

"At present, surgery for AF most commonly is performed as a concomitant procedure in patients with AF undergoing open heart surgery for coronary artery disease or valvular disease. A stand-alone surgical procedure for AF may be appropriate for patients who have not had a successful outcome from catheter ablation, who are not good candidates for catheter ablation, or who prefer a surgical procedure over catheter ablation." Some physicians are following up the modified MAZE procedure with "touch up" catheter ablation months later. A DDD pacemaker would be contraindicated in persistent AF, because there would be no good A wave to track.
See: Braunwald chapter on AF

10. The recommended therapy for patients that have a history of VT and an EF <30% due to prior MI but have NEVER had a cardiac arrest is:
   a. ICD for primary prevention of SCD
   b. ICD for secondary prevention of SCD
   c. Antiarrhythmic drugs for primary prevention of SCD
   d. Antiarrhythmic drugs for secondary prevention of SCD

ANSWER: a. ICD for primary prevention of SCD. Braunwald says, "the ICD is now the preferred therapy for survivors of cardiac arrest at risk for recurrences and for primary prevention in patients in a number of high-risk categories: See: Braunwald chapter on Sudden Cardiac Death.

11. Which fluoroscopic view is the most utilized to visualize the LAA for a closure procedure?
   a. RAO cranial
   b. RAO caudal
   c. LAO cranial
   d. LAO caudal

ANSWER: b. RAO caudal. "For the WATCHMAN device, the 14-F access sheath is advanced deep into the LAA using a pigtail (5- to 6-F) before device introduction. RAO 20° to 30° caudal 20° to 30° angulation typically allows good visualization of the distal lobes for sheath advancement and device deployment."
See: Saw, J., & Lempereur, M. (2014, November 17). Percutaneous left Atrial Appendage Closure: Procedural techniques and outcomes. Retrieved May 08, 2021, from: https://www.sciencedirect.com/science/article/pii/S1936879814012382#fig6

12. Why might doppler be utilized with ICE during PVI?
   a. Guide transseptal access
   b. Observe lesion formation
   c. Monitor for pericardial effusion
   d. Check for pulmonary vein stenosis

ANSWER: d. Check for pulmonary vein stenosis. PV stenosis may occur with RF ablation to close to the ostium or inside the vein itself.

13. While mapping atrial tachycardia, what would the unipolar signal look like at the best area for ablation?
   a. RS wave
   b. R wave
   c. QR wave
   d. QS wave

ANSWER: d. QS wave. If the electrode is at the earliest site, or focus, all of the activation will be traveling away from it. This would create a QS deflection. Recall, an impulse moving away from a positive pole will create a negative deflection (towards a positive pole creates a positive deflection). If the electrode is at the site of origin, the activation will be traveling away from the positive pole creating a QS deflection (negative) on the unipolar electrogram.

14. How would you assess conduction while the patient is in junctional rhythm observed during RF slow pathway ablation?
   a. **Pace the atrium**
   b. **Pace the ventricle**
   c. **Come off ablation**
   d. **Perform parahisian pacing**

ANSWER: a. Pace the atrium. What we are concerned with during ablation of the slow pathway for AVNRT is maintaining antegrade conduction from the atrium to the ventricle. We are unable to observe this if the patient is in junctional rhythm. Junctional rhythm is commonly seen and the desired effect of a slow pathway ablation with RF energy. To assure that antegrade conduction is still present, the physician may request atrial pacing to watch each signal conduct to the ventricle.

15. After ablation of a left posterior accessory pathway, the following ECG was recorded. What is observed?
   a. **Hyperkalemia**
   b. **Cardiac Memory**
   c. **Cardiac Ischemia**
   d. **Pericardial Effusion**
   e. **Myocardial Infarction**

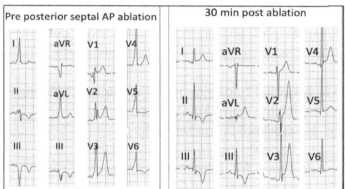

ANSWER: b. Cardiac Memory. "Cardiac memory (CM) refers to the persistent T-wave changes on the ECG after a period of wide QRS rhythms that become evident once a normal ventricular activation pattern is restored. It is related to the term ventricular electric remodeling sometimes used in basic science literature. Although CM itself is considered as an adaptive reaction to the change in the ventricular activation sequence, its manifestations (usually T-wave inversions, TWIs) are often confused with pathological conditions, such as myocardial ischemia or infarction. CM signature consisting of the specific combinations of negative and positive T waves can give a clue to the presence and localization of intermittent wide QRS rhythms including pre-excitation, ventricular tachycardia, and conduction abnormalities. The ECG recorded 30 minutes after the bypass tract ablation demonstrates tall, peaked T waves across the precordium as well as inferior TWI corresponding to the vector of the delta wave. Tall positive memory T waves in the right precordial leads can be easily confused with hyperkalemia or ischemia." See: Shvilkin, A., et al. (2015, April 01). Cardiac memory. Retrieved May 07, 2021, from https://www.ahajournals.org/doi/full/10.1161/circep.115.002778

16. Why should the operator and EP staff continue to observe the electrogram/ECG after RF energy is stopped?
Monitor for:
   a. **Coagulum Buildup**
   b. **Thermal Latency**
   c. **Tissue Adhesion**
   d. **Steam Pop**

ANSWER: b. Thermal Latency. The temperature of the tissue may continue to rise after ablation is stopped. If performing an ablation near the AV node and PR prolongation is noticed, the operator may abruptly stop applying energy, but the tissue will continue to heat. This thermal latency is due to the conductive heating of the tissue. It is much like if you are roasting a turkey, once the turkey is removed from the oven, the thermometer will continue to rise.

17. The Lariat, Watchman, and Amulet (etc.) are devices used in atrial fibrillation patients to:
   a. **Ablate the Pulmonary veins and reduce AF**
   b. **Cardiovert AF to increase CO and reduce risk of stroke**
   c. **Occlude the left atrial appendage and reduce risk of stroke**
   d. **Ablate AV node to reduce risk of rapid ventricular response**

ANSWER: c. Occlude the left atrial appendage and reduce risk of stroke.
All these devices cut off blood flow into the LA appendage, which is the major source of blood clots leading to stroke in patients with atrial fibrillation. These procedures are an alternative to troublesome blood thinners, such as Coumadin.

Chapter 13
Miscellaneous Tachycardia & Ablation

EP Essentials LLC

Supraventricular Arrhythmias:

AT: Kusumoto says, "In atrial tachycardias, the automatic site(s) or reentrant circuit is located within atrial tissue. A straightforward way to think of this is that if the ventricles and AV node region were separated from the atria, the tachycardia would continue.

AFL: A stable reentrant circuit within the atria is traditionally called atrial flutter, while a point source of abnormal automaticity is called focal atrial tachycardia.

AF: A tachycardia due to several foci firing rapidly within the atria is called multifocal atrial tachycardia, and chaotic irregular activation of the atria is called atrial fibrillation. Tachycardias from junctional tissue can be due to reentry or automaticity.

AVNRT: The most common cause of regular supraventricular tachycardia in your adults is development of reentry within the AV node and adjacent atrial tissue. Logically, this type of SVT is called AV Nodal reentry. Abnormal automaticity from junctional tissue is less commonly observed and is usually called junctional ectopic tachycardia."

AVRT: "The final anatomic type of SVT is due to the presence of an accessory pathway.... The presence of an AP connecting atrial and ventricular tissue is the classic example for initiation of reentry since the accessory pathway and the AV node form parallel pathways that connect atrial and ventricular tissue. Accessory pathways can be associated with SVT if a reentrant circuit develops that activates the ventricles (antegrade conduction) via the AV node and activates the atria (retrograde conduction) via the accessory pathway. This type of SVT is often called atrioventricular (AV) reentry [**AVRT**] to emphasize that both atrial and ventricular tissue are part of the reentrant circuit. Another term that is commonly added to describe this SVT is orthodromic AV reentry. **"Orthodromic"** refers to normal conduction (ortho means straight/correct in Greek) over the AV node and normal depolarization of the ventricles. Unfortunately, having multiple names for the same tachycardia adds to the confusion for the newcomer to electrophysiology." This is the only type of SVT that <u>requires</u> that the ventricle participate in the circuit. It may conduct orthodromic – down the AV node and up the pathway or antidromic – down the pathway and up the AV node. WPW is when the pathway manifests itself on the ECG with the appearance of the delta wave which shows conduction antegrade down the pathway; however, during tachycardia it may still be conducted in the orthodromic manner.

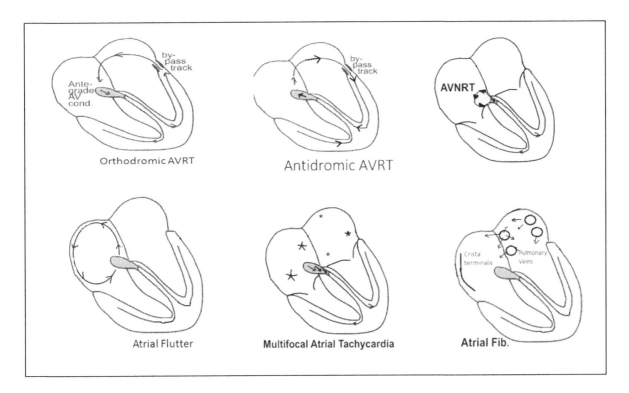

1. **Which arrhythmia most closely resembles an "itch of the heart" in acutely ill patients?**
   a. **Automatic arrhythmias**
   b. **Triggered arrhythmias**
   c. **Reentry arrhythmias**
   d. **SVT arrhythmias**

ANSWER: a. Automatic arrhythmias. These arrhythmias are due to abnormal acceleration of phase 4 activity. It accounts for less than 10% of tachycardias. Fogoros says, "Of all the tachyarrhythmias, automatic arrhythmias resemble an "itch of the heart" the most closely, and it is tempting to apply the salve of antiarrhythmic drugs...should be treated by identifying and reversing the underlying metabolic cause. Automatic tachyarrhythmias cannot be induced by programmed pacing techniques, so these arrhythmias are generally not amenable to provocative study in the EP laboratory." .... Automatic tachycardias often display a warm-up and warm-down rate when the arrhythmia begins and ends. Analogous to sinus tachycardia, automatic tachycardias also have metabolic causes, such as acute cardiac ischemia, hypoxemia, hypokalemia, hypomagnesemia, acid-base disorders, high sympathetic tone, and sympathomimetic agents. Therefore, automatic arrhythmias are often seen in acutely ill patients, often in the intensive care setting, with all the attendant metabolic abnormalities." See: Fogoros chapter on Principles of the Electrophysiology Study

2. Which tachycardia is most associated in a patient with a history of congestive heart failure, stroke, and increased hospitalization?
   a. **Ventricular tachycardia**
   b. **Atrial Fibrillation**
   c. **AVNRT**
   d. **AVRT**

ANSWER: b. Atrial Fibrillation. "Atrial fibrillation (AF) is one of the most common clinical arrhythmias affecting about 1.5-2% of the general population in developed countries. Several complications, including congestive heart failure, stroke, and hospitalization, were associated with AF. At present, there are two main therapeutic strategies for AF, namely, antiarrhythmic drugs and radiofrequency catheter ablation. The use of the former is limited because of the accumulative proarrhythmic risk. A radiofrequency catheter ablation guided by a three-dimensional (3D) mapping system has been introduced recently, and its superiority in safety and efficacy has been reported in many studies."
See: Zhou, et al, Catheter ablation of paroxysmal atrial fibrillation using high-density mapping-guided substrate modification. Pacing and Clinical Electrophysiology, 2018.

3. During an EP study for SVT a supraventricular reentry tachycardia was easily initiated with an Isuprel drip. This suggests that the _____ participates in the reentry loop.
   a. **Coronary sinus tissue**
   b. **Pulmonary vein**
   c. **SA node**
   d. **AV node**

ANSWER: d. AV node. Fogoros says: "In the case of supraventricular arrhythmias, if reentry depends on automatic tone, that is strong evidence that the AV node participates in the reentrant loop." This suggests AVRT or ANVRT both of which rely on the AV node to complete the reentry loop. Isuprel as sympathomimetic to speed AV conduction and heart rate. See: Fogoros chapter on Principles of the Electrophysiology Study

4. A 20-year-old male patient with a wide complex tachycardia (WCT) was brought for an EP study and ablation. The differential diagnosis includes all the following except:
   a. **AVNRT**
   b. **AVRT**
   c. **1:1 Atrial Flutter**
   d. **Ventricular Tachycardia**
   e. **All the above are possible**

Answer: e. AVNRT, AVRT, 1:1 Atrial Flutter, and Ventricular tachycardia are all possible and further testing is needed. Any rhythm may cause a wide QRS complex if there is aberrant conduction down the bundle branches due to the rapid ventricular rate.

Brugada says, "Current criteria for the differential diagnosis between supraventricular tachycardia with aberrant conduction and ventricular tachycardia are frequently absent or suggest the wrong diagnosis. The absence of an RS complex in all precordial leads is easily recognizable and highly specific for the diagnosis of ventricular tachycardia. When an RS complex is present in one or more precordial leads, an RS interval of more than 100 ms is highly specific for ventricular tachycardia. This new stepwise approach may prevent diagnostic mistakes." See: A new approach to the differential diagnosis of a regular tachycardia with a wide QRS complex. P Brugada; J Brugada; L Mont; J Smeets; E W Andries

5. Which two patients below, with a narrow complex tachycardia and heart rate over 150 bpm, should be cardioverted (biphasic) starting at low energy (e.g., 50 J)?
(Select 2 answers below)
   a. **Ventricular Fibrillation**
   b. **Ventricular Tachycardia (polymorphic)**
   c. **Atrial Flutter**
   d. **Supraventricular AVNRT**
   e. **Chronic Atrial Fibrillation**

ANSWER: c & d. Atrial flutter and supraventricular AVNRT. These rhythms have a strong narrow QRS complex necessary to trigger the Cardioverter, and the atrial muscle mass being smaller than ventricular can be converted with smaller amounts of energy. These rhythms are not usually emergencies, so you have time to optimize the ECG leads and the patient's condition.

Ventricular fibrillation and pulseless ventricular tachycardia should receive emergency defibrillation. Asystole cannot be converted with high voltage shock (unless it is fine VF). Synchronized cardioversion must not be used for treatment of VF as the device may not sense a QRS wave and thus a shock may not be delivered. Synchronized cardioversion should also not be used for pulseless VT or polymorphic (irregular VT). These rhythms require delivery of high-energy unsynchronized shocks (i.e., defibrillation doses)."

Issa says, "If AVNRT cannot be terminated with intravenous drugs [or vagal maneuvers], DC cardioversion can always be used. Energies in the range of 10 to 50 J are usually adequate.... Direct current cardioversion of atrial flutter to sinus rhythm has a high likelihood of success. With use of a monophasic shock, it also requires as little as 25 J, although at least 50 J is recommended because it is more often successful. Because 100 J is virtually always successful and virtually never harmful, it should be considered as the initial shock. Even less energy is required in using a biphasic shock to achieve cardioversion." See, Issa, chapter on AVNRT

The recommended initial biphasic energy dose for cardioversion of adult atrial fibrillation is 120 to 200 J (Class IIa, LOE A). Cardioversion of adult atrial flutter and other supraventricular tachycardias generally requires less energy; an initial energy of 50 J to 100 J is often sufficient. If the initial shock fails, providers should increase the dose in a stepwise fashion." See: ACLS manual chapter on "Defibrillation."

6. This EGM shows induction of SVT. What do the last A waves indicate?

  a. **Atrial flutter 1:1 conduction**
  b. **Accessory pathway AVRT**
  c. **Jump to slow pathway**
  d. **AV nodal echo beats**

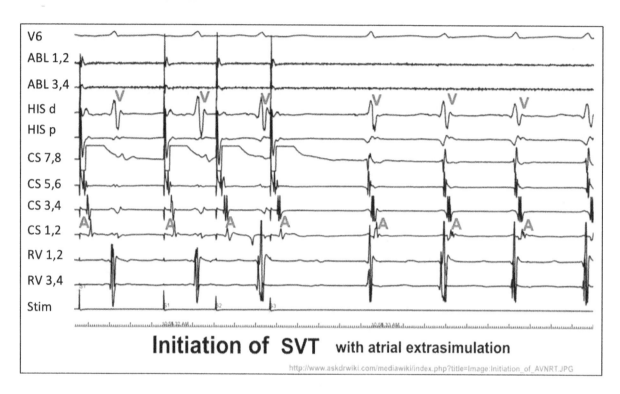

Initiation of SVT with atrial extrasimulation

http://www.askdrwiki.com/mediawiki/index.php?title=Image:Initiation_of_AVNRT.JPG

ANSWER: d. AV nodal echo beats. This EGM shows initiation of AVNRT with a "jump" and echo beats following each narrow AVNRT QRS, each caused by the slow-fast AVN reentry loop. Issa says, "Atrial echoes and AVNRT usually occur while dual pathways are revealed." Note that as the reentry loop hits the AVN the impulse splits, with half going down the slow pathway to the AV node and half rising retrograde up the fast path into the atrium. This retrograde A is called an "AV nodal echo beat." The antegrade potential reaches the ventricle about the same time as the retrograde echo potential reaches the ventricle. Thus, the A & V may be superimposed. The typical CCW AVNRT cycle can be summed up by down the slow (to the AV node) and up the fast (retrograde to the atrium). The AV nodal echo A waves are labeled on the CS 1,2 electrode, but not seen in other leads.

7. Match the SVT with its response to adenosine administration.

  a. **AT**   1. Ruled out if SVT continues with AV block
  b. **AVRT**   2. SVT terminates with an A as the last event
  c. **AVNRT**   3. SVT continues but with AV block

CORRECTLY MATCHED ANSWERS ARE:
   a. AT   3. SVT continues but with AV block
   b. AVRT   1. Ruled out if SVT continues with AV block
   c. AVNRT   2. SVT terminates with an A

In Atrial tachycardia, since adenosine won't affect the atrial rate, A waves will continue unaffected. After a period of AV block and ventricular asystole SVT will resume. In AVRT, the AV node is necessary for the macroreentry. If AV block occurs and the atria continues beating, it cannot be AVRT. This is most obvious if you pace the ventricle and then give adenosine. A retrograde accessory pathway will conduct up, but the resulting A will not conduct down the AV node and His.

In AVNRT adenosine blocks the upper AV node and slow pathway and will thus usually break the SVT. After the period of ventricular asystole sinus rhythm may resume. "Reproducible termination of the SVT with a QRS not followed by a P wave excludes orthodromic AVRT using a rapidly conducting AV BT as the retrograde limb (adenosine blocks the AVN and not the BT), is unusual in typical AVNRT (adenosine blocks the slow pathway but does not affect the fast pathway), and is consistent with AT, PJRT, or atypical AVNRT." Issa, chapter on "Approaches to Paroxysmal SVT" and Fig.5.24 of Kusumoto chapter on SVT

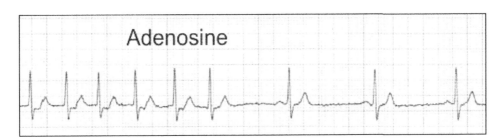

8. Match the SVT to its usual AV relationship:
   a. **AT**   **1. VA longer than AV interval**
   b. **AVRT**   **2. Simultaneous A & V**
   c. **AVNRT**   **3. VA shorter than AV interval**

CORRECTLY MATCHED ANSWERS ARE:
   a. AT   1. VA longer than AV interval
   b. AVRT   3. VA shorter than AV interval
   c. AVNRT 2. Simultaneous A & V

In atrial tachycardia, you expect short AV intervals (short PR), and a longer ventricular refractory period (longer VA). Kusumoto says, "Atrial activity usually precedes ventricular activity but can be "anywhere" - with the specific location dependent on the atrial rate and AV node conduction properties." Read carefully. Here, the VA interval is described first and the AV interval last.

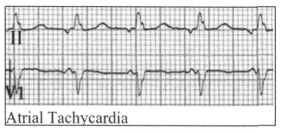
Atrial Tachycardia

In AVRT the A waves are retrograde and behind the V. "Atrial activation will occur after ventricular activation." In AVNRT, the A's are commonly buried in the V's because of the echo beats. "Typically, the atrial and ventricular signals will be simultaneous, but almost any relationship can be seen in atypical forms." See: Table 5.2 of Kusumoto chapter on SVT

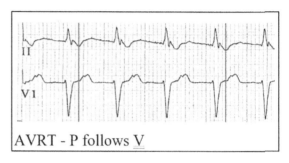
AVRT - P follows V

9. Which micro-reentrant arrhythmia is caused by a blocked fast pathway and conduction through a slow pathway?
  a. AVRT
  b. AVNRT
  c. Mobitz I AV block
  d. Mobitz II AV block

ANSWER: b. AVNRT. Cohen says, "One of the most common types of supraventricular tachycardias is AV-nodal reentrant tachycardia. (AVNRT). As the name indicates, this is a micro reentrant tachycardia that involves the AV node. In approximately 25% of patients, there is more than one AV nodal pathway. These patients often have a fast (alpha) pathway and a slow (beta) pathway." This is a setup for a reentry tachycardia. See: Cohen, chapter on AV-Nodal Reentrant Tachycardia.

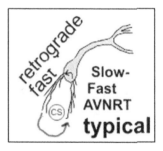

10. Which arrhythmia reveals a sudden decrease in the A2-H2 interval with progressively early atrial extrastimuli graph as shown in the diagram?
  a. AVRT
  b. AVNRT
  c. Mobitz I AV block
  d. Mobitz II AV block

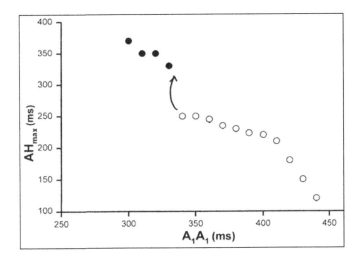

ANSWER: b. AVNRT. Cohen says, "In AVNRT programmed atrial stimulation (A1A2) typically reveals the presence of a "jump" in which progressive earlier extrastimuli demonstrate a jump in the A2H2 interval indicative of refractoriness in the fast AV nodal pathway. Elimination of the slow pathway (post ablation) reveals no evidence of a jump and only a single curve. See: Cohen, chapter on AV-Nodal Reentrant Tachycardia.

11. Which tachycardia typically starts by warming-up and then cooling-down (rate speeds at beginning and slows later)?
   a. AVRT
   b. AVNRT
   c. Atrial Flutter
   d. Atrial Fibrillation
   e. Atrial Tachycardia

ANSWER: e. Atrial tachycardia. Focal automatic ATs start with a P wave identical to the P wave during the arrhythmia and the rate generally increases gradually (warms up) over the first few seconds. In comparison, interatrial reentry or triggered-activity AT is usually initiated by a P wave from a premature atrial complex (PAC) that differs in morphology from the normal P wave during the established arrhythmia.
Automatic AT cannot be entrained by atrial pacing. Rapid atrial pacing results in overdrive suppression of the AT rate. The AT resumes after cessation of atrial pacing but at a slower rate and gradually speeds up (warms up) to return to the tachycardia CL. Occasionally, overdrive pacing produces no effect at all on automatic AT.

12. What type of narrow complex tachycardia commonly has a regular ventricular rate around 150 bpm?
   a. AF
   b. AVRT
   c. AVNRT
   d. AFL with 2:1 block

ANSWER: d. AFL with 2:1 block. This 2:1 AFL heart rate is 140 bpm, just under 150 bpm. Zipes says, "The rate of the untreated tachycardia often narrows diagnostic possibilities, and patients should be instructed in how to count their radial or carotid pulse rate. Ventricular rates of 150 beats per minute should always suggest the 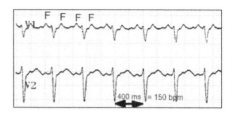 potential diagnosis of atrial flutter with 2:1 AV block, whereas most supraventricular tachycardias, such as those caused by AVNRT or AVRT, usually occur at rates exceeding 150 beats per minute."

"Knowledge about the typical onset and termination of tachycardia is helpful. Abrupt, paroxysmal onset is consistent with tachycardia such as AV nodal reentrant tachycardia (AVNRT) whereas gradual speeding and slowing are more in keeping with a sinus tachycardia. Termination by Valsalva maneuver or carotid sinus massage suggests a tachycardia incorporating nodal tissue in the reentrant pathway, such as sinus node reentry, AVNRT or AV reentrant tachycardia (AVRT), and idiopathic right ventricular outflow tract tachycardia."
See: Zipes, chapter on Diagnostic Evaluation, Palpitations

13. Identify the tachycardia shown in this EGM, after CSM (carotid sinus massage).
   a. **Sinus tachycardia**
   b. **Atrial tachycardia**
   c. **AVRT**
   d. **AVNRT**

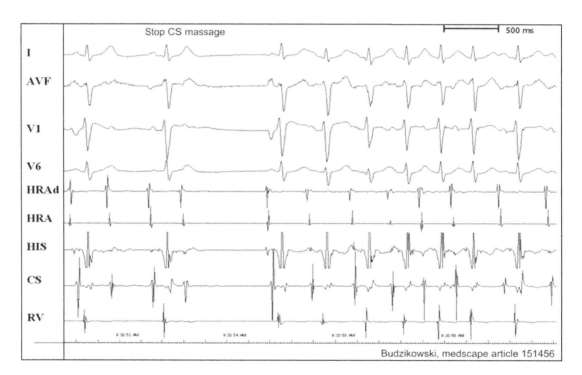

ANSWER: b. Atrial tachycardia. CSM (carotid sinus massage) causes AV block in the 1st half of the tracing with slowing of the heart rate. This tachycardia originates in the HRA, but initial P waves show different morphologies from the sinus beats shown.

Since the HRA A waves continue during CSM the arrhythmia is not dependent on the AV node. If it were AVNRT or AVRT the A waves would terminate during AV block. Often CSM or Adenosine will break AVNRT or AVRT. Medscape says, "Note that the atrial activities originate from the right atrium and persist despite the atrioventricular block. These features exclude atrioventricular nodal reentry tachycardia and atrioventricular tachycardia via an accessory pathway. Note also that the change in the P wave axis at the onset of tachycardia makes sinus tachycardia unlikely." See: http://emedicine.medscape.com/article/151456-overview

14. Patients in the CONFIRM trail all had a history of symptomatic:
   a. **Atrial Tachycardia**
   b. **Atrial Fibrillation**
   c. **Atrial Flutter**
   d. **AVRT**

ANSWER: d. Atrial Fibrillation. "The CONFIRM (Conventional Ablation for Atrial Fibrillation with or Without Focal Impulse and Rotor Modulation) trial identified that ablation of rotor and focal sources reduces the late recurrence of AF compared with trigger ablation alone." Zhou, et al, Catheter ablation of paroxysmal atrial fibrillation using high-density mapping-guided substrate modification. Pacing and Clinical Electrophysiology, 2018.

15. On this 21-year-old patient with hypertrophic obstructive cardiomyopathy, what are we trying to induce?
   a. **Atrial Tachycardia**
   b. **AVNRT**
   c. **AVRT**
   d. **VT**

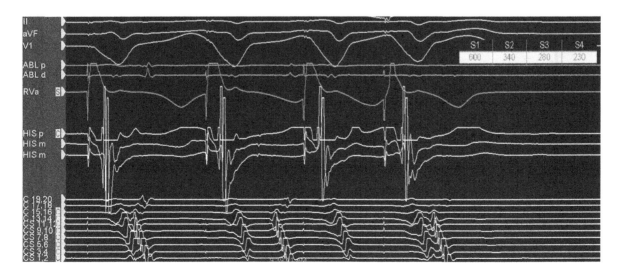

ANSWER: b. VT. A HOCM patient is at a higher risk of having VT due to hypertrophy and disarrayed myocardial fibers. This shows the typical induction technique for VT. An 8 beat drive train (S1) followed by 1,2, or 3 PVCs. Each PVC is brought in tighter (closer) until it begins to block. If this is unsuccessful at the RV apex, the catheter may be repositioned in the outflow tract. Keeping in mind, the more aggressive the pacing (3 PVCs at short 180 cycle lengths) the less specific it is - more false positives.

Murgatroyd says: "Sustained Monomorphic VT is considered a specific finding however it is induced. The induction of nonsustained polymorphic VT or ventricular fibrillation by triple or quadruple extrastimuli may be a nonspecific finding, not necessarily related to underlying heart disease or arrhythmic risk. The induction of polymorphic VT or VF by single or double extrastimulus is in a 'grey zone' and is considered specific by some. Similarly, the use of a second stimulation site and the infusion of isoproterenol during testing improves sensitivity, but at the expense of specificity. For risk assessment, it is our practice to limit testing to the use of three extrastimuli at two drive cycle length and two stimulation sites. However, if the purpose of EP testing is to induce a known arrhythmia so that it can be studied or ablated, more aggressive methods are used, as necessary. "See: Murgatroyd, chapter on VT
Braunwald says, "Left Ventricular hypertrophy is an independent risk factor of SCD, goes with many causes of SCD, and may be a physiological contributor to mechanisms of potentially lethal arrhythmias.... patients with severely hypertrophic ventricles are particularly susceptible to arrhythmic death. Among patients who have the obstructive form up to 70 percent of all deaths are sudden."
See: Braunwald, chapter on Cardiac Arrest and Sudden Death

16. During an EP study on this 32-year-old patient; initial testing shows _____.
   a. **Accessory Pathway ERP**
   b. **Initiation of AVNRT**
   c. **AVNERP**
   d. **AERP**

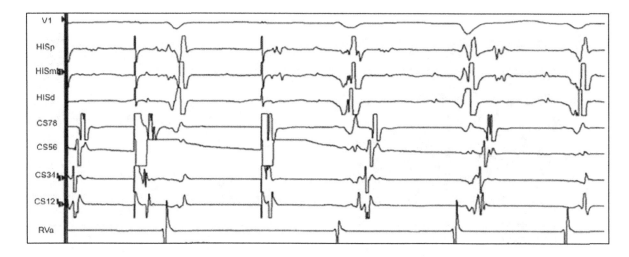

ANSWER: b. Initiation of AVNRT. Pacing is in the atrium via the proximal CS. There is a critical prolongation before "typical" AVNRT starts. Here the impulse blocks in the fast pathway and jumps to the slow. By the time it conducts down the slow pathway and travels to the V, the fast pathway has recovered, and it can go up the fast pathway to the A. This is an echo beat. When it repeats over and over it is called AVNRT.

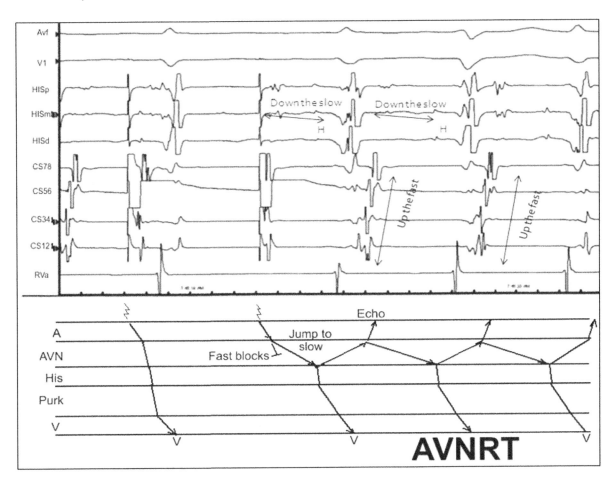

17. This 58-year-old patient complained of palpitations that get faster and faster; then after a few minutes it slows down, and then it stops. This tachycardia was induced in the lab and felt just like her symptoms at home. What is the rhythm in this example?
   a. **Atrial Tachycardia**
   b. **RVOT**
   c. **AVNRT**
   d. **WPW**

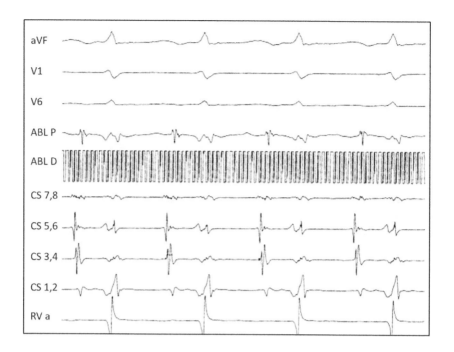

ANSWER: a. Atrial Tachycardia. We see distinct A waves preceding each V with appropriate intervals. Atrial tachycardia typically warms up and cools down. You need to determine is the A driving the V (atrial tachycardia), or the V is driving the A (possible AVRT). This is one of those arrhythmias where it is nice to see the induction. Atrial tach initiates with an A (typically VAAV initiation); unlike the AVNRT initiation seen in the previous question.

Fogoros says, "Focal atrial tachycardia can be paroxysmal or incessant, and, depending on their frequency, duration, and rate, they can produce symptoms that are anywhere from mild to severe. These arrhythmias can be caused by automatic foci, foci of triggered activity, or micro reentrant circuits. Because they are focal, atrial tachycardias can often be mapped and are thus amenable to ablation. The site of atrial tachycardia is often associated with anatomic structures, most commonly the crista terminalis in the right atrium, the ostia of the pulmonary veins in the left atrium, the ostium of the coronary sinus, and the tricuspid annulus." See: Fogoros chapter on SA Node, AV Node, and His-Purkinje system

18. A young woman complains of palpitations that would rapidly start and stop. The following tachycardia was induced without Isuprel infusion. What is the most likely rhythm?
   a. **Atrial Tachycardia**
   b. **Junctional Escape**
   c. **Concealed AVRT**
   d. **AVNRT**

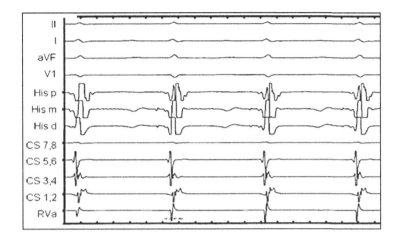

ANSWER: d. AVNRT. Notice there are the same number of A's and V's. AVNRT usually starts and stops suddenly, unlike atrial tachycardia, which typically warms up to a faster rate. In AVNRT usually there is 1:1 AV conduction; however, you may see block in the A or the V, and it will not terminate the tachycardia. Since the tachycardia is confined within the AV node, it does not need participation of the atrium or ventricle. AV interval is <60 ms which is a characteristic of AVNRT. The rate is too fast for Junctional Escape rhythm.

Since the reentry loop is within the AV node, vagal maneuvers are first line therapy to interrupt the tachycardia. If vagal maneuvers fail, adenosine is the initial drug of choice. Long term drug therapy involves beta blockers, Ca antagonists, or digitalis. However, RF ablation is more than 95% curative. See: Fogoros chapter on SA Node, AV Node, and His-Purkinje system

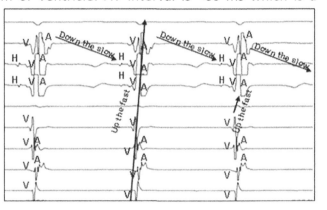

19. This 78-year-old patient with complaints of dizzy spells was brought to the EP lab.

What arrhythmia was induced?

a. Junctional Escape
b. Atrial Flutter
c. AVNRT
d. RVOT

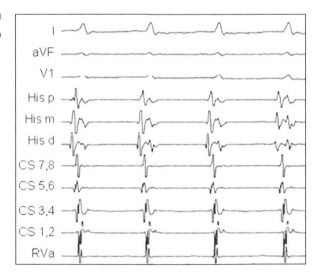

ANSWER: c. AVNRT. This is way too fast to be Junctional Escape (rate 40-60 bpm).
If this were RVOT VT (Right Ventricular Outflow Tract Ventricular Tachycardia), there would be a wide QRS complex on the surface ECG. Typical AVNRT has this typical look, where all the A's and V's line up close together. There is an exception to every rule... such as it could be atrial tachycardia with a 1st degree HB in which the A in the 1st beat goes with the V in the 2nd beat (rare). In such a situation an underlying 1st degree HB would be noticed.

BiosenseWebster.com says on AVNRT, "This type of abnormal rhythm arises from malfunctioning of the AV node. In most people, the AV node conducts impulses along a single pathway. In AVNRT, a second conducting pathway arises, confusing the electrical signals traveling from atria to ventricles. As a result, both the atria and ventricles beat at the same time instead of in sequence. This creates a fast heart rate — 120-250 beats per minute. Although the heartbeat is typically regular, rather than erratic, the heart is not pumping efficiently. Most AVNRT patients do not have underlying heart disease."
See: BiosenseWebster.com

20. What is the rate of this tachycardia (paper speed: 200mm/sec)?
   a. **125 bpm**
   b. **150 bpm**
   c. **170 bpm**
   d. **200 bpm**

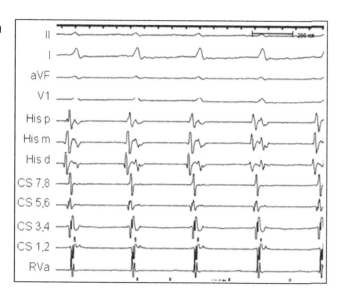

ANSWER: c. 170 bpm with a cycle length of 347 ms. Use paper to measure the RR interval. Then hold it up to and count the timelines in one cycle. I measure 5.2 lines.
The paper speed is 200 ms/3 timelines. By multiplying (200/3) x 5.2 we get 347 ms.
HR = 60,000/BCL = 60,000/347 = 173 bpm.

21. After giving the following 78-year-old patient Isuprel and rapid atrial burst pacing, this EGM was recorded. What is the most likely rhythm?
   a. **Atrial Tachycardia**
   b. **Manifest AVRT**
   c. **Typical AVNRT**
   d. **RVOT**

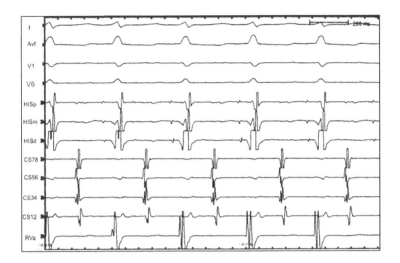

ANSWER: a. Atrial Tachycardia. We see regular A waves on the CS channel, followed by an H on the His channel, followed by Vs on the His & RV channels. Wrong answers are: Manifest AVRT would show (or "Manifest") itself with a delta wave – no delta wave is observed. Typical AVNRT would have a VA interval <60. This is much greater than 60 ms. RVOT would have a wide QRS complex.

Ablating atrial tachycardia requires activation mapping. Look for the earliest atrial deflection that precedes the P wave on the surface ECG. Thus, successful mapping depends on one's ability to induce an atrial tachycardia during the ablation procedure or the presence of incessant or very frequent tachycardia. Ablation should occur during

tachycardia. See: Fogoros: chapter on, Transcatheter Ablation: Therapeutic Electrophysiology.

22. Post slow path ablation testing revealed the following EGM. What is observed?
   a. **Ventricular pacing initiating tachycardia**
   b. **Atrial pacing initiating AVNRT**
   c. **Post successful SVT ablation**
   d. **Parahisian pacing**

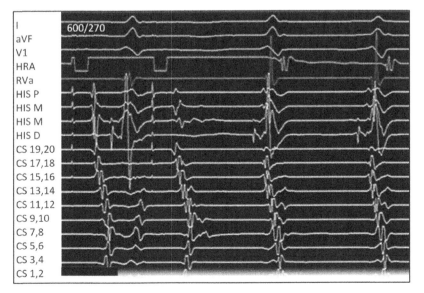

ANSWER: b. Atrial pacing initiating AVNRT. Note the long AH interval (jump) after S2. Note the drawing of the circular movement in the AV node, going down the slow path to the His & V, and up the fast pathway to reenter and echo in the atria.

INCORRECT ANSWERS: V pacing would have a wide QRS complex and pacing artifact. Parahisian pacing would have pacing artifact and capture on the His catheter. The HRA is paced the impulse conducting down the slow pathway (notice AH jump) then conducts to the H & V. At the same time the Fast pathway recovers, and conducts retrograde to trigger A. The echoing A (retrograde) and conducted V (antegrade) are almost superimposed. It was not a successful ablation since we induced the arrhythmia again as shown.

Fogoros says, "When the anatomy of dual AV nodal pathways (AVNRT) was first recognized most attempts at curing AV nodal reentry focused on ablating the fast pathway. This had a high incidence of complete heart block. In recent years they now accomplish this by ablation of the slow pathway." See: Fogoros chapter on SA Node, AV Node, and His-Purkinje system

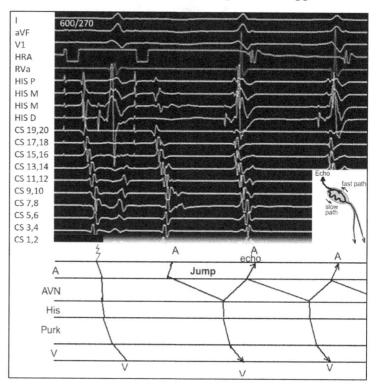

23. What is the rhythm?
a. **Orthodromic AVRT**
b. **Atrial Tachycardia**
c. **Typical AVNRT**
d. **Antidromic AVRT**

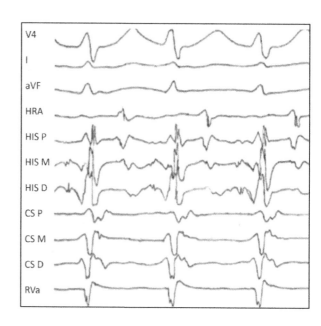

ANSWER: a. Orthodromic AVRT. The QRS is narrow with no preexcitation, this rules out Antidromic AVRT with uses the accessory pathway from the atrium to the ventricle. The VA interval is >60 ms which is observed with typical AVNRT.

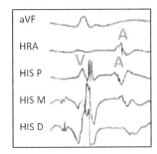

24. Where is the approximate accessory pathway location?
 a. **Right Mid Anterior**
 b. **Right Free Wall**
 c. **Left Lateral**
 d. **Septal**

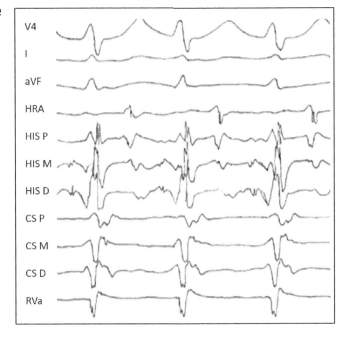

ANSWER: c. Left Lateral. As you recall, the CS runs along the AV groove with the distal electrodes located near the lateral left atrium. Notice the fusion on CS d (distal) and the eccentric conduction from distal to proximal. Here, the VA interval is fused showing the earliest atrial activation and the pathway location.

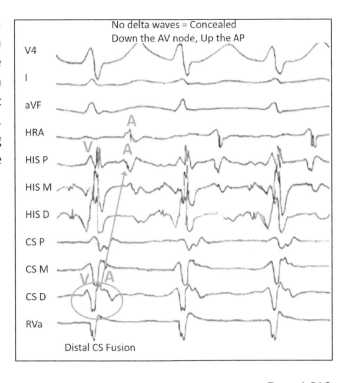

25. What is the rhythm induced in the electrogram after the physician performed ventricular pacing?
   a. **Antidromic / Manifest AVRT**
   b. **Orthodromic AVRT**
   c. **Atrial Tachycardia**
   d. **AVNRT**

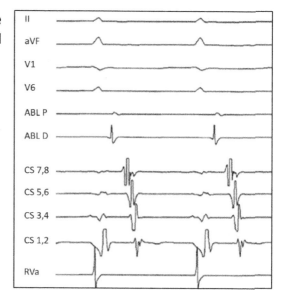

ANSWER: b. Orthodromic AVRT where the impulse passes down AV node (ortho) with a normal QRS, then up the accessory pathway, which appears to be right sided, since CS records the A moving proximal to distal.

INCORRECT answers are: Antidromic / Manifest AVRT would show a delta wave, not present. -Does not appear to be Atrial tach where the A would drive the V. Here the V is driving the A. (The exception to this would be atrial tachycardia with a first-degree heart block which would be noticed on the underlying rhythm. Further testing such as entrainment would help rule out atrial tachycardia. Also, atrial tachycardia is unlikely to be induced by V pacing.)
-AVNRT the VA interval would be <60 ms.

The two main treatment approaches to WPW syndrome are (1) pharmacotherapy and (2) EPS with RF catheter ablation. EPS with ablation is the first-line treatment for symptomatic WPW syndrome and for patients with high-risk occupations. It has replaced surgical treatment and most drug treatments. Drug therapy can be useful in some instances, such as in patients who refuse RF ablation and in temporizing patients with a higher risk of ablation-related complications (e.g., AV block with pacing requirement for anteroseptal or mid-septal pathways). In choosing drug therapy, keep in mind that class Ic and class III antiarrhythmic medications will slow AP (Accessory pathway) conduction, facilitating blockage of SVT. If the patient has a history of AF or atrial flutter, an AV nodal blocking medication should also be used.

26. This 23-year-old patient had complaints of palpitations that would come on suddenly with exercise. What does this extrastimulus test show?
   a. **RV pacing inducing RVOT**
   b. **CS pacing inducing AVNRT**
   c. **Loss of capture**
   d. **AVNERP**

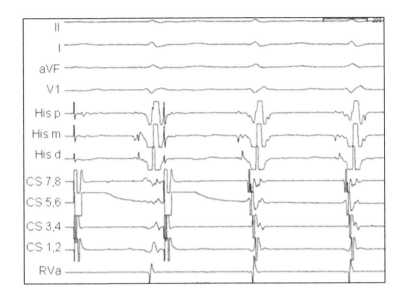

ANSWER: b. CS pacing inducing AVNRT. Pacing was occurring in the proximal CS capturing the atrium resulting in a narrow QRS, then a jump in AH interval after S2. Notice the long AH which indicates conduction down the slow pathway to the V. By the time it is through the slow pathway the fast pathway has recovered and is able to conduct the impulse back up to the A (at the same time the impulse is going to the V). This cycle continues…. AVNRT.

Murgatroyd says, "AVNRT can take several forms, with a confusing variety of accompanying names. Typical AVNRT (classical type) is seen in approximately 90% of patients with AVNRT." See Murgatroyd, chapter on AVNRT

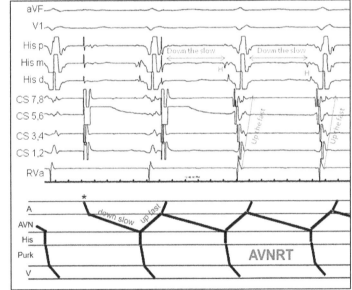

This is an example of typical AVNRT where the impulse goes down the slow pathway and up the fast pathway. In other forms the impulse may go down the fast pathway and up the slow pathway.
See: Murgatroyd chapter on Differential Diagnosis of SVT

27. After atrial extrastimulus testing, this rhythm was initiated. What is the rhythm?
   a. **Ventricular Tachycardia**
   b. **Atrial Flutter**
   c. **AVNRT**
   d. **AVRT**

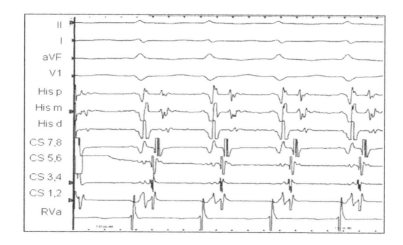

ANSWER: d. AVRT. Notice on CS 3,4 there is AV fusion. This accessory pathway is displaying orthodromic conduction on the left side of the heart, as indicated by the distal to proximal A movement on the CS catheter (but not left lateral which would have the earliest A on CS 1,2 assuming traditional catheter placement). AVRT requires 1:1 (V:A) conduction, but this may be seen in the other tachycardias as well.

Incorrect answers include:
- AVNRT: No jump seen here. Short AH interval. VA interval >60 ms (AVNRT VA interval typically is <60 ms).
- VT would have a wide QRS complex.

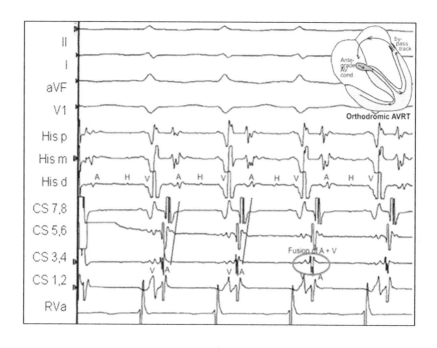

28. On this 14-year-old patient we noticed this 73-bpm rhythm after isoproterenol administration. What is the rhythm?

a. Multifocal atrial arrhythmia
b. Accelerated Junctional
c. Orthodromic AVRT
d. Typical AVNRT

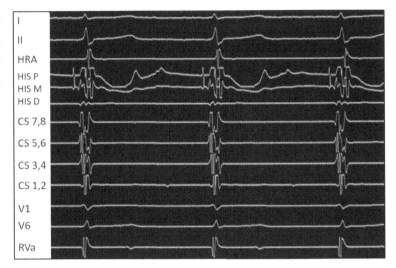

ANSWER: b. Accelerated Junctional. Junctional rhythms originate in the AV junction, so it "looks" similar to AVNRT. The impulse goes up to the A and down to the V at the same time. Note the H with no preceding A. Retrograde A is buried in QRS. Notice the different layout of the channels, always familiarize yourself with the display before committing to an answer. According to Medscape, "An accelerated junctional rhythm (rate >60) is a narrow complex rhythm that often supersedes a clinically bradycardic sinus node rate. Less commonly, the AV junction develops abnormal automaticity and exceeds the sinus node rate at a time when the sinus rate would be normal. These junctional tachycardias are most often observed in the setting of digitalis toxicity, recent cardiac surgery, acute myocardial infarction, or isoproterenol infusion." In this example the junctional rhythm is caused by the Isoproterenol infusion that was given post ablation to try to reinduce the AVNRT that was ablated earlier.

29. This EGM suggests:

a. Typical AVNRT induced
b. Accessory Pathway
c. Bundle Branch Block
d. Loss of Capture

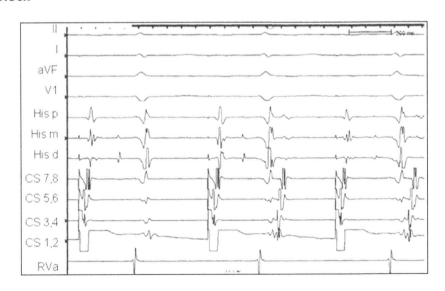

ANSWER: b Accessory pathway. The impulse conducts down AV node, giving a narrow QRS and then as noted in the ladder diagram the V conducts immediately back into the atrium eccentrically. This is an accessory pathway "echo." If it were to continue, a reentry loop tachycardia would result (Orthodromic AVRT).

Incorrect answers are:

- Typical AVNRT uses the slow pathway, so it would have an AH "jump," not the normal AH seen here.

- Notice that there is no delta wave which would be seen in antidromic or manifest AVRT. Antidromic AVRT uses the accessory pathway down (broad QRS) and the AV node up. When thinking of orthodromic think of "ortho" meaning correct. (Like orthodontists – correct teeth); therefore, the impulse would go down the AV node (correct way) and up the accessory pathway.

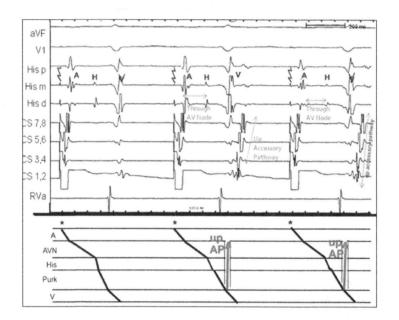

30. What is the pacing cycle length? (sweep speed: 200 mm/sec)

    a. 400 ms
    b. 500 ms
    c. 600 ms
    d. 700 ms

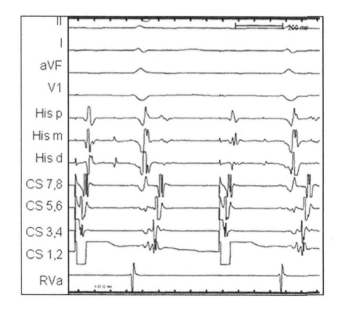

ANSWER: c. 600 ms. There are 9.0 timelines between pacer spikes. At speed 200 ms/3 timelines, 9 x 200/3 = 600 ms. With a rate of 100 bpm.

31. After burst pacing the atrium on this 18-year-old patient, what was the rhythm induced?
  a. **AVRT**
  b. **RVOT**
  c. **WPW**
  d. **AVNRT**

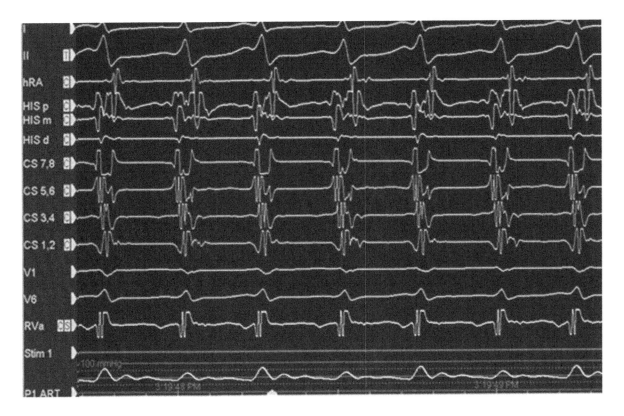

ANSWER: d. AVNRT. Notice how the V and A seem to line up on all the channels. This is the "look" of typical AVNRT. The VA interval in typical AVNRT should be <60 ms. AVNRT may be induced in many ways; typically, this is done by atrial extrastimulus testing (drive train of 8 beats than a PAC), isoproterenol may be helpful in this maneuver. In some cases, AVNRT can be induced with incremental atrial pacing, incremental ventricular pacing, or VEST. Since the tachycardia is located within the AV node, you may notice block in either the atrium or the ventricle without disruption of that tachycardia.

As we already have learned, AVNRT is a type of reentrant tachycardia. It is the mechanism in up to 60% of patients presenting with SVT. The circuit is usually enclosed within the AV node and needs neither atrium nor ventricle to participate in the loop. AV nodal reentry is seen in all age groups and the incidence of underlying heart disease in patients with this arrhythmia is no greater than in the normal population.

The tachycardia zone in AV nodal reentry is from the ERP of the fast pathway to the ERP of the slow pathway. In this arrhythmia, the tachycardia zone tends to be quite reproducible. See Fogoros: Supraventricular Tachyarrhythmias.

32. In your EP lab after many induction techniques and the use of Isuprel, this EGM was recorded. What is the rhythm?
   a. **Multifocal Atrial Tachycardia**
   b. **AVNRT**
   c. **AVRT**
   d. **RVOT**

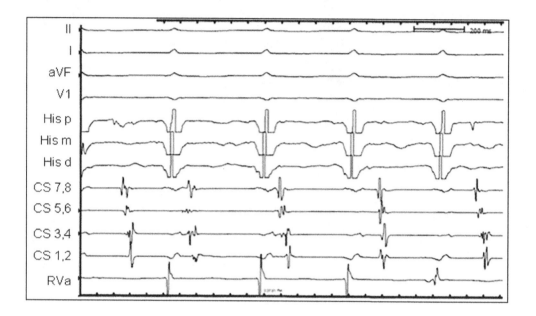

ANSWER: b. Multifocal Atrial tachycardia. This is a narrow complex tachycardia with an A preceding each V. Notice the A wave morphology varies depending on the atrial focus. Also, the A-to-A interval is quite variable showing several different foci. Ablating is challenging in that once one focus is ablated, another area may start firing, and another.

Fogoros says, "Multifocal atrial tachycardia is a form of automatic atrial tach characterized by multiple P wave morphologies and irregular PP intervals. It is thought to be due to multiple atrial automatic foci which are firing at differing rates. Multifocal atrial tachycardia is often seen with acute pulmonary disease and may be related to theophylline use." See: Fogoros, chapter on SVT

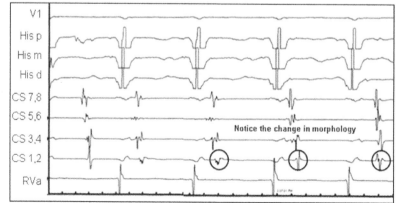

33. In this EGM, what happened after atrial extrastimulus testing was performed?
   a. **Accessory pathway Echo**
   b. **Junctional Escape**
   c. **AV Nodal Echo**
   d. **PVC**

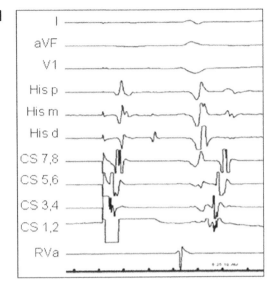

ANSWER: a. Accessory pathway echo. In this example the AH interval appears to be within the normal range.

INCORRECT answers are: Not AVNRT, because in a typical AV nodal echo you would see an AH jump 1st and the VA would be <60 ms. Also in a typical AV nodal echo beat, the A and V would be <60 ms on all CS channels and His catheter. In this example the VA is fused in CS 1,2 (distal / left sided) and out about 100 ms in the His-p channel. Notice in the VA interval, the proximal CS, and His it is clearly <60 ms. A junctional escape would not come in that quick and typically the VA would be <60 ms in all channels. Even though the V does come 1st, it is not a PVC because the QRS is narrow.

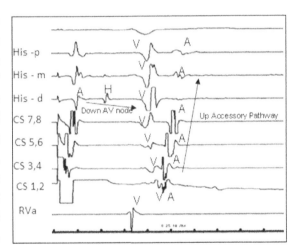

34. Following ventricular extrastimulus testing what rhythm was induced?
   a. **Atrial Tachycardia**
   b. **Atrial Flutter**
   c. **AVNRT**
   d. **AVRT**

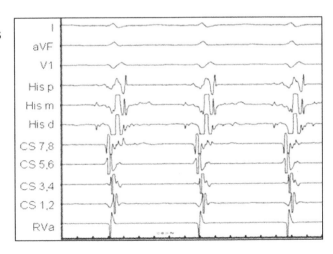

ANSWER: c. AVNRT; The A & V are happening almost simultaneously and there is a long AH interval. Although this is the usual look of typical AVNRT, many pacing maneuvers were used to prove this. Such as, entraining the tachycardia (sometimes referred to as Morady maneuver or ventricular overdrive pacing) and observing whether the response is VAV or VAAV.

35. After rapid atrial pacing, the following rhythm was induced. The RA catheter is positioned along the lateral right atrium (RA 9,10 HRA and RA 1,2 on the low lateral RA). What is the rhythm?
   a. **Counterclockwise AFL**
   b. **Clockwise AFL**
   c. **AVNRT**
   d. **AVRT**

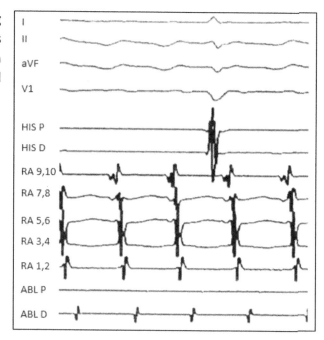

ANSWER: a. Counterclockwise Atrial Flutter. Notice there are more A's than V's.
The activation sequence is from proximal to distal on the RA catheter or from HRA, lateral wall, and then low RA. Murgatroyd says, "Multi-electrode recordings have demonstrated that typical atrial flutter is a macroreentrant circuit confined to the right atrium. Left atrial activation is entirely passive. For the rhythm to continue there must be a slow zone of conduction. With Typical Atrial Flutter this slow zone is between the tricuspid annulus and inferior vena cava. [isthmus]" This is where ablation is usually done, to break the circuit. Murgatroyd chapter on Atrial Arrhythmias

"In Atrial Flutter the physician may like to demonstrate entrainment. This is proof that an arrhythmia is due to a reentrant circuit and depending on the post pacing interval one can tell if their catheter is located within the circuit (Within 25 ms of the tachycardia cycle length). Catheter ablation is the electrophysiologist treatment of choice for atrial flutter and has a high success rate in relieving patients of the symptoms." See: Biosensewebster.com.

36. Typical atrial flutter is usually caused by a/an:
   a. **Wavelets from pulmonary veins**
   b. **Automatic focus in the atria**
   c. **Dual AV node physiology**
   d. **Large RA reentry loop**

ANSWER: d. Large RA reentry loop. Multi-electrode recordings have proven that typical atrial flutter is a macro-reentrant RA circuit, and LA activation is entirely passive." See: Murgatroyd chapter on Atrial Arrhythmias.

37. This rhythm was induced multiple times with atrial pacing, with occasional 2:1 conduction (not observed here). What is the rhythm?
   a. **Atrial Flutter**
   b. **Typical AVNRT**
   c. **Concealed AVRT**
   d. **Atrial Tachycardia**

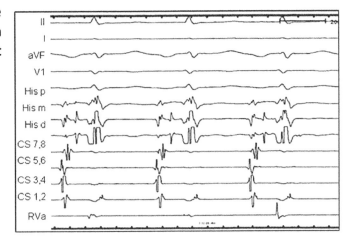

ANSWER: d. Atrial Tachycardia. Normal AV conduction as indicated by the normal AH & HV intervals. Automatic atrial tachycardia typically displays a warmup cool down period. Ablation of atrial tachycardia requires mapping of the earliest atrial activation preceding the surface P wave.
Incorrect answers are:

- AV interval is >60 ms ruling out typical AVNRT.
- There is no apparent VA fusion that you would see in concealed AVRT, and the A is "driving" the V. AVRT requires participation of both the A and V, so if there is block this is ruled out.

Murgatroyd says, "Ectopic atrial tachycardias are regular arrhythmias arising from regions of the atria other than the sinus node. They arise from a small area of tissue but can be caused by several mechanisms: Micro-reentry, triggered or abnormal automaticity. Truly focal atrial tachycardia may be the result of triggered activity or abnormal automaticity. Triggered activity is suggested when the arrhythmia is inducible by rapid pacing, but there is no other evidence of reentry. Abnormal automaticity is suggested when the arrhythmia cannot be induced or terminated by pacing. Pharmacological measures, such as isoproterenol infusion, are often needed to induce automatic arrhythmias in the electrophysiology laboratory."
See: Murgatroyd chapter on Atrial Arrhythmias

38. What rhythm was induced on this EGM?
   a. **Atrial Tachycardia**
   b. **Fast Pathway ERP**
   c. **Typical AVNRT**
   d. **WPW**

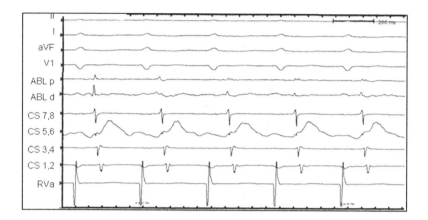

ANSWER: a. Atrial Tachycardia with long PR interval. An A precedes every V by >200 ms. Notice the earliest atrial deflection on the ablation distal electrode; this is a good spot for ablation. There is no delta wave which rules out WPW. The VA interval is >60 ms ruling out typical AVNRT. There are no non-conducted impulses, ruling out the fast pathway ERP.

39. This 32-year-old female was brought into the EP lab. Looking at the sinus beat on the left and a tachycardia beat on the right. What is the most likely tachycardia?
- a. **Sinus node reentry**
- b. **Atrial Fibrillation**
- c. **Concealed AVRT**
- d. **AVNRT**

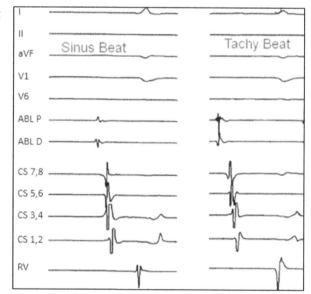

ANSWER: a. Sinus Node reentry. The tachycardia beat has the identical morphology as the Sinus rhythm beat. Sinus node reentry is a paroxysmal arrhythmia with abrupt onset and termination. During an EP study, the arrhythmia can be initiated and terminated with atrial extrastimuli. The earliest atrial activation is in the sinus node region. Zipes says, it is "presumed to be due to micro-reentry in tissue near the sinus node or perinodal region (superior Crista terminalis)." It is treated with antiarrhythmic drugs.
See: Zipes, chapter on Atrial Tach.

40. What is the rhythm in the following electrogram? The duodecapolar is in the RA and labeled from distal (1,2) to proximal (19,20) as it descends the RA lateral wall. The CS is displayed with distal first.

a. Counterclockwise AFL
b. Atrial tachycardia
c. Clockwise AFL
d. AVNRT

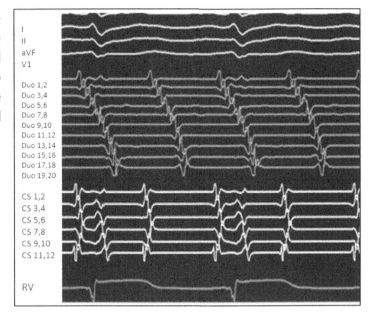

ANSWER: c. Clockwise Atrial Flutter. The impulse starts at 1,2 (distal) and loops around to 19,20 (proximal) traveling clockwise. Labeling of poles always starts with distal…. Distal 1,2, then numbers higher assigned to the more proximal electrodes. Tip is always #1. Remember that most EP catheters are a bipolar configuration, using 2 poles, a positive and negative, for pacing and recording signals in the heart. The negative pole is distal to the proximal pole, like a pacing wire where the distal electrode is − and the more proximal electrode +. In this example, 1 is the negative pole and 2 is the positive pole on that electrode pair, and the pattern continues. See: Fogoros Electrophysiologic Testing.

41. What is the rhythm on this 52-year-old female patient?

a. Atrial Fibrillation
b. Atrial Flutter
c. AVNRT
d. AVRT

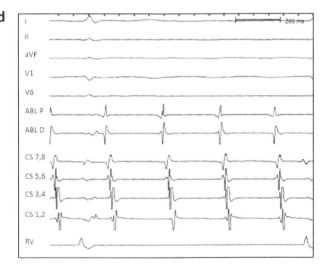

ANSWER: b. Atrial Flutter with 4:1 block. AF is not this organized. Incorrect answers are:

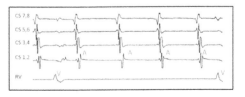

- AVNRT you would see the A and V "lineup" or a VA interval <60 ms.
- AVRT is not possible without 1:1 conduction.

42. What is the rhythm on this EGM?
    a. **Accelerated Junctional Tachycardia**
    b. **Atrial Tachycardia**
    c. **Atrial Fibrillation**
    d. **Atrial Flutter**

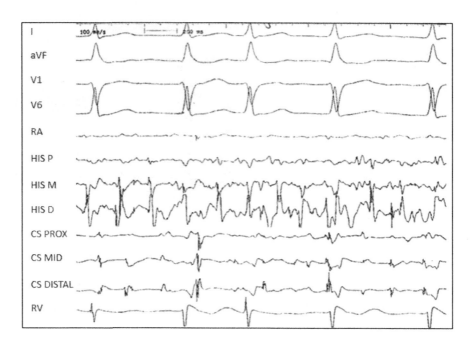

ANSWER: c. Atrial Fibrillation. AF will show more atrial than ventricular activity. The atrial activity is very irregular and chaotic with an irregular ventricular response. Although there seem to be discrete A waves on the HIS channel, they do not have a fixed AV interval, indicating variable conduction with a narrow QRS.

Murgatroyd says, "AF was originally thought to be caused by multiple atrial ectopic foci. In the last two decades, an alternative model has dominated; in which multiple wavelets of depolarization propagate within the atria. These can divide, coalesce, and extinguish each other as they travel in a random fashion, seeking tissue that is excitable. Another hypothesis is that AF is not purely self-sustaining but driven by a stable focus or reentrant circuit. The activation arising from this focus is too rapid to be conducted uniformly throughout the atria and propagation of the wave fronts therefore breaks up into irregular wavelets."
See: Murgatroyd chapter on SVT

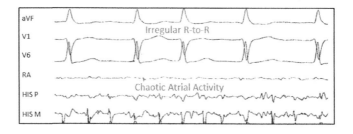

43. What is the tachycardia shown in this EGM?
 a. **Atrial Flutter with WPW**
 b. **Left-sided AVRT**
 c. **Typical AVNRT**
 d. **AF with WPW**

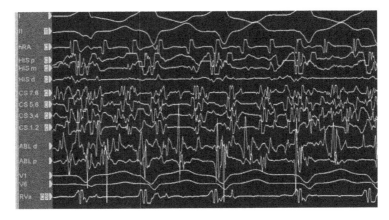

ANSWER: a. Atrial Flutter with WPW and a 3:1 AV block. Note broad QRS with delta waves on surface leads. There is a slight variation in the A-to-A interval which may be seen in Atrial Flutter, but it is not the irregular chaotic activity as seen in AF. Incorrect answers are:

- Not typical AVNRT because the VA interval would be less than 60 ms.
- Not AF because of the clearly seen A waves in the HRA catheter.
- Not left sided AVRT because you would notice fusion on CS 1,2 which is in the distal CS... left side of the heart. No fusion is noticed on any of the channels. We cannot determine from this where the ablation catheter is located, although the accessory bypass tract is right-sided or septal. Further mapping is needed to know the exact location.

44. On a patient with a known antegrade conducting accessory bypass tract, the physician intentionally induced atrial fibrillation. Knowing that AF could lead to VF on this type of patient, why was this done?
 a. **MD wants to do PVI (pulmonary vein isolation)**
 b. **See how fast the AP conducts**
 c. **Serial drug testing**
 d. **Atypical VT study**

ANSWER: b. See how fast the AP conducts or determine the accessory pathway ERP.
This patient has WPW as noted by the delta wave (slurred upstroke of the QRS). The danger of AF on WPW patient is VF. Unlike the AV node which slows down the impulses before they reach the ventricle, accessory pathways do not decrement. If the accessory pathway conducts fast enough, this AF could lead to VF. With extrastimulus testing we get an idea of the AP (accessory pathway) ERP, but until it is bombarded with impulses, such as in AF, you don't truly know how fast it can conduct. This patient could conduct at 260 ms which is at moderate risk of sudden death.

45. What is the tachycardia in this example? Catheter locations are as shown.

    a. **Right-sided atrial flutter**
    b. **Left-sided atrial flutter**
    c. **Atrial tachycardia**
    d. **AVNRT**

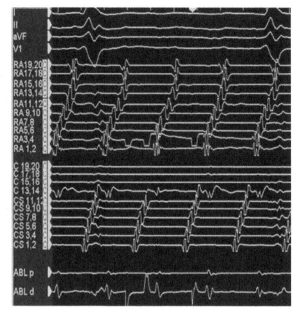

ANSWER: b. Left-sided Atrial Flutter. Remember RA 1,2 is the distal electrode pair (at the catheter tip). This is typically positioned just across the isthmus. CS 1,2 is also the distal pair of electrodes located on the left side of the heart. The earliest atrial activation in this example is on CS 1,2 which is on the left side of the heart, then it travels to the right side of the heart. Quite often this can be seen in patients after pulmonary vein isolation or other extensive ablations or surgery which causes scar. Scar tissue acts like the cavotricuspid isthmus on the right side that has an area of slow conduction which is needed for the flutter reentry circuit.

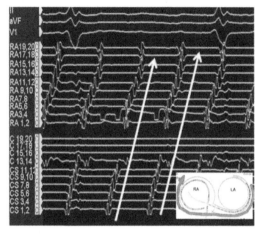

46. AVNRT is most common in _____. AVRT is the most common in_____.

    a. **Women, women**
    b. **Women, men**
    c. **Men, women**
    d. **Men, men**

ANSWER: b. Women, men. AVNRT is twice as common in women as it is in men. The incidence of AVRT with accessory pathways is just the opposite, occurring mostly in young men. This diagram shows the proportion of EP ablation cases diagnosed with AT, AVNRT and AVRT (AP). Issa says, "AV nodal reentrant tachycardia (AVNRT) has a 2:1 female-to-male predominance, and accessory pathways are twice as common in men. There is a striking 2:1 predominance of women in the AVNRT group.... Of 557 consecutive patients referred to the Heart Rhythm Institute at the University of Oklahoma Health Sciences Center for catheter ablation for treatment of AVNRT, 436 (78%) were female." See: Issa, chapter on PSVT, Epidemiology

47. From this X-ray, what is the ablation that is being performed on this 86-year-old patient with persistent SVT?
   a. **Orthodromic AVRT**
   b. **Antidromic AVRT**
   c. **AV Node**
   d. **AVNRT**

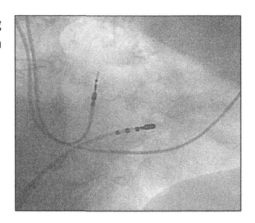

ANSWER: c. AV Node ablation. The AV node is normally positioned on the right side of the heart at the apex of the triangle of Koch. This is an anterior structure in contrast to the posterior CS ostium. The ablation catheter shown with the large tip is directed at the AV node. The patient already has support for CHB with a dual chamber pacemaker.

AV node ablations may be performed on patients with rapid ventricular rates due to AF. However, this patient has a dual chamber PPM, so the patient more than likely has paroxysmal AF or SVT. You may do an AV node ablation on this SVT patient due to advanced age and the fact that they already have a PPM in place. This is "pace and ablate," where the AV node is destroyed and thereafter the AV pacer controls the AV delay.

48. From the EGM and Xray shown, what type of ablation is being performed?
   a. **Retrograde AV node**
   b. **Transseptal AVRT**
   c. **RVOT VT**
   d. **AVNRT**

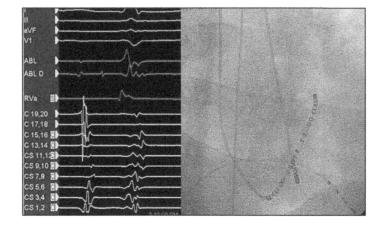

ANSWER: a. Retrograde AV node. First, notice the His signal on the ABL D channel. Second, notice that the ablation catheter comes in from above, unlike the RVa catheter. The RVA catheter comes up from the IVC, whereas the ablation catheter goes up the AO, down through the AO valve - not across the septum. This is referred to as the retrograde approach since the insertion is opposite to blood flow.

Murgatroyd says, "Catheter ablation of the AV node, to cause complete AV block, is chiefly used in patients with permanent atrial fibrillation and poorly controlled ventricular rates. The principal goal is an improvement in quality of life due to a reduction in tachycardia-related symptoms, but a hemodynamic improvement may also occur. A successful result eliminates the need for antiarrhythmic drugs but creates life-long pacemaker dependence. The procedure is therefore best suited to older patients, for whom it is a simple treatment, necessitating a very brief hospital stay, with an excellent outcome. Conversely, it is considered a treatment of last resort in younger patients. A location is sought where the atrial and ventricular electrograms are of comparable amplitude, and the His potential is just visible. If the ablation is performed in AF, it is sometimes not possible to identify the His electrogram, and anatomical landmarks are instead used. Allowance must also be made for the lower amplitude of atrial electrograms in AF compared with sinus rhythm. The anatomy of the AV node varies between patients. Even at the successful site, complete heart block may take 10 to 20 seconds or more of RF energy to occur. If energy delivery at the location described is unsuccessful, a more aggressive approach may be necessary, aiming nearer the His bundle itself. Occasionally, it is necessary to ablate the His bundle from the left side, using a retrograde approach."

49. What type of ablation is being performed on the displayed electrogram?
  a. **Atrial tachycardia**
  b. **Concealed AP**
  c. **Manifest AP**
  d. **AVNRT**
  e. **Need more information to determine**

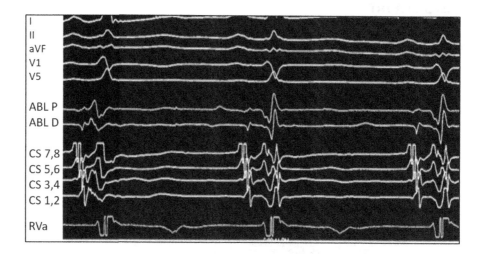

ANSWER: c. Manifest accessory pathway or bypass tract. On the first beat, notice the AV fusion on the ablation catheter, especially on ablation distal. This is the appearance of an accessory pathway when your catheter is sitting on the site of the pathway. Sometimes an accessory pathway potential (or sharp spike) will be seen in between the A and V on the ablation catheter. The evidence of a pathway potential is the best area to ablate.

50. Where is the location of the ablation catheter in the electrogram?
   a. **Anterior septal aspect of RA**
   b. **Lateral aspect of LA**
   c. **Slow pathway area**
   d. **Crista terminalis**
   e. **Near CS ostium**

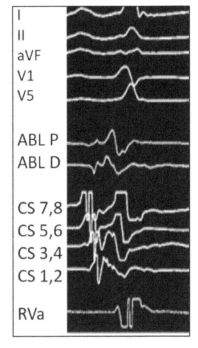

ANSWER: b. Lateral aspect of the left atrium. Now consider the location of the pathway. Remember that the CS catheter travels in between the atrium and ventricle on the posterior aspect of the left atrium. There is AV fusion on CS 1,2; this suggests that those electrodes are near the accessory pathway. If the CS catheter is positioned correctly, the distal CS electrodes should be near the left lateral aspect of the left atrium. Since the site is not well bracketed (meaning that fusion is at the most distal electrode displayed), further mapping should be done more distal to CS 1,2 to make sure the earliest site is found. After RF energy is applied, there is an AV split on the ablation and CS channels. Now a clear A and V may be seen on the ablation catheter. This nicely demonstrates that the catheter is sitting on the mitral valve ring. Huang says, "The rates of success for left free wall AP ablations are the highest of any AP location and are typically greater than 90%.... The recurrence rates for left free wall APs are the lowest of any location at 2%-5%." See: Catheter Ablation of Cardiac Arrhythmias by Huang and Wood's chapter on Free Wall Accessory Pathways.

51. On the displayed electrogram, what happens on the third beat into ablation?
   a. **Ablation of an accessory pathway**
   b. **Ablation of the slow pathway**
   c. **Ablation of fast pathway**
   d. **AV node ablation**

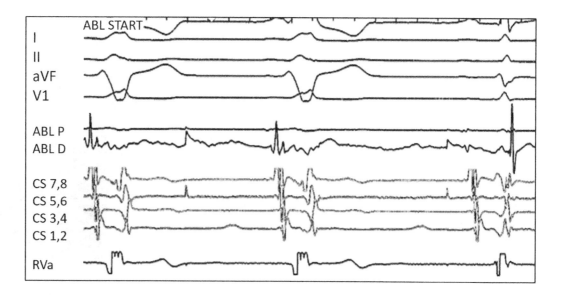

ANSWER: a. Ablation of an accessory pathway. There is a delta wave on the first two beats which is gone on the third beat into ablation. Also, there is AV fusion on the first two beats which is separated on the third. This is either an anterior septal or a right sided accessory pathway. The CS and AV intervals appear normal. There is no structure on the right side to aid in mapping, like the CS aids us for left sided ablations. Accessory pathway ablations are typically successful in the first 10-15 seconds of ablation. If not, the ablation should be attempted at a different location.

Regarding septal pathways Kibos says, "The application [of RF energy] should be stopped if no success is observed after 15-20 sec…. APs are usually superficial in this area and lack of success is usually due to wrong site or poor tissue contact. Use of higher energies, larger tip catheters, or irrigation to make bigger lesions is not appropriate in this region." See: Cardiac Arrhythmias: From Basic Mechanism to State-of-the-Art Management by Kibos, Knight, Essebag, Fishberger, Slevin, and Tintoiu.

Chapter 14
Advanced Skills

1. Differential Pacing (pg. 533)
2. Atrial Flutter Entrainment (pg. 540)
3. Advanced Electrograms (pg. 548)

EP Essentials LLC

Differential Pacing

1. When an EP electrode senses an electrogram different from the site of its contact, E.g., when an atrial electrogram shows a V wave, this is termed:
    a. **Ventricular overdrive**
    b. **Near-field sensing**
    c. **Atrial aberration**
    d. **Far-field sensing**

ANSWER: d. Far-field sensing. Hayes, dictionary says: "far-field sensing. Phenomenon in which an electrophysiologic catheter or pacemaker lead senses an electrogram different from the electrogram generated at the site of myocardial contact with the lead."
See: Hayes, Dictionary of Cardiac Pacing, Defibrillation, Resynchronization, and Arrhythmias

2. Entrainment mapping is most useful in:
    a. **Atrial fibrillation with RVR (rapid ventricular response)**
    b. **Ischemic VT**
    c. **AVNRT**
    d. **AVRT**

ANSWER: b. Ischemic VT. Entrainment mapping is useful in reentrant circuits such as Atrial Flutter and Ischemic VT. By measuring the post pacing interval, the physician can tell if their ablation catheter is in the tachycardia circuit." Entrainment mapping is a variation of pace mapping. The idea is to pace from various areas within the ventricle during sustained ventricular tachycardia, at a length slightly shorter than that of the tachycardia" It is also useful in other macroreentry rhythms like AFL to define an isthmus.
See: Fogoros, chapter on Transcatheter ablation.

3. Pacing different sites to match a previously recorded tachycardia morphology is termed:
   a. **Propagation mapping**
   b. **Activation mapping**
   c. **Isochronal mapping**
   d. **Voltage mapping**
   e. **Pace mapping**

ANSWER: e. Pace map by moving a mapping electrode around until you find the spot where the waveform morphology is the same as the recorded tachycardia.
   - Pace mapping compares the paced morphology of a site with the previously recorded tachycardia morphology.
   - A voltage map displays peak-to-peak voltages sampled on the endocardial surface.
   - Activation map of local activation times is a timing map, usually looking for the earliest site of activation or reentrant activation.
   - Isochronal maps depict all the points with an activation time within a specific range on a shell of the geometry
   - Propagation maps show electrical activation waves spreading as a continuous animated loop on a shell

See: Issa, chapter on "Mapping and Navigation Modalities"

4. Where is pace mapping most useful?
   a. **Accessory Pathways**
   b. **Atrial Fibrillation**
   c. **Focal VT or AT**
   d. **Reentry AFL**
   e. **AVNRT**

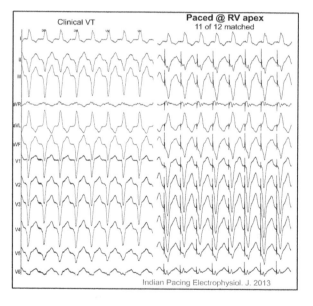

Indian Pacing Electrophysiol. J. 2013

ANSWER: c. Focal VT or AT. Issa says, "Pace mapping has been shown to be an effective corroborative method to regionalize the site of origin of VT and define potential exit sites along the border of any low-voltage region. Pace mapping with the paced QRS morphology mimicking that of VT on the 12-lead ECG can help find the site of origin of the VT..."

"When atrial activation originates from a point-like source, such as during focal AT or during pacing from an electrode catheter, the resultant P wave recorded on the surface ECG is found by the sequence of atrial activation, which is determined to a considerable extent by the initial site of myocardial depolarization. Additionally, analysis of specific P wave configurations in multiple leads allows estimation of the pacing site location to within several square centimeters. Therefore, comparing the paced P wave configuration with that of AT is particularly useful for finding a small arrhythmia focus in a structurally normal heart." See: Issa, chapter on "Other VTI"

5. What is the term for the type of mapping described? Capturing of the reentrant circuit of a tachycardia without interrupting the tachycardia. After cessation of pacing, the spontaneous reentrant tachycardia is still present.
   a. **Spontaneous pulse train reentry pacing**
   b. **Synchronous overdrive pacing**
   c. **Extrastimulus testing**
   d. **Continuous resetting**
   e. **Entrainment**

Answer: e. Entrainment. This is a case of Typical Clockwise AFL where the ablation catheter was used to Entrain the tachycardia. The Intrinsic CL=243. The return Post Pacing Interval (PPI) CL=243 (Measured from the last stim to the return tachycardia on the stim catheter). So, 243 – 243 = 0. In other words, the Ablation catheter is in the circuit of the tachycardia/flutter. Be sure to examine the tachycardia during entrainment and make sure your pacing has accelerated the tachycardia to the pacing CL. This example shows pacing at 225 ms., just faster than the AFL. Entrainment is used on every AFL case and is one of the most difficult concepts to understand in EP. Note: PPI=Tachycardia Cycle Length-The Return Cycle Length.

Issa says, "Entrainment is the continuous resetting of a reentrant circuit by a train of capturing stimuli.... Entrainment is used to estimate qualitatively how far the reentrant circuit is from the pacing site..." See: Issa, chapter on Electrophysiological Mechanisms

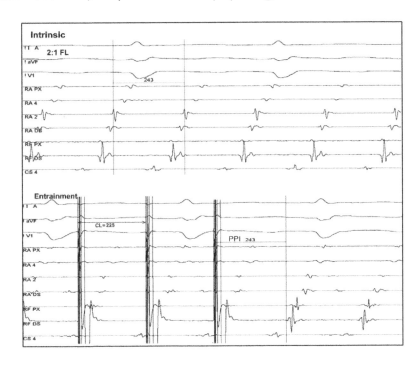

6. What is the post overdrive ventricular pacing (entrainment) response demonstrated in the EGM?

a. **VAAV**

b. **VAV**

c. **VVA**

d. **Not entrained**

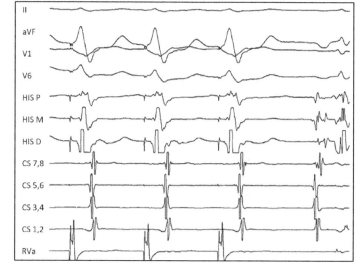

ANSWER: a. VAAV. Fixed rate pacing captures the V, and each is followed by a retrograde A. But, after the pacing stops an additional A appears, then V, hence VAAV.

To perform ventricular overdrive pacing, you must:

a. Pace the ventricle 10-20 ms faster than the tachycardia cycle length

b. Must capture the V and speed the A up to the same rate.

c. When pacing stops the tachycardia must continue.

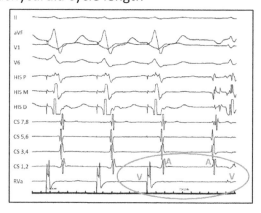

VAAV response is seen in atrial tachycardia. This makes sense because atrial tachycardia always has a leading A. VAV is seen in AVNRT and AVRT, a PPI-TCL measurement will differentiate the two. AVNRT has a PPI-TCL >115ms and AVRT is <115ms.

7. What is the post ventricular overdrive pacing response in this EGM?

a. **VAAV**

b. **VAV**

c. **VVA**

d. **Not Entrained**

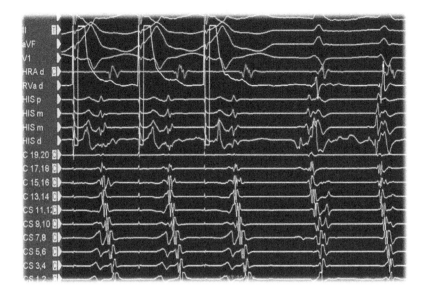

ANSWER: b. VAV. You can tell the tachycardia was entrained by the fact that the paced V to V speeds up the A-to-A. (as in the arrows). Every V pace, drives every A. Then after pacing has stopped the tachycardia continues with a narrow complex tachycardia. Fred Morady MD FACC discovered this maneuver. The purpose of Dr. Morady's study was to determine the atrial response after pacing stops during supraventricular tachycardia. The results showed a VAV response in AVRT and AVNRT. The results also showed a VAAV response in Atrial tachycardia.

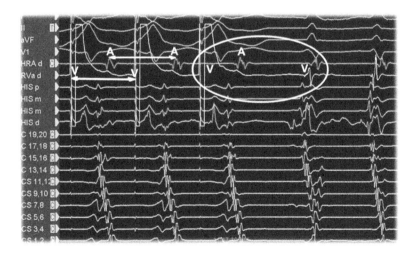

8. What is the post entrainment (ventricular overdrive pacing) response?
   a. **VAAV, Atrial Tachycardia**
   b. **VAAV, AVNRT or AVRT**
   c. **VAV, Atrial Tachycardia**
   d. **VAV, AVNRT or AVRT**

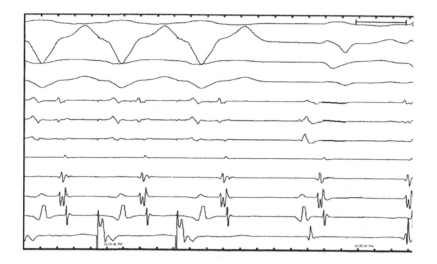

ANSWER: d. VAV, suggesting AVNRT or AVRT. Most EP docs like to see this repeated over again, just to double check the entrainment. The RV channel is the most reliable place to look for V's. Remember V-A-V response implies AVNRT or AVRT. The V-A-A-V response implies atrial tachycardia.

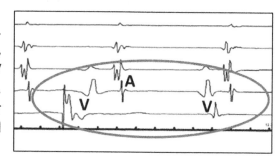

9. What is the post entrainment (ventricular overdrive pacing) response?
   a. **VAAV, suggesting atrial tachycardia**
   b. **VAAV, suggesting AVNRT or AVRT**
   c. **VAV, suggesting atrial tachycardia**
   d. **VAV, suggesting AVNRT or AVRT**
   e. **Not completely entrained.**

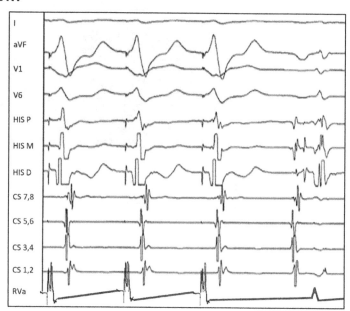

ANSWER: a. VAAV, suggesting atrial tachycardia. The resulting arrhythmia has A's leading all V's, as expected in atrial tachycardia. The tachycardia appears to be atrial tachycardia by this result. Atrial tachycardia often initiates the same way: VAAV (Not seen in this example)

Remember to always check for true entrainment. While pacing the V faster than the atrial rate one must reliably capture the ventricle. Also, the atrial rate must speed up to the rate of the paced V. The tachycardia must then continue after pacing ceases.

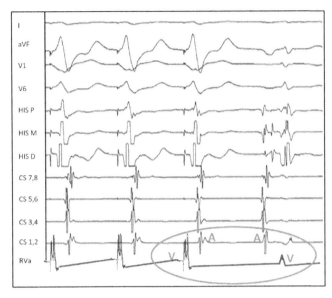

10. During atrial pacing this tachycardia was induced. What pattern is noticed during initiation?

    a. **VAV, AVNRT**

    b. **VAV, AVRT**

    c. **VAAV, AVNRT**

    d. **VAAV, Atrial Tachycardia**

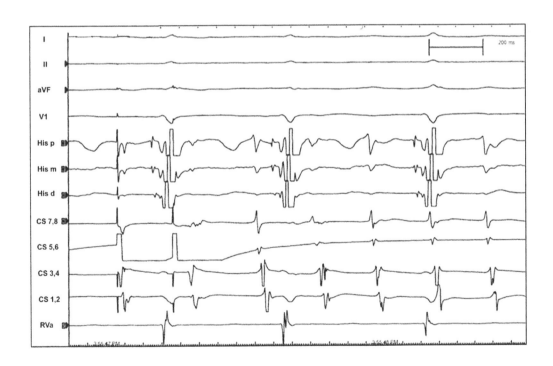

ANSWER: d VAAV – Atrial tachycardia typically has a VAAV initiation. Remember, AVNRT and AVRT are typically a VAV response. Also notice that after initiation there is a period of 2:1 atrial conduction which would also rule out AVRT which needs both atrial and ventricular participation.

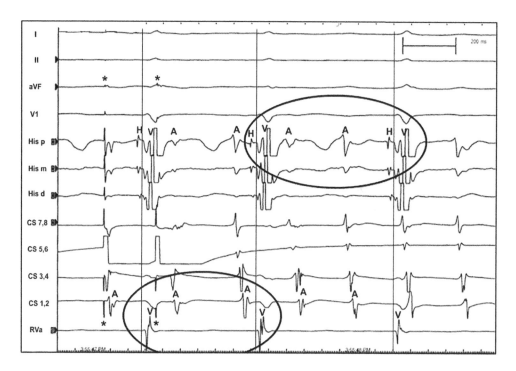

Atrial Flutter Entrainment

1. In AFL entrainment mapping, you reliably capture (entrain) the atrium at a rate faster than the flutter cycle length. When you stop pacing, the post pacing interval (PPI) on that electrode is an indication of:
   a. **Proximity to the cavotricuspid isthmus**
   b. **Proximity to the primary reentry loop**
   c. **Refractory period of the loop**
   d. **Pulse train cycle length**

ANSWER: b. Proximity to the primary reentry loop. Ideally the post pacing interval (PPI) should equal the reentry loop cycle length. In this diagram, the macro-reentry loop of interest is 300 ms around. We are entraining at 290 ms with our exploring catheter in three different loops, 300 ms to go around it, and 40 ms to return to our electrode. So, the first native beat after we stop pacing will be 380 ms long. That PPI is too long. If we move our catheter to position #2 then it takes even longer to enter and exit the loop, so our last beat will be 420 ms long. Finally, if we position within the reentry loop at #3, it takes no time to get to or return from the loop, so the PPI is 300 ms long - the same as the native reentry loop. That's what we want. We now know position #3 is in the loop. Hopefully, this catheter position #3 is in a narrow isthmus, so we can ablate here and break the loop.

In AFL, the first catheter position to try is usually the cavotricuspid isthmus, because that is the normal location to ablate. But, if the macro-reentry loop is elsewhere, we may need to assess many locations in both atria. It's like a blind man locating a wall by yelling at it and waiting for the return echo. A long echo means the wall is far away; immediate return would be close to the wall.

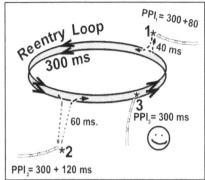

Issa says, "The PPI is the time interval from the last pacing stimulus that entrained the tachycardia to the next non-paced recorded electrogram at the pacing site.... the PPI (measured from the pacing site recording) should be equal (within 30 milliseconds) to the tachycardia CL.... The greater the difference between the PPI and the tachycardia CL, the longer the conduction time between the pacing site and reentry circuit."
See: Issa, chapter on electrophysiological Mechanisms of Cardiac Arrhythmias

2. During entrainment mapping of typical AFL, pacing from the cavotricuspid isthmus results in: (Note the "PPI-Tachycardia CL" is a mathematical formula in ms.)
   a. **Manifest atrial fusion where (PPI—tachycardia CL) > 30 ms**
   b. **Manifest atrial fusion where (PPI—tachycardia CL) < 30 ms**
   c. **Concealed atrial fusion where (PPI—tachycardia CL) > 30 ms**
   d. **Concealed atrial fusion where (PPI—tachycardia CL) < 30 ms**

ANSWER: d. Concealed atrial fusion and (PPI—tachycardia CL) < 30 ms. This means the paced F waves should be identical to the patient's AFL waves, and the post pacing interval (PPI) should be within 30 ms of the patient's normal flutter cycle length. Issa says, "Entrainment is used to estimate qualitatively how far the reentrant circuit is from the pacing site. Pacing from a protected isthmus inside the circuit results in concealed entrainment:

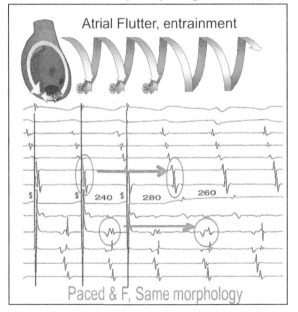

Atrial Flutter, entrainment

Paced & F, Same morphology

- Concealed atrial fusion (i.e., paced atrial waveform on the surface ECG and intracardiac recordings are identical to the tachycardia waveform) PPI - AT CL < 30 ms
- The interval between the stimulus artifact to the onset of P wave on surface
- ECG equals the interval between the local electrogram on the pacing site to the onset of the P wave on the surface ECG."
See: Issa, chapter on Isthmus-dependent AFL

3. What is the effect of CS pacing in this EGM?
  a. **Entrainment of typical RA flutter**
  b. **Entrainment from proximal CS**
  c. **Entrainment from distal CS**
  d. **Entrainment did not occur**

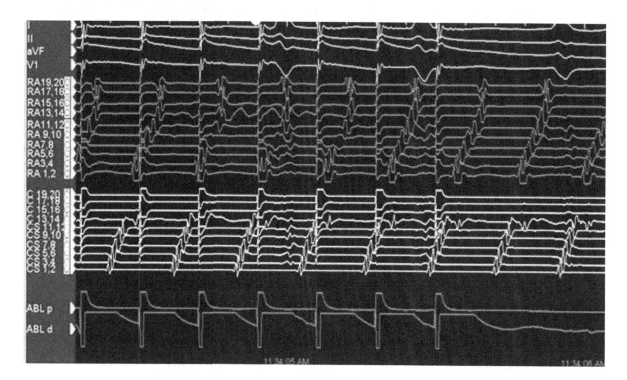

ANSWER: d. Entrainment did not occur. This is in reference to a different type of entrainment that in the earlier questions. The rules for entrainment are the same as in the Morady maneuver, there is just a different diagnostic use which will be discussed in the following questions. Pacing in this example occurs on a proximal CS channel, most likely 19,20. Consistent capture is not seen. Notice the pacing spikes marching through without affecting the underlying tachycardia. None of the pacing spikes in this example captured the atrium; therefore, it supplies no information regarding entrainment.

4. What happens in the following EGM with attempted entrainment? Pacing is from the ablation catheter in the cavotricuspid isthmus of the right atrium.
The duodecapolar catheter is in the standard location in the RA.
  a. **Ablation catheter is in the tachycardia circuit**
  b. **Entrainment of typical RA flutter**
  c. **Tachycardia not CTI dependent**
  d. **Entrainment did not occur**

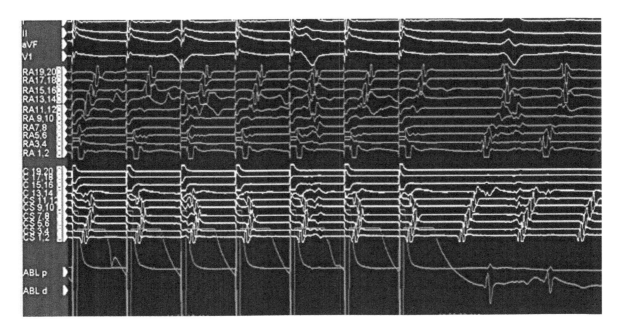

ANSWER: c. Tachycardia not CTI dependent. The tachycardia located on the right of the screen appears to be atrial flutter. There are more A's than V's and the atrial depolarizations are organized unlike Atrial Fibrillation.

Entrainment shows whether the ablation (mapping) catheter is located within the tachycardia circuit. This is a common technique used for Atrial Flutter such as in this example. It is also quite helpful in other macro reentrant tachycardias such as Ischemic VT. When looking at this example, one must first decide whether entrainment did occur. Pacing is faster than the underlying tachycardia, (underlying seen at the right side) and all pacing artifacts capture the atrial tissue. The pacing rate speeds up the underlying

tachycardia (of 230) to the pacing rate of 200 ms. Also, the tachycardia continues after pacing ceases; however, notice that the atrial activation during pacing is completely different than the underlying tachycardia. So, the tachycardia was entrained, but the ablation catheter is not close to the tachycardia circuit. To further show this look at the PPI (post pacing interval). If the PPI is short, the catheter is within the tachycardia circuit. If the PPI is long, then the catheter is not within the circuit. To measure the PPI, first measure the underlying tachycardia rate which here is 230 (this information is not displayed in this example) and the rate that we are pacing at is 200 ms.

Once pacing stops, measure from the last pacing spike on the catheter you are pacing from to the next intrinsic signal on that catheter. In this Atrial Flutter example, we will measure to the next intrinsic A wave on the ablation channel. From this number (318 in this ex.) subtract the tachycardia cycle length (230). This gives you a PPI (post pacing interval) of 88. This PPI is large which shows that our catheter is not within the circuit. This shows that the catheter is not dependent on the cavotricuspid isthmus. Therefore, an ablation line from the IVC to the tricuspid ostium, which is typically performed for typical atrial flutter, will not terminate the tachycardia. Further mapping is needed to figure out the tachycardia location. A lot of information was given in this example. This will be broken down in the other questions.

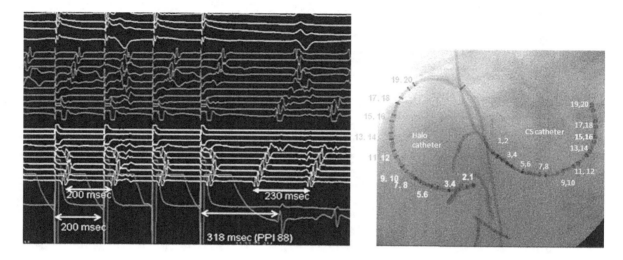

5. On the same patient, there is pacing on CS 11,12 which the physician described at mid CS. What can be said about the entrainment attempt below?
EGM shows lead V1, RA duodecapolar, CS and ablation catheters
   a. **Unable to be determined from the information supplied**
   b. **Entrainment of an atypical right atrial flutter**
   c. **Entrainment did not occur**
   d. **Entrainment did occur**

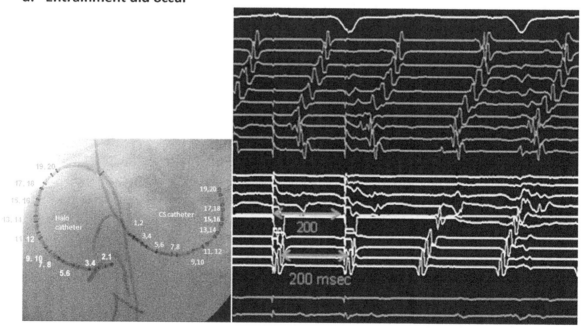

ANSWER: d. Entrainment did occur. The pacing rate is clearly faster than the underlying tachycardia which you recall was 230 ms. The atrial tissue was captured. The pacing not only captures the atrial tissue, but also speeds up the atrium to the pacing interval of 200 ms. After pacing ceases the tachycardia continues. More information on this example will be provided in the next question.

6. On the same patient as in the previous questions, there is pacing on CS 11,12 which the physician described at mid CS. The underlying tachycardia cycle length is 230 ms in this example. What does this successful entrainment attempt show?

 a. **Entrainment of atypical right atrial flutter**
 b. **Entrainment of typical right atrial flutter**
 c. **Entrainment of a cavotricuspid flutter**
 d. **None of the above**

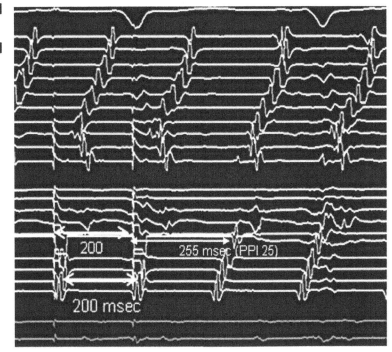

ANSWER: d. None of the above. We already discussed that successful entrainment occurred. Now notice the PPI (post pacing interval). This was found by measure from the last pace to the first intrinsic A wave on the same channel that we paced from (CS 11,12). That number was 255 ms minus the underlying tachycardia cycle length which was 230 ms. 255 - 230 = 25ms

A PPI-TCL of 25ms shows that we are pacing to a site that is closer to the tachycardia's circuit as compared to pacing the ablation catheter located on the cavotricuspid isthmus in the previous question. Therefore, the tachycardia is not located on the right side since the further we pace from the right atrium the smaller the PPI. However, further mapping is still necessary. Notice how the pacing atrial activation is still slightly different than the tachycardia atrial activation.

7. On the same patient as in the previous questions, there is pacing on CS 1,2 which the physician described at distal CS. The underlying atrial cycle length is 230 ms. From this EGM, did entrainment occur?

 a. **Yes, entrainment did occur**
 b. **No, entrainment did not occur**
 c. **Unable to determine with information given**

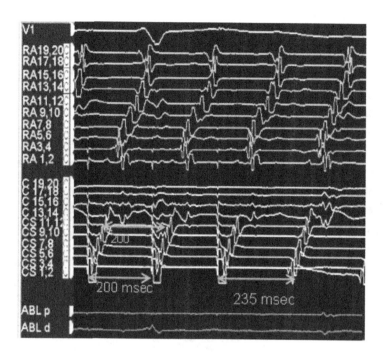

ANSWER: a. Yes, entrainment did occur. As describe previously, pacing is faster than the underlying tachycardia cycle length of 230, capture did occur, the atrial activation speeds up to the pacing rate, and tachycardia continued after pacing stopped.

8. From the EGMs in the previous two questions what type of AFL is it?
   a. **Atypical Flutter located on the atrial septum**
   b. **Atypical Flutter around the crista terminalis**
   c. **Left Atrial Flutter**
   d. **Typical Cavotricuspid Flutter**

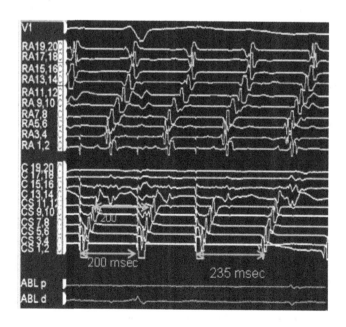

ANSWER: c. Left Atrial Flutter. The PPI (post pacing interval in this example is 5ms. 235 – 230 = 5 ms. This is when we were pacing on the distal CS which is located on the far-left side of the LA. This small PPI shows that our catheter is in the tachycardia circuit. Also, notice that the activation with pacing is the exact same as the tachycardia itself. This is referred to as "concealed entrainment."

INCORRECT ANSWERS:

- Atypical flutter on the atrial septum would have a smaller PPI on the proximal CS rather than the distal CS. Atypical flutter around the crista terminalis would have a smaller PPI with right atrial pacing since it is a RA structure.

- Cavotricuspid isthmus dependent flutter would have had a small PPI with pacing on the ablation catheter which was located at that location.

- With atypical flutters, further mapping is necessary to determine the circuit of the tachycardia whether it is scar related or around the LA structures themselves. 3D mapping techniques are valuable in this type of patient. LA scar related flutters are more common in patients post LA surgeries or extensive LA ablations such as PVI (pulmonary vein isolation). The diagram shows a clockwise LA flutter and a CCW RA flutter.

- Typical counterclockwise Atrial flutter is like what is displayed below in which the impulse travels through the cavotricuspid isthmus, up the septal wall and down the lateral wall. The cavotricuspid isthmus is the area between the IVC and the tricuspid valve. That is why an ablation line from the IVC to the tricuspid annulus will stop the atrial flutter from continuing if the line is complete.

- Flutter may also propagate clockwise and in many atypical ways. E.g., around the crista terminalis or areas of scar (slow conduction) on either the right or left side of the heart. See: Murgatroyd's chapter 8.7

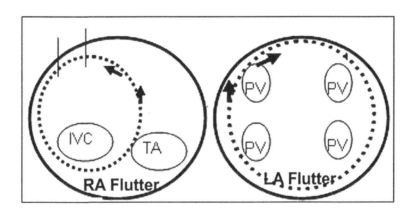

Advanced Electrograms:

1. This tachycardia was induced on a 34-year-old patient with a history of presyncope. How does the tachycardia terminate in the last beat?
   a. **Septal PVC**
   b. **Sinus beat**
   c. **Left-sided PAC**
   d. **Right-sided PAC**

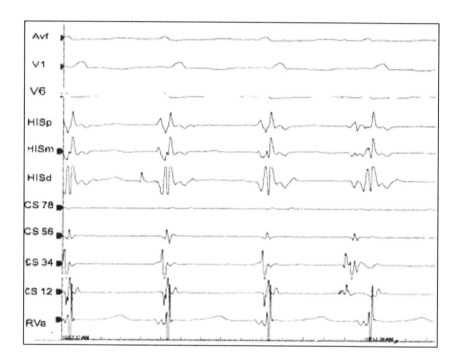

ANSWER: c. Left-sided PAC. A PAC ended the tachycardia not a PVC because the A comes first, and it is a narrow QRS complex. Now where did the PAC originate?

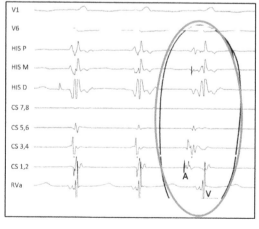

- It comes early on CS 1,2 (distal) which is on the left lateral LA.
- Without an HRA catheter you only have the CS and His to utilize in the determination.
- If it were a right sided sinus beat, you would notice the A earliest on the His. It is not RVOT, because this is a narrow complex QRS. Atypical AVNRT is a possibility, but it would have a rapid onset. No Delta waves are present which rules out WPW.

2. During atrial extrastimulus testing on this patient with suspected WPW, the circled beat shows:

    a. **First beat of orthodromic tachycardia**

    b. **Accessory Pathway Echo**

    c. **Junctional Escape**

    d. **AV Nodal Echo**

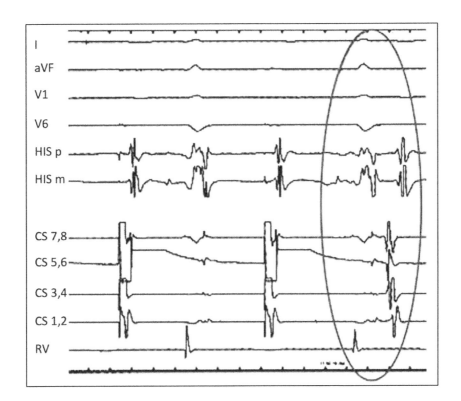

ANSWER: b. Accessory pathway echo. The incorrect answers are: In a typical AV nodal echo, you would see an AH jump first and the VA would be <60 ms. Junctional escape would not come in that quick, and typically the VA would be <60 ms. Even though the V does come first, it is not a PVC. Because the QRS complex looks the same as the previous atrial paced beats. The CS catheter shows A wave and V waves, and finally an RVa catheter with just the V signal. When answering questions, see how the suspected diagnosis (WPW) might fit the EGM or one of the answers.

3. After RV catheter placement, threshold testing was done to ensure RV capture. What does the CS catheter show in the last beat?
    a.   **Shift in atrial conduction**
    b.   **Shift in ventricular conduction**
    c.   **VERP**
    d.   **AERP**

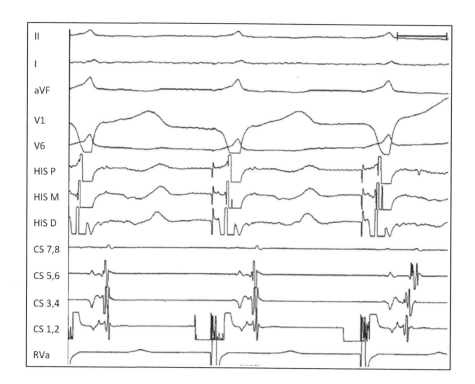

ANSWER: a. Shift in atrial conduction. Notice the atrial deflection appears first on the distal CS (CS 1,2), which is on the left side of the heart. Then the A works its way back proximal (sloping eccentric A conduction differs from previous two beats). Normally during RV pacing the A should first go retrograde up the AV node nearest the proximal CS electrodes. Note the eccentric conduction. This suggests an accessory pathway conducting the A up the left side of the AV ring.

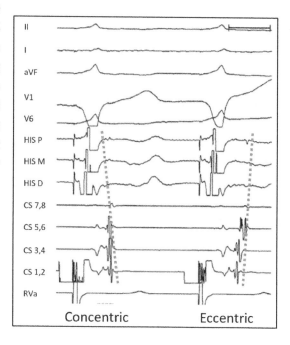

4. What happens in the last half of this EGM?
   a. **Defibrillation of VT**
   b. **Atrial Flutter**
   c. **Successful ATP**
   d. **Unsuccessful ATP**

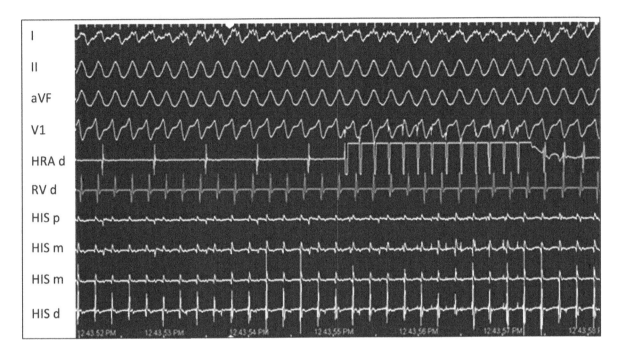

ANSWER: d. Unsuccessful ATP. Wide QRS and more V's than A's suggesting VT. The ATP (antitachycardia pacing) attempt was unsuccessful… why?? The patient was being paced in the atrium, NOT the ventricle. When ATP is successful it is nice to avoid shocking the patient, especially if they are not "fully sedated." If defibrillation is delayed too long, it may cause hemodynamic collapse or degenerate to VF. With ATP there is also the risk of accelerating the VT. Some electrophysiologists feel that pre-ICD testing is extremely useful to characterize the nature of the patient's sustained VT. They evaluate the VT rate, how well it is tolerated, and what kinds of pacing sequences reliably terminate it. Other electrophysiologists point out that the characteristics of a patient's induced VT are often quite different from their spontaneous tachycardia, and that the odds of successfully pace terminating a patient's induced arrhythmia are small. See: Fogoros Ventricular Arrhythmias.

5. During atrial extrastimulus testing on this patient with a history of palpitations at rest, what is the circled beat?

    a. **Typical AV Nodal Echo**
    b. **Intra-atrial Reentry**
    c. **Junctional**
    d. **PVC**

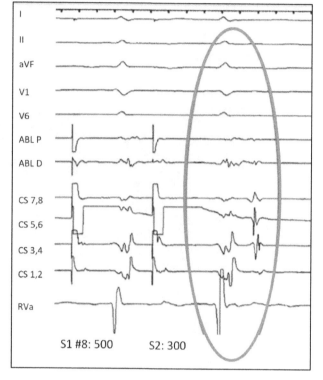

ANSWER: b. Intra-atrial reentry. The first beat is paced in the A (CS), then conducts down to the V. The second beat is paced in the A (CS) and conducts down to the V, then back up to the A (on the CS channel). Intra-atrial reentrant refers to any macroreentrant atrial reentry that does not utilize the cavotricuspid isthmus as a critical pathway. There is also Intra-atrial reentrant tachycardia (IART) that is associated with post-surgical or ablation scar.

Incorrect answers: In a typical AV nodal echo and a Junctional beat, you would see the VA interval much shorter; typically, less than 60 ms. A PVC would have a wide QRS complex. In this example, the QRS complex is narrow, like the underlying rhythm.

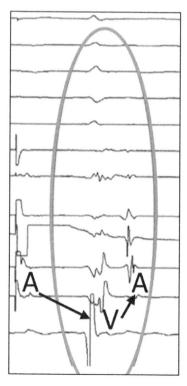

6. In the second paced beat the stimulator mA was increased. Where is the physician pacing in this EGM?

   a. **CS**
   b. **RV**
   c. **HIS**
   d. **HRA**

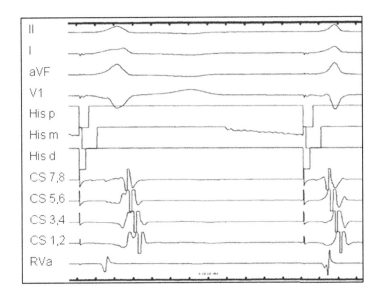

ANSWER: c. HIS. (Parahisian pacing) The QRS is a wide complex on the first beat which would lead one to believe that we are pacing on the RVa catheter; however, looking at the RVa channel there is clearly no pacing spike. The HIS channel is pegged, suggesting pacing from that catheter. The His bundle is anatomically deep and well insulated, so you must pace at a high output to truly capture the His (narrow QRS complex). When you turn the mA down until you just lose His capture, you can still capture the ventricle, which will result in a wide complex as shown on the left. With this high amplitude V pacing, the impulse must travel down through the myocardium (wide complex) and back up through the Purkinje system and AV node to get back to the atrium (Late retrograde A). The retrograde A shown on the CS channel spreads concentrically from the proximal to distal electrodes.

This diagram does not show conduction through an accessory pathway. We do parahisian pacing when looking for an antero-septal accessory pathway. If there were early retrograde activation with both high and low His pacing, it would suggest an anteroseptal pathway. For more information on Parahisian pacing. See: Murgatroyd's chapter on Accessory Pathways and AV Reentry

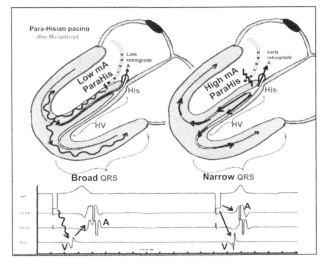

THE BELOW ELECTROGRAM IS USED FOR THE NEXT TWO QUESTIONS

7. During tachycardia, the physician added a PVC at the exact time as the His deflection in the third beat. What was the effect of the stimulation?
   a. **PVC did not advance the A**
   b. **Tachycardia terminated**
   c. **PVC advanced the A**
   d. **AV Block**

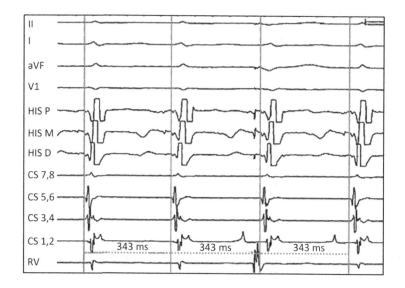

ANSWER: a. PVC did not advance the A or alter conduction.

8. What does this result of the question above mean?
   a. **Unable to determine if there is an accessory pathway**
   b. **There are no dual nodal pathways**
   c. **There is an accessory pathway**
   d. **There are dual nodal pathways**

ANSWER: a. Unable to determine if there is an AP. A PVC is placed at the exact time of the His so that the His is refractory to conduct the impulse up to the atrium. So, if the impulse cannot go through the AV node, but somehow still reaches the atrium (advances the next A) then it must have arrived via an accessory pathway.

When the PVC advances the A (by rapid conducting into the atria) it shows there is an accessory pathway. But if it does not advance the A (as here) it doesn't necessarily mean there is no pathway. The pathway may just be far enough away that PVC doesn't get there in time. If you place a PVC closer to the pathway location, you should see the A advance or come earlier.

THIS ELECTROGRAM IS USED FOR THE NEXT TWO QUESTIONS

9. Where is the physician pacing in the electrogram?
  a. HRA
  b. CS
  c. RV
  d. HIS

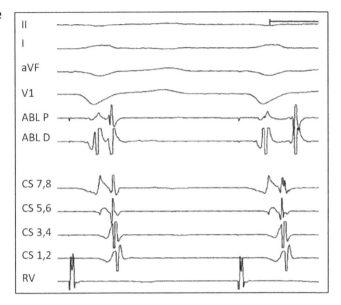

ANSWER: c. RV. Note the pacer spike in the His catheter, timed with the RVa spike, preceding a broad QRS.

10. The previous EGM suggests:
  a. Intermittent pathway
  b. AVNERP
  c. VAERP
  d. Echo

ANSWER: a. Intermittent pathway visualization. Note a wide QRS and pacing spike on the RVa with the RV impulse coming first shows that we are pacing in the RV. Notice the shift in conduction on the His catheter (fifth and sixth line from the top).

The vertical lines are drawn to help show the earliest site of activation.

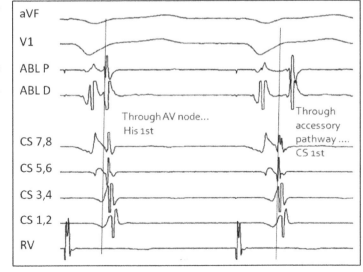

11. Note pacing on the His channel timed to H. What SVT is the physician trying to rule out with this pacing technique?
   a. **Bundle Branch Reentry**
   b. **Septal Pathway**
   c. **AVNRT**
   d. **RVOT**

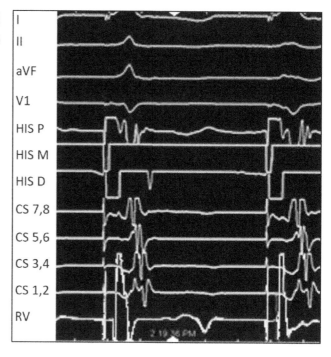

ANSWER: b. Septal pathway. Note the pacing on the His channel. A physician may parahisian pace to rule out a septal pathway. If we pace the His (which requires a high output due to insulation) the impulse will get to the atrium quickly through the His / AV node. When we turn down the mA until we just lose His capture, then we can capture the ventricular tissue at that spot. This is sometimes a location for a septal pathway. If the impulse takes a long time to reach the atrium, then it went through the ventricular tissue down to the Purkinje system where it could travel back up the bundle branches through the His to the atrium. If it reaches the atrium quickly when pacing the ventricular tissue (loss of HIS capture) then it took a short cut and went up through an accessory bypass tract.... A septal pathway. is pacing technique (Parahisian pacing) can be helpful in these situations.

See: Murgatroyd's chapter on Accessory Pathways and AV Reentry.

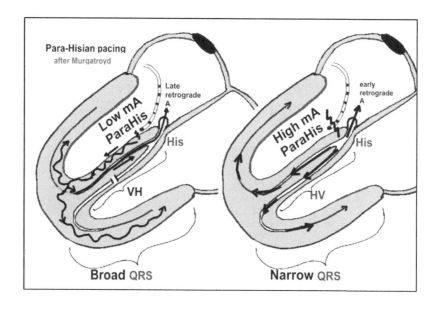

12. An Isuprel infusion is started on your SVT patient. What happens near the end of the EGM?
   a. **Spontaneous Initiation of AF**
   b. **Initiation of AVNRT**
   c. **Successful PVI**
   d. **CHB**

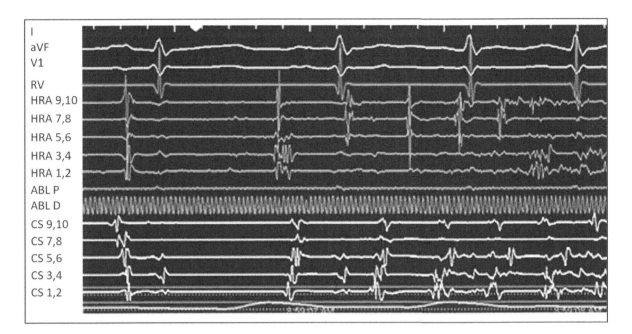

ANSWER: a. Spontaneous AF. Chaotic atrial activity with more A's than V's is characteristic of atrial fibrillation. It appears to have started with a left sided PAC. Notice how the earliest A is on CS 1,2 (distal CS) electrodes. The catheter marked A is a circular mapping catheter, the patient is in the EP lab for an AF ablation.

13. While performing atrial extrastimulus testing (drive train of eight beats then adding a PAC) in the CS, the delayed A wave shown is termed:

    a. **Failure to capture**

    b. **AVNERP**

    c. **Latency**

    d. **AERP**

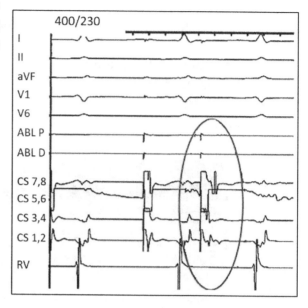

ANSWER: c. Latency. Notice the delay between the pacing spike and atrial capture after S2. The delay is termed "latency," because it is "LATE." With the extrasystole, the atrium is nearing its refractory period and beginning to fatigue. An earlier S2 may show more marked latency (see diagram) or block totally (refractory). Pacing faster than this would either lead to AF or simply block (AERP). With the chance of inducing AF most physicians would stop pacing here and "park" the S2 about 20 ms higher, add an S3, and start coming down on the S3. Latency may also occur in Ventricular extrastimulus testing.

It is important to watch for latency, especially in performing measurements. When measuring for an AH jump (in this example one would measure from the A to the V since no His catheter is available); if one did not account for the latency and measure at the actual start of the atrial deflection rather than the pacing spike, there may appear to be a jump to the slow pathway when there actually is not. This also can be a factor when measuring the post pacing interval (PPI) for entrainment. If latency is not considered, one could incorrectly measure the PPI.

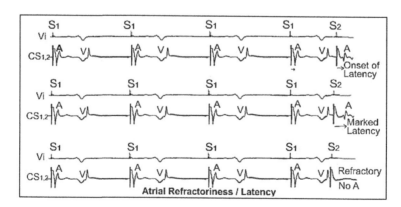

14. What happens after S2 in the second electrogram?
   a. **Infrahisian Block**
   b. **AH Jump**
   c. **VH Jump**
   d. **AERP**

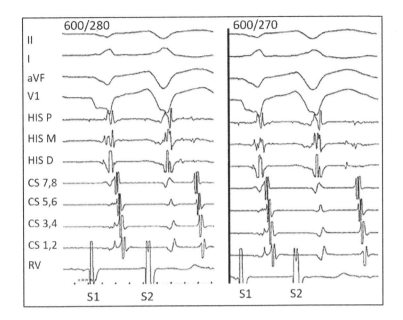

ANSWER: c. VH jump. With S2 note the His in each tracing. The VA and VH intervals are longer in the second EGM suggesting a "jump." It is unusual to see a VH jump. This example shows a block in the bundle branch – this is important because this rules out an accessory pathway. If the bundle blocks, the impulse can cross the septum and go up to the His. If there was a pathway it would have passed up into the atrium and presented itself by this point.

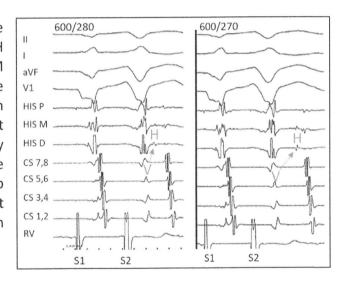

THIS ELECTROGRAM IS USED FOR THE NEXT TWO QUESTIONS

15. This 16-year-old patient arrived in the EP lab after complaints of palpitations. During the EP study, the physician gave 6 mg of Adenosine IV while pacing the RVa. What happens in the EGM?
   a. **Failure to capture**
   b. **Infrahisian block**
   c. **VA block**
   d. **AV block**

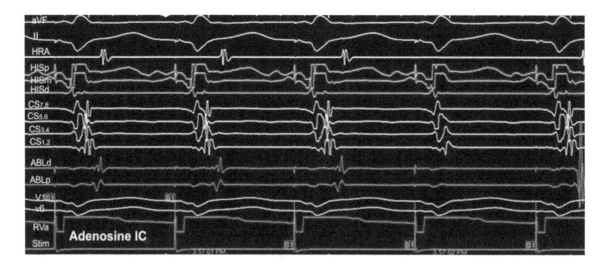

ANSWER: c. VA block. The fourth pacing spike on this screen shows ventricular pacing and capture, but no A following the fourth beat on any channel. This is the easiest to see on the HRA channel. The first three beats show V pacing and capture immediately followed by retrograde A waves. In the fourth beat, the retrograde A passes up through the Bundle branches and His was blocked (VA block) and is absent. WHY? Adenosine causes AV node refractoriness/ block. In individuals suspected of suffering from supraventricular tachycardia (SVT), adenosine is used to help identify the rhythm. Certain SVTs can be successfully terminated with adenosine. This includes any reentrant arrhythmias that require the AV node for the reentry, e.g., AV reentrant tachycardia (AVRT), AV nodal reentrant tachycardia (AVNRT). In addition, atrial tachycardia can sometimes be terminated with adenosine.

16. Continued from last question, what does this essentially rule out when you see VA block after adenosine administration?
    a. **Atrial tachycardia**
    b. **Atrial fibrillation**
    c. **RVOT VT**
    d. **AVRT**

ANSWER: d. AVRT. Adenosine affects the AV node resulting in block. If we are pacing the ventricle and do not see VA block after repeated adenosine administrations (dosage will go up with each bolus). Then somehow the impulse finds a way from getting from the V to the A without the use of the AV node. This is by an accessory bypass tract which is required for AVRT. If you do get AV or VA conduction with adenosine, it is via an accessory pathway. There are rare situations in which adenosine may block the pathway at the same time as the AV node, but rare.

heart.bmj.com says, "Not all patients who suffer from atrioventricular reciprocating tachycardia has a delta wave on their resting ECG. Concealed pathways only conduct retrogradely, while in latent pre-excitation the accessory pathway has a net conduction time to the ventricle (that is, intra-atrial conduction plus AP conduction times) greater than the net conduction time via the atrioventricular (AV) node. Latent conduction may be unmasked by blocking AV nodal conduction with adenosine (adenosine testing)" See: heart.bmj.com

17. These two EGMs were recorded pre and post PVI ablation with pacing in the distal CS. The catheter labeled "A" is a circular mapping catheter in the pulmonary vein. The post ablation EGM shows:

   a. **AV Dissociation**
   b. **Entrance Block**
   c. **Exit Block**
   d. **CHB**

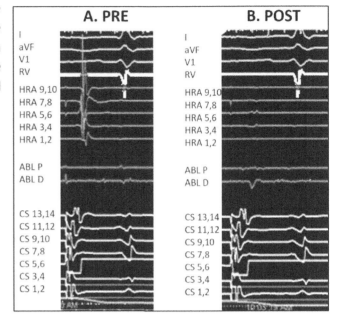

ANSWER: b. Entrance block – In this example, pacing the distal CS (closest to the left veins) the impulse does not "enter" into the pulmonary vein. Exit block cannot be determined from this slide. This would be done with PACs from a circular mapping catheter that do not "exit" to the CS. See diagram.

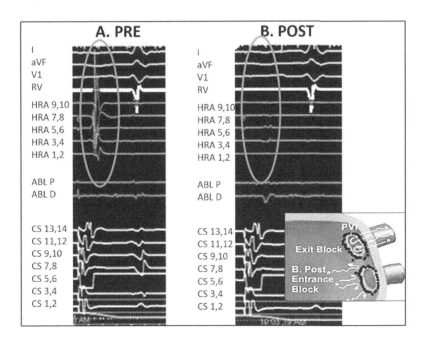

18. This 12-lead ECG is from a 76-year-old patient with near syncopal spells. The tachycardia shown was documented at 173 bpm. What is the most likely tachycardia?
   a. **Atrial Tachycardia**
   b. **Orthodromic AVRT**
   c. **Antidromic AVRT**
   d. **AVNRT**

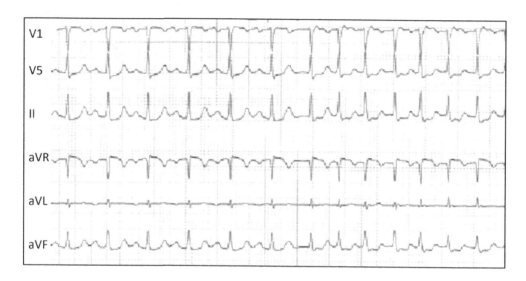

ANSWER: d. AVNRT. Notice the onset of the tachycardia on the 7th beat.

Incorrect answers are: Atrial tachycardia would start with a PAC, and one would observe two P waves prior to initiation (VAAV initiation). Antidromic AVRT would go over the pathway and up the AV node, so it would have a wide complex. In AVRT the VA time is typically greater than 60 ms, where this appears much shorter. AVNRT   VA time is typically less than 60 ms which this appears to be. Notice during the tachycardia the inverted P wave following the QRS complex. It is less the 60 ms from the QRS. The P wave is inverted due to the activation of the atrium is low to high, unlike high to low when coming from the SA node.

However, when AVNRT initiates you should see a jump to the slow pathway. The T waves have the same morphology as the underlying rhythms T waves. There is no evidence of a P wave buried in the T wave.... except... in V1. Notice that the T wave in V1 looks more like a P wave. That is the P wave buried in the T wave.... initiating the jump to the slow pathway. Therefore, it is important to look at all the leads, otherwise vital information will be missed.

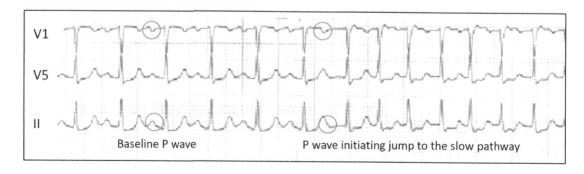

Baseline P wave   P wave initiating jump to the slow pathway

19. What is this arrhythmia seen on this EGM, ECG and Xray?
   a. **Counterclockwise AFL with 2:1 block**
   b. **AF with rapid ventricular response**
   c. **Atrial tachycardia with 2:1 block**
   d. **Clockwise AFL with 2:1 block**

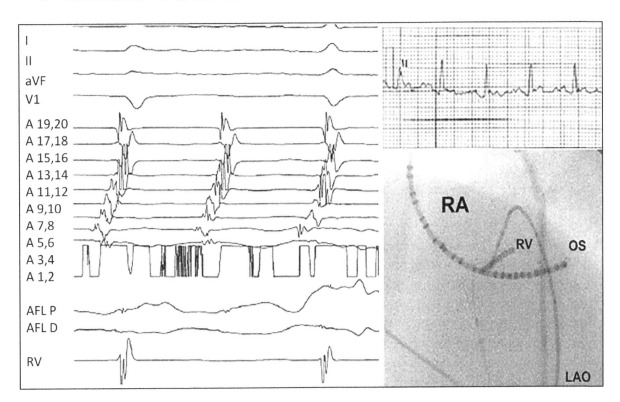

ANSWER: d. Clockwise AFL with 2:1 block. Note above the 2:1 Atrial flutter, with 2 As for every V. This is AFL in an unusual clockwise direction. The EGM shows atrial signals moving from A3,4 to A19,20 - distal to proximal in a clockwise direction. Note that on the duodecapolar catheter the A's move clockwise, up to the left, like the movement of a clock's hands. Most AFL (90%) moves the other direction, counterclockwise. The loop is entirely in the RA and usually cavotricuspid isthmus dependent, where ablation can interrupt the loop. The lead II ECG shows an irregular baseline that looks deceptively like AF.

USE THIS EGM FOR THE NEXT 2 QUESTIONS:

20. In this EGM, which catheter are we pacing from?
    a. **HRA**
    b. **His**
    c. **CS**
    d. **RVa**

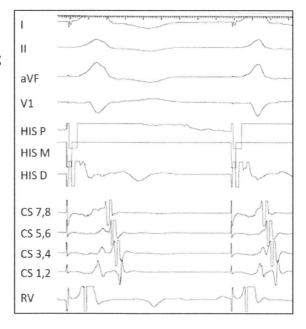

ANSWER: b. His. The largest pacing spikes arise from the His catheter. If we were pacing and capturing the RVa there would be a pacer artifact such as that shown on the His catheter and a wide QRS complex before both beats. The pacer artifact would be followed by an immediate ventricular signal on the RVa catheter and the QRS complexes would be uniformly wide. Here there is a delay between the pacing stimulus and the V signal on the RVa channel. This is an example of parahisian pacing. Note the second QRS is narrower because the His is captured.

21. In the above EGM of parahisian pacing, the second paced beat shows pacing the His at:
    a. **Lower mA output with an H response**
    b. **Lower mA output with an H + V response**
    c. **Higher mA output with an H response**
    d. **Higher mA output with an H + V response**

ANSWER: c. Higher mA output with an H response. The complex is narrower, suggesting more rapid conduction in the AV node (H). In parahisian pacing capturing the His requires higher output, because it is harder to capture than the V. There is more insulation around the RBB so the His has a higher stimulation threshold requiring more mA. As the mA is turned up (beat #2) the H is captured resulting in a narrower QRS because it proceeds mostly down the His and bundle branches. When the His capture threshold is found, the physician may go back and forth between the high mA (H narrow QRS response) and the low mA (V + H wide QRS response). In this EGM the operator is turning UP the mA, so we see the narrow H response last.

Issa says, "Parahisian pacing is helpful in determining whether retrograde conduction is occurring over the AV node versus a septal accessory pathway. A minimum of two catheters are required, one at the His position and another in the right atrium. High-output pacing is performed, and the stimulus-atrial time is analyzed with and without His capture. During His capture, both the specialized conduction system and the basal right ventricular myocardium are captured, resulting in a relatively narrow QRS. At lower output, only the ventricular myocardium is captured, due to the higher capture threshold of the His bundle, yielding a wide QRS."

"If the stimulus-atrial time is the same irrespective of His capture, this indicates retrograde conduction over a septal accessory pathway. During an "AV nodal" response to parahisian pacing, the stimulus-atrial interval is shorter when the His is captured. Such a response suggests that retrograde activation depends upon capture of the specialized conduction system. The reason that the stimulus-atrial time is longer when the His bundle is not captured is that the atria can only be activated after depolarization of the right ventricular myocardium, followed by engagement of distal ramifications of the His-Purkinje system, the His bundle, and the AV node. During His bundle capture, however, the atrial activation occurs earlier, because the impulse needs to conduct only from the very proximal aspect of the specialized conduction system. Parahisian pacing also is helpful in determining whether a septal accessory pathway has been successfully ablated."

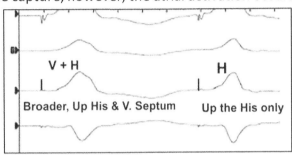

See: Issa, chapter on Approach to Paroxysmal SVT

22. In the above EGM of parahisian pacing, the A waves are:
   a. **Antegrade and eccentric**
   b. **Antegrade and concentric**
   c. **Retrograde and eccentric**
   d. **Retrograde and concentric**

ANSWER: d. Retrograde and concentric. The A waves are retrograde because they consistently follow the V waves. They come up the AV node into the septum and spread from proximal to distal CS electrodes concentrically around the LA. Note V and A waves as marked.

Concentric LA conduction is normal conduction from the septum outward and lateral. It appears like this, with the A wave moving down to the right (\). Eccentric conduction is opposite and abnormal, moving up to the right (/). E.g., a left sided accessory pathway will enter the LA through an AP and move eccentrically toward the septum.

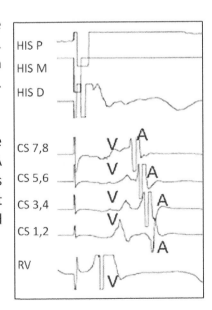

23. Describe the AFL pattern shown in these two EGMs:
   a. **#1 is the typical clockwise (CW) AFL, #2 is a typical counterclockwise (CCW) AFL**
   b. **#1 is the typical counterclockwise (CCW) AFL, #2 is the typical clockwise (CW) AFL**
   c. **#1 is the atypical clockwise (CCW) AFL, #2 is the typical counterclockwise (CCW) AFL**
   d. **#1 is the typical clockwise (CCW) AFL, #2 is the atypical counter-clockwise (CW) AFL**

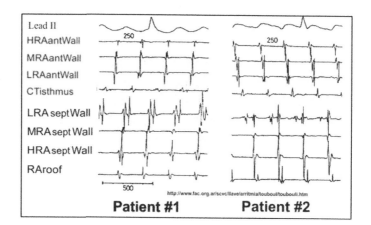

ANSWER: c. #1 is the typical clockwise (CCW) AFL, #2 is the typical counterclockwise (CCW) AFL. Issa says, "Typical AFL is of two types, counterclockwise and clockwise. In counterclockwise AFL, activation proceeds up the septal side of the tricuspid annulus toward the crista terminalis and moves along the lateral wall of the RA to reach the lateral tricuspid annulus, after which it propagates through the isthmus defined by the IVC, CS, and tricuspid annulus (counterclockwise as viewed in the left anterior oblique [LAO] view from the ventricular side of the tricuspid annulus).The circuit is entirely in the RA."

"Left atrial activation occurs as a bystander and follows transseptal conduction across the inferior CS-left atrium (LA) connection, Bachmann's bundle, and/or fossa ovalis. In clockwise (reverse typical) AFL, activation propagates in the opposite direction." Note Pt. #2 has downward pointing flutter waves. Typical CCS FL has downward pointed flutter waves in leads II, III and aVF, and upward pointing in V1. See: Issa, chapter on Isthmus Dependent AFL EGM

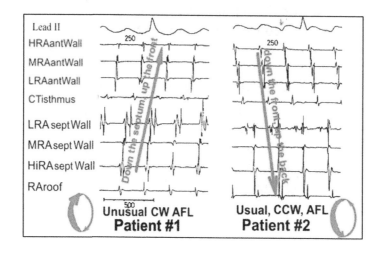

24. Identify EGMs taken before and after successful ablation of CCW atrial flutter. These four EGMs were taken before and after ablation of CCW AFL of the cavotricuspid isthmus. The duodecapolar catheter (Labeled H) circles the tricuspid annulus in the usual configuration with distal electrode #1 being low lateral RA. Match each electrogram recording (A, B, C, & D) from the CS and Duodecapolar (H) catheters to its description.

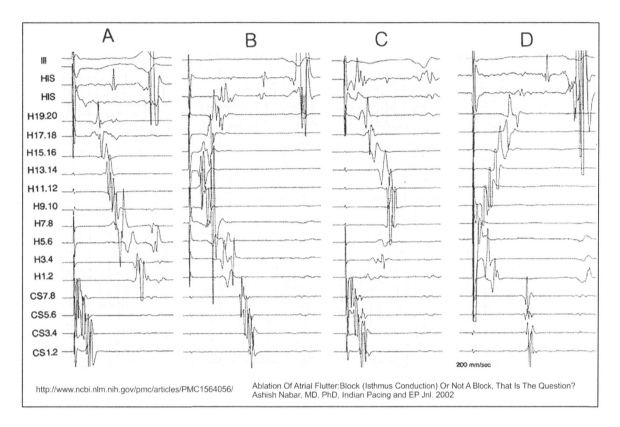

http://www.ncbi.nlm.nih.gov/pmc/articles/PMC1564056/

Ablation Of Atrial Flutter:Block (Isthmus Conduction) Or Not A Block, That Is The Question? Ashish Nabar, MD, PhD, Indian Pacing and EP Jnl. 2002

1. **Pre-ablation, pacing CS ostium**
2. **Pre-ablation, pacing low lateral RA**
3. **Post-ablation, pacing CS ostium**
4. **Post-ablation, pacing low lateral RA**

CORRECTLY MATCHED ANSWERS ARE: A=3, B=2, C=1, D=4

The four circles represent the tricuspid annulus in the LAO view. The burn lesions are drawn as brown ablation dots below the IVC in the CTI. Numbers in the circle represent the approximate location of the duodecapolar catheter electrodes. The pacing electrode is marked with a red asterisk. The small circle is the CS. The curved black line connecting the SVC & IVC is the crista terminalis (CT), which normally acts as a conduction barrier. Pre-ablation, when the CTI is untreated or incompletely blocked, the atrial activation line is < or > shaped as shown. EGMs B & C show incomplete block, where activation passes in 2 directions unimpaired around the atrium until the two waves meet and extinguish each other. Tracings A & D were taken post CTI ablation. In A & C pacing from the CS catheter shows immediately on the CS electrodes, while RA pacing shows last on the CS electrodes in B &D. When cavotricuspid isthmus block is complete the duodecapolar electrograms will stack up in one diagonal line (A or D). The line slants left or right depending on which side of the CTI you are pacing from. EGM D shows most of the depolarizations nicely stacked diagonally, except for H1-H6 which are below the lateral pacing electrode. You will soon learn to be happy when you see the straight diagonal lines, because it is a successful endpoint of CTI ablation for AFL.

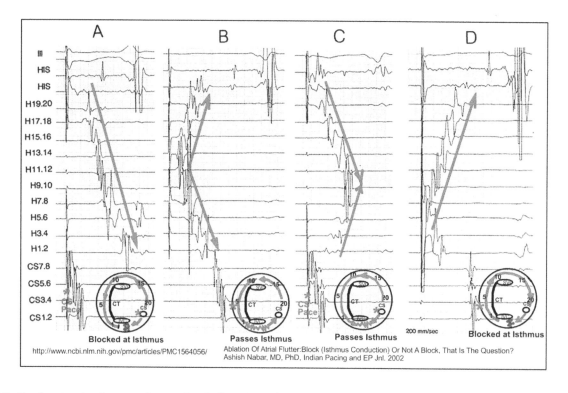

Ablation Of Atrial Flutter:Block (Isthmus Conduction) Or Not A Block, That Is The Question?
Ashish Nabar, MD, PhD, Indian Pacing and EP Jnl. 2002

25. Evaluate the intervals on the following electrogram. Mark all that apply.
   a. **Short HV**
   b. **Short PR**
   c. **Short AH**
   d. **Long QT**
   e. **Long AV**

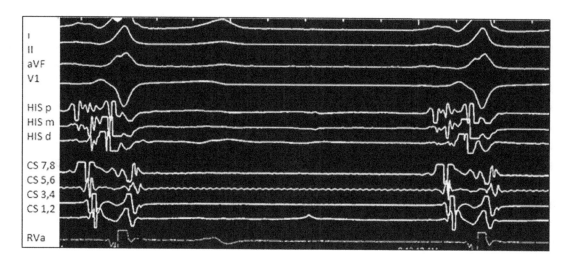

ANSWER: a. Short HV, b. Short PR, and c. Short AH. This patient has a delta wave which is shown by the slurred upstroke of the QRS complex. Even without calipers the AH interval is short. The AH interval shows the time through the AV node. The AV node takes more time than what is shown; so, a short AH interval such as this suggests an accessory pathway. With timelines of 0.1 sec, this PR interval is 0.07 sec. Normal is 0.12-0.20 sec, so it's noticeably short.

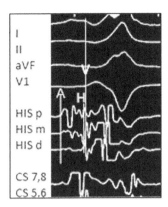

The HV interval is almost zero when measured from HIS p to the earliest ventricular activation on the surface lead I or V1. This suggests that the ventricular myocardium is getting activated early without going through the AV node. This is an accessory bypass tract conducting antegrade and bypassing the AV node. Normal HV int. is 35-55 ms. Normal AH is 50-120 ms

26. In the EGM displayed, what occurs with CS 5,6 pacing?
   a. **Rate related BBB**
   b. **Preexcitation**
   c. **AVNERP**
   d. **APERP**

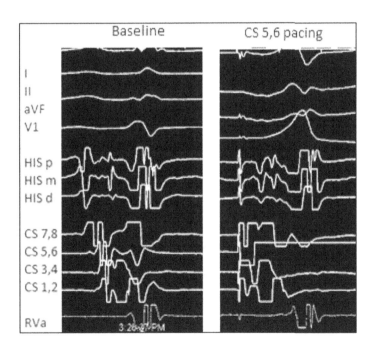

ANSWER: b. Preexcitation. In the baseline EGM the surface ECG and the HIS channels all appear to be normal. The CS appears slightly abnormal on CS 1,2 and CS 3,4 with a shorter AV interval than expected. However, when pacing the CS at 5,6 there is an obvious change on the surface ECG as well as the intracardiac EGMS. Notice the slurred upstroke on the QRS complex, this is a delta wave. Next, note the short AH interval on the HIS channels and the almost fused AV interval on the CS channels (CS 3,4 and unable to tell on CS 5,6). This suggests an accessory pathway that can conduct in the antegrade direction (over the AP from atrium to ventricles). Many times, it may be difficult to see an accessory pathway if the conduction of the AV node is quick or if the accessory pathway is a longer distance from the AV node, such as a left lateral pathway. Pacing closer to the pathway will show more preexcitation as the impulse will reach the pathway before the AV node. Slowing down conduction over the AV node would also demonstrate a similar appearance. Therefore, it may be beneficial to pace the atrium at various sites rather than just via the HRA catheter.

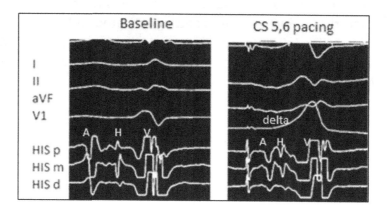

27. This EGM was recorded during extrastimulus testing. Each example is the last beat (the extrastimulus or S2) while pacing CS 5,6. What is demonstrated in this test?
- a. **Evidence of dual AV nodal physiology**
- b. **Manifest Accessory Pathway**
- c. **Concentric conduction**
- d. **Wenckebach**

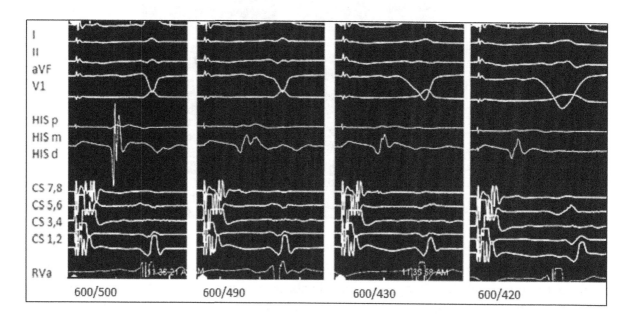

ANSWER: b. Manifest Accessory Pathway. With every extrastimulus pacing run, notice the changes occurring to the QRS complex. The HIS catheter also demonstrates changes in which demonstrate more of the impulse conducting down to the ventricle via the accessory pathway; however, there is not an obvious H wave in which case watch the AV interval. The AV interval becomes fused (shortens) on the His catheter with more aggressive pacing. Also, the delta wave becomes more pronounced with more aggressive pacing. This is because the impulse is slowing or decrementing in the AV node (like normal) with faster pacing; therefore, the activation is more pronounced over the accessory pathway. Accessory pathways do not (with rare exception) decrement like the AV node does. APs are an all or none response. Notice that the AV interval is fused on the His catheter rather than the CS catheter. This demonstrates a pathway closer to the AV node, anteroseptal. "Differential atrial pacing can also be used to help locate accessory pathways. With left—sided pathways, the stimulus to delta interval is shorter with pacing from the CS than with pacing from the high right atrium. With right-sided pathways, pacing at various sites along the tricuspid annulus can be used to locate the site with the shortest stim to delta interval."

See: Murgatroyd's Handbook of Cardiac Electrophysiology chapter on AVRT.

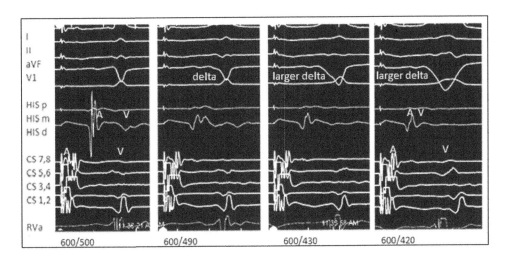

28. A 23-year-old athlete presented to the ER with the following rhythm after drinking an energy drink. The recording was taken from defibrillator paddles.
What is the probable cause of ventricular fibrillation?
  a. Atrial flutter with 1:1 conduction
  b. Dual AV nodal physiology
  c. Brugada syndrome
  d. WPW

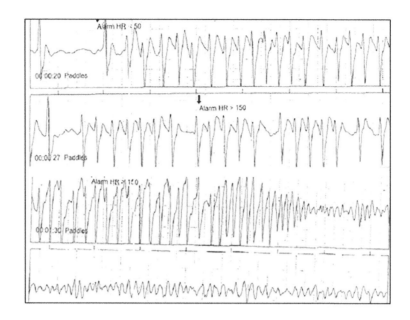

ANSWER: d. WPW. It is difficult to discern clear delta waves due to the fast rhythm and because the ECG was recorded from the defibrillator paddles. This is the risk of an antegrade pathway or WPW in a patient that goes into atrial fibrillation.

Zipes says, "Supplements from energy drinks…. are commonly used by athletes… Energy drinks such as Monster and Red Bull are broadly marketed to athletes across the world and indeed sponsor athletic events. Energy drinks contain caffeine, taurine, and glucuronolactone. Caffeine causes epinephrine and acetylcholine release and direct stimulation of the muscle cell and reduces the perception of fatigue. Caffeine at standard doses has little potential toxicity; however, at higher doses, agitation, tremors, and arrhythmias may result. The benefits of taurine and glucuronolactone are much less clear, as is their potential toxicity. Several deaths have reputably been linked to energy drinks; thus, several European countries have banned them." The effect of energy drinks combined with an accessory pathway can be life threatening. See: Cardiac Electrophysiology: From Cell to Bedside by Douglas P Zipes chapter on Sudden cardiac deaths in athletes.

29. Match the following answers with the correct beat in this mid ablation electrogram.
   a. **Retrograde conduction through the accessory pathway**
   b. **Conduction through the AV node**
   c. **VA block**

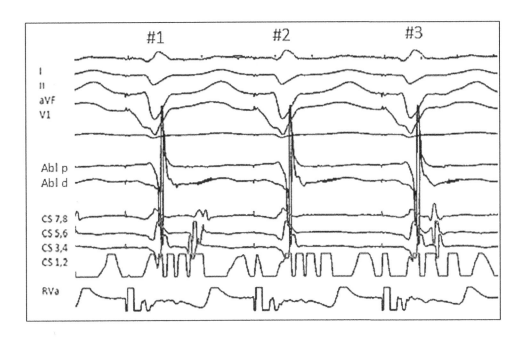

CORRECTLY MATCHED ANSWERS ARE:
#1: a. Retrograde conduction through the accessory pathway
#2: c. VA block
#3: b. Conduction through the AV node

The patient is being paced via the RV apex catheter. This is demonstrated with a ventricular signal seen before the atrial signal with earliest on the RVa, saturation of the RVa channel, and a wide complex QRS that is preceded by a pacing artifact. Antegrade conduction over the accessory pathway or AV node is unable to be demonstrated while pacing the RVa. To demonstrate antegrade conduction, there would need to be native conduction or atrial pacing. There is evidence of an accessory pathway on beat #1. The earliest atrial activity is seen on CS 1,2. If the impulse were to go through the AV node the earliest atrial defection would be seen on the His catheter (if there is one in place) followed by the proximal CS. Somehow the impulse is reaching the atrial tissue on the left side of the heart before going through the bundle of His. This is only seen when there is an accessory pathway (exceptions would be a PAC originating from the LA). Beat #2 was blocked as seen by a ventricular signal with no atrial signal to follow. Beat #3 was conducted retrograde through the AV node as demonstrated by the earliest atrial activity occurring on the proximal CS. Notice there is no longer a "V" appearance on the CS catheter. At a successful ablation site, there would be VA fusion on the ablation catheter which is not well demonstrated in this example. The catheter may be past the mitral valve more on the ventricular aspect (small A), the retrograde approach may have been used with ablation on the ventricular side, or it may be a slant pathway and the ventricular insertion.

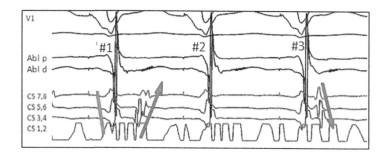

USE THE FOLLOWING EGM FOR THE NEXT TWO QUESTIONS.

30. Where is the physician pacing in the following electrogram?

a. HRA
b. RV
c. LV
d. CS

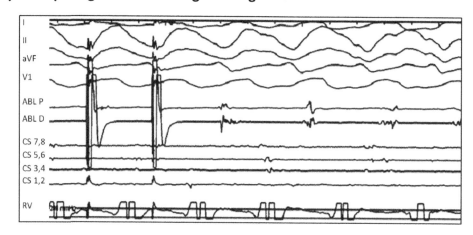

ANSWER: c. LV pacing. Pacing is via the RF ablation catheter which is in the LV.
Notice the wide complex immediately following the pacing artifact on the surface ECG. There is a delay on the RVa catheter from the time of the pacing spike to RV signal.

31. What arrhythmia was initiated in the previous electrogram?

a. AF in a WPW patient
b. VT
c. AVRT
d. CHB

ANSWER: b. VT. Also, looking at the surface ECG, the paced QRS complex as a RBBB morphology which indicates that the LV is depolarizing first, and the RV is delayed. Pacing occurs from higher in the ventricle such as the base of the LV or LVOT as indicated by the positive QRS in leads II and aVF. II, III, and aVF are inferior leads in which the positive pole is at the foot. An impulse moving towards a positive pole makes a positive deflection and an impulse moving away from a positive pole makes a negative deflection.

USE THE FOLLOWING EGM FOR THE NEXT FOUR QUESTIONS

32. Where are we pacing from in EGM #115?
   a. **Proximal His**
   b. **Distal His**
   c. **Proximal CS**
   d. **Distal CS**

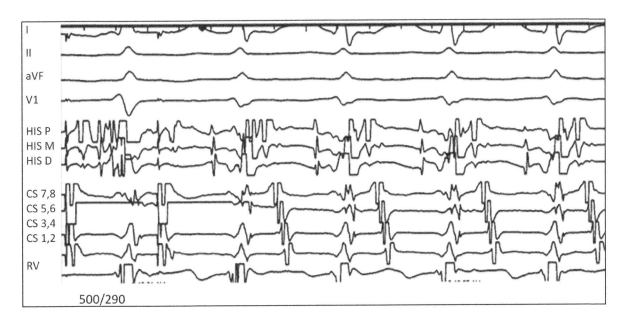

ANSWER: c. Proximal CS. Notice the pacing artifact on CS 5,6. An atrial deflection is unable to be seen immediately following the pacing spike on CS 5,6 due to saturation of the pacing channel, but capture is apparent by looking at all the other EGMs. All catheters are numbered starting at the distal tip. The distal electrode is 1 and, on this catheter, the most proximal electrode is 8. This is an octapolar or 8 electrode catheter.

33. What type of pacing is being performed in the previous electrogram?
   a. **Extrastimulus Testing**
   b. **Decremental**
   c. **Ramp**
   d. **Burst**

ANSWER: a. Extrastimulus testing, even with seeing only two paced beats, you are still able to determine that extrastimulus testing is being performed by the 500,290 listed below the example. This number is usually displayed in the pacing log of the EP system. This is the method of using a drive train of eight beats and then adding a PAC or PVC (extrastimulus). This is a common form of pacing to induce arrhythmias.

34. What rhythm is induced in the previous electrogram?
   a. **Orthodromic AVRT**
   b. **Antidromic AVRT**
   c. **Typical AVNRT**
   d. **Atrial Flutter**

ANSWER: a. Orthodromic AVRT. The rhythm induced is AVRT, more specifically, orthodromic AVRT. In orthodromic AVRT the impulse travels from atrium, AV node, ventricle, and then back to the atrium via the accessory pathway. In antidromic AVRT the wavefront would be traveling over the accessory pathway down to the ventricle; therefore, depolarizing the ventricle early without going through the AV node displaying a wide complex or delta wave. It is not typical slow-fast AVNRT as the AH interval is short (unable to see if there is a "jump" as the previous drive train is not displayed). Also, in typical AVNRT the VA interval is <6070 ms as the impulse is just reentering within the AV node. In AVRT, the circuit is much larger and must travel through the ventricular myocardium which takes longer than 70 ms. "VA interval of <70 ms or a ventricular-to-high RA interval of <95 ms during SVT excludes orthodromic AVRT, and is consistent with AVNRT, but can occur during AT with a long PR interval."
See: Clinical Arrhythmology and Electrophysiology by Issa, Miller, and Zipes.

35. In the same EGM, where is the approximate location of the accessory pathway?
   a. **Anteroseptal**
   b. **Posteroseptal**
   c. **Left lateral**
   d. **None of the above**

ANSWER: a. Anteroseptal. When localizing an accessory pathway during tachycardia we are looking for VA fusion. When the ablation catheter is at the pathway location, the VA interval will be fused and/or have an accessory pathway potential. In this example the earliest atrial deflection is seen on the His catheter. We know that the His is and anterior structure, however without any other right sided catheters displayed, we need to do additional mapping. The CS is a posterior structure and CS 7,8 is the proximal pair of electrodes. Therefore, if there was a posterior septal pathway, the earliest atrial activation would be on CS 7,8. Left lateral accessory pathways would show VA fusion on the distal CS electrodes (CS 1,2). This is all dependent on the positioning of the CS catheter. If the CS catheter is not advanced far, CS distal would not be a good representation of the lateral wall and so forth.

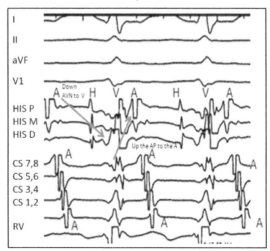

USE THE FOLLOWING EGM FOR THE NEXT TWO QUESTIONS.

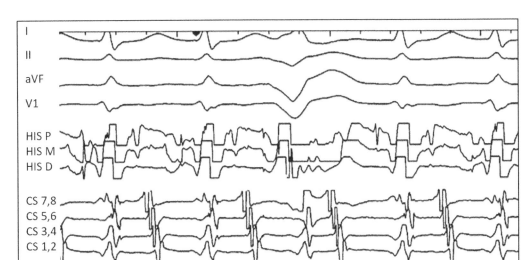

36. The pacing maneuver performed in the above electrogram may be used to help determine which of the following tachycardias?
   a. **Atrial Tachycardia**
   b. **Atrial Flutter**
   c. **AVNRT**
   d. **AVRT**

ANSWER: d. AVRT. This maneuver or test may be used to help determine if the tachycardia is due to an accessory pathway that can be conducted in the retrograde direction. What the physician did was add a PVC during the tachycardia when the His was refractory. If the His is refractory, it cannot accept another impulse, so the PVC will not make it up to the atrium in a normal patient. However, with an accessory pathway, when a PVC is placed at the same time, the His is refractory. If it advances the next atrial signal, that is proof that there is an accessory pathway. As in other pacing maneuvers, the tachycardia must continue after the test is performed otherwise the results may not be accurate. displayed.

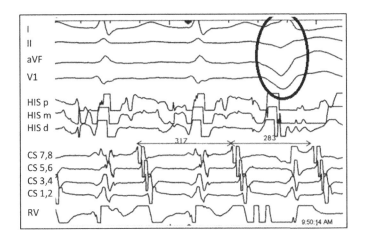

37. Was the test in the displayed electrogram a positive response?
   a. Yes
   b. No

ANSWER a. Yes. The PVC circled in the EGM was timed at the critical point at which the Bundle of His is refractory. The following atrial signal is "advanced" or came early. This is not possible unless there is an accessory pathway. If the pathway is a long distance from the site of pacing, the PVC may not advance the A, such as a left lateral pathway and a RV PVC. So, a negative test does not rule out an accessory pathway, but a positive test is evidence of a pathway. One may also add a PVC in the LV which would help demonstrate a left sided pathway. See: Murgatroyd's chapter on AVRT.

38. Where is the location of the accessory pathway in the electrogram displayed?
   a. **Right free wall**
   b. **Anteroseptal**
   c. **Posteroseptal**
   d. **Left lateral**

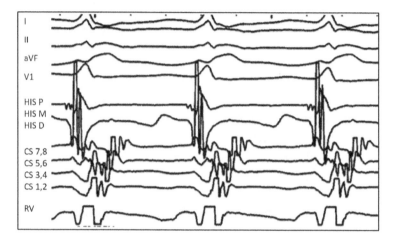

ANSWER: d. Left Lateral. The earliest atrial activation is on CS 1,2 which is on the distal tip of the CS catheter. CS 1,2 sits at the left lateral aspect of the heart. Left lateral pathways are the easiest to pick out as the activation is very eccentric. Normal activation should go through the AV node, so earliest on the His catheter, then proximal CS, with the distal CS being last.

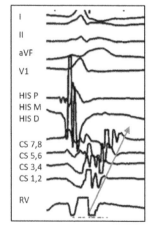

39. Spontaneous termination of orthodromic AVRT typically ends with a/an:
   a. A wave
   b. H wave
   c. V wave
   d. Delta wave

ANSWER: a. A wave. In orthodromic AVRT block occurs in the AV node. Therefore, the last impulse would be an A, as it is still able to travel up the accessory pathway to the atrium. Antidromic AVRT typically terminates with a ventricular signal as it travels down the pathway but is blocked from going up the AV node to the atrium. AVNRT will typically terminate with an atrial deflection as the impulse travels up the fast pathway to the atrium and down the slow pathway to the ventricle. Therefore, if the last impulse is a ventricular event during ablation, damage to the fast pathway may have occurred.

Kibos says, "Spontaneous termination of AVNRT and AVRT is typically caused by anterograde block in the AV node. As a result, tachycardia termination in this setting ends with a P wave that is not premature and is not followed by a QRS." See: Cardiac Arrhythmias: From Basic Mechanism to State –of-the-Art Management by Kibos, Knight, Essebag, Fishberger, Slevin, and Tintoiu.

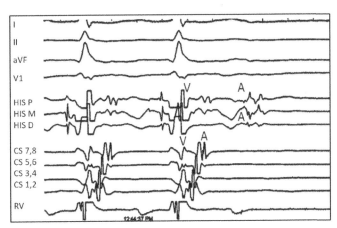

40. The post-entrainment response in EGM 123 (below) helps to rule out:
    a. Atrial Tachycardia
    b. Septal Pathway
    c. AVNRT
    d. AVRT

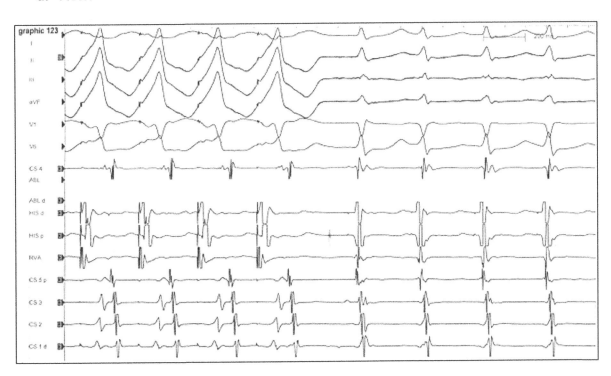

ANSWER: a. Atrial Tachycardia. This form of entrainment is referred to as the Morady maneuver. As discussed previously, to be able to interpret these results, the ventricular pacing must capture, speed up the atrium, and the tachycardia must continue after pacing is terminated. All these stipulations were met in this example. The post

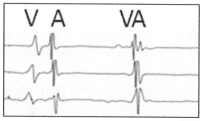

entrainment response is VAV which rules out atrial tachycardia. Atrial tachycardia will display a VAAV response since it is not affected by conduction in the AV node or ventricle. When pacing stops in atrial tachycardia, that atrial ectopic focus will begin to fire again leaving the VAAV response. The resulting tachycardia appears to be typical AVNRT due to the short VA interval. The VA interval is longer in AVRT due to the time the impulse takes to travel through the ventricular myocardium.

41. The following electrogram is an example of:
    a. **Morady Maneuver**
    b. **Entrainment**
    c. **Coumel Law**
    d. **PVCs on His**

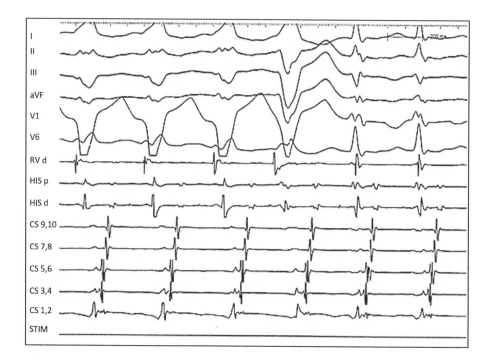

ANSWER: c. Coumel Law. The rhythm appears to be AVRT as the VA interval is longer than the <60-70 ms seen in typical AVNRT and more importantly, the earliest atrial signal appears on CS 1,2 or CS 3,4. The distal CS is on the left side of the heart and that all normal conduction should go up through the AV node unless there is an accessory pathway. You might look at this EGM and think it is a left sided atrial tachycardia because of the eccentric atrial conduction. However, Coumel's law disproves that. Compare the rate during aberrant bundle branch conduction with the rate after the bundle branch block resolves. The rate is much faster when there is no bundle branch block. Coumel's law states that when the BBB occurs on the same side as the accessory pathway (ipsilateral) the tachycardia rate will be slower. This is because the impulse takes longer (due to the block) to make the circuit. However, if it were a RBBB, the rate of the tachycardia would be unchanged as the right bundle is not a critical part of the circuit. This for one would rule out atrial tachycardia as the bundle branches and ventricular myocardium are not required so the tachycardia rate would not change. But also, this would tell us that the pathway is on the left side of the heart. This is apparent with the CS catheter; however, would be very helpful to properly inform the patient pre-procedure on risk factors, such as if we must go transseptal.

The Europace article below says, "Coumel not only introduced the technique of programmed electrical stimulation of the heart...., but also described criteria to determine the mechanisms and pathways of AV junctional reciprocating tachycardias. By reporting findings such as (1) the paradoxical capture and (2) prolongation of tachycardia VA conduction times during bundle branch block ipsilateral to the location of the accessory pathway, and by showing preexcitation of the atria by an appropriately timed ventricular premature extrastimulus during supraventricular tachycardia with the bundle of His refractory...." See: http://europace.oxfordjournals.org/content/6/5/464

Innovations in CRM says, "It is not unusual to observe aberration during SVT. The rapidity of the conduction can lead to functional block in one of the bundles. Development of left bundle branch block (BBB) favors the diagnosis of AVRT with a positive predictive value of 92%. An increase in the VA interval of more than 20 ms during development of BBB has a positive predictive value of nearly 100% for AVRT and helps with the localization of the accessory pathway. In the setting of AVRT, sudden aberration with prolongation in the VA time localizes the involved accessory pathway to the side on which the functional block is occurring (Coumel's Law)." See: http://www.innovationsincrm.com/cardiac-rhythm-management/2013/april/430supraventricular-tachycardia-in-the-electrophysiology-laboratory

42. Once catheters were placed on this EP case the following EGM was recorded. Peak QRS markers are shown. This suggests a diagnosis of:

a. **Ventricular tachycardia**
b. **1:1 Atrial Flutter**
c. **AVNRT**
d. **AVRT**

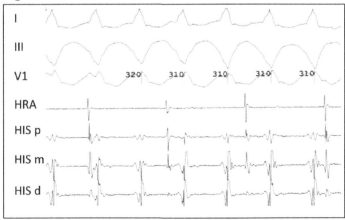

ANSWER: a. Ventricular Tachycardia. Many times, it is difficult to observe the appearance or lack of P waves on a surface ECG at a rapid rate. Ventricular tachycardia is not the finding in a young patient; however, with the intracardiac catheters in position, there are clearly approximately 2 ventricular events for every atrial event. QRS is broad with RBB pattern in V1, suggesting LV origin. This is diagnostic for ventricular tachycardia.

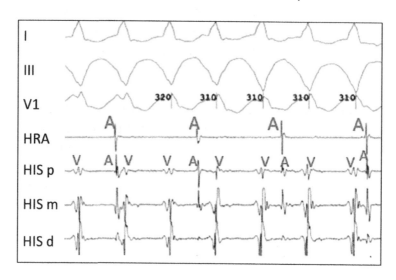

43. What is the rhythm in the displayed EGM?
  a. **Accelerated Idioventricular**
  b. **2:1 Atrial tachycardia**
  c. **2:1 AVNRT**
  d. **2:1 AVRT**

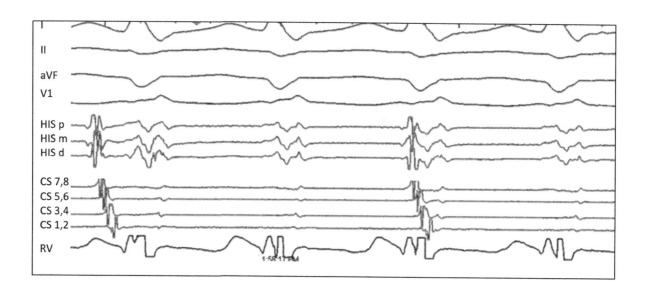

ANSWER: a. Accelerated Idioventricular Rhythm. The rhythm is a slow ventricular tachycardia, since no sweep speed is displayed it is difficult to determine the rate. Notice the wide RBBB morphology QRS complex on the surface ECG and many more ventricular signals than atrial signals. Although it is possible to have 2:1 Atrial tachycardia and AVNRT, this is not possible in the EGM shown. 2:1 SVTs would have more atrial than ventricular signals. (AVNRT with 2:1 V:A is very uncommon, but possible). The 2:1 conduction on this EGM is more consistent with VT or CHB as in the atrial and ventricular waveforms are unrelated. The atrial rate is marching through at a completely different rate. In AVRT, it is not possible to have 2:1 conduction because the atrium, AV node, ventricle, and accessory pathway are all critical components to the tachycardia circuit. Blocking in any of those four areas would cause the tachycardia to terminate. "Ventricular tachycardia (VT) is ≥ 3 consecutive ventricular beats at a rate ≥ 120 beats/min...Some experts use a cutoff rate of ≥ 100 beats/min for VT. Repetitive ventricular rhythms at slower rates are called accelerated idioventricular rhythms or slow VT." See: The Merck Manual. VT

Chapter 15
New Ablation Technology

1. Pulsed Field Ablation (pg. 585)

EP Essentials LLC

Pulsed Field Ablation:

1. This is a benefit of pulsed field ablation (electroporation) for treatment of cardiac arrhythmias.
   a. **Preservation of surrounding structures**
   b. **Expansion of conductive heating**
   c. **Increase in resistive heating**
   d. **Single point focal lesions**

ANSWER: a. Preservation of surrounding structures. Electroporation is referred to as pulse field ablation in the cardiac space. "Irreversible electroporation (IRE) is a well-established treatment modality for solid tumors and is particularly alluring as a method for cardiac ablation when compared to RF as it can create lesions without the consequences of thermal heating and preserve surrounding structures (nerves, vessels). The application of IRE to cardiac tissue is an area of exponentially increasing interest and to date has been successfully applied to a range of cardiac tissues in animal studies."

Sugrue, A., Maor, E., Ivorra, A., Vaidya, V., Witt, C., Kapa, S., & Asirvatham, S. (2018). Irreversible electroporation for the treatment of cardiac arrhythmias. Expert Review of Cardiovascular Therapy, 16(5), 349–360. doi: 10.1080/14779072.2018.1459185

2. Pulsed field ablation has this effect on the cell membrane.
   a. **Direct heating of the cell membrane**
   b. **Direct cooling of the cell membrane**
   c. **Increases permeability**
   d. **Decreases permeability**

ANSWER: c. Increases permeability of the cell membrane to ions and molecules.
Sugrue, et al. Irreversible electroporation for the treatment of cardiac arrhythmias. 2018

3. During pulsed field ablation, the cell membrane is changed when it is exposed to this.
   a. **Magnetic waves**
   b. **Thermal energy**
   c. **Electric fields**
   d. **Microwaves**

ANSWER: c. Electric fields. "Electroporation (pulsed field ablation) is a process in which a cell membrane permeability to ions and molecules is increased when the cell is exposed to high electric fields. Usually, these electric fields are applied in the form of short DC pulses with an increase in cell permeability attributed to the formation of nanometric pores in the cell membrane, hence the term electroporation. Depending upon the electric field applied, the effect of electroporation can be transient and result in viable cells after electric field exposure. In this case, the term reversible electroporation is applied. On the other hand, when the cells die due to prolonged electroporation, either because of permanent permeabilization leading to cell lysis or severe disruption of cell homeostasis during transient permeabilization, the term IRE is applied."

Sugrue, et al. Irreversible electroporation for the treatment of cardiac arrhythmias. 2018

4. What type of energy is utilized during pulsed field ablation?
   a. **Radiofrequency**
   b. **Direct Current**
   c. **Cryo**
   d. **Laser**

ANSWER: b. Direct Current. "At a cellular level, the initiation of electroporation depends on the cell transmembrane voltage (TMV), with electroporation occurring when the externally applied electric field (DC energy) induces a TMV that overcomes a cell's threshold. The threshold value depends on the characteristics of the electric field. This would be the number of pulses, frequency, duration, and shape of the pulses, and on how electroporation (pulsed field ablation) is assessed. Most authors report TMV threshold values in the range from 200 mV to 1 V."

Sugrue, et al. Irreversible electroporation for the treatment of cardiac arrhythmias. 2018

5. Once the transmembrane voltage threshold is overcome, the formation of this will increase the cell membrane permeability.
   a. **Additional Na+ pump channels**
   b. **Nanopores**
   c. **Necrosis**
   d. **Edema**

ANSWER: b. Nanopores. Once the cell is exposed to a high electric field (from short DC pulses) and the transmembrane voltage threshold is overcome, then nanometric pores in the cell membrane are formed.

"The cell membrane permeabilization (through the formation of nanopores) increases during the electric field exposure and rapidly drops after exposure cessation but, in cells, the permeabilization remains significantly high for seconds or several minutes."

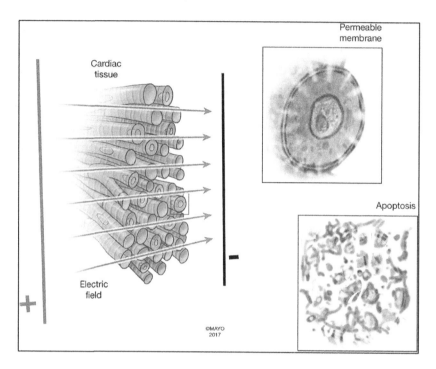

Sugrue, et al. Irreversible electroporation for the treatment of cardiac arrhythmias. 2018

6. This is the type of heating from the dissipation of electric power. (Select all that apply)
   a. **Joule heating**
   b. **Ohmic heating**
   c. **Resistive heating**
   d. **Conductive heating**

ANSWER: a, b, and c. "Electric power is always dissipated as heat at any conductor. This is known as Joule heating, but it is also referred to as ohmic heating or resistive heating because of its relationship with Ohm's law. If one were to provide a single pulse of 100 µs at a magnitude of 1000 V/cm, the maximum temperature increase that must be expected to occur in living tissues is about 0.36°C. For 2000 V/cm, the maximum increase would be about 1.44°C. Such increases in temperature are unlikely to produce any thermal effects on tissue considering the threshold for thermal injury is reported at 50°C."

Sugrue, et al. Irreversible electroporation for the treatment of cardiac arrhythmias. 2018

7. Pulsed field ablation may be safer to utilize near these structures. (Select all that apply)
   a. **Near the coronary arteries**
   b. **Phrenic Nerve**
   c. **His bundle**
   d. **Esophagus**

ANSWER: a, b, c, and d. "There is a multitude of concerns with thermal based approaches in cardiac ablation. Based upon current animal studies to date, electroporation offers a unique approach which addresses and avoids these limitations."

Sugrue, et al. Irreversible electroporation for the treatment of cardiac arrhythmias. 2018

8. This is a potential adverse consequence of pulsed field ablation.
   a. **Pulmonary vein stenosis**
   b. **Vagal nerve injury**
   c. **Triggering VF**
   d. **Thrombus**

ANSWER: c. Triggering VF. "An adverse consequence of electroporation delivery is the risk of triggering VF or other cardiac arrhythmias. Fortunately, a solution was envisioned quite early in the field of electrochemotherapy: pulses can be synchronized with the electrocardiogram (ECG) signal so that they are delivered when all myocardium cells are in the absolute refractory period. Currently, all IRE treatments near the heart are delivered with ECG synchronization."

An addition adverse consequence during the time of the journal posting (2018):
"IRE protocols typically consist of series of DC pulses with lengths ranging from 10 to 100 µs. Unless preventive measures are taken, these pulses are likely to cause acute pain and strong muscle contractions due to the capture of nearby efferent and afferent nerves. This is particularly relevant when monopolar electrode configurations are attempted due to the wider 'antenna' inherent to monopolar stimulation. A commonly used workaround includes administration of local and general anesthesia along with muscle relaxants or neuromuscular blockade [113]. This leads to an increase in the complexity of the whole clinical procedure that may limit the applicability of electroporation-based treatments. To overcome this drawback, Davalos proposed a novel IRE pulsing protocol consisting of bursts of short (1–5 µs) bipolar square pulses. This protocol, labeled high-frequency irreversible electroporation (H-FIRE), very substantially reduces muscle contractions, hence preventing the need for neuromuscular blockade. However, this protocol has not been studied for cardiac ablation."

Sugrue, et al. Irreversible electroporation for the treatment of cardiac arrhythmias. 2018

Chapter 16
Ultrasound

EP Essentials LLC

Ultrasound Principles

1. Ultrasound transducers are composed of a/an:
   a. **Electromagnetic induction coil**
   b. **Bonded Strain gauge**
   c. **Piezoelectric crystal**
   d. **Capacitance array**

ANSWER: c. Piezoelectric crystal. Transducers convert one form of energy into another. Ultrasonic transducers convert electric signals into ultrasonic energy. This is transmitted into the tissues, and some of it bounces back. The reflected ultrasonic waves are then converted by the same crystal into electric energy. The time for a signal to be reflected back is a measure of the depth of the structure off which it was reflected. The thickness of the ultrasound crystal transducer determines its resonant frequency. The crystal is "struck" with a sharp voltage spike, and just like a pipe in a pipe organ, it resonates at one natural frequency. Typically, a 1 mm thick crystal resonates at 2 MHZ. See: Curry, Chapter on "Ultrasound."

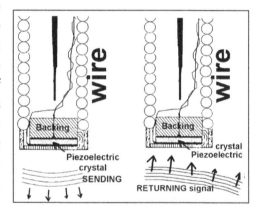

2. A change in electrical charge on a crystal following mechanical stress is termed/the:
   a. **Crystalloid ionization**
   b. **Photoelectric effect**
   c. **Piezoelectric effect**
   d. **Crystallization**

ANSWER: c. Piezoelectric effect. Ultrasound waves hitting a crystal deform it, causing it to generate an electric charge on its surface. This charge is measured by an amplifier and is displayed as a tissue interface on the echogram. Crystals can transform energy in both directions, from mechanical to electrical and from electrical to mechanical. Ultrasonic transducers typically first generate ultrasound vibrations that are transmitted into the tissues. Some of these vibrations bounce back and are then converted by the same crystal into electric energy that reads out on the echocardiogram machine. See: Reynolds, chapter on "Elementary Principles"

3. The Doppler transducer for taking BP and identifying arteries employs:
   a. **A single piezoelectric element that both sends and receives**
   b. **Two piezoelectric elements one to send one to receive**
   c. **A sector scanner array**
   d. **A mechanical scanner**

ANSWER: a. A single piezoelectric element that both sends and receives. Such systems must send out an ultrasound signal, then turn it off while they wait for a return signal. In cardiac flows, this is a very short time. The numeric difference between the outgoing and the returning signals is the Doppler shift. This difference is the frequency displayed on Doppler - sending & receiving the screen and that we hear with our ears.
See: Curry, Chapter on "Ultrasound."

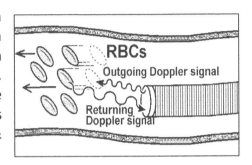

4. When Doppler ultrasound senses flow away from the transducer, the returning ultrasound wave has a:
   a. **Higher relative frequency**
   b. **Lower relative frequency**
   c. **Higher relative amplitude**
   d. **Lower relative amplitude**

ANSWER: b. Lower relative frequency. Doppler measures velocity of any reflecting object/fluid by evaluating the frequency change of the reflected ultrasound. You have heard a Doppler frequency shift. When a whistling train approaches, you hear the "eeee" sound. As soon as it passes, the frequency of the whistle suddenly drops to a "oooo." This change to a lower pitch is an indication that approaching objects compress the sound waves to make them sound higher pitch. Objects moving away, slow the sound waves bouncing from them. They thus sound lower in pitch. The more parallel the moving object is the ultrasound beam the greater the change in pitch. Objects perpendicular to the beam do not shift the frequency.
See: Curry, Chapter on "Ultrasound."

5. In cardiovascular Doppler, what is the usual target off which the ultrasound waves are reflected?
   a. Endocardium and/or pericardium
   b. Red blood cells
   c. Cardiac valves
   d. Plasma eddies

ANSWER: b. Red blood cells. Doppler is used to measure blood flow or velocity. The RBCs carried within the blood reflect the sound waves. RBCs moving away from the transducer decrease the reflected velocity and the pitch of the Doppler sound heard. The difference in frequency between the outgoing and returning signal is the actual Doppler signal heard and displayed. It is proportional to the velocity of the RBCs within the vessel.

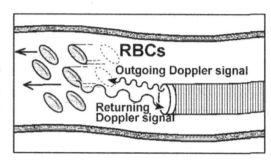

See: Braunwald, Chapter on Echocardiography

6. The diagram at the right represents five standard transducer imaging locations used in echocardiography. What imaging position is labeled at #3 on the diagram?
   a. Apical
   b. Subcostal
   c. Parasternal
   d. Suprasternal
   e. Trans-esophageal

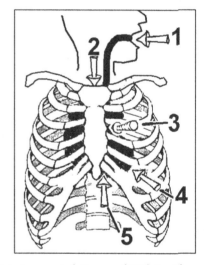

ANSWER: c. Parasternal = alongside the sternum, usually 2-4 Intercostal Space (ICS) to the left of the sternum. The heart can only be seen through echocardiographic windows, through soft tissue and between the bony part of the chest. When a transducer on an esophageal probe is swallowed by the patient, echograms may be taken from inside the chest.

CORRECTLY MATCHED ANSWERS ARE:
   1. Transesophageal (TEE)
   2. Suprasternal (above sternum)
   3. Parasternal (next to sternum, a Transthoracic Echo, TTE)
   4. Apical (a Transthoracic Echo, TTE)
   5. Subcostal (below costal cartilage/rib cage)
   6. See: Braunwald, chapter on Echocardiography

7. What type of ultrasound test is the best way to rule out atrial thrombi prior to PVI?
  a. ICE (Intracardiac Echo)
  b. TTE (Transthoracic echo)
  c. TEE (Transesophageal echo)
  d. Contrast cardiac CT scan
  e. Contrast cardiac MRI scan

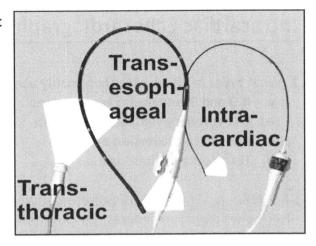

ANSWER: c. TEE (Transesophageal echo). Since the esophagus runs right behind the heart it gives the best ultrasound images of left atrial and atrial appendage. Issa says, "Preprocedural Evaluation: Heart failure, myocardial ischemia, and electrolyte abnormalities should be treated and adequately controlled before any invasive EP testing is undertaken. Patients with critical aortic stenosis, severe hypertrophic cardiomyopathy, left main or severe three-vessel coronary artery disease, or decompensated heart failure are at high risk of complication. Induction of sustained tachyarrhythmias in these patients can cause severe deterioration. Anticoagulation for 4 weeks before the procedure, transesophageal echocardiography (to exclude the presence of intracardiac thrombus), or both, is required before studying patients who have persistent atrial fibrillation (AF) and atrial flutter (AFL)." See, Issa, chapter on "Periprocedural Management"

"TEE is frequently performed in patients with AF. The primary purpose of TEE is to detect LA appendage thrombi and to identify patients at increased risk for cardiogenic embolism. Patients at moderate risk for both stroke and hemorrhagic complications with anticoagulation may benefit from risk stratification with TEE. Compared with TTE, TEE provides a superior assessment of the LA appendage in most patients." See: Issa, chapter on Echocardiography in AF

Intracardiac Echocardiography (ICE)

1. What types of EP lab cases commonly use intracardiac echo (ICE)?
   a. ICD and Biventricular lead implant
   b. CRT coronary vein lead placement
   c. Prior to cardioversion of AF
   d. Transseptal catheterization

ANSWER: c. Transseptal catheterization. Watson says, "ICE has been used for electrophysiologic procedures, guiding radio frequency ablations, trans-septal punctures, evaluating aortic aneurysms and aortic stent-graft procedures." TEE is often used pre-cardioversion, looking for LA thrombi. See: Watson, chapter on "Invasive Ultrasound: Beyond Angiography"

2. A major advantage to using intracardiac echocardiography (ICE) has over TEE is:
   a. Tissue characterization (4 color images)
   b. General anesthesia is not needed
   c. Three dimensional images
   d. It is disposable

ANSWER: b. General anesthesia is not needed. Local anesthesia used in standard percutaneous entry has no anesthesiologist, no complications due to anesthetic, less time for induction, and less discomfort to the patient. The diagram shows 3 types of phased array echo transducers used in cardiology. All produce a pie-shaped sector scan. Being disposable is not an advantage, due to added expense. Many labs resterilized their ICE catheters. See: Watson, chapter on Invasive Ultrasound

3. Intracardiac echocardiography uses _____ as an injectable contrast agent to view shunts or distinguish the right heart from the left heart chambers.
   a. Low osmolar angiographic contrast
   b. Radioisotope tagged red cells
   c. Doppler shifted plasma
   d. Agitated saline

ANSWER: d. Agitated saline. This technique is termed a "bubble study. It looks like a dust storm in the chamber where they are injected as each bubble reflects ultrasound. The technique uses a saline solution which is agitated by mixing it back and forth quickly between two syringes [connected with a stopcock]. This creates very small bubbles in the saline which, when injected intravenously into the arm, can be seen as they pass through the heart's chambers. These bubbles can be followed in the heart ultrasonically, to determine if any bubbles do not follow the normal blood flow pathways. It is also termed a "Contrast-enhanced ultrasound (CEUS)." The bubbles are filtered out in the lungs and produce no ill effects. Some labs mix the saline with small amounts of blood for slightly better visualization.

4. An ICE catheter is in the RA. Of the four drawings shown, identify what is shown in image #1.
   a. **Eustachian & Tricuspid valve**
   b. **Intraatrial septum & SVC**
   c. **AO & PA**
   d. **LA & LV**

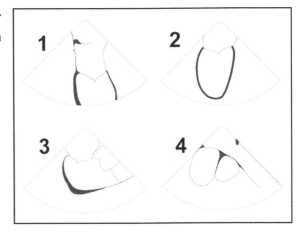

ANSWER: a. #1 shows the Eustachian ridge remnant of the eustachian valve, and tricuspid valve isthmus. To observe this, withdraw the catheter to the inferior RA. The isthmus is between the eustachian ridge and the TV. Remember an isthmus is a piece of land between two land masses, like the isthmus of Panama connects N. & S. America.

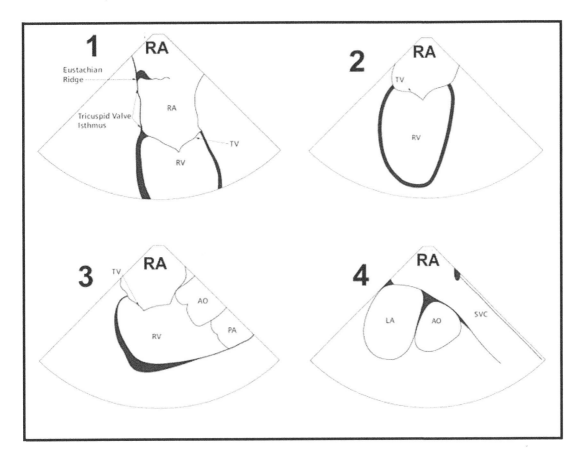

5. Which of the four images above is the HOME or starting view for an ICE exam?

    a. #1
    b. #2
    c. #3
    d. #4

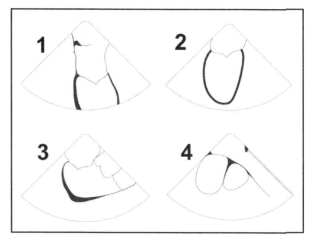

ANSWER: b. Position #2 is termed the "Home view" showing the RA, TV, and RV. The scan plane is facing anteriorly in a neutral position. This is where you always start.

#3 this position shows the RA, TV, RV, AO & PA, where the transducer is rotated slightly clockwise from the anterior home view.

#4. This position shows the IAS & SVC with the catheter withdrawn to the inferior RA, tilted posteriorly with slight right rotation. See:
https://www.medical.siemens.com/siemens/en_US/gg_us_FBAs/files/brochures/AcuNav/Instructional_Guide.pdf

6. The ICE catheter is located on the right side of the heart. Of the four ICE drawings, identify the view labeled #1.

    a. LA & LA appendage, MV, LV
    b. Coronary sinus ostium
    c. LV short axis
    d. LV long axis

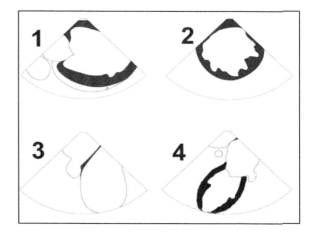

ANSWER: #1. d. LV Long axis view. Advance the ICE catheter into the RV and rotate clockwise to see the intraventricular septum. LV is on the other side.

#2. c. Is the LV short axis view. From the LV long axis view, tilt the steering knob until the circular LV and papillary muscles are seen.

#3. b. Is the Coronary Sinus Ostium seen from the RA by rotating clockwise and looking inferiorly.

#4. a. Is the LA appendage, mitral valve and LV view. Rotate clockwise past the AO/PA view with some left tilt. See: Siemens.com

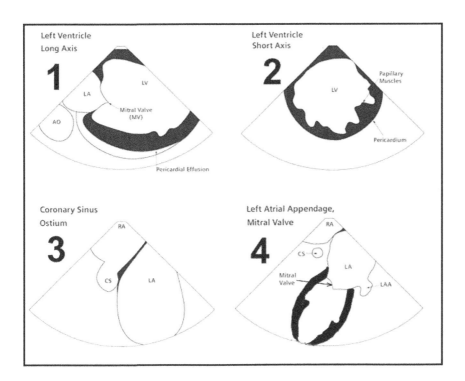

7. The ICE catheter is in the right atrium with slight clockwise rotation. Identify the cardiac structure labeled #3.

    a. **Coronary sinus**
    b. **Tricuspid valve**
    c. **AO valve**
    d. **PA valve**

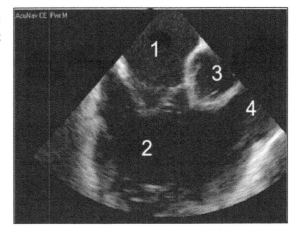

ANSWER: c. AO valve. The transducer is rotated slightly clockwise from the anterior home view. The ICE image is rotated 90 degrees to make it like the drawing that shows the same structures.

Structures shown are:

    1. RA
    2. RV
    3. AO root/valve
    4. Pulmonic outflow/valve

The tricuspid valve is seen between the RA & RV. See: King, chapter on ICE

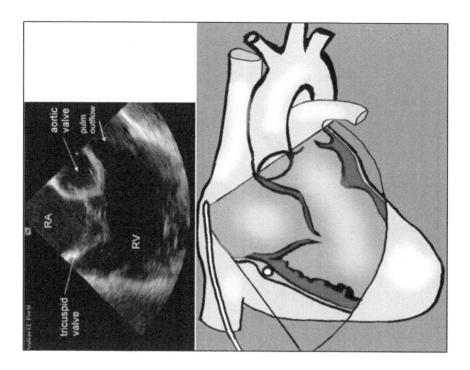

8. What structure is seen at #3 on this ICE image acquired from the RA?

    a. RV moderator band

    b. RV trabeculations

    c. Coronary Sinus

    d. LA appendage

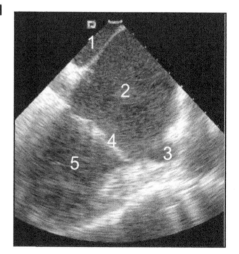

ANSWER: d. LA appendage. This is view #4 from the illustrated ICE views in the earlier question. The coronary sinus might have shown up on the left below the RA. Of course, in real time you can see the mitral valve opening and closing, which helps identify structures.

See: Practical Intracardiac Echocardiography in Electrophysiology, by Jian-Tang Ren, et. al.

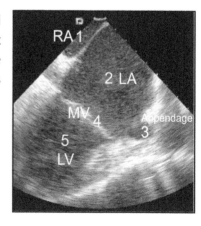

9. What is shown at the arrow on this ICE image in the RA *Home View* just superior to the IVC?
   a. **Eustachian ridge & valve**
   b. **Inferior vena cava**
   c. **Interatrial septum**
   d. **Tricuspid valve**

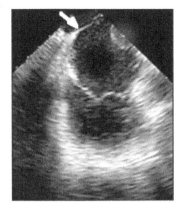

ANSWER: a. Eustachian ridge & valve. These are seen from the default position in the RA. In this view we also see the RA, tricuspid valve, and RV chamber. The eustachian ridge and valve are a remnant venous valve over the IVC. The Thebesian valve is a remnant valve over the coronary sinus. These valves can become obstacles during EP studies.

The valve of the inferior vena cava (eustachian valve) lies at the junction of the inferior vena cava and right atrium. In fetal life, the Eustachian valve helps direct the flow of oxygen-rich blood through the right atrium into the left atrium via the foramen ovale (preventing blood flowing into the right ventricle). While the Eustachian valve persists in adult life, it does not have a specific function. Most commonly, it is a crescentic fold of endocardium arising from the anterior rim of the IVC orifice. The lateral horn of the crescent tends to meet the lower end of the crista terminalis, while the medial horn joins the thebesian valve, a semicircular valvular fold at the orifice of the coronary sinus.
See: King, chapter on Intracardiac Echocardiography in the Catheterization and Laboratory.

10. What is observed in the following ICE image?
   a. **Clot**
   b. **Home View**
   c. **Pericardial Effusion**
   d. **Transseptal Puncture**

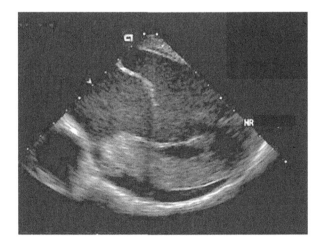

ANSWER: c. Pericardial Effusion. Blood/fluid will appear black on ultrasound. In this view, the physician is looking at the left ventricle. Notice the black space outside of the myocardium. This is a pericardial effusion. Often before any procedure that requires transseptal access, the physician will check for an effusion both before puncture as well as at the end of the procedure.

Chapter 17
Medications

EP Essentials LLC

Sympathetic & Parasympathetic Systems:

1. Match the autonomic receptor sites below with their effect in the box.

    a. **Alpha adrenergic**
    b. **Beta-1 adrenergic**
    c. **Beta-2 adrenergic**
    d. **Cholinergic**

    1. **Lung broncho-dilation**
    2. **Cardiac stimulation**
    3. **Vasoconstriction**
    4. **Cardiac depression**

CORRECTLY MATCHED ANSWERS ARE:
1. Lung broncho-dilation   c. Beta-2 adrenergic
2. Cardiac stimulation   b. Beta-1 adrenergic
3. Vasoconstriction   a. Alpha adrenergic
4. Cardiac depression   d. Cholinergic

The parasympathetic autonomic nervous system is the "vegetative" system which liberates acetyl choline. Thus, the term "cholinergic." The SA and AV nodes are richly innervated with parasympathetic fibers, but not the ventricles. Parasympathetic stimulation depresses the heart rate and contractility. The main drug in this category is atropine, which blocks the cholinergic or parasympathetic system. Atropine thus stimulates the heart rate.

The adrenergic system has three important types of receptors: alpha (α) adrenergic, beta-1 (β1) and beta-2 (β2). The effects of each respectively are vasoconstriction, cardiac stimulation, and lung broncho-dilation.

Remember alpha (α) adrenergic as follows: the Greek letter (α) alpha looks like a knot in a suture tied Adrenergic receptors around a vessel - constricting it.

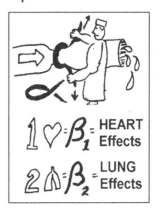

To remember the two types of Beta receptors like the acronym "We have one heart, two lungs." This reminds us that Beta 1 (one heart) causes cardiac stimulation, and beta 2 (2 lungs) causes bronchial dilation and some vascular dilation of skeletal muscle.

See: Underhill, Chapter on "Pharmacologic Management of Patient with Coronary Artery Disease" & Todd, Vol. I, #168

2. Match each class of autonomic drug in the box with its effect below.
- a. **Sympathomimetic**
- b. **Cholinergic**
- c. **Vagal Blocker**
- d. **Beta Blocker**

1. **Atropine**
2. **Propranolol (Inderal)**
3. **Norepinephrine**
4. **Acetylcholine**

CORRECTLY MATCHED ANSWERS: AUTONOMIC DRUGS and their CLASS
1. Atropine: c. Vagal Blocker (Blocks Vagal discharge)
2. Propranolol (Inderal): d. Beta Blocker (Blocks Sympathetic discharge)
3. Norepinephrine: a. Sympathomimetic (Causes Fight or Flight)
4. Acetylcholine: b. Cholinergic (Causes depression of heart)

Inderal is a common anti-hypertensive. It blocks Norepinephrine/Epinephrine at the sympathetic nerve endings. This causes slowing of the heart and lowering of the BP. See: Underhill, Chapter on "Pharmacologic Management of Patient with CAD."

3. Match the autonomic receptor sites with their chief stimulating effect.
- a. **+ Chronotropic and + inotropic**
- b. **- Chronotropic**
- c. **Arteriolar vasoconstriction**
- d. **Bronchodilation (lung)**

1. **Alpha$_1$ adrenergic**
2. **Beta$_1$ adrenergic**
3. **Beta$_2$ adrenergic**
4. **Parasympathetic**

CORRECTLY MATCHED ANSWERS
1. Alpha$_1$: c. α1, Arteriolar vasoconstriction (increase arterial blood pressure)
2. Beta$_1$ adrenergic: a. + chronotropic and + inotropic (speed HR and contractility)
3. Beta$_2$ adrenergic: d. bronchodilation (lung)
4. Parasympathetic: b. - chronotropic (slow HR)

Remember alpha (α) adrenergic as follows: the Greek letter (α) alpha looks like a knot in a suture tied around a vessel - constricting it. Stimulation of these receptors can come either from a sympathetic neural discharge or from circulating norepinephrine stimulating the heart. Thus, a total sympathetic discharge would prepare you for "fight or flight" by stimulating these receptors. These are important because the actions of many of the cardiac drugs effect these receptor site.

See: Underhill, Chapter on "Pharmacologic Management of Patient with Coronary Artery

4. Stimulation of different autonomic receptor sites causes specific hemodynamic effects. When you stimulate parasympathetic receptors, what hemodynamic effect does it cause?
   a. **Vasoconstrict vascular smooth muscle (peripheral arteriolar arterioles...)**
   b. **Slow heart rate and AV node conduction**
   c. **Stimulate heart muscle & AV node**
   d. **Dilate lung bronchioles**

ANSWER: b. Slow heart rate and AV node conduction.
Alpha$_1$: c Vasoconstrict vascular smooth muscle (peripheral arteriolar vasoconstriction...)
Beta$_1$: b. Stimulate heart muscle & AV node (catecholamine effect)
Beta$_2$: a. Dilate lung bronchioles (reverse broncho-constriction in asthma)
Parasympathetic: d. Slow heart rate and AV node conduction

Remember alpha (α) adrenergic as follows: the Greek letter (α) alpha a look like a knot in a suture tied around a vessel - constricting it. Effects of sympathetic and parasympathetic systems have opposite effects; sympathetic - speeds, parasympathetic - slows. Like your cars gas pedal (speeds) and brake (slows). When your reflexes tell you to stop, you remove your foot from the gas and hit the brake. In the same way, the sympathetic and parasympathetic systems provide push/pull control. See: Opie, Drugs for the Heart, Chapter on "Beta Blockers"

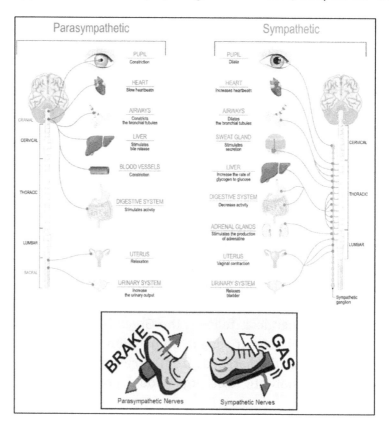

5. What beta-adrenergic agonist medication is used in the EP lab to stress patient's hearts? It primarily increases heart rate. Because it increases MVO2 it is not recommended for patients with myocardial ischemia.
   a. **Norepinephrine (Levophed)**
   b. **Isoproterenol (Isuprel)**
   c. **Retavase (Reteplase)**
   d. **Dopamine (Intropin)**

ANSWER: b. Isoproterenol (Isuprel). This stimulant is commonly used to precipitate symptoms such as angina, gradients, or stimulate arrhythmias as needed to make a diagnosis. In therapy, it may be used to increase HR in severe bradycardia if atropine administration is ineffective. Isuprel is contraindicated for patients in cardiac arrest, and MI because it increases MVO2. It has recently been de-emphasized by AHA.

The ACLS manual says: "Use isoproterenol, if at all, with extreme caution. At low doses it is a Class IIb (possibly helpful); at all other doses it is a Class II (harmful) intervention... Patients who are ill enough to need isoproterenol are probably too ill to tolerate it." Note that an agonist is a drug that stimulates receptors in the body. E.g., When you stimulate beta receptors, they speed the heart rate. An antagonist blocks those receptors, like a beta blocker slows the heart rate. See: ACLS manual

6. Cardiovascular Alpha-Adrenergic receptors are associated with the _____ nervous system primarily affects the _____:
   a. **Parasympathetic; Peripheral vascular resistance**
   b. **Sympathetic; Peripheral vascular resistance**
   c. **Sympathetic; SA and AV nodes**
   d. **Parasympathetic; Myocardium**

ANSWER: b. Sympathetic; peripheral resistance vessels. Alpha adrenergic receptors are chiefly in the arteriolar sphincters of the skin, mucosa, intestine, and kidney. When stimulated they cause vasoconstriction, reduce blood flow to those organs, and raise the peripheral resistance and the blood pressure. Most vasopressors (constrictors)work this way.
 Sympathomimetic amine drugs like "dopamine" mimic catecholamines through stimulation of these alpha receptors. See: Underhill, Chapter on "Pharmacologic Management of Patient with Coronary Artery Disease."

7. Stimulation of sympathetic nerves liberates _____ as an end site chemical mediator.
   a. **Norepinephrine**
   b. **Acetylcholine**
   c. **Dobutamine**
   d. **GP IIb/IIIa**

ANSWER a. Norepinephrine. Sympathetic nerves when stimulated liberate norepinephrine as a synaptic mediator. This catecholamine speeds all heart activity. In the diagram note that there are no parasympathetic nerves supplying the ventricles. That's why in a vagal attack slows the HR and AV conduction, not lowering of the BP neuro-humoral transmitters.

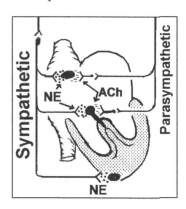

8. Beta blockers are potentially dangerous to:
   a. **Patients with peripheral vascular disease**
   b. **Patients with bronchospasm or asthma**
   c. **Patients with allergies to iodine**
   d. **Patients post heart transplant**
   e. **Patients on MAO inhibitors**

ANSWER: b. Asthmatics. A common side effect of beta -blockers is bronchospasm. This would be especially bad for an asthmatic patient. Asthmatics may need the beta stimulation of epinephrine to dilate their bronchioles. If the beta sites are blocked, it may precipitate an asthmatic crisis. Opie says: "Pulmonary absolute contraindications are severe asthma or bronchospasm. . .. No patient may be given a beta-blocker without questions about past or present asthma. Fatalities have resulted when this rule is ignored. Relative: Mild asthma or bronchospasm or chronic airways disease. Use agents with cardio-selectivity plus beta2stimulants (by inhalation)." See: AHA, ACLS Provider Manual, chapter on "Acute Coronary Syndromes"

9. The effect of beta-blockers like propranolol (Inderal) is to block the effects of:
   a. **Cholesterol on the vascular epithelium**
   b. **Nitric oxide on the vascular epithelium**
   c. **Adrenalin, epinephrine**
   d. **Renin, angiotensin**

ANSWER: c. Adrenalin, epinephrine is blocked at the sympathetic nerve endings by Beta Blockers, like Propranolol (Inderal). Inderal is a common anti-hypertensive. It causes slowing of the heart and lowering of the BP. See: Underhill, Chapter on "Pharmacologic Management of Patient with CAD.

10. The two primary cardiac responses associated with a PARASYMPATHETIC neural discharge are ____ heart rate and _____.
   a. **Increased HR, Increased AV conduction**
   b. **Increased HR, Reduced AV conduction**
   c. **Reduced HR, Increased AV conduction**
   d. **Reduced HR, Reduced AV conduction**

ANSWER d. Reduced HR, reduced AV conduction. The vagus nerve inhibition is mainly supraventricular. It depresses the SA node, atrial myocardium, & AV conduction. It's depressing effect on ventricular myocardium is less pronounced. That is why a vagal response usually appears initially as bradycardia and only later as low BP or hypotension. See: Berne and Levy, Chapter on "Regulation of the Heartbeat."

11. What is atropine's effect on the autonomic nervous system?
   a. **Parasympathetic blocker (anti-cholinergic)**
   b. **Sympathetic blocker (adrenergic blocker)**
   c. **Parasympathetic stimulant (cholinergic)**
   d. **Sympathetic stimulant (adrenergic)**

ANSWER: a. Parasympathetic blocker (anticholinergic). Atropine (Belladonna) increases all supraventricular parameters - rate and AV conduction. It does this by blocking the parasympathetic system. Remember the parasympathetic system slows everything, so if it is blocked - things speed up. It's like having one foot on your car's gas (sympathetic) and another on the brake (parasympathetic). The balance of the two determines whether you are speeding or slowing.

Dosage

1. What is the normal dose of IV ibutilide in AF?
   a. **10 mg over 10 minutes**
   b. **1 mg over 10 minutes**
   c. **10 mg bolus**
   d. **1 mg bolus**

ANSWER: b. 1 mg over 10 minutes. "Ibutilide is administered IV 1 mg over 10 minutes. 10 to 15% of the patients with new onset AF may convert to sinus rhythm with ibutilide alone. When cardioversion is performed after administration of ibutilide, the success rate may approach 100% and the amount of energy required may also be less." See Abedin, chapter on SVT "Ibutilide is an antiarrhythmic drug... marketed for the rapid conversion of atrial fibrillation and atrial flutter. After intravenous administration, ibutilide is moderately effective in achieving prompt cardioversion to sinus rhythm, with greater efficacy in patients who have atrial flutter. Like other drugs that prolong ventricular repolarization, ibutilide administration carries a risk of excessive QT prolongation, or the acquired long-QT syndrome, with associated polymorphic ventricular tachycardia (torsade de pointes), necessitating careful patient selection and clinical monitoring during drug administration."
See: "Cardiovascular Drugs, Ibutilide" Murray, Circulation 1998,

2. Match each premedication to its average adult dosage:

a. **125 mg IV**	1. **Valium (Diazepam)**
b. **5-10 mg IV or PO**	2. **Cimetidine (Tagamet)**
c. **(10-50 mg IV) 25-50 mg PO**	3. **Benadryl (Diphenhydramine)**
d. **(50-300 mg IV) 300 mg PO**	4. **Solu-Medrol (Methylprednisolone)**

CORRECTLY MATCHED ANSWERS:

1. Valium (Diazepam): 5-10 mg IM, IV, or PO Benzodiazepine, anti-anxiety drug

2. Cimetidine (Tagamet):(50-300 mg Iv) 300 mg PO given to decrease esophageal reflux

3. Benadryl (Diphenhydramine) (10-50 mg IV) 25-50 mg PO Antihistamine, given to prevent allergic reactions

4. Solu-Medrol (Methylprednisolone): (125 mg IV) Steroid given to patients with contrast allergy. See: Pepine, Chapter on "Cath Techniques." & Yaniga, chapter on premeditations

3. For patients in atrial fibrillation, the therapeutic range of coumadin/warfarin is an INR of:
   a. **0.8 - 1.5**
   b. **2.0 - 3.0**
   c. **4.0 - 5.0**
   d. **6.0 - 10.0**

ANSWER: b. 2.0 - 3.0. INR is the International Normalized Ratio, or the prothrombin time compared to normal for that lab. Braunwald says: "The optimal therapeutic range of warfarin for the prevention of venous thromboembolism and systemic embolism from atrial fibrillation and tissue heart valves target an INR of 2.0 to 3.0." Remember a normal (uncoagulated) INR is 1.0.

Issa says about AF anticoagulation: "The recommended target international normalized ration (INR) is 2.5, (range 2.0 to 3.0). It has been suggested that it may be prudent to aim for an INR higher than 2.5 before cardioversion to provide the greatest protection against embolic events.... After cardioversion, it is recommended to continue warfarin therapy for at least 4 weeks, with a target INR of 2.5 (range 2.0 to 3.0) .... The risk of stroke doubles when the INR falls to 1.7, and values up to 3.5 do not convey an increased risk of bleeding complications. A higher goal (INR between 2.5 and 3.5) is reasonable for patients at particularly high risk for embolization." See: Braunwald, chapter on "Hemostasis & Thrombosis" and Assa chapter on "Atrial Fibrillation"

4. Prior to an EP study, the patient should be in a baseline state. It is most important to remove the patient from nonessential:
   a. **Electrolyte controlling medications**
   b. **Cardiac ischemia medications**
   c. **Antiarrhythmic medications**
   d. **Heart failure medications**

ANSWER: c. Antiarrhythmic medications. Fogoros says: "Ideally, the electrophysiologic evaluation should be performed while the patient is in a baseline state - nonessential drugs should be withdrawn (especially antiarrhythmic agents), and cardiac ischemia or heart failure maximally treated, electrolytes controlled, and every effort made to prevent excessive anxiety, which can cause excessive sympathetic tone." See: Fogoros chapter on Principles of the Electrophysiology Study

5. Many drugs have antagonists that can counteract their action. Match each drug to its antagonist.

a. Narcan	1. Heparin antagonist
b. Protamine	2. Demerol/morphine antagonist
c. Romazicon	3. Midazolam (Versed) antagonist
d. Embouchure	4. Thrombolytic (tPA) antagonist
e. Vitamin K	5. Warfarin (Coumadin) antagonist

CORRECTLY MATCHED ANSWERS:
1. Heparin antagonist = b. Protamine
2. Demerol/morphine antagonist =a. Naloxone (Narcan)
3. Midazolam (Versed)antagonist =c. Romazicon (Mexican, flumazenil)
4. Thrombolytic (tPA) antagonist = d. Aminocaproic Acid (Embouchure)
5. Warfarin (Coumadin) antagonist = e. Vitamin K

Flumazenil (Romazicon) rapidly reverses the effects of Versed. It binds to benzodiazepine receptors in the CNS and blocks them. It may cause rapid withdrawal, which is shorter acting than the Versed itself - leading to delayed re-sedation. Side effects are panic attacks, seizures, cardiac ischemia, and pulmonary edema. Narcan (naloxone) is an antagonist to opiate medications such as Demerol, fentanyl, and morphine. However, it is shorter acting than the drug itself and may need an additional dose.

The thrombolytic (tPA) can be reversed with aminocaproic Acid (Embouchure). Warfarin can be reversed with vitamin K or infusion of fresh frozen plasma. However, these 2 drugs do not completely reverse the primary drug effect.
Loebl, The Nurses Drug Handbook, Chapter on "Thrombolytic drugs"

6. Match each cardiovascular drug below to its classification.

a. Lidocaine, Procainamide	1. Pressor
b. Verapamil, Adenosine	2. Chronotropic
c. Digitalis, Dobutamine	3. Inotropic
d. Isoproterenol, Atropine	4. Ventricular Antiarrhythmic
e. Norepinephrine, Dopamine (high dose)	5. Supraventricular Antiarrhythmic

CORRECTLY MATCHED ANSWERS ARE:
1. Pressor: e. Norepinephrine, Dopamine (high dose). Vasopressors vasoconstrict peripheral arterioles raising the BP
2. Chronotropic: d. Isoproterenol, Atropine. Chrono- means rate. These drugs primarily increase heart rate. Isoproterenol (Isuprel) stimulates beta-1 receptors. Atropine blocks vagal bradycardia to speed the heart rate.
3. Inotropic: c. Digitalis, Dobutamine. Inotropism increases inherent contractility of myocardial fibers
4. Ventricular Antiarrhythmic: a. Lidocaine, Procainamide. Decrease automaticity in SA node and conduction velocity in reentry loops
5. Supraventricular Antiarrhythmic: b. Verapamil, Adenosine. Verapamil blocks slow inward movement of Ca into the cell. (Ca channel blocker). Adenosine slows AV conduction and interrupts AV nodal reentry pathways.

See: ACLS Manual

7. The correct IV dose for procainamide in cardiac arrest is:
   a. **Infusion of 1 mg for 6 hours, then 0.5 mg for 24 hours**
   b. **20-50 mg/min slowly for total of 17 mg/kg**
   c. **1 mg push every 3-5 minutes**
   d. **1.5 mg/kg over 1 hour**

ANSWER: b. 20-50 mg/min slowly for a total of 17 mg/kg. ACLS guidelines say: "Procainamide hydrochloride suppresses both atrial and ventricular arrhythmias.... Procainamide hydrochloride may be given in an infusion of 20 mg/min until the arrhythmia is suppressed, hypotension ensues, the QRS complex is prolonged by 50% from its original duration, or a total of 17 mg/kg (1.2 g for a 70-kg patient of the drug has been given. Bolus administration of the drug can result in toxic concentrations and significant hypotension.... The maintenance infusion rate of procainamide hydrochloride is 1 to 4 mg/min....Precipitous hypotension may occur if the drug is injected too rapidly.)" See: AHA Guidelines ...Consensus on Science. Supplement to chapter on "Pharmacology I"

8. The physician has ordered a heparin drip infusion for your patient who weighs 90kg. A pre-mixed infusion is available with a concentration of 25,000 units heparin/250cc NS. You are to begin the infusion at 18units/kg/hr. What is the infusion rate in cc/hr?
   a. **0.18 cc/hr**
   b. **1.6 cc/hr**
   c. **16.2cc/hr**
   d. **18 cc/hr**

ANSWER: c. 16.2cc/hr. 18 units/kg/hr. = 1620 units/hr. (simply multiply 18units x pt. weight of 90kg) Now you need to know the concentration given. 25,000 units/250 cc = 100 units/cc. 1620 units/hr. / (100 units/cc) = 16.2 cc/hr. (Note how the units cancel) Or

25,000 u   = 1620 u/hr.
250 cc x

To solve for x: Cross multiply 250 x 1620 = 405,000
Then divide: 405,000/25,000 = 16.2

9. Your patient completed a bypass track ablation. He is allergic to fish and peanuts. At the end of the case your physician requests you to counteract 2000 unit of heparin. You should:
   a. **Give 4 cc of Protamine (10 mg/cc) slowly over 5 minutes**
   b. **Remind the physician about the patient's peanut allergy**
   c. **Remind the physician about the patient's fish allergy**
   d. **Give 2 cc of Protamine (10 mg/cc) by rapid IV push**

ANSWER: c. Remind the physician about the patient's fish allergy. In patients who are allergic to fish, it can cause significant histamine release resulting in hypotension and bronchoconstriction and may cause pulmonary hypertension. Infusion should be slow to minimize these side effects. The physician must be made aware of the potential for side effects due to the fish allergy. In normal concentrations 1 cc of protamine counteracts each 1 cc of heparin. Grossman says: "If systemic heparinization is used, its effects must be reversed at the termination of the left heart catheterization and associated angiography. This is usually accomplished by the administration of protamine (1 mL = 10 mg of protamine for every 1,000 IU of heparin). When giving protamine, administer it slowly (over 5 minutes), since more rapid administration can provoke severe back pain of unknown etiology."
See: Grossman, Chapter on "Percutaneous Approach."

10. What is the adult dose of isoproterenol (Isuprel)?
   a. **5 to 10 mg/min**
   b. **1 to 20 mg/ min**
   c. **5 to 10 mcg/min**
   d. **1 to 20 mcg/ min**

ANSWER: d. 1 to 20 mcg/ min. "DOSE: 1 to 20 mcg/ min. should be started at the lowest recommended dose and the rate of administration gradually increased if necessary while carefully monitoring the patient. Peak Effect: 1 Min., Duration: 1 to 5 Min. Beta 1 Effects: Increases SA Node Rate, AV Conduction Velocity, Increases Heart Rate, Decreases Refractory Periods, Worsens Ischemia and can cause angina (Sinus tachycardia and ventricular arrhythmias), may be used to induce atrial and ventricular tachycardias.
See:
http://www.pana.org/Power%20Point%20Presentations/WilliamsCardiac%20Electrophysiol ogy%20-p1.pdf

11. The electrophysiologist has ordered an Isuprel drip to infuse at 5 mcg/min. The infusion is pre-mixed as a 4:1 drip (4 mg/1 liter fluid). Select the correct infusion rate in cc/hr.
   a. **15 cc/hr**
   b. **30 cc/hr**
   c. **75 cc/hr**
   d. **100 cc/hr**

ANSWER: c. 75 cc/hr. Note that "mcg" is a simplification of "microgram." Infusions that are mixed in a 4:1 ratio (4/1 liter) should infuse at 15cc/hr. for each mcg per minute. This is because 60/4=15; where there are 60 min/hr. and 4 units of the drug in every liter of IV fluid. This doesn't have to be a calculation question; it is simply testing the nurse's or the tech's knowledge on infusion rates of Isuprel.

- The calculation follows:
- Remember that 1000 mcg. (Or micrograms) = 1 mg.
- 4,000 mcg/1000cc = 4 mcg/cc; Conc. x vol = amt; Conc. x rate = amt/min; (4 mg/cc) (X cc/min) = 5 mcg. /min.; Solving for X:
- X = (5 mg/min) / (4 mg/cc) = 1.25 cc/min; then convert minutes to hours (1.25 cc/min) (60 min/hr.) = 75 cc/hr.

See: Craig, Clinical Calculations Made Easy, Chapter on "Solving Problems Using Dimensional Analysis"

12. The electrophysiologist has just ordered a Lidocaine infusion to run at 3mg/min. The infusion is pre-mixed as a 4:1 drip (4gms of Lidocaine in 1 liter of fluid). How fast (cc's/hr.) should you run the drip?
   a. **15cc/hr**
   b. **30cc/hr**
   c. **45cc/hr**
   d. **60cc/hr**

ANSWER: c. 45 cc/hr. Infusions that are mixed in a 4:1 ratio (4/1 liter) should infuse at 15cc/hr. for each mcg or mg per minute.
The calculation: 4,000 mg/1000cc = 4 mg/cc; Conc. x vol = amt; Conc. x rate = amt/min; (4 mg/cc) x (X cc/min) = 3 mg./min.
X = (3 mg/min) / (4 mg/cc) = .75 cc/min; then convert minutes to hours:
(0.75 cc/min) / (hr./60 min) = 45 cc/hr.
See: Craig, Chapter on "Solving Problems Using Dimensional Analysis"

13. What is the standard adult dosage for Atropine given IV?
   a. **0.5-1.0 mg bolus every 2 min to a maximum of 5-10 mg**
   b. **0.5-1.0 mg bolus every 5 min to a maximum of 2-3 mg**
   c. **2-5 mg bolus every 2 min to a maximum of 10-20 mg**
   d. **2-5 mg bolus every 5 min to a maximum of 5-10 mg**

ANSWER b. 0.5-1.0 mg. bolus every 5 min. to a maximum of 2-3 mg or 0.04 mg/kg. This dose could reach 4 mg in a 100 Kg. victim. Whether you give 0.5 or 1.0 mg with each bolus depends on the severity of the symptoms. Do not give less than 0.5 mg because these small doses mg can cause paradoxical bradycardia - just the opposite of what you want. Atropine is a parasympathetic blocker which increases the heart rate by reducing vagal tone. For stable bradycardia, the "live" dose is 0.5 mg IV every 3 to 5 minutes to a total dose of 0.04 mg/kg. See: http://www.druglib.com/druginfo/atropine/indications_dosage/ AHA, ACLS Guidelines Chapter on "Pharmacology I"

14. A patient has been on oral amiodarone for 2 years for SVT. His SVT is resumed, and an EP study is planned. To eliminate the residual effects of amiodarone on the study, prior to the study he should:
   a. **Cut this normal dose in half, 2 weeks prior to the study**
   b. **DC it 3-6 months prior to the procedure**
   c. **DC it 2-3 days prior to the procedure**
   d. **No need to discontinue (DC)**

ANSWER: b. DC it 3-6 months prior to the procedure. Murgatroyd says, "Antiarrhythmic drugs should be discontinued for at least 4 half-lives (for most drugs 2-3 days) prior to an EP procedure, with the possible exception of AV node ablation. Amiodarone presents a particular problem in this respect because of its long half-life." Opie says that the pharmacokinetics of amiodarone differs from other cardiac drugs. It is slowly absorbed and slowly eliminated with a half-life of 25-110 days. See: Murgatroyd chapter on Patient Preparation

15. What is the elimination half-life of amiodarone?
   a. **20-40 min**
   b. **12-24 hours**
   c. **2-3 days**
   d. **4-8 weeks**

ANSWER: d. 4-8 weeks. Remington says: "Amiodarone is an antiarrhythmic agent (medication used for irregular heartbeat) used for various types of tachyarrhythmias (fast forms of irregular heartbeat), both ventricular and supraventricular (atrial) arrhythmias.... Elimination half-life average of 58 days (ranging from 25-100 days for amiodarone and 36 days for the active metabolite), ...therefore, if an individual was taking amiodarone on a chronic basis, if it is stopped it will remain in the system for weeks to months." See: Remington: The Science and Practice of Pharmacy 21st edition

15. Your EP study patient is an NPH insulin dependent diabetic. On the morning of her EP study, she should be kept NPO and be administered:
   a. **Quarter dose Metformin instead**
   b. **Oral Metformin instead**
   c. **Half dose NPH insulin**
   d. **No NPH insulin**

ANSWER: c. Half dose insulin. Kern says, "For patients taking subcutaneous insulin (NPH, regular), an overnight fast with their normal dose insulin would cause hypoglycemia. The dose of NPH insulin should be decreased by 50% for patients coming to the catheterization laboratory when they are NPO in the early morning." See: Kern, Chapter on "Introduction to the Catheterization Laboratory"

16. The EP lab nurse gives your patient a bolus injection of Procainamide. Too rapid an injection of Procainamide may cause:
   a. Bradycardia
   b. Tachycardia
   c. Hypotension
   d. Hypertension

ANSWER: c. Hypotension. When procainamide is administered intravenously, a loading dose should first be given of 100mg IV bolus given slowly over 5 minutes. Too rapid an infusion causes transient high plasma levels and temporary but severe lowering of blood pressure. Use should be discontinued after the dysrhythmia is suppressed, if hypotension ensues, if the QRS complex widens by 50% or more, or maximum dose is achieved.... Max dose is 17 mg/kg. See: http://www.drugs.com/sfx/procainamide-side-effects.html#ixzz0vDwS5Nhr

17. This medication affects the K^+ channels, Na^+ channels, a beta-blockade effect, and some degree of Ca^{++} channel blockade.
   a. Amiodarone
   b. Metoprolol
   c. Flecainide
   d. Digoxin

ANSWER: Amiodarone. Amiodarone is a class III medication but has properties of all four of the antiarrhythmic classes.
   • Class I: Mild-to-moderate blockade of the sodium channels
   • Class II: Noncompetitive beta blockade
   • Class III: Blockade of the potassium (K+) channels
   • Class IV: Some degree of calcium (Ca++) channel blockade

"It is classified as a Class III antiarrhythmic drug because its major electrophysiologic effect is a homogenous prolongation of the action potential, and therefore of refractory periods, due to blockade of the potassium channels. The drug has this Class III effect in all cardiac tissues." See: Fogoros: Antiarrhythmic Drugs – chapter on Class III antiarrhythmic drugs.

18. Which of the following action potential changes corresponds with the administration of class IV medications?

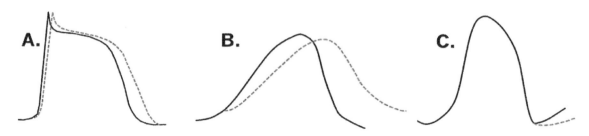

ANSWER: b. Example B. Class IV antiarrhythmics are referred to as calcium channel blockers. These medications slow the calcium channels, which are responsible for depolarization in the SA and AV node. Verapamil and diltiazem are the most utilized Class IV medications. See: EP Essentials – Understanding EP: A Comprehensive Guide – chapter on antiarrhythmics.

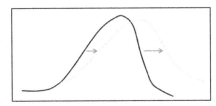

19. **Which class of medications will decrease the refractory period of the action potential?**
    a. **Class Ia**
    b. **Class Ib**
    c. **Class Ic**
    d. **Class II**

ANSWER: b. Class Ib. EP Essentials says, "Class Ib antiarrhythmics are used for the suppression of ventricular arrhythmias and have a minimal effect on atrial tissue. These medications suppress automaticity and decrease the refractory period duration. They have a weaker effect on the Na+ channels." See: EP Essentials – Understanding EP: A Comprehensive Guide – chapter on antiarrhythmics.

20. **When a patient is on flecainide, additional medication from this class is often utilized.**
    a. **Class Ia**
    b. **Class II**
    c. **Class III**
    d. **Class IV**

ANSWER: b. Class II. EP Essentials says, "... [Flecainide] is often given along with an AV nodal blocking agent. This is because it may slow an atrial flutter (for example) to a 1:1 conduction, allowing for rapid conduction to the ventricles; therefore, the AV node must be slowed as well." See: EP Essentials – Understanding EP: A Comprehensive Guide – chapter on antiarrhythmics.

Anticoagulants

1. **A 66-year-old patient with new AF (one week) is scheduled for cardioversion. When is oral anticoagulation recommended for this patient?**
    a. **If TEE shows he is clot free immediately pre-procedure, no anticoagulation is required before or after cardioversion**
    b. **4 weeks prior and 4 weeks after**
    c. **None prior, 4 weeks after**
    d. **4 weeks prior, none after**

ANSWER: b. 4 weeks prior and 4 weeks after cardioversion. Even if the TEE shows the patient free of LA thrombus, cardioversion may stun the atrium, making it more prone to LAA thrombus afterward. It is recommended to anticoagulate everyone post cardioversion. Issa says, "The rationale for anticoagulation prior to cardioversion is that more than 85% of LA thrombi resolve after 4 weeks of warfarin therapy. Thromboembolic events have been reported in 1% to 7% of patients who did not receive anticoagulation before cardioversion."
See: Issa, chapter on AF
Abedin says, "Anticoagulation for conversion to sinus rhythm:
- If AF is less than 48 hours in duration, cardioversion can be attempted [without anticoagulation].
- The presence of AF for more than 48 hours necessitates 3-4 weeks of therapeutic anticoagulation prior to conversion unless TEE demonstrates absence of a clot in the left atrium and its appendage.
- Regardless of whether a TEE is performed, systemic anticoagulation is required for 3 weeks following cardioversion in all patients with atrial fibrillation of greater than 48 hours duration."
See: Abedin, chapter on SVT

2. What is the latest recommended practice for anticoagulation during a case requiring transseptal puncture with ICE guidance?
   a. **In enlarged atria give IIB/IIIA glycoprotein receptor blockers or clopidogrel**
   b. **Give heparin only if going retrograde across the aortic valve**
   c. **Give heparin only after a successful transseptal puncture**
   d. **Don't give heparin if the patient is to continue Warfarin**
   e. **Give heparin immediately after gaining venous access**

ANSWER: e. Give heparin immediately after gaining venous access, is the latest recommendation, although most labs wait until after transseptal puncture.
"Once vascular access is achieved, intravenous heparin (bolus of 100 U/kg, then infusion of 10 U/kg/hr.) is administered. During the initial experience with AF ablation, anticoagulation with heparin was delayed until after LA access had been achieved because of fear of complications with transseptal puncture. Later, it became evident that such a strategy can allow thrombus formation on sheaths, catheters, and in the RA before transseptal puncture, and these thrombi could potentially travel to the LA. More recently, experienced operators have favored complete heparinization after vascular access, and clearly before transseptal puncture, especially when intracardiac echocardiography (ICE) is used to guide transseptal puncture. Even in patients fully anticoagulated with warfarin therapy at the time of ablation, it is still recommended to administer intravenous heparin during the ablation procedure.... To reduce the risk of bleeding complications, antiplatelet therapy (especially IIB/IIIA glycoprotein receptor blockers and clopidogrel) should be avoided, if possible."
See: Issa, chapter on "Catheter Ablation of AF"

3. Heparin blocks clot formation by interfering with the enzymatic conversion of:
  a. **Thromboplastin to Prothrombin**
  b. **Prothrombin to Thrombin**
  c. **Plasminogen to Plasmin**
  d. **Fibrinogen to Fibrin**

ANSWER: b. Prothrombin to Thrombin. In the heparinized patient prothrombin cannot be converted to thrombin. Because of this thrombin cannot combine with fibrinogen to form fibrin, clotting cascade and clotting fails.
See: Todd's, CV Review Book: Vol. I

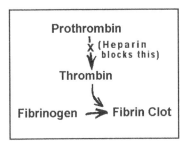

4. Patients with an INR of 0.5 are prone to _____. Patients with an INR of 1.0 are ___.
  a. **Bleeding, Prone to Clotting**
  b. **Clotting, Prone to Bleeding**
  c. **Normal, Prone to Bleeding**
  d. **Clotting, Normal**

ANSWER: d. Clotting, Normal. A low INR of 0.5 suggests there is a high chance of having a clot, whereas a high INR level such as INR=5 indicates that there is a high chance of bleeding. Normal range for a healthy person is 0.9–1.3, and for people on warfarin therapy, 2.0–3.0, although the target INR may be higher situations, such as for those with a mechanical heart valve, or bridging warfarin with a low-molecular weight heparin (such as enoxaparin) perioperatively.

5. At the beginning of a short EP procedure a patient was given 2500 units of IV heparin. What amount of Protamine (10 mg/cc) should be given to reverse 2500 units of heparin?
  a. **1.25 cc**
  b. **2.5 cc**
  c. **5 cc**
  d. **10 cc**

ANSWER: b. 2.5 cc. Grossman recommends 10 mg (1.0 cc) of Protamine to counteract every 1000 units of heparin. It's easy to remember because they react 1:1 by volume, or 1000μ:10 mg. by dosage. If the concentrations are standard (1000 units heparin = 1 cc and 10 mg. Protamine = 1 cc), then each 1 cc of protamine counteracts each 1 cc of heparin.

Grossman says: "If systemic heparinization is used, its effects must be reversed at the termination of the left heart catheterization and associated angiography. This is usually accomplished by administration of protamine (1 ml = 10 mg of protamine for every 1,000 units of heparin) The operator should be watchful for potential adverse reactions to protamine, characterized by hypotension and vascular collapse... Protamine reactions are more common insulin-dependent diabetics." Because of this, many physicians are reducing the amount of Protamine because of these several potentially lethal side effects. Since the half-life of heparin is 40 minutes, only a fraction of the total reversal dose of protamine may be administered. E.g., Some give 25 mg Protamine for 5000 unit's heparin at the end of a 40-minute case. Grossman recommends withholding Protamine on insulin dependent patients, and just letting the heparin effect wear off. See: Grossman, Chapter on "Percutaneous Approach."

6. During an EP ablation procedure, the patient was converted from chronic AF to NSR. Postoperative medications should include:
   a. **Beta blockers and ACE inhibitors**
   b. **Statins and nitroglycerine**
   c. **Heparin and Warfarin**
   d. **Dual antiarrhythmics**

ANSWER: c. Heparin and Warfarin. Cohen says, "If a patient is cardioverted from chronic atrial fibrillation during the procedure, postoperative heparin and warfarin must be initiated in order to avoid complications (i.e., transient ischemic attack or cerebrovascular accident)." See: Cohen, chapter on Preoperative Checklist

7. Many physicians discontinue Dabigatran (Pradaxa) or Xarelto (rivaroxaban) on AF patients prior to a PVI procedure. The main problem with continuing these anticoagulants at the time of a PVI procedure is:
   a. **No bleeding time monitoring**
   b. **No known reversal agent**
   c. **Reduced AF inducibility**
   d. **Increased risk of stroke**

ANSWER: b. There is no known reversal agent for these two new anticoagulants, needed in case of a bleeding complication. This could be a problem if the patient develops a brain bleed or pericardial tamponade. Drugs.com says, "Surgery and Interventions: If possible, discontinue Pradaxa 1 to 2 days (CrCl (creatine clearance) =50 mL/min) or 3 to 5 days (CrCl <50 mL/min) before invasive or surgical procedures because of the increased risk of bleeding." (CrCl = Creatinine Clearance) See: http://www.drugs.com/pro/pradaxa.html
If such bleeding occurs, Weingart recommends only "Mechanical compression, Surgical intervention, Fluid replacement and hemodynamic support, Blood product transfusion, Oral charcoal application, or Hemodialysis. Thrombin Time is probably the best available way to monitor this drug." See: http://emcrit.org/misc/bleeding-patients-on-dabigatran/

8. Match the generic name with the trade name of the following oral anticoagulants.
   a. **Eliquis**
   b. **Xarelto**
   c. **Pradaxa**

   1. **Dabigatran**
   2. **Rivaroxaban**
   3. **Apixaban**

CORRECTLY MATCHED ANSWERS ARE:

3. Eliquis (Apixaban) Manufactured by Pfizer and Bristol-Myers Squibb

2. Xarelto (Rivaroxaban) Manufactured by Bayer

1. Pradaxa (Dabigatran) Manufactured by Boehringer Ingelheim

9. What oral thrombin inhibitor drug may be used in place of warfarin/coumadin to anticoagulate patients in AF?
   a. **Eptifibatide (Integrilin)**
   b. **Bivalirudin (Angiomax)**
   c. **Dabigatran (Pradaxa)**
   d. **Clopidogrel (Plavix)**

ANSWER: c. Dabigatran (Pradaxa) is an oral anticoagulant from the class of the direct thrombin inhibitors. It is being studied for various clinical indications and in some cases, it offers an alternative to warfarin as the preferred orally administered anticoagulant ("blood thinner") since it does not require frequent blood tests for international normalized ratio (INR) monitoring while offering similar results in terms of efficacy. There is no specific way to reverse the anticoagulant effect of dabigatran in the event of a major bleeding event, unlike warfarin…. Dabigatran is used to prevent strokes in those with atrial fibrillation due to non-heart valve causes, and at least 1 additional risk factor for stroke (congestive heart failure, hypertension, age, diabetes, and prior stroke). Patients already taking warfarin with excellent INR control may have little to gain by switching to dabigatran in atrial fibrillation." The costs of this new anticoagulant ($3000/year) are higher than those of warfarin ($48/year), even after addition of the extra cost of INR testing and provider visits for warfarin dose adjustment. This is 60 times higher.

Additional antiplatelet information:
Clopidogrel (Plavix) is an oral antiplatelet agent like aspirin used to inhibit blood clots in coronary artery disease, peripheral vascular disease, and cerebrovascular disease. Its onset of action is slow, so a loading-dose of 300 mg is usually administered.

10. Which NOAC anticoagulant is a direct thrombin inhibitor?
   a. **Xarelto (Rivaroxaban)**
   b. **Pradaxa (Dabigatran)**
   c. **Warfarin (Coumadin)**
   d. **Eliquis (Apixaban)**
   e. **Heparin**

ANSWER: b. Pradaxa (Dabigatran). Dabigatran is a direct oral anticoagulant (DOAC) that works at the end of the final pathway to prevent formation of fibrin. DOACs offer an alternative to warfarin as the preferred orally administered anticoagulant. Drugs.com says, "Thrombin inhibitors are anticoagulants that bind to and inhibit the activity of thrombin and therefore prevent blood clot formation. Thrombin inhibitors inactivate free thrombin and the thrombin that is bound to fibrin. Thrombin has many important functions in the clotting pathway, so it is a good target for anticoagulants drugs."

The other DOACs, Eliquis (Apixaban) & Xarelto (Rivaroxaban), are factor Xa inhibitors further up the coagulation cascade (see diagram), that prevent conversion of prothrombin into thrombin. Factor Xa occupies a pivotal position in the coagulation cascade at the convergent point of extrinsic and intrinsic pathway leading to coagulation. Heparin is also a factor X inhibitor. See: Drugs.com

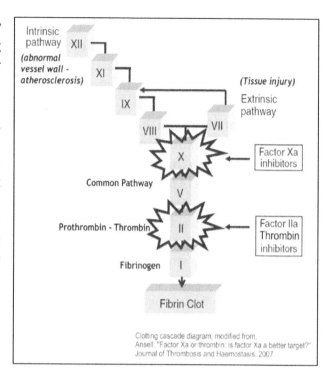

Clotting cascade diagram, modified from, Ansell, "Factor Xa or thrombin: is factor Xa a better target?" Journal of Thrombosis and Haemostasis, 2007

11. Match these blood thinners with their mechanism of action.
   a. **Anticoagulant, Direct thrombin inhibitor**
   b. **Anticoagulant, Direct factor Xa inhibitor**
   c. **Anticoagulant, Vitamin K antagonist**
   d. **Antiplatelet - COX/Thromboxane inhibitor**
   e. **Antiplatelet -Glycoprotein IIb/IIIa inhibitor**

   1. Dabigatran
   2. Rivaroxaban & Apixaban
   3. Abciximab, Eptifibatide, Tirofiban
   4. Coumadin, Warfarin
   5. Dipyridamole & Aspirin

CORRECTLY MATCHED ANSWERS ARE:
1. Anticoagulant, Direct thrombin inhibitor = 1. Dabigatran (DOAC)
2. Anticoagulant, Direct factor Xa inhibitor = 2. Rivaroxaban & Apixaban (DOACs) Heparin & Enoxaparin are also Factor Xa inhibitors
4. Anticoagulant, Vitamin K antagonist = 4. Coumarin, Warfarin
5. Antiplatelet - COX/Thromboxane inhibitor = 5. Dipyridamole & Aspirin
3. Antiplatelet -Glycoprotein IIb/IIIa inhibitor = 3. Abciximab, Eptifibatide, Tirofiban
   Each blood thinner has its place in treating or preventing clots.

12. Some physicians stop a patient's oral anticoagulation medication prior to their PVI procedure, then switch the patient to heparin for the ablation pre-procedure, and finally resume oral anticoagulation post procedure. This strategy of periprocedural anticoagulation is termed:
   a. Provisional anticoagulation
   b. Cross-over anticoagulation
   c. Stop-gap anticoagulation
   d. Bridging anticoagulation

ANSWER: d. Bridging anticoagulation. Verma says, "To date, the two most employed strategies for periprocedural anticoagulation have been the bridging strategy and the continuous warfarin strategy. In the bridging strategy, warfarin is discontinued for 2-4 days prior to the ablation and the patient is covered with full dose low molecular weight heparin (LMWH). Post-ablation, warfarin is resumed the same day with a few days of post-ablation LMWH often given in half dose. "

"In the continuous warfarin strategy, warfarin is continued right through the ablation while keeping the international normalized ratio (INR) ideally between 2.0-2.52." See: http://afibprofessional.cardiosource.org/Article-of-the-Month/2012/05/Anticoagulants-fo r-Periprocedural-Anticoagulation-for-AFib.aspx 'Atul Verma, M.D. May 10, 2012

13. The following statements regarding aspirin are true: (circle two).
   a. Inhibits platelet aggregation
   b. Increases Thromboxane A2
   c. Reduces pain of ischemia
   d. Indirect antithrombotic
   e. Lyses clots

ANSWER: a. Inhibits platelet aggregation, and d. Indirect antithrombotic. Opie says: "There is general agreement that aspirin should be given both in the acute and follow-up phases. [of AMI] Although aspirin reduces AMI and death, even in doses as low as 75 mg daily it does not consistently decrease anginal pain.... Aspirin removes all the platelet cyclo-oxygenase activity for the life span of the platelet. [irreversible platelet inhibition] Therefore, aspirin stops the production of pro-aggregatory thromboxane A2 and eventually acts as an indirect antithrombotic agent." See: Opie, Drugs for the Heart, Chapter on Antiarrhythmic Agents.

14. Aspirin anticoagulant works in blood because it interferes with:
   a. Prostaglandin synthesis of thromboxane A2
   b. Binding of thrombin to fibrinogen
   c. Conversion of fibrinogen to fibrin
   d. Angiotensin II receptors
   e. ADP receptors

ANSWER: a. Prostaglandin synthesis of thromboxane A2. Aspirin (or Acetylsalicylic acid abbreviated ASA) has an antiplatelet effect by inhibiting the production of thromboxane, which binds platelets together to patch damaged blood vessels. In layperson terms, thromboxane is the glue that makes platelets sticky and aspirin dissolves this glue.

Low dose aspirin is used long-term to help prevent heart attacks, strokes, and blood clots. Low dose aspirin is recommended for 1 to 6 months after placement of stents and for years after a coronary artery bypass graft. Full dose Aspirin (325 mg) is also one of the first drugs given in acute coronary syndrome and MI to reduce platelet aggregation. It is a very important antiplatelet drug.

15. Which of the following subcutaneous anticoagulants is a direct thrombin inhibitor?
   a. Hirudin (Desirudin, Bivalirudin, Hirulog, Argatroban)
   b. Tirofiban (Aggrastat)& Eptifibatide (Integrilin)
   c. Ticlopidine (Ticlid) & Clopidogrel (Plavix)
   d. Abciximab (ReoPro)

ANSWER: a. Hirudin (Desirudin, Bivalirudin, Hirulog Argatroban) are direct thrombin inhibitors. These, unlike heparin, inactivate both free thrombin and clot-bound thrombin. Hirudin is the prototype of these direct thrombin inhibitors and was originally isolated from leech saliva. The remaining drugs are all platelet inhibitors. Abciximab (ReoPro) is a large molecule GP IIb/IIIa inhibitor while Tirofiban (Aggrastat) & Eptifibatide (Integrilin) are small molecule GP IIb/IIIa inhibitors. Ticlopidine (Ticlid) & Clopidogrel (Plavix) are oral antiplatelet agents more related to aspirin.

See: Kandarpa or Watson, Chapter on "Commonly Used Medications"

16. All the following are anti-platelet drugs EXCEPT?
   a. Acetylsalicylic acid (Aspirin)
   b. Enoxaparin (Lovenox)
   c. Clopidogrel (Plavix)
   d. Ticagrelor (Brilinta)
   e. Ticlopidine (Ticlid)

ANSWER: b. Enoxaparin (Lovenox) is NOT an anti-platelet drug. It is a low molecular weight heparin that is used for "bridging" away from coumadin prior to ablation for AF. It is short acting and administered subcutaneously.

Antiplatelet drugs: Ticlopidine (Ticlid - for patients allergic to Plavix), Ticagrelor (Brilinta), Clopidogrel (Plavix), Prasugrel (Effient), and Aspirin are all antiplatelet drugs used post PCI. Antiplatelet drugs decrease platelet aggregation and inhibit thrombus formation. They are commonly given along with aspirin. They are effective in arterial circulation, where anticoagulants are less effective. Prevention of clotting in arteries is often done with antiplatelet drugs, which act by a different mechanism from warfarin (which has no effect on platelet function).

17. Platelet-rich plasma or fresh frozen plasma may be administered:
   a. **When shock develops following blood loss**
   b. **To patients with hemorrhagic disorders**
   c. **In place of plasma expanders**
   d. **In place of whole blood**

ANSWER: b. To patients with hemorrhagic disorders. Fresh Frozen Plasma (FFP) which contains many clotting factors, including platelets. See: Grossman, Chapter on Complications.

18. Which vitamin is necessary for the formation of clotting factors and may be given to neutralize coumadin?
   a. **Vitamin A**
   b. **Vitamin C**
   c. **Vitamin D**
   d. **Vitamin K**

ANSWER: d. Vitamin K. Guyton says, " Vitamin K is required . . . for normal formation of prothrombin as well as four other clotting factors . . . Therefore, the lack of vitamin K can decrease the prothrombin level so low that a bleeding tendency results." An important long-term anticoagulant coumadin functions by inhibiting vitamin K. In fact, giving vitamin K reverses coumadin's anticoagulant effect. See: Guyton, chapter on Hemostasis and Blood Coagulation

19. All the following are benefits of low molecular weight heparin (LMWH) EXCEPT:
   a. **Lower risk of bleeding complications**
   b. **Less need of laboratory monitoring**
   c. **More effective anticoagulant**
   d. **More predictable dosing**
   e. **More cost effective**

ANSWER: e. More cost effective is NOT true. It currently costs more than unfractionated heparin. Braunwald says: "LMWH [low molecular weight heparin] has been considered theoretically superior to standard heparin in several additional ways.

   - First, unlike unfractionated heparin, it can inhibit platelet-bound factor Xa and therefore should be a more effective anticoagulant. For many flashcards on medication See: www.gwhizmobile.com
   - Second, LMWH binds less readily to plasma proteins .... This produces a longer plasma half-life, more predictable bioavailability, and more favorable pharmacokinetics than standard heparin.
   - Third, LMWH has less pronounced effects on platelet function and vascular integrity, properties that contribute to its lower risk of bleeding complications than standard heparin. The longer plasma half-life and more predictable anticoagulant response of LMWH preparations allow their administration as fixed-dose, once-daily or twice-daily subcutaneous injections, without need for laboratory monitoring."

See: Braunwald, chapter on "Acute Myocardial Infarction"

20. Low Molecular Weight Heparin (LMWH) is different from unfractionated heparin in that: (select two answers)
  a. LMWH cannot be completely reversed with Protamine
  b. LMWH has an increased risk of thrombocytopenia
  c. LMWH must be monitored with PPT not ACT
  d. LMWH is administered subcutaneously
  e. LMWH is degraded by contact with light

ANSWERS: a. & d. LMWH is administered subcutaneously, while heparin is given IV. Protamine's effect on LMWH is limited, while heparin is completely reversible with protamine sulfate. Some LMWH drugs are Enoxaparin (Lovenox) & Dalteparin (Fragmin).
Waksman says "Laboratory monitoring of LMWH is unnecessary except in high-risk patients.... LMWH does not significantly affect the partial thromboplastin time or activated clotting time [anti-Xa may be used to monitor its action] .... One limitation of the use of LMWH is that there is no antidote that has been consistently shown to neutralize its action in the case of bleeding. Protamine, which is used to reverse anticoagulation with heparin, has been shown to neutralize only 60% of the anti-factor Xa activity of LMWH. Nonetheless, if reversal is necessary... Protamine can be administered at a dose of 1 mg per mg of enoxaparin.... A second dose of protamine can be administered at 0.5 mg for every 1 mg given if the bleeding persists...."

Because it can be given subcutaneously and does not require PTT monitoring, LMWH permits outpatient treatment of conditions such as deep vein thrombosis or pulmonary embolism that previously mandated inpatient hospitalization for IV heparin administration. Because LMWH has more predictable pharmacokinetics and anticoagulant effect, LMWH is recommended over unfractionated heparin for patients with massive pulmonary embolism, and for initial treatment of deep vein thrombosis. See: Waksman and Ajani, Pharmacology in the Catheterization Laboratory, chapter on "Low Molecular Weight Heparin..."

21. ACLS guidelines recommend heparin in patients with acute injury pattern on 12 lead ECG and unstable angina. What is the maximum heparin dose for full anticoagulation in patients over 70 kg?
  a. Heparin 2500 U bolus IV followed by 500 U/hr IV drip
  b. Heparin 4000 U bolus IV followed by 1000 U/hr IV drip
  c. Heparin 6000 U bolus IV followed by 1500 U/hr IV drip
  d. Heparin 10000 U bolus IV followed by 1000 U/hr IV drip

ANSWER: b. 4000 U bolus IV followed by 1000 U/hr. IV drip. ACLS guidelines say: "To reduce the incidence of [Intracranial hemorrhage] ICH, the 1999 update to the ACC/AHA Guidelines for the Management of Myocardial Infarction recommends a lower dose of heparin than was previously recommended. The current recommendations now call for a bolus dose of 60 U/kg followed by infusion at a rate of 12 U/kg per hour (a maximum bolus of 4000 Units and infusion of 1000 U/h for patients weighing >70 kg). A PTT of 50 to 70 seconds is considered optimal. Increased rates of bleeding and ICH have been related to more intensive heparin therapy and higher PTTs (>70 seconds). The incidence of stroke is increased in patients with a large anterior wall infarction and thrombus significant L V dysfunction atrial fibrillation, and a previous embolic event. Treat these high-risk patients with heparin for an extended period; warfarin therapy may be initiated in some. ... LMWH [low molecular weight heparin] is an acceptable alternative to IV UFH [regular Unfractionated Heparin]. Enoxaparin is preferable to UFH. UFH is recommended for use with GP IIb/IIIa inhibitors until data on safety and efficacy regarding combination with LMWH is available."

See: AHA, ACLS Provider Manual, chapter on "Acute Coronary Syndromes"

22. A patient with occasional bouts of non-valvular AF has a CHADS2 score of 0. He should be treated with:
  a. **Receive anticoagulation on either a warfarin or antiplatelet drug depending on patient preference.**
  b. **Receive long term warfarin or other anticoagulant drugs**
  c. **Aspirin or other antiplatelet therapy**
  d. **Receive no anticoagulation therapy**

ANSWER: c. Aspirin or other antiplatelet therapy. Issa says, "Patients with a CHADS2 score of 0 are at low risk of embolization (0.5% per year in the absence of Warfarin) and can be managed with aspirin."

23. What type of anticoagulation should PVI patients receive? Select all true answers.
  a. **Prior to PVI all patients should receive oral anticoagulation for 3 months.**
  b. **After transseptal puncture Heparin should be administered to ACT of 300 sec.**
  c. **After successful PVI all patients should receive Oral anticoagulation for 4-6 months.**
  d. **4-6 months after successful PVI, CHADS 1 patients who have had no recurrence of AF may be converted to Aspirin and antiplatelet therapy.**
  e. **After successful PVI, a patient with a mechanical mitral valve who has no recurrence of AF after 4-6 months should remain on oral anticoagulants indefinitely.**

ANSWERS: a, b, c, d & e are all true. Zipes says: "Pre-ablation Anticoagulation Issues: Like patients with permanent AF, patients at risk (patients with persistent AF or those with paroxysmal AF or with associated risk factors) require oral anticoagulation therapy with at least 3 weeks of documented INR values and should undergo bridging with intravenous heparin or subcutaneous low molecular weight heparin before ablation. We also recommend TEE for any patient presenting in AF who has not undergone oral anticoagulation therapy with bridging before ablation."

"Anticoagulation Therapy during the Ablation Procedure: Anticoagulation should be established after transseptal puncture, and in some cases, ACT can be tailored up to 300 seconds if necessary to reduce sheath thrombus risk. "See: Zipes, chapter on PVI for AF

Patients with mechanical or prosthetic heart valves are anticoagulated for life due to thrombogenicity of the valve. Biological valves (pig valves) have a reduced risk of clotting, and do not usually require lifelong anticoagulation.

Hussein, et. al. says, "Radiofrequency ablation is feasible and safe for patients with MVR. It allowed restoration of sinus rhythm in a substantial proportion of patients undergoing ablation. An abnormal atrial substrate underlies recurrences in these patients." Hussein, et. al., RF ablation of AF patients with mechanical MVP, J Am Coll Cardiol. 2011

24. A 70-year-old man in mild CHF is treated for paroxysmal AF with amiodarone and dabigatran (Pradaxa). He shows no other symptoms, except his QT has increased from 465 to 505 ms. You should recommend:
   a. **Reduce amiodarone dosage and recheck ECG in 1 week**
   b. **Discontinue dabigatran (Pradaxa) and switch to coumadin**
   c. **Discontinue amiodarone and switch to another antiarrhythmic**
   d. **Nothing more, this is common side-effect with amiodarone with few consequences**

ANSWER: d. Nothing more, this is a common side-effect with amiodarone with few consequences. Amiodarone is a class III agent which is expected to prolong the action potential and lengthen the QT interval. Dabigatran is a novel anticoagulant for the prevention of stroke or systemic embolism in patients with AF. It has fewer bleeding complications than warfarin and does not lengthen the QT interval.

Drugs.com says, "Amiodarone increases the cardiac refractory period without influencing resting membrane potential, except in automatic cells where the slope of the prepotential is reduced, reducing automaticity. These electrophysiologic effects are reflected in a decreased sinus rate of 15 to 20%, increased PR and QT intervals of about 10%, the development of U-waves, and changes in T-wave contour. These changes should not require discontinuation of Amiodarone as they are evidence of its pharmacological action, although Amiodarone can cause marked sinus bradycardia or sinus arrest and heart block. On rare occasions, QT prolongation has been associated with worsening of arrhythmia."

Crouch says, "When a patient develops QT prolongation, one should consider the heart rate-corrected QT, or QTc, for risk assessment. A relationship exists between QTc prolongation and the development of torsade de pointes, ... If a drug-drug interaction is present, it should be immediately eliminated. Small extensions in the QTc (< 10 ms) are acceptable if there are no predisposing risk factors. If QT prolongation becomes more marked, one should consider decreasing the dosage of the offending agent and monitor the patient more closely. In addition to the QTc, the uncorrected QT interval should be considered. When the QT exceeds 500 ms, it implies substantial risk to the patient, irrespective of heart rate, and the offending agent should be withdrawn immediately. The only exception would be amiodarone. Amiodarone frequently prolongs the QT interval but has a low frequency of torsade de pointes.... [However,] The most concerning situation, which typically requires immediate

management, is when QT prolongation progresses to torsade de pointes…. Direct current shock may be performed if the patient is hemodynamically unstable."
See: Crouch, et. al., Clinical Relevance and Management of Drug-Related QT Interval Prolongation, http://www.medscape.com/viewarticle/458868_4

25. During an arterial access procedure, after administering heparin use ___ to monitor the level of blood clotting and keeping it above _____.
   a. **PT (Prothrombin Time), >30 sec**
   b. **PTT (aPPT), >12 sec**
   c. **ACT, >300 sec**
   d. **INR, >2**

ANSWER: c. ACT, >300 sec. Issa says: "The lower level of anticoagulation should be maintained at an ACT of at least 300 to 350 seconds throughout the period of mapping and ablation in the LA." See: ClinLab navigator says, "the ACT is the recommended test for monitoring heparin in interventional cardiology procedures. The ACT correlates with the anticoagulant effect of heparin at the higher heparin levels used in these procedures. The aPTT is unsuitable at this level of heparinization, as it is frequently prolonged beyond the measurable range." The INR is used to monitor Coumadin levels. The PT test is the basis of the ACT. But, since it varies so much between labs, INR is the ratio of the measured PT to normal PT. An INR of 1 means the measured PT clotting time is the same as the normal clotting time- in other words normal. See: http://clinlabnavigator.com/activated-clotting-time-act.html

26. Match the coagulation test to its use and normal value:
   1. **PT (Protime)**
   2. **PTT or aPTT (activated Partial Thromboplastin Time)**
   3. **INR (International Normalized Ratio)**
   4. **ACT (Activated Clotting Time)**

   a. **Monitor Coumadin anticoagulation, approximately 1.0 (Anticoagulation values should be >2.0)**
   b. **Monitor high dose complete heparin anticoagulation, approximately 100 sec. (Anticoagulation values should be >250)**
   c. **Monitor extrinsic (tissue damage) coagulation pathway approximately 12 sec.**
   d. **Monitor intrinsic (surface contact coagulation pathway), approximately 30 sec. Anticoagulation values should be >3 times normal**

CORRECTLY MATCHED ANSWERS ARE:
   1. PT   = c. Monitor extrinsic (tissue/endothelial damage)
   2. PTT = d. Monitor intrinsic (surface contact pathway)
   3. INR = a. Monitor Coumadin
   4. ACT = b. Monitor High dose Heparin

Coagulation has two sequential pathways, intrinsic and extrinsic, either of which leads to a final common pathway that generates fibrin and the clot. The Intrinsic pathway is within blood itself (happens slowly), while the extrinsic pathway may be due to injured endothelium or other tissues (happens quickly). There are many interactions and proteins involved in the clotting cascade.

PT or Pro-Time stands for prothrombin time, sometimes called pro-time. This test measures how long it takes the plasma part of your blood to clot once a tissue factor is added. The PT test evaluates the extrinsic and common pathways of the coagulation cascade. The normal level for people not on anti-coagulation drugs ranges between 11 and 13.5 seconds.
PTT stands for partial thromboplastin time. The PTT test evaluates the intrinsic and common pathways. For people who are not on anti-coagulation therapy, it should take between 25 to 35 seconds for normal blood to clot. If you are on anti-coagulation therapy, that number should be at least three times higher or even more.

INR stands for International Normalized Ratio; The INR is used to monitor the effectiveness of the anticoagulant warfarin (COUMADIN®). For the average person, that number typically runs at about 0.8 to 1.1. For most people on anti-coagulation therapy, it should be at 2 and some people are supposed to keep it above 2.5.

ACT stands for Activated Clotting time and is intended to monitor anticoagulant effect of unfractionated heparin especially during interventional procedures when heparin lengthens the clotting time. Activated clotting time (ACT) depends on the test device used, and [normal values] it can vary from 80 to 160 seconds. During anti-coagulation, the ACT should exceed 250.

27. If 5000 units of heparin was given at the start of an PVI case, how long should you wait before pulling arterial and venous sheaths after a case?
   a. **Wait 20 minutes or until INR normalizes**
   b. **Arterial ACT<185, Venous ACT<165**
   c. **Arterial ACT<165, Venous ACT<185**
   d. **Wait 10 minutes**

ANSWER: c. Arterial <165, Venous <185. Clinlabnavigator.com recommends ACT <165 for arterial sheath pulls or <185 for venous sheath pulls. INR is not appropriate for heparin monitoring. See: http://clinlabnavigator.com/activated-clotting-time-act.html

Conscious Sedation:

1. Hemodynamic effects of morphine include _____ venous capacitance and _____ peripheral vascular resistance.
   a. Increased, Increased
   b. Increased, Decreased
   c. Decreased, Increased
   d. Decreased, Decreased

ANSWER: b. Increased venous capacitance, decreased peripheral vascular resistance. The ACLS manual states, "Morphine is effective in the treatment of ischemic chest pain and for acute pulmonary edema. It manifests both analgesic and hemodynamic effects. It increases venous capacitance and reduces systemic vascular resistance, relieving pulmonary congestion. In doing so, it reduces intramyocardial wall tension, which decreases myocardial oxygen requirements." Thus, by reducing preload and afterload, morphine reduces both venous and arterial pressures. See: ACLS chapter on "CV Pharmacology I"

2. Match the following drugs with their mechanism of action?
   1. **Prophylaxis for contrast reaction**   a. Diphenhydramine (Benadryl)
   2. **Prevent and treat nausea**   b. Midazolam (Versed)
   3. **Sedation and amnesia**   c. Fentanyl Citrate (Sublimaze)
   4. **Analgesia**   d. Zofran (Ondansetron)

CORRECTLY MATCHED ANSWERS:
1. Prophylaxis for contrast reaction: a. Diphenhydramine (Benadryl)
2. Prevent and treat nausea: d. Zofran (Ondansetron)
3. Sedation and amnesia: b. Midazolam (Versed)
4. Analgesia: c. Fentanyl Citrate (Sublimaze)
See: Kandarpa or Watson, Chapter on "Commonly Used Medications"

3. What is the generic name for Versed?
   a. Diphenhydramine
   b. Meperidine
   c. Midazolam
   d. Diazepam
   e. Atropine

ANSWER: c. Midazolam is the generic name for Versed. Commonly given during interventional procedures. The onset of its action is rapid (1-2 min), and its duration of action is only 30 minutes following a normal 2 mg IV dose. This short duration of action makes it an ideal sedative for EP procedures. Midazolam wears off soon after the procedure terminates. Note that the RCES exam uses only generic names. Be able to match all answers:

COMMON NAME	GENERIC NAME
1. Demerol	Meperidine
2. Valium	Diazepam
3. Versed	Midazolam
4. Benadryl	Diphenhydramine
5. Belladonna	Atropine

See: Grossman, chapter on "Complications and Optimal Use of Adjunctive Pharmacology"

4. When conscious sedation (E.g., Versed) is administered, the patient usually:
   a. **Can follow simple instructions but cannot recall later what happened**
   b. **Becomes difficult to arouse and may require intubation**
   c. **Is semi-conscious but remembers later what happened**
   d. **Loses consciousness and is unresponsive to stimuli**

ANSWER: a. Can follow simple instructions but doesn't remember later what happened. Versed is a benzodiazepine that reduces anxiety and diminishes recall. It should be used with analgesia because Versed is not an analgesic and does not eliminate the pain experienced by the patient. Loebl says: "Because of amnesic effects patients may not remember . . . post procedure instructions or remember the results of the procedure, even though they seem wide awake." See: Loebl, chapter on "Antianxiety drugs"

5. Versed used in conscious sedation has all the following effects EXCEPT:
   a. **Drowsiness**
   b. **Pain relief**
   c. **Hypnotic**
   d. **Amnesia**

ANSWER: b. Pain relief- No. That is the function of analgesic medications like Fentanyl not a sedative/amnesiac like Versed. That is why Versed, and Fentanyl are usually given together. Fentanyl reduces the pain, versed relaxes the patient and helps them forget the procedure (amnesia). And like other benzodiazepines Versed is termed a "hypnotic". See: Loebl, The Nurses Drug Handbook, Chapter on Antianxiety drugs

6. Current monitoring standards during conscious sedation drug administration require:
   a. **Vital signs and level of consciousness documentation every 5-15 min (Aldrete score)**
   b. **Vital signs & level of consciousness documentation every 20-30 min (Aldrete score)**
   c. **Eyelid sensitivity (Apgar score) and pain sensitivity documentation every 5-15 min**
   d. **Eyelid sensitivity (Apgar score) & pain sensitivity documentation every 20-30 min**

ANSWER: a. Vital signs and level of consciousness documentation every 5-15 minutes. Monitoring should be done every 5-15 minutes and should document vital signs, cardiac rhythm, pulse oximetry (SAO2), and level of consciousness. AORN standards recommend ETCO2 (End-Tidal Carbon Dioxide) monitoring. The Aldrete score is used to evaluate the level of conscious sedation with level 10 being normal. The Apgar score is to evaluate premature children. See: Loebl, Chapter on "Antianxiety drugs"

7. The most important side effect to watch for with narcotic and benzodiazepine over-sedation is:
   a. **Respiratory depression (decreased rate and depth of breathing)**
   b. **Cardiac arrhythmias (both atrial and ventricular)**
   c. **Allergic reaction with skin rash and paresthesia**
   d. **Diarrhea, nausea, and vomiting**

ANSWER: a. Respiratory depression (decreased rate and depth of breathing). Yaniga says: "Narcotics, analgesic combinations and general anesthetics cause respiratory depression and are contraindicated in patients with pulmonary disease or respiratory depression from any cause. Respirations, SaO2 and BP must be monitored closely...Both Versed and Valium may cause respiratory depression and hypotension...." See: Yaniga, Leslie, RCIS, Cardiac Catheterization Medications Guide, Smith Notes, 1998, chapter on "Analgesics, Anesthetic and Narcotic medications and reversal agents"

8. In the EP lab, the most sensitive patient parameter to monitor for over sedation is:
   a. **Eyelid twitch response**
   b. **Respiratory rate**
   c. **Blood pressure**
   d. **O2 saturation**
   e. **Pulse rate**

ANSWER: d. O2 saturation. Patient monitoring during conscious sedation must be performed by a trained and licensed health care professional. This clinician must not be involved in the procedure but should have primary responsibility of monitoring and attending to the patient. Equipment must be in place and organized for monitoring the patient's blood pressure, pulse, respiratory rate, level of consciousness, and, most important, the oxygen saturation with a pulse oximeter. The oxygen saturation is the most sensitive parameter affected during increased levels of conscious sedation. Vital signs and other pertinent recordings must be monitored before the start of the administration of medications, and then at a minimum of every five minutes thereafter until the procedure is completed. After the procedure has been completed, monitoring should continue every 15 minutes for the first hour after the last dose of medication(s) was administered. After the first hour, monitoring can continue as needed. Use as little sedation as possible as too much suppresses the arrhythmia you are trying to induce. See: surgeryencyclopedia.com

9. Which of the following drugs is a benzodiazepine?
   a. **Midazolam (Versed)**
   b. **Fentanyl (Sublimaze)**
   c. **Nifedipine (Procardia)**
   d. **Flumazenil (Romazicon)**

ANSWER: a. Midazolam (Versed) is a short-acting drug in the benzodiazepine class that is used for inducing sedation (calming) and amnesia (forgetting) before medical procedures. It has potent anxiolytic, amnesic, hypnotic, anticonvulsant, skeletal muscle relaxant, and sedative properties. Midazolam is ineffective for pain and has no analgesic effect during conscious sedation. Midazolam has a fast recovery time and is the most used benzodiazepine as a premedication for sedation.

10. Which sedative usually wears off within 30 minutes following IV infusion?
   a. Valium
   b. Versed
   c. Benadryl
   d. Demerol

ANSWER: b. Versed, or Midazolam is a short-acting benzodiazepine CNS depressant. The onset of its action is rapid (1-2 min), and its duration of action is only 30 minutes following a normal 2 mg IV dose. This short duration of action makes it an ideal sedative for angiographic procedures. And it wears off soon after the procedure terminates. It is eliminated 10 times faster than Valium. It is contraindicated in patients with narrow-angle glaucoma. See: Kandarpa, ch. on "Commonly Used Medications."

11. IV Flumazenil (Romazicon) is used to:
   a. Reverse Fentanyl (Sublimaze)
   b. Reverse Midazolam (Versed)
   c. Induce Analgesia
   d. Induce Amnesia

ANSWER: b. Reverses Midazolam (Versed). Versed is a short-acting drug in the benzodiazepine class that is used for inducing sedation (calming or reduced irritability) and amnesia (forgetting) before medical procedures. It has potent anxiolytic, amnestic, hypnotic, anticonvulsant, skeletal muscle relaxant, and sedative properties. Midazolam has a fast recovery time and is the most used benzodiazepine as a premedication for sedation.... Flumazenil is a benzodiazepine antagonist drug that can be used to treat an overdose of midazolam as well as to reverse sedation.

12. What is the reversal agent for Fentanyl/Sublimaze?
   a. Flumazenil (Romazicon)
   b. Naloxone (Narcan)
   c. Protamine
   d. Vitamin K

ANSWER: b. Naloxone is a drug used to counter the effects of opiate overdose, for example morphine or Fentanyl overdose. Naloxone is specifically used to counteract the life-threatening depression of the central nervous system and respiratory system that can result from opioids. It is marketed under various trademarks including Narcan and Naloxone.

13. Fentanyl (Sublimaze) is primarily a:
   a. **Muscle relaxant**
   b. **Amnesiac**
   c. **Painkiller**
   d. **Sedative**

ANSWER: c. Painkiller. Fentanyl (Sublimaze) is a synthetic primary opioid agonist and a potent narcotic analgesic (pain killer) with a rapid onset and short duration of action. The analgesic effects of all opioids are decreased perception of pain, decreased reaction to pain as well as increased pain tolerance. Fentanyl is approximately 100 times more potent than morphine. Intravenous fentanyl is extensively used for anesthesia and analgesia, especially in combination with a benzodiazepine, such as midazolam, to produce procedural sedation for cardiac catheterization and EP procedures.

14. All the following agents are anxiolytics (not analgesics) used for conscious sedation EXCEPT: (Which is a narcotic?)
   a. **Versed / Midazolam**
   b. **Valium / Diazepam**
   c. **Fentanyl / Sublimaze**
   d. **Ativan / Lorazepam**

ANSWER: c. Fentanyl/ Sublimaze is an artificial narcotic (opiate) used for analgesia (pain relief). It is commonly given with Versed which is an anxiolytic (relaxes) and hypnotic medication. Midazolam, diazepam, and lorazepam are benzodiazepines (end in "am").
Fentanyl is approximately 100 times more potent than morphine. See: Watson, Chapter on "Cardiac Pharmacology"

15. A long-acting benzodiazepine sedative is:
   a. **Acetylsalicylic Acid (Aspirin)**
   b. **Midazolam (Versed)**
   c. **Diazepam (Valium)**
   d. **Morphine**

ANSWER: c. Diazepam (Valium) has an elimination half-life of 1–3 days.... but it has a fast onset of action, about 1–5 minutes for IV administration and 15–30 minutes for IM administration. The duration of diazepam's peak pharmacological effects is 15 minutes to 1 hour for both routes of administration. It is a benzodiazepine derivative drug commonly used for treating anxiety and insomnia. It may also be used as a preop before cardiac catheterization to reduce tension and anxiety, and in some surgical procedures to induce amnesia. It possesses anxiolytic, anticonvulsant, hypnotic, sedative, skeletal muscle relaxant, and amnestic properties.

16. When you are administering deep conscious sedation to a patient, how can you best tell they are having pain?
   a. Sweating and nervousness
   b. Positive Babinski reflex
   c. Facial expression
   d. Ask them

ANSWER: c. Facial expression. Patients should be instructed to tell you if they are in pain. However, under deep conscious sedation the patient may not be able to answer appropriately. The Patient Safety Council has standards for the "Non-Verbal Reporting of Pain: For patient's unable to self-report pain, observable behavioral/facial expressions (e.g., grimacing) and physiological indicators (e.g., tachycardia, hypertension) represent important indices for the assessment of pain." One 10-point Non-Verbal Pain Scale rates these 5 observations from 0-2: Facial expression, Activity (restlessness), guarding (rigidity), Physiologic parameters (BP), Respiratory rate."
See: http://www.chpso.org/meds/sedation.pdf

17. Which of the following medications are opioids? (Select all that apply)
   a. Meperidine
   b. Flumazenil
   c. Fentanyl
   d. Benadryl
   e. Valium
   f. Versed
   g. Naloxone

ANSWERS: a. Meperidine and c. Fentanyl. Meperidine may be better known as the brand name Demerol. Romazicon/Flumazenil is a reversal agent for benzodiazepines (valium/versed) and Narcan/Naloxone is a reversal for opioids.

Antiarrhythmics:

1. In the Vaughan Williams classification, match each class with an example antiarrhythmic drug.

a.	Procainamide, Quinidine	1.	Class Ia
b.	Diltiazem, Verapamil, Nifedipine	2.	Class Ib
c.	Lidocaine	3.	Class Ic
d.	Amiodarone, Sotalol	4.	Class II
e.	Flecainide, Propafenone	5.	Class III
f.	Inderal (Propranolol), Timolol, Metoprolol	6.	Class IV

CORRECT ANSWERS:
1. Class Ia = a. Procainamide, quinidine (Na blocker medium fast onset, reduces Vmax and prolongs action potential duration)
2. Class Ib = c. Lidocaine (Na blocker of fast onset, shortens action potential duration)
3. Class Ic = e. Flecainide, propafenone (Na blocker - fast acting, slows conduction)
4. Class II = f. Inderal (propranolol), timolol, metoprolol (Beta1 channel blockers)
5. Class III = d. Amiodarone, Sotalol (Block potassium channel & prolong repolarization)
6. Class IV = b. Diltiazem, Verapamil, Nifedipine (Block slow Calcium channel)

Braunwald says: "The Vaughan Williams classification is widely known and provides a useful communication shorthand. It is listed here, but the reader is cautioned that the drug actions are more complex than those depicted by the classification."

Opie says, "Such compounds (Class 1) can cause proarrhythmic complications by prolonging the QT-interval in certain genetically predisposed individuals or by depressing conduction and promoting reentry.... Currently there is no evidence that class I agents reduce death,... (but) there is such evidence favoring B-blockers (Class II agents) especially in ischemic heart disease, and there is increasing evidence that Amiodarone (Class III agent) is effective against a wide spectrum of arrhythmias, but [still] being inferior to implantable cardioverter defibrillators (ICDs) in the highest risk patients...." Remember acronym. "So Be Pot Cautious" for Sodium, Beta Potassium, and Calcium blockers. See: Opie, chapter on "Antiarrhythmics" and See: Braunwald, chapter on "Management of Patients with Cardiac Arrhythmias"

2. Which class of antiarrhythmics works on the sodium channel?
   a. **Class I**
   b. **Class II**
   c. **Class III**
   d. **Class IV**

ANSWER: a. Class I antiarrhythmics affect the Na channel, while Class II are Beta Blockers, Class III antiarrhythmics block the K+ channel, and Class IV are Calcium Channel Blockers. Remember acronym "So Be Pot Cautious" Sodium blockers are class 1.

3. Class I antiarrhythmics cause _____ conduction velocity and are termed _____.
   a. **Increased, Beta blockers**
   b. **Decreased, Beta blockers**
   c. **Increased, Membrane stabilizing agents**
   d. **Decreased, Membrane stabilizing agents**

ANSWER: d. Decreased, Membrane stabilizing agents. The class I antiarrhythmic agents interfere with the fast sodium channel (phase 0) and thus reduce conduction velocity. As a group class I agents are called "Membrane Stabilizers." Lidocaine is so stabilizing that it is also a local anesthetic.

Vaughan Williams classification:

- Class 1A lengthens the action potential (right shift): Quinidine, Procainamide, Disopyramide.
- Class 1B shortens the action potential (left shift) and prolongs QT interval: Lidocaine, Phenytoin, Mexiletine.
- Class 1C slows the fast Na current in phase 0: Flecainide, Propafenone, Moricizine

Opie says, "Such compounds (Class 1) can [also] cause proarrhythmic complications by prolonging the QT-interval in certain genetically predisposed individuals or by depressing conduction and promoting reentry.... Currently there is no evidence that class I agents reduce death," See: Opie, chapter on "Antiarrhythmics"

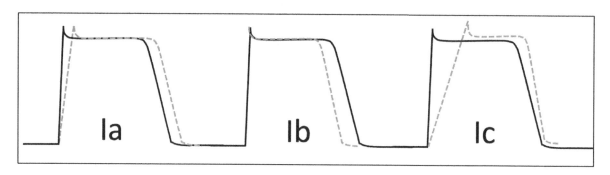

4. Class 1 drugs that block the fast sodium channel in cardiac tissue cause:
   a. **Decreased conduction velocity**
   b. **Increased conduction velocity**
   c. **Decreased automaticity**
   d. **Increased automaticity**

ANSWER: a. Decreased conduction velocity. In "Class 1 antiarrhythmic drugs ...it takes longer to depolarize the cell (the slope of phase 0 is decreased). Because the speed of depolarization determines how quickly adjacent cells will depolarize (and therefore the speed of impulse propagation), class I drugs as a group tend to decrease the conduction velocity of cardiac tissue." The diagram shows a normal action potential followed by a dotted action potential with slowed phase 0 upstroke. Note how the slow upstroke affects conduction velocity in the lower diagram. This slowing may even up the two sides of a reentry loop in diseased tissue where one side is already damaged and slowed. This "evening out" often prevents reentry tachycardias. But, in the oval diagram where the two velocities are uneven, it may allow reentry. The slow signal may exit the loop after the fast signal because its refractory phase has passed. That upper signal may then pass retrograde to the left through the lower loop and start a clockwise reentry circus (circular) movement and tachycardia. If a Class 1 drug caused this problem, it would be called proarrhythmic. See: Fogoros chapter on Treatment of Arrhythmias

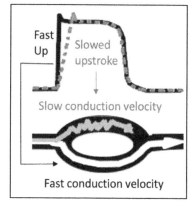

5. Drugs that affect phase 0 of action potential are what class of antiarrhythmic in the Vaughan Williams classification?
   a. 0
   b. I
   c. II
   d. III
   e. IV

ANSWER: b. Class I antiarrhythmic agents interfere with the sodium channel (phase 0) and thus reduce conduction velocity and stabilize myocardial cell membranes. Opie says, "Currently there is no evidence that class I agents reduce death, [but] there is such evidence favoring Beta-blockers (Class II agents) especially in ischemic heart disease, and there is increasing evidence that Amiodarone (Class III agents) is effective against a wide spectrum of arrhythmias, but being inferior to implantable cardioverter defibrillators (ICDs) in the highest risk patients... Such compounds (Class 1) can cause proarrhythmic complications by prolonging the QT-interval in certain genetically predisposed individuals or by depressing conduction and promoting reentry." See: Opie, chapter on "Antiarrhythmics"

6. In the Vaughan Williams classification, class II antiarrhythmics are termed:
   a. **Sodium Channel blockers**
   b. **Alpha blockers**
   c. **Ace inhibitors**
   d. **Beta blockers**

ANSWER: d. Beta blockers. Remember that beta (ß) is the second letter in the Greek alphabet (α, β, Γ, & Δ), and the second class of antiarrhythmic drugs. Beta blocker drugs (also termed ß-blockers, beta-adrenergic blocking agents, beta-adrenergic antagonists, or beta antagonists) block the effect of epinephrine in the fight or flight effect, thus slowing and relaxing the heart. Many drugs given after MI (BBs & ARBs) block the bad effect of increased catecholamines on the heart. See: Opie, chapter on "Antiarrhythmics"

7. All the following antiarrhythmic medications are in Vaughan Williams Class III EXCEPT?
   a. **Amiodarone (Cordarone)**
   b. **Procainamide (Pronestyl)**
   c. **Dofetilide (Tikosyn)**
   d. **Sotalol (Betapace)**
   e. **Ibutilide (Covert)**

ANSWER: b. Procainamide is a class Ia drug. The class III drugs extend the repolarizing potassium current and prolong the QT interval.
Antiarrhythmics: class III members, remember the mnemonic BIASeD: for: Bretylium, Ibutilide, Amiodarone, Sotalol. Remember mnemonic "So Be Pot Cautious" for the four Vaughan Williams classes.

Opie says, "Procainamide...has a wide spectrum of antiarrhythmic activity, without serious side effects except for hypotension and QRS and QT widening, making it an attractive class I agent for IV use." See: Opie, chapter on Antiarrhythmic Drugs

8. Which of the following is a class III antiarrhythmic that is administered over 10 minutes by IV infusion, and if that is ineffective may be repeated over another 10 minutes?
   a. **Diltiazem**
   b. **Ibutilide**
   c. **Sotalol**
   d. **Lidocaine**

ANSWER: b. Ibutilide. Ibutilide can convert atrial fibrillation (AF) and flutter. Opie says, "The recommended dose for treatment of atrial arrhythmias is 1 mg administered by IV infusion over 10 minutes. If the arrhythmia is not terminated within 10 minutes after end of the first infusion, the infusion may be repeated." Wrong answers are:
   • Diltiazem (Cardizem) is a class IV Calcium blocker
   • Sotalol is a class II beta blocker
   • Lidocaine is a class Ib Sodium channel blocker See: Opie chapter on Antiarrhythmics

9. Which class of antiarrhythmics has the most effect on depressing the action potential of the AV and SA nodes?
   a. **Class II, Alpha blockers**
   b. **Class II, Beta blockers**
   c. **Class IV, Potassium channel blockers**
   d. **Class IV, Calcium channel blockers**

ANSWER: d. Class IV, Calcium channel blockers. "In cardiac pharmacology, calcium channel blockers are considered class IV antiarrhythmic agents. Since calcium channels are especially concentrated in the sinoatrial and atrio-ventricular nodes, these agents can be used to decrease impulse conduction through the AV node, thus protecting the ventricles from atrial tachyarrhythmias.... Many calcium channel blockers also slow down the conduction of electrical activity within the heart, by blocking the calcium channel during the plateau phase of the action potential of the heart. This results in a negative chronotropic effect, or a lowering of heart rate. This can increase the potential for heart block. The negative chronotropic effects of calcium channel blockers make them a commonly used class of agents in individuals with atrial fibrillation or flutter in whom control of the heart rate is a goal. Negative chronotropy can be beneficial when treating a variety of disease processes because lower heart rates represent lower cardiac oxygen requirements. An elevated heart rate can result in significantly higher 'cardiac work', which can result in symptoms of angina." Remember acronym "So Be Pot Cautious." See: Braunwald, chapter on "Management of Patients with Cardiac Arrhythmias"

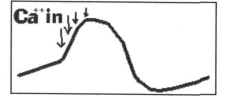

10. Class IV antiarrhythmics like verapamil and diltiazem mainly _____ conduction through the AV node, and _____ SA & AV tissue refractory periods:
   a. **Slow, increases**
   b. **Slow, decreases**
   c. **Speed, increases**
   d. **Speed, decreases**

ANSWER: a. Slows AV node conduction and increases nodal refractory periods. Fogoros says: "Class IV includes the calcium channel blockers, whose effects are mainly on the SA and AV nodes (because these structures are almost exclusively depolarized by the slow calcium channels)." Class IV drugs include diltiazem and verapamil. See: Fogoros chapter on Treatment of Arrhythmias, also Opie 247

11. In the Vaughan Williams classification of antiarrhythmic drugs, which type of blockers fit into class IV?
   a. **Potassium channel blockers**
   b. **Calcium channel blockers**
   c. **Sodium channel blockers**
   d. **Beta$_1$ channel blockers**

ANSWER: b. Calcium channel blockers
Class I. = c. Block fast Sodium channel (slow Na from entering cell during phase 0)
Class II. = d. Beta$_1$ channel blockers (block adrenergic sites) - most end in "-olol."
Class III. = a. Potassium channel blockers (prolong repolarization)
Class IV. = b. Block slow Calcium channel.
Braunwald says: "the Vaughan Williams classification is widely known and provides a useful communication shorthand. It is listed here, but the reader is cautioned that the drug actions are more complex than those depicted by the classification."

Note in the diagram, it is easy to remember class I and III, because they change that part of the action potential with their name. Class I effects phase 0 & 1. Class III effects phase III. Class IV effects phase II where Ca enters the cell. Class II contains beta blockers with effects on phase IV by slowing the heart rate. See: Braunwald, chapter on "Management of Patients with Cardiac Arrhythmias"

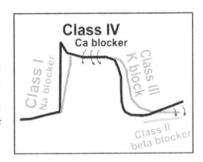

12. Most antiarrhythmic drugs (especially Class I and III) work by:
   a. **Changing bidirectional block into unidirectional block**
   b. **Changing the shape of the cardiac action potential**
   c. **Blocking beta parasympathetic tone**
   d. **Suppressing automatic ectopic sites**

ANSWER: b. Changing the action potential. Fogoros says, "Antiarrhythmic drugs are not arrhythmia suppressants in the same way that menthol is a cough suppressant. They do not work by soothing irritable areas. In fact, most antiarrhythmic drugs work merely by changing the shape of the cardiac action potential. By changing the action potential, these drugs alter the conductivity and refractoriness of cardiac tissue. Thus, it is hoped, the drugs will change the critical electrophysiologic characteristics of reentrant circuits to make reentry less likely to occur." See: Fogoros chapter on Treatment of Arrhythmias

13. The action of class III antiarrhythmics like amiodarone and sotalol is to:
   a. **Decrease the refractory period in cardiac tissue**
   b. **Increase the refractory period in cardiac tissue**
   c. **Block the beta parasympathetic system**
   d. **Block the alpha-adrenergic system**

ANSWER: b. Increase the refractory period. "Class III drugs (amiodarone, Bretylium, N-acetylprocainamide, sotalol and ibutilide) increase the action potential duration and therefore refractory periods and have relatively little effect on conduction velocity." The diagram shows a normal action potential behind a dotted action potential with long refractory period. Note the longer refractory period in the lower diagram - upper loop. This longer tail may even-up the two sides of a reentry loop in diseased tissue where one side is already damaged and lengthened. This "evening up" often prevents reentry tachycardias.

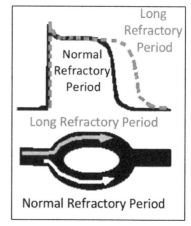

However, in the diagram shown, where the two arrows are uneven, it may allow reentry if the upper (long) signal appears on the right side after the fast signal and its refractory phase have passed. Since the lower loop's refractory phase has passed, it is ready to fire again. A signal may then pass retrograde to the left through the lower loop and start a clockwise reentry circus movement and tachycardia. Longer refractory period (Type III antiarrhythmics) may also break up reentry loops. Drugs with different mechanisms. See diagram. See: Fogoros chapter on Treatment of Arrhythmias

14. A mixed class III antiarrhythmic that is like amiodarone in the prevention of recurrent VT and AF is:
   a. **Procainamide (Pronestyl)**
   b. **Magnesium sulfate**
   c. **Sotalol (Betapace)**
   d. **Lidocaine**

ANSWER: c. Sotalol (Betapace) and amiodarone are active against a wide variety of ventricular and atrial arrhythmias. They help prevent monomorphic VT or VF which was inducible with an EP study. They are also used to prevent recurrent AF after cardioversion.

Since they both are class III agents, and thus lengthen the action potential, their Achilles heel is the possible side effect of torsade des pointes.

Two other class III agents not mentioned in the question, Ibutilide and dofetilide may be used to convert atrial fibrillation to sinus rhythm. Lidocaine is a class Ib ventricular antiarrhythmic that acts on ischemic tissue by blocking (numbing) conduction thereby interrupting reentry circuits. It is used in MI patients with frequent PVCs that depress hemodynamics. Procainamide (Pronestyl) is a class IA agent, like quinidine, but does not prolong the QT-interval. Magnesium sulfate may be the treatment of choice in torsades de pointes VT.

15. This ECG is on a hemodynamically stable man with complaints of palpitations. He has a normal ECG at baseline with no evidence of a delta wave. What is the most appropriate therapy?
   a. **Cardioversion**
   b. **Defibrillation**
   c. **Adenosine**
   d. **Verapamil**
   e. **Amiodarone**

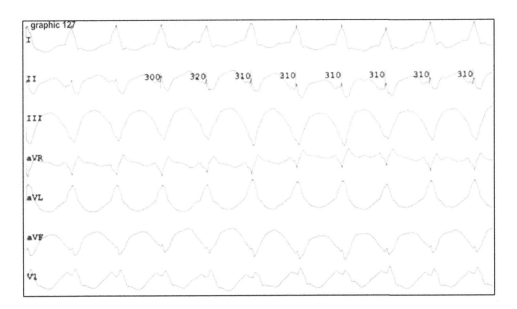

ANSWER: e. Amiodarone. The patient is in stable condition with only complaints of palpitations; therefore, cardioversion and/or defibrillation are not an appropriate treatment of choice. Adenosine is an excellent option to rule out whether the AV node is participating in the tachycardia circuit. Adenosine would terminate AVNRT or AVRT. Also, by blocking the AV node, the physician would be able to see if there are underlying flutter waves, such as in Atrial Flutter with 1:1 conduction. However, this would be potentially life threatening in a patient with a Manifest AVRT. In Manifest AVRT, or a patient that has a pathway that conducts antegrade over the pathway and up the AV node, blocking the AV node would allow for pure conduction down the pathway to the ventricle. If this patient had an underlying AF with RVR (rapid ventricular response) this could be life threatening.

Tullo says," The acute treatment of sustained AVRT is the same as AVNRT. Since the AV node is part of the circuit, AVRT should terminate with intravenous adenosine or verapamil. To prevent recurrent episodes, AV nodal blocking agents can be used. In addition, Class IA, Class IC, and Class III antiarrhythmic agents have been used to affect conduction in the accessory pathway (which is sodium-dependent). Atrial fibrillation with rapid conduction down an accessory pathway in a patient with WPW Syndrome should never be treated with verapamil since this can increase the rate of conduction down to the ventricles and may result in ventricular fibrillation."
See: Advanced Concepts in Arrhythmias by Nicholas G. Tullo, MD, FACC, FHRS.

16. Diltiazem or verapamil are used to treat the following heart rhythm:
   a. **ST-segment elevation MI with frequent PVCs**
   b. **Third-degree heart block**
   c. **Ventricular Fibrillation**
   d. **Atrial Fibrillation**

ANSWER: d. Atrial Fibrillation. Calcium channel blockers slow the rate and increase conduction time at the AV node. They are not used in "dead" patients (i.e., VF). ACLS manual says: "Intravenous Verapamil is effective for terminating narrow-complex PSVT and may also be used for rate control in patients with AF. Adenosine, however, is the drug of choice for terminating narrow-complex PSVT....Verapamil should be given only to patients with narrow complex PSVT or Arrhythmias known with certainty to be of supraventricular origin. Verapamil should not be given to patients with impaired ventricular function or heart failure." Braunwald says: "We do not recommend the routine use of either verapamil or diltiazem in AMI." If used with wide complex tachycardias they may worsen the rhythm by turning VT into VF. And 9 times out of 10 apparent wide complex SVT is VT. See: AHA, ACLS Guidelines Chapter on "Pharmacology I"

17. IV Lidocaine is used to:
   a. **Treat chronic recurrent ventricular arrhythmias**
   b. **Treat ventricular arrhythmias in acute MI**
   c. **Prophylactically prevent VT and VF**
   d. **Inhibit the slow calcium channel**

ANSWER b. Treat ventricular arrhythmias in acute MI. IV Lidocaine inhibits the fast sodium channel and is used only for ventricular arrhythmias especially those associated with AMI. Braunwald says, "Lidocaine significantly reduces the action potential duration and the effective refractory period of Purkinje fibers and ventricular muscle due to blocking of the... sodium channels and decreasing entry of sodium into the cell. It has little effect on atrial fibers and does not affect conduction in accessory pathways."

Opie says, "Lidocaine has become the standard IV agent for suppression of serious ventricular arrhythmias associated with AMI and cardiac surgery. The concept of prophylactic lidocaine to prevent VT and VF in AMI is now outmoded...has no role in control of chronic recurrent ventricular arrhythmias."
See: Braunwald, chapter on "Management of Cardiac Arrhythmias"

18. Accepted cardiac use of IV Lidocaine is:
   a. **Before attempted defibrillation of ventricular arrhythmias**
   b. **Prophylactically to prevent PVCs in acute MI patients**
   c. **When frequent PVCs or VT significantly drop the BP**
   d. **To break most reentry SVTs**

ANSWER: c. When frequent PVCs or VT significantly drop the BP. Opie says, "The concept of prophylactic lidocaine to prevent VT and ventricular fibrillation (VF) in AMI is now outmoded. This IV drug has no role in the control of chronic recurrent ventricular arrhythmias. 1. Should lidocaine be administered routinely to all patients with AMI? Increasingly the answer is no.... meta-analysis has shown that lidocaine reduces VF but adversely affects mortality rates, therefore lidocaine should not routinely be used in AMI.... 2. Should lidocaine be used routinely before attempted defibrillation of ventricular tachyarrhythmias? The answer is no - any benefits are cancelled by the greater delays involved in achieving defibrillation. When can it be used? When tachyarrhythmias or very frequent PVCs seriously interfere with hemodynamic status in patients with AMI (especially when already beta-blocked) and during cardiac surgery or general anesthesia." It is strictly for ventricular arrhythmias, not atrial.
See: Opie, chapter on Antiarrhythmic Drugs & Strategies

19. What oral Class I medication has effects most like intravenous lidocaine?
   a. **Procainamide**
   b. **Mexiletine**
   c. **Flecainide**
   d. **Quinidine**

ANSWER: b. Mexiletine. Mexiletine is like an oral lidocaine that does not degrade as fast as the injectable version. See, Wilson, Cardiac EP Exam Preparation, chapter on Antiarrhythmic drugs. Drugs.com says, "Mexiletine is a Class 1B antiarrhythmic compound with electrophysiologic properties in patients like lidocaine, but dissimilar from quinidine, procainamide, and disopyramide.... Mexitil (mexiletine hydrochloride, USP) is a local anesthetic, antiarrhythmic agent, structurally like lidocaine, Mexitil did not prolong ventricular depolarization (QRS duration), or repolarization (QT intervals) as measured by electrocardiography. Theoretically, therefore, Mexitil may be useful in the treatment of ventricular arrhythmias associated with a prolonged QT interval." See: drugs.com

20. Antiarrhythmic meds have many side effects and special considerations. Match each drug to its side effect/precaution.

a. CNS effects (numbness, tingling...)

b. Don't shake ampule, Pulmonary Fibrosis

c. Muscle paralysis, flush, sweating

d. Do not mix with other meds

e. Bradycardia, widens QRS, vasodilation, Lupus-like effects

1. Amiodarone
2. Lidocaine
3. Procainamide
4. MgSO4
5. Sodium Bicarbonate

ANSWERS:
1. Amiodarone =   b. Don't shake ampule, Pulmonary Fibrosis
2. Lidocaine = a. CNS effects (numbness, tingling...)
3. Procainamide = e. Bradycardia, wide QRS, vasodilation, Lupus-like effects
4. MgSO4=   c. Muscle paralysis, flushing, sweating
5. Sodium Bicarbonate = d. Do not mix with other meds

See: AHA, ACLS Provider Manual, chapter on "VF/Pulseless VT"

21. An antiarrhythmic drug was ineffective on a patient. The physician orders an increased dose of the same antiarrhythmic medication. This leads to even more arrhythmia. When this happens, it is termed (a):

a. Refractoriness

b. Proarrhythmia

c. Dysrhythmia

d. Overdrive

ANSWER: b. Proarrhythmia. Fogoros says: "Although proarrhythmia is a common occurrence, it was until recently only poorly recognized by many physicians who use antiarrhythmic drugs. Failing to recognize that the drug is worsening arrhythmias frequently leads to inappropriate therapy (such as increasing or adding to the offending drug), and sometimes leads to death. Herein lies the problem with considering antiarrhythmic drugs to be simply arrhythmic suppressants. Proarrhythmia is an inherent property of antiarrhythmic drugs. The mechanism that controls reentrant arrhythmias is the same mechanism that can worsen arrhythmias."
See: Fogoros chapter on Treatment of Arrhythmias

22. The most common toxic effect of antiarrhythmic drugs is:

a. Electrolyte imbalance

b. Rash and fever

c. Proarrhythmia

d. CNS effects

ANSWER: c. Proarrhythmia. Fogoros says: "Proarrhythmia is probably the most important, and is certainly the most universal, type of toxicity seen with antiarrhythmic drugs."
See: Fogoros chapter on Treatment of Arrhythmias

23. What is the first line drug recommended by ACLS guidelines to terminate narrow complex tachycardia in the stable patient?
   a. **Amiodarone**
   b. **Adenosine**
   c. **Diltiazem**
   d. **Esmolol**

ANSWER: b. Adenosine. Braunwald says: "Adenosine has become the drug of first choice to terminate an acute SVT such as AV node or AV re-entry. Adenosine can produce AV block or terminate atrial tachycardias and sinus node reentry. It results in transient AV block ... Because of its effectiveness and extremely short duration of action, adenosine is preferable to verapamil in most instances...." See: Braunwald, chapter on "Management of Patients with Cardiac Arrhythmias" and ACLS Providers Manual

24. Which first line, Class 1c oral antiarrhythmic drug is commonly used on symptomatic AF patients with recent onset of AF that have no structural or ischemic heart disease. This antiarrhythmic may be proarrhythmic and should be started only with close monitoring with regular ECGs for several days, followed by Holter monitoring. It has been used as a "Pill-in-the-Pocket" antiarrhythmic for recent onset AF.
   a. **Amiodarone**
   b. **Flecainide**
   c. **Dofetilide**
   d. **Ibutilide**

ANSWER: b. Flecainide. The other three drugs are class III agents usually reserved for chronic AF patients with structural heart disease. Opie says of Flecainide, "The drug should be started under careful observation, using a gradually increasing low oral dose with regular ECGs to assess QRS complex duration and occasional serum levels. Once steady state treatment has been reached... it is advisable to perform a 24-hour Holter analysis or a symptom limited exercise stress test to detect potential arrhythmias during maximum effort.... In [AF] patients with no minimal structural heart disease, the first-line agents are flecainide, propafenone, or sotalol. Amiodarone or dofetilide are secondary options. In patients with CHF only amiodarone and dofetilide are known to be effective.... A single dose of flecainide (200-300 mg) ... when an episode begins - the 'Pill-in-the-pocket technique' - may be effective in selected patients with AF and no structural heart disease."
See: Opie chapter on Antiarrhythmics

25. In AF patients with mild or no heart disease, the "pill-in-the-pocket" approach to rhythm control utilizes:

   a. Flecainide or Propafenone, taken when AF symptoms begin
   b. Amiodarone or Dofetilide, taken following cardioversion
   c. Verapamil or Diltiazem, taken when AF symptoms begin
   d. Verapamil or Diltiazem, taken following cardioversion

ANSWER: a. Flecainide or Propafenone (Class 1c agents:), taken when AF symptoms begin. Some AF patients carry Flecainide or Propafenone around with them to take immediately when they feel the symptoms. These Class IC antiarrhythmics may convert AF to sinus rhythm in few hours and prevent having to go to the hospital.

Issa say, "flecainide and propafenone are preferred for patients with no or minimal heart disease, whereas amiodarone and dofetilide are preferred for patients with reduced LV EF or heart failure and sotalol for patients with coronary artery disease....Class 1C agents are reserved to treat patients without a structural cardiac abnormality, and may be prescribed for patients with acute conversion of paroxysmal AF i.e., the so-called Pill in the pocket approach.... amiodarone...causes substantial noncardiac toxic effects and is therefore generally reserved for second-line therapy."

Class IV agents Verapamil or Diltiazem are AV nodal Ca++ blockers that are used for rate control. See, Issa, chapter on AF and NEJM, "Outpatient Treatment of Recent-Onset Atrial Fibrillation with the "Pill-in-the-Pocket" Approach Dec 2004

UCLA.edu says: "In selected patients, the oral antiarrhythmic agents, propafenone or flecainide, can effectively cardiovert recent onset (within 48 hours) AF. Oral pharmacologic conversion can be considered in those patients who are hemodynamically stable and experience abrupt onset of palpitations and no symptoms of dyspnea, lightheadedness, or syncope.... These patients may take the drug shortly after the onset of recurrent atrial fibrillation. If symptoms persist more than 6-8 hours or if the patient experiences new symptoms after ingestion of the medication, further medical evaluation should be taken.... To assess safety for "a pill in the pocket" approach, ... The initial treatment is administered using a single oral dose based on weight.... The recommended oral dosage of flecainide is 200 mg for patients under 70 kg and 300 mg otherwise. For propafenone, the oral dosage is 450 mg for patients under 70 kg and 600 mg for patients with weight equal to or greater than 70 kg. Cardiac observation should be performed for eight hours thereafter, monitoring for adverse effects, including hypotension, dysrhythmia, and cardiopulmonary symptoms. Pharmacologic cardioversion is usually anticipated within six hours after oral administration." See: "A Pill in the Pocket Approach for Recent Onset Atrial Fibrillation in a Selected Patient Group" at http://www.med.ucla.edu/modules/wfsection/article.php?articleid=525

26. The effective half-life of IV adenosine is approximately:
   a. **5 seconds**
   b. **30 seconds**
   c. **10-20 minutes**
   d. **2-6 hours**

ANSWER: a. 5 seconds. Braunwald says: "The body's elimination systems result in very rapid clearance of adenosine from the circulation. Elimination half-life is 1 to 6 seconds. Most of adenosine's effects are produced during its first passage through the circulation."
See: Craig, Clinical Calculations Made Easy, Chapter on "Solving Problems Using Dimensional Analysis"

27. Your awake and asymptomatic patient has a very regular, monomorphic wide complex (>0.12 sec) tachycardia. Your physician orders an adenosine IV bolus. Why?
   a. **It may terminate the tachycardia if it's an SVT with aberrancy (not VT)**
   b. **Adenosine should not be given in wide-complex tachycardia**
   c. **A period of asystole may convert VT to NSR**
   d. **To prepare the patient for cardioversion**

ANSWER: a. It may terminate the tachycardia if it is an SVT with aberrancy (not VT). Since SVT with aberrancy may look like monomorphic VT, IV adenosine can distinguish between VT and SVT. Current guidelines say, "Adenosine is recommended in the initial diagnosis and treatment of stable, undifferentiated regular, monomorphic wide-complex tachycardia... It is important to note that adenosine should not be used for irregular wide-complex tachycardias because it may cause degeneration of the rhythm to VF."

Braunwald says, "Adenosine may be useful to help differentiate among causes of wide QRS tachycardias because it terminates many SVTs with aberrancy or reveals the underlying atrial mechanism...." See: Braunwald chapter on Therapy for Cardiac Arrhythmias" http://static.heart.org/eccguidelines/pdf/ucm_317350.pdf

28. Which IV bolus medication may cause the patient to go into a short period of ventricular asystole?
   a. **Calcium channel blockers**
   b. **Amiodarone**
   c. **Adenosine**
   d. **Diltiazem**

ANSWER: c. Adenosine has adverse effects such as: "PVCs, transient sinus bradycardia, sinus arrest and AV block are common when an SVT abruptly terminates." It is such a good AV blocker that it may cause a short period of complete heart block or asystole. However, the effect of adenosine normally lasts only a few seconds.
See: Braunwald, chapter on "Management of Patients with Cardiac Arrhythmias"

29. Your electrophysiologist asks you to draw up 12 mg of adenosine. How much should you draw up from the bottle shown (60 mg/20 ml)?
   a. **4 ml**
   b. **6 ml**
   c. **12 ml**
   d. **15 ml**

ANSWER a. 4 ml. This is a simple unit conversion problem. You can do it by looking at the concentration in parentheses on the box. It is 3 mg/ml, and you need 12 mg, so you should draw up 4 ml. Here is the unit cancellation way to solve the problem.

Desired amount

12 mg	20 ml	==240	== 4 ml
	60 mg	== 60	

See: Braunwald, chapter on "Management of Patients with Cardiac Arrhythmias"

30. In SVT if the initial dose of adenosine is ineffective, after 2 minutes administer:
   a. **12 mg adenosine rapid IV push x2**
   b. **6 mg adenosine rapid IV push x2**
   c. **Transcutaneous pacing**
   d. **DC cardioversion**

ANSWER: a. 12 mg adenosine rapid IV push x2. Opie says about adenosine: initial dose is 6 mg, given as a fast intravenous/intraosseous infusion push "The drug is given as an initial rapid intravenous bolus ... followed by a saline flush to obtain high concentrations in the heart. If it does not work within 1 to 2 minutes, a 12 mg bolus is given that may be repeated..." twice for a maximum of 30 mg.
See: Opie, Drugs for the Heart, Chapter on Antiarrhythmic Agents.

31. A patient has arrived from the ER with asymptomatic narrow QRS complex tachycardia. The first treatment should be:
   a. **Try vagal maneuvers**
   b. **Give Amiodarone**
   c. **Give Lidocaine**
   d. **Cardiovert**

ANSWER: a. Try vagal maneuvers first to increase parasympathetic tone and slow the HR and AV conduction. Vagal nerve stimulation may be achieved by having the patient perform one of the vagal maneuvers: holding the breath for a few seconds, dipping the face in cold water, coughing, or tensing the stomach muscles as if to bear down for a bowel movement (Valsalva maneuver). Patients with supraventricular tachycardia (SVT) and atrial fibrillation (AF) may be trained to perform vagal maneuvers to slow these tachycardias. Treatment of symptomatic SVTs is cardioversion.

32. Which antiarrhythmic drug has the most extensive toxic effects on many organ systems such as: bradyarrhythmias, pneumonitis, thyroid effects, CNS effects, and liver toxicity.
   a. **Ibutilide**
   b. **Lidocaine**
   c. **Amiodarone**
   d. **Procainamide**

ANSWER: c. Amiodarone. Fogoros says: "Amiodarone, a class III drug, deserves special recognition as a drug that is uniquely toxic not only among antiarrhythmic drugs but also among all drugs used legally in the United States. Amiodarone has a singular spectrum of toxicities (it can affect virtually every organ system) that can be subtle in onset and difficult to recognize (the drug is accumulated slowly in many organs and toxicity may be related to the cumulative lifetime dose) and can be difficult to treat (the half-life of amiodarone may be up to 100 days). The only reason amiodarone is used, given this toxic potential, is that most authorities consider it to be the most efficacious drug yet marketed for the treatment of serious cardiac arrhythmias. In carefully selected patients, the use of amiodarone is appropriate and quite helpful." See: Fogoros chapter on Treatment of Arrhythmias

33. All the following are side effects of amiodarone EXCEPT:
   a. **Shortens action potential duration (<QTc)**
   b. **Photosensitivity (corneal granules)**
   c. **Pigmentation of skin (blue gray)**
   d. **Pulmonary alveolitis and fibrosis**
   e. **Peripheral neuropathy**

ANSWER: a. Shortens action potential and QTc is incorrect because its action is based on prolonging the action potential and QT interval. Note the side effects start with the letter "P." Another common side effect is to alter the thyroid hormone levels.

Opie says, "Amiodarone is a unique "wide spectrum" antiarrhythmic agent, chiefly class III but with also powerful class I activity and ancillary class II and class IV activity. In general, the status of this drug has changed from that of a "last ditch" agent to one that is increasingly used when life-threatening arrhythmias are being treated. Its established antiarrhythmic benefits and potential for mortality reduction need to be balanced against, first, the slow onset of action of oral therapy and may require large oral loading does. Second, the many serious side effects, especially pulmonary infiltrates, and thyroid problems, dictate that there must be a fine balance between the minimum antiarrhythmic effect of the drug and the potential for the side effects." See: Opie chapter on Antiarrhythmic Drugs

34. In symptomatic sinus bradycardia or A-V block, which of the following medications is contraindicated?
   a. Amiodarone
   b. Epinephrine
   c. Dopamine
   d. Atropine

ANSWER: a. Amiodarone. Opie says, "Amiodarone may inhibit the SA or AV node, which can be serious in those with prior sinus node dysfunction or heart block.... Amiodarone is a unique "wide spectrum" antiarrhythmic agent... In general, this drug has changed from that of a 'last ditch' agent to one that is increasingly used when life-threatening arrhythmias are being treated." See: Opie, chapter on "Antiarrhythmics"

35. Magnesium sulfate is used in the treatment of: (Select two answers)
   a. Torsades de pointes
   b. Refractory VF
   c. Heart block
   d. Acute MI
   e. CHF

ANSWER: b. Refractory VF and b. Torsades de pointes. ACLS guidelines say: "Severe magnesium deficiency is associated with cardiac arrhythmias, symptoms of cardiac insufficiency, and sudden cardiac death. Anecdotal experience suggests that magnesium may be an effective treatment for antiarrhythmic drug-induced Torsades de pointes even in the absence of magnesium deficiency.... The routine administration of magnesium in AMI is no longer recommended." See: ACLS Manual

36. Side effects of procainamide indicating that it should be discontinued, or the dosage reduced include: (Select three answers)
   a. Decreases contractility
   b. QRS widens by > 50%
   c. Hypotension
   d. Tachycardia
   e. Numbness
   f. PVCs

ANSWER: a. Hypotension, c. QRS widens by > 50%, d. Decreases contractility. ACLS guidelines say: "Procainamide hydrochloride suppresses both atrial and ventricular arrhythmias.... Procainamide hydrochloride may be given in an infusion of 20 mg/min until the arrhythmia is suppressed, hypotension ensues, the QRS complex is prolonged by 50% from its original duration, or a total of 17 mg/kg (1.2 g for a 70-kg patient) of the drug has been given." IV administration side effects are: Hypotension, QRS widening, QT widening, ST elevation, and infra-His block. See: AHA Guidelines

Braunwald says, "Procainamide can block conduction in the accessory pathway of patients with the Wolff-Parkinson-White syndrome and may be used in patients with atrial fibrillation and a rapid ventricular response related to conduction over the accessory pathway. It can produce His-Purkinje block and is sometimes administered during an electrophysiologic study (EPS) to stress the His-Purkinje system in evaluating the need for a pacemaker.... It has been used to facilitate VT induction at EPS when the arrhythmia could not be initiated in the baseline state." See: Braunwald chapter on RX for Cardiac arrhythmias

37. RVOT triggered VT is most likely to be converted to NSR with intravenous:
   a. **Adenosine or Nitroglycerine**
   b. **Ibutilide or Nitroglycerine**
   c. **Adenosine or Verapamil**
   d. **Ibutilide or Verapamil**

ANSWER: c. Adenosine or Verapamil. Zipes says, "The signature characteristic of sustained RVOT and LVOT tachycardia is termination by adenosine. Sensitivity of ventricular tachycardia to blockade of the L-type calcium channel current (ICa, L) with verapamil is another distinguishing feature." See, Zipes, chapter on "VT in Structurally Normal Hearts." That is why RVOT is termed an "adenosine-sensitive" arrhythmia.

Remember how the AV node is very sensitive to adenosine, another Ca blocker. Since RVOT & LVOT are due to Ca overload, Calcium blockers usually break these arrhythmias. Adenosine is sometimes called a class "IV like" agent. But the problem is not breaking RVOT tachycardia, it is often difficult to initiate in the EP lab. Rapid burst pacing and isoproterenol are usually required. Issa says, "Most forms of outflow tract VTs are adenosine-sensitive and are thought to be caused by catecholamine cyclic adenosine monophosphate (cAMP)–mediated delayed afterdepolarizations (DADs) and triggered activity, Heart rate acceleration facilitates VT initiation. This can be achieved by programmed stimulation, rapid pacing from either the ventricle or atrium, or infusion of a catecholamine alone or during concurrent rapid pacing. Additionally, termination of the VT is dependent on direct blockade of the dihydropyridine receptor by calcium channel blockers or by agents or maneuvers that lower cAMP level" See: Issa, chapter on Idiopathic VT

38. All the following drugs are contraindicated in a patient with WPW EXCEPT?
   a. **Flecainide & Procainamide**
   b. **Verapamil & Nicardipine**
   c. **Digoxin & Lidocaine**
   d. **Inderal & Labetalol**

ANSWER: a. Flecainide & Procainamide may be helpful in WPW. Any drugs that block the AV node increase the risk of rapid bypass pathway conduction and could lead to VF if AF develops. The mnemonic to remember what drugs to avoid in WPW is ABCD, for Adenosine, Beta blockers, calcium channel blockers, and Digoxin.

Medscape says, "The use of digoxin or verapamil for long-term therapy appears to be contraindicated for many patients with WPW syndrome, because these medications may enhance antegrade conduction through the AP by increasing the refractory period in the AV node. In addition, digoxin may shorten the refractory period of the AP, further enhancing its antegrade conduction." See: http://misc.medscape.com/pi/android/medscapeapp/html/A159222-business.html

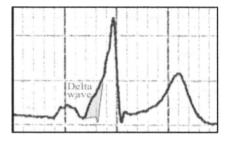

39. What are the two main types of rhythm control drugs (antiarrhythmics) for AF & AFL? (Select two answers)
   a. Class 1a drugs, Amiodarone or Sotalol
   b. Class 1a drugs, Quinidine or Procainamide
   c. Class 1c drugs, Amiodarone or Sotalol
   d. Class 1c drugs, Dronedarone, Propafenone or Flecainide
   e. Class III drugs, Amiodarone or Sotalol
   f. Class III drugs, Dronedarone, Propafenone or Flecainide

ANSWERS: d. Class 1C drugs, Dronedarone, Propafenone or Flecainide and answer e. Class III drugs, Amiodarone or Sotalol. The 1C drugs are used in patients with normal LV function or EF. The class III drug Amiodarone is the only antiarrhythmic that can be recommended to all AF patients whether have abnormal LV function. The aim of rhythm control is to convert AF into sinus rhythm. Of course, the ultimate rhythm control is catheter ablation PVI. See, http://www.ncbi.nlm.nih.gov/pmc/articles/PMC3576947/

40. What are the two main types of rate control drugs for AF & AFL? (Select two answers)
   a. Class 1c drugs, Dronedarone, Propafenone or Flecainide
   b. Class 1c drugs, Amiodarone or Sotalol
   c. Class II drugs, any drug ending in -olol
   d. Class II drugs, any drug ending in - amide
   e. Class IV drugs, Verapamil, Diltiazem
   f. Class IV drugs, Amiodarone or Sotalol

ANSWERS: c. Class II drugs, any drug ending in -olol (beta-blockers) and answer e. Class IV drugs, Verapamil, Diltiazem (Calcium blockers). Remember, the beta blockers all end in olol (labetalol, metoprolol, Propranolol). They block the stimulating effects of catecholamines. The Ca blockers slow the Ca channels in the SA & AV nodes. So, both class II and class IV drugs slow the heart and AV conduction in AF and may be prescribed together. In addition to these above 2 classes of drugs Digoxin may also be prescribed to slow the rate and improve LV function in patients with CHF. The aim or rate control in AF is not to convert from AF, but to reduce the ventricular rate to under 100 bpm.
See: http://www.ncbi.nlm.nih.gov/pmc/articles/PMC3576947/

41. What is the recommended therapy for asymptomatic patients with long QT syndrome?
   a. Exercise program, low fat diet and take beta blockers
   b. Avoid exercise and stress, and take beta blockers
   c. Exercise program, low fat diet and receive an ICD
   d. Avoid exercise and stress, and receive an ICD

ANSWER: b. Avoid exercise, stress, and take beta blockers. Ellenbogen says, "This is group of genetically determined diseases.... Affected individuals have a structurally normal heart but an increased risk of syncope and sudden cardiac death (SCD) caused by ventricular tachycardia (VT) or ventricular fibrillation (VF).... Current guidelines suggest that all patients diagnosed with LQTS should avoid triggers of arrhythmias (exercise, emotional stress, loud noises) as well as drugs that prolong the QTc interval. Patients should receive ß-blockers.... Several studies support the role of ICDs in preventing or reducing SCD in high-risk patients with LQTS. However, most patients do not belong to this subgroup and remain at a relatively low risk of cardiac events; these patients may be appropriately protected from arrhythmic events by a combination of noninvasive and simple measures."
See: Ellenbogen, chapter on Channelopathies

42. All the following cardiac medications may lengthen the QTc and increase the risk of Torsade de Pointes EXCEPT:
   a. Procainamide
   b. Disopyramide
   c. Amiodarone
   d. Dofetilide
   e. Quinidine
   f. Ibutilide
   g. Esmolol
   h. Sotalol

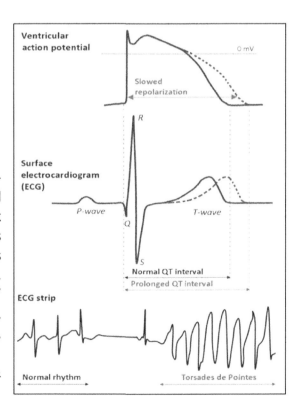

ANSWER: g. Esmolol is a class II drug (beta-blocker.) Note that the offending drugs all lengthen the action potential which is a key risk for Torsade de Pointes. They are either in class IA (the -amide drugs, Sodium blockers) or class III (Amio & -ide drugs, potassium blockers). Mnemonic is "Long Qt Dogs should be SPAID" for (Q, D, SPAID) = Quinidine, Dofetilide, Sotalol, Procainamide, Amiodarone, Ibutilide, Disopyramide.
See: Opie chapter on Antiarrhythmic Drugs & Strategies

43. Patients with Long QT Syndrome should avoid taking what two classes of drugs?
   (Select two best answers)
   a. Class 1a drugs
   b. Class 1b drugs
   c. Class 1c drugs
   d. Class II drugs
   e. Class III drugs
   f. Class IV drugs

ANSWER: a. Class 1a drugs and e. Class III drugs. Long QT and Torsade de pointes can be drug induced. Both 1a (Quinidine, Procainamide) and class III (dofetilide, ibutilide, sotalol, amiodarone) drugs prolong the QT interval and lengthen repolarization. Because their long QT interval is already too long, drugs that prolong it further exacerbate the problem. Several Antipsychotic medications are also implicated in LQT and torsade de pointes.

Ellenbogen says, "Current guidelines suggest that all patients diagnosed with LQTS should avoid triggers of arrhythmias (exercise, emotional stress, loud noises) as well as drugs that prolong the QTc interval. Patients should receive ß-blockers...." See: Ellenbogen, chapter on Channelopathies

Zipes says, "QT prolongation has attracted considerable attention in recent years due to their association with life-threatening cardiac arrhythmias, such as torsade de pointes. Antiarrhythmic drugs with class III action, which prolong cardiac repolarization by blocking potassium channels, were among the first to be linked to this arrhythmogenic syndrome. The incidence of torsade de pointes in patients who receive quinidine is estimated to range between 2.0% and 8.8%. Therapy with dl-sotalol has been associated with an incidence ranging from 1.8% to 4.8%. A similar incidence has been described for newer class III agents, such as dofetilide and ibutilide." See: Zipes chapter on Drug-induced Channelopathies

44. You should most closely monitor the QTc in patients taking:
   a. Quinidine & Procainamide
   b. Flecainide & Propafenone
   c. Lovastatin & Simvastatin
   d. Diltiazem & Verapamil

ANSWER: a. Quinidine, Procainamide, and other Class Ia drugs. Class III drugs like Amiodarone (less likely with Sotalol) increase the refractory period; therefore, may lengthen the QTc on the surface ECG.

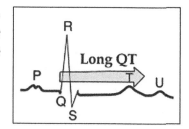

45. After successful defibrillation of an unstable patient with torsade de pointes what drug is indicated?
- a. Procainamide
- b. Beta blocker
- c. Amiodarone
- d. Magnesium

ANSWER: d. Magnesium 1-2 gm IV. Ecgguru.com says, "Clinically — it "does" and it "does not" make a difference if the rhythm is truly torsades [with long QT on baseline ECG or another Polymorphic VT]. I say this because practically speaking — initial management is the same. IF the patient is unstable — SHOCK! You can't synchronize polymorphic VT [PMVT] (or torsades) — so this is unsynchronized shock that is needed. IF the patient goes in-and-out of the irregular wide complex tachycardia rhythm, Magnesium Sulfate is indicated regardless of whether the rhythm is PMVT or torsades. One starts with 1-2 gm IV Mg^{++} and repeats this up to doses of 4-8 gm IV every few minutes as needed. IV Mg^{++} infusion may be needed to prevent recurrence. Adverse effects from IV Mg^{++} are minimal and many patients will respond to this medication regardless of whether serum Mg^{++} levels are normal or low."

Stimulants & Vasoactive Drugs:

1. All the following are cardiac active sympathomimetic catecholamines EXCEPT:
- a. Norepinephrine
- b. Isoproterenol
- c. Dobutamine
- d. Epinephrine
- e. Dopamine
- f. Histamine

ANSWER: f. Histamine is released during an allergic reaction in tissue. We give antihistamines to reduce the swelling and permeability caused when histamines are released during allergic reactions. E.g., Benadryl is an antihistamine. Catecholamines are produced in the adrenal medulla and circulated in the blood (hormones) or generated at the nerve endings of the sympathetic nerves. Catecholamines are often called "adrenergic" after adrenalin or "sympathomimetic" because they mimic the sympathetic nervous system. They are responsible for the "fight or flight" response. In therapeutic doses they all increase the BP (pressors) and contractility (inotropes) of the heart. Note the mnemonic "DINED" for the main five catecholamines.

2. All the following are contraindications and pathologies where caution is indicated when giving patients beta-blockers EXCEPT: (which is indicated)

    a. **Block (heart block & bradycardia)**
    b. **Post MI ventricular arrhythmias**
    c. **Diabetes mellitus**
    d. **Extremities (PVD)**
    e. **Asthma**
    f. **COPD**

ANSWER: b. Post MI ventricular arrhythmias is an indication for beta-blockers not a contraindication. Opie says, "In postinfarction patients, beta-blockers outperformed other antiarrhythmics and decreased arrhythmic cardiac deaths.... At present, beta-blockers are the closest to an ideal class of antiarrhythmic agents for general use because of their broad spectrum of activity and established safety record.... beta-blockade may precipitate diabetes.... Cardiac absolute contraindications to beta-blockade include severe bradycardia, preexisting high-degree heart block, sick sinus syndrome, and overt left ventricular failure unless already conventionally treated and stable. Pulmonary contraindications are overt asthma or severe bronchospasm, ... Active peripheral vascular disease with rest ischemia is another contraindication." Beta-blockers mnemonic for main contraindications & cautions is: ABCDE.

See: Opie, chapter on beta-blocking agents.

3. All the following medications are inotropic agents used in the treatment of heart failure EXCEPT:

    a. **Digitalis (Lanoxin, Digoxin...)**
    b. **Dobutamine (Dobutrex)**
    c. **Milrinone (Primacor)**
    d. **Verapamil (Isoptin)**

ANSWER: d. Verapamil (Isoptin) has a negative inotropic effect - to decrease the force of contraction. It would NOT be used in heart failure because it would decrease cardiac contractility even further. Calcium channel blockers like Verapamil, Nifedipine, and Diltiazem block the excitation contraction coupling of smooth muscle. They depress the heart's function and relax it. Calcium channel blockers like verapamil cause vasodilation and are used to treat high blood pressure.

The other positive inotropic agents listed (Digitalis, Dobutamine, Milrinone) are used in the treatment of heart failure because they enhance myocardial contractility. An entirely new and higher Starling curve is created as shown. This will increase cardiac performance and cardiac output. But, by increasing myocardial oxygen consumption this may also exacerbate existing ischemia.

Milrinone is an "ino-dilator" because it not only increases contraction (inotropic), but it also increases vasodilation thereby reducing both preload and afterload. It is a short-term IV medication for CHF. See: Underhill, chapter on "Pharmacologic Management."

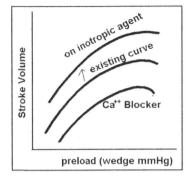

4. The use of diuretics in the treatment of congestive heart failure are intended to:
  a. **Decrease contractility**
  b. **Increase afterload**
  c. **Decrease preload**
  d. **Increase CO**

ANSWER: c. Decrease preload. Diuretics make you "diuresis" or "pee." Eliminating water from the system reduces the elevated blood volume and brings less blood back into the veins. This is reflected in lower venous pressures and lower preload. Diuretics can help with the "edema" problem, but by reducing preload they may make the heartbeat weaker.
Diuretics are often given with Digitalis to strengthen the weakened contractility. See: Braunwald, chapter on "Pathology of Heart Failure."

5. Epinephrine has all the following properties EXCEPT:
  a. **Vasoconstrictor**
  b. **Bronchodilator**
  c. **Chronotropic**
  d. **Vagolytic**

ANSWER: d. Vagolytic. Epinephrine does NOT stimulate the vagal or parasympathetic nerves. It does the opposite; it stimulates the sympathetic (fight or flight) nerves. Epinephrine (also known as adrenaline) is a hormone and a neurotransmitter. Epinephrine has many functions in the body, regulating heart rate, blood vessel and air passage diameters, and metabolic shifts; epinephrine release is a crucial component of the fight-or-flight response of the sympathetic nervous system. It is one of the catecholamines.

6. Isoproterenol is a catecholamine whose main cardiac effect is as a_____ used to increase the heart's _____.
  a. **Alpha agonist, chronotropic effect**
  b. **Beta agonist, chronotropic effect**
  c. **Beta antagonist, irritability**
  d. **Alpha blocker, irritability**

ANSWER: b. Beta agonist, chronotropic effect increases heart rate. Remember, an antagonist is someone who fights against you, just as an antagonistic drug block or neutralizes another.

So, an agonist is the opposite, a chemical that activates another. Another related term is "chronotropic" where the "Chrono" prefix means time or speed. Because it speeds the heart and shortens the refractory periods it also may induce arrhythmias, which is the effect we usually want in the EP lab.

Opie says, "Isoproterenol (Isuprel): This pure beta-stimulant (B1>B2) .... Its cardiovascular effects closely resemble those of exercise including a positive and vasodilatory effect." Without Isuprel's vasodilatory effect the BP would elevate due to the increase in CO. Remember on exercise the HR increases, but the BP does not, because of the vasodilation. "Inotropic" refers to increased cardiac contractility. See: Opie chapter on Antiarrhythmic Drugs & Strategies.

ACLS manual says, "Isoproterenol hydrochloride is a pure beta-adrenergic agonist with potent inotropic and chronotropic effects. It increases myocardial oxygen consumption, cardiac output, and myocardial work and can exacerbate ischemia and arrhythmias in patients with ischemic heart disease, CHF, or impaired ventricular function. ... Isoproterenol is not indicated in patients with cardiac arrest or hypotension." Isuprel is also used to vasodilate the bronchial tree in asthma (Beta2 effect) or broncho-constriction. Remember beta1 effects are on the heart (1 heart) beta2 effects are on the lungs (2 lungs). See, AHA, Guidelines for CPR & ECC The effect of a dopamine drip varies significantly with the rate of administration.

7. Match the effect of the dopamine IV dosage in the box to its expected effect.
   a. **Dilate renal & mesenteric vessels**
   b. **Peripheral vasoconstrictor**
   c. **Increase CO (beta-1 effect)**

   1. **Low dose (1-2 µg/kg/min)**
   2. **Moderate dose (2-10 µg/kg/min)**
   3. **High dose (>10 µg/kg/min)**

CORRECTLY MATCHED ANSWERS ARE:
Dopamine IV:
   1. Low dose (1 - 2 µg/kg/min): a. Dilates renal and mesenteric vessels
   2. Moderate dose (2 - 10 µg/kg/min): c. Increases CO (beta-1 effect) with only moderate increase in peripheral resistance.
   3. High dose (> 10 µg/kg/min): b. Peripheral vasoconstrictor with significant increase in BP like norepinephrine

See: ACLS manual

8. How fast should dopamine be administered to produce 5 µg/kg/min from a concentration of 1600 µg/ml on a patient weighing 220 lb. (100 kg)?
   a. **0.31 ml/min**
   b. **0.8 ml/min**
   c. **1.75 ml/min**
   d. **8.0 ml/min**

ANSWER: a. 0.31 ml/min. First, you must determine the dose based on the patient's weight.

Dose rate = [5 µg/kg/min] x 100 kg =500 µg/min (note how the kg units cancel out)
Then, Use the given formula: Amt./min = Conc. x Vol/min
Vol/min = [Amt./min]/ [Conc.] = [500 µg/min] / [1600 µg/ml]   = 0.31 ml/min Note how the
µg cancels out. This ml/min would then have to be changed into micro drops/min from the
IV used or set on the infusion pump. Know these formulas: Amt./min = Conc. x Vol/min.
See: ACLS Manual

9. Vasopressin has several advantages over Epinephrine in VF/pulseless VT.
   Select three advantages of vasopressin.
   a. **Increased alpha and beta stimulation**
   b. **Reduced cardiac ischemia and irritability**
   c. **More effective in Asystole and PEA**
   d. **One-time dose simplifies administration**
   e. **Reduced propensity for VF**
   f. **Shorter half-life**

ANSWER: b, d, & e. Reduced cardiac ischemia and irritability (Epi. should be given cautiously
in MI because its beta effects make the heartbeat faster and harder, whipping the heart,
which may lead to ischemia and irritability). One-time dose simplifies administration (Yes, you
can only give it once, whereas epinephrine must be given every 3-5 minutes)
Reduced propensity for VF (High catecholamine state may make the heart return to VF)

The ACLS manual says: "Vasopressin produces the same positive effects as epinephrine in
terms of vasoconstriction and increasing the blood flow to the brain and heart during CPR.
Moreover, vasopressin does not have the negative, adverse effects of epinephrine on the
heart, such as increased ischemia and irritability and paradoxically, the propensity for VF....
Give vasopressin as a single, 1-time dose (40 u IV) a regimen based on the much longer half-
life of vasopressin (10 to 20 minutes) compared with epinephrine (3 to 5 minutes)....higher
epinephrine doses may contribute to return of spontaneous circulation, but they have also
been associated with greater post resuscitation myocardial dysfunction, and they may create
a "toxic hyperadrenergic state." Many hospitals give vasopressin first and then start epi. and
antiarrhythmics after 10 minutes when the vasopressin wears off. See: AHA, ACLS Provider
Manual, chapter on "VF/Pulseless VT"

10. How should vasopressin be administered?
   a. **80 Units IV, followed by 40 U every 3-5 minutes**
   b. **40 Units IV push, 1-time dose**
   c. **1.0 - 1.5 Mg/Kg/min**
   d. **3.0 Mg/Kg IV push**

ANSWER: b. 40 Units IV push, 1-time dose. It may only be given by IV push. Flush in with 20
mL saline. After its half-life has elapsed (10 minutes) you may start epinephrine and
antiarrhythmics. See: AHA, ACLS Provider Manual, chapter on "VF/Pulseless VT"

11. In the EP lab you are treating a patient in persistent VF arrest. After several attempted defibrillations, you consider using vasopressin. Which of the following guidelines for use of vasopressin is true?
   a. Give vasopressin 40 U every 3 to 5 minutes
   b. Give vasopressin for better vasoconstriction and adrenergic stimulation than provided by epinephrine
   c. Give vasopressin as an alternative to epinephrine in shock-refractory VF
   d. Give vasopressin as the first-line pressor agent for clinical shock caused by hypovolemia

ANSWER: c. Give vasopressin as an alternative to epinephrine in shock-refractory VF. It is a vasoconstrictor and pressor agent with a longer half-life than epinephrine which simplifies the cardiac arrest algorithm because it is only given once. Many ACLS providers prefer it as the first drug after 3-stacked shocks in VF/Pulseless VT cardiac arrest. It has the same effect as epi. with fewer side effects. It may be given before epinephrine. Then, when it wears off in 10 minutes start with epinephrine. Vasopressin is given as a 40 U given IV push in a single dose, not repeated. Hypovolemia is best treated with fluid administration. See: AHA, ACLS Provider Manual, chapter on "VF/Pulseless VT"

12. The ACLS guidelines recommend vasopressin as a first line ACLS medication. Which algorithm does NOT recommend vasopressin?
   a. VF/pulseless VT
   b. Bradycardia
   c. Asystole
   d. PEA

ANSWER: b. Bradycardia. It is an alternative therapy to epinephrine in the VF/pulseless VT, Asystole, and PEA algorithms, but not bradycardia. Vasopressin produces the vasoconstrictive effects of epinephrine but without cardiac toxicity. It is indicated in each of the other algorithms as a replacement for either the 1st or 2nd dose of epinephrine at a dosage of 40 units. Additional catecholamine needs are continued with Epi. There is no scientific based evidence that states Vasopressin is more effective than Epinephrine, or vice versa. Vasopressin, a peripheral vasoconstrictor is not recommended in the treatment of bradycardia. See: AHA, ACLS Provider Manual, chapter on "VF / Pulseless VT"

13. Examples of a pressor agents are:
   a. Ticlopidine (Ticlid) & Clopidogrel (Plavix)
   b. Cardizem (Diltiazem) & Verapamil (Isoptin)
   c. Lopressor (Metoprolol) & Propranolol (Inderal)
   d. Dopamine (Intropin) & Aramine (Metaraminol)

ANSWER: d. Dopamine (Intropin) & Aramine (Metaraminol). These are vasoconstrictors that "press" the arterioles and increase peripheral resistance. Dopamine is a vasopressor at high dosages. It stimulates dopaminergic receptors, which increase arteriolar resistance and BP.

Aramine is an adrenergic alpha stimulant that also increases BP. See: Kandarpa or Watson, Chapter on "Commonly Used Medications"

14. How much of this Nitroglycerine bottle (50 mg/10 ml) should go into a 500 ml IV bag to mix an IV with a concentration of 100 mcg/ml of nitroglycerin?
   a. **5 ml (half the bottle)**
   b. **10 ml (entire bottle)**
   c. **20 ml (2 bottles)**
   d. **50 ml (5 bottles)**

ANSWER: b. 10 ml (entire bottle).
   - Amt = Conc x Vol.
   - Amt = (100 mcg/ml) x (500 ml) = 50,000 mcg
   - Now convert the micrograms to milligrams
   - 50,000 mcg x (1 mg/1000 mcg) = 50 mg

As you can see from the bottle it contains exactly 50 mg.
See: Craig, Clinical Calculations Made Easy, Chapter on "Solving Problems Using Dimensional Analysis"

15. Your pharmacy dispenses premixed nitroglycerin in a solution of 50 mg of NTG in 250 ml ofD5W. The cardiologist in the lab orders a drip to be started at a rate of 33 mcg/min. What rate do you set for the infusion?
   a. **5 ml/hr**
   b. **10 ml/hr**
   c. **33 ml/hr**
   d. **50 ml/hr**
   e. **100ml/hr**

ANSWER: b. 10 ml/hr. There are several unit conversions and one formula needed. You need to know there are 1000 mcg in one mg and the formula Amount = Concentration x Volume. Start with the unit conversion: 50 mg = 50,000 mcg. This is put in 250 ml for a dilution of 50,000 mcg/250 ml = 200 mcg/ml. One can see intuitively that 33 mcg is 1/6 of a ml of this solution (or 0.166 ml). To do this mathematically use Amount = Concentration x Volume: 33 mcg/min = X (200 mcg/ml): solve for X= (33 mcg/min) / (200 mcg/ml) = 0.166 ml/min. Then convert this to hours with 60 min/hr.: (0.166 ml/min) (60 min/hr.) = 10 ml/hr.
When the units cancel out correctly you know you have done it correctly.

1/Concentration		dose rate	Desired units			
250 ml	1 mg	33 mcg 's	60 min	= 250 x 33 x 60	=495000	=9.9 ml
50 mg	1000 mcg's	1 min	1 hr.	= 50 x 1000 x1 x1	=50000	

See: Craig, Clinical Calculations Made Easy, Chapter on "Solving Problems Using Dimensional Analysis"

16. The general action of most cardiac nitrate-based medications (nitro-) is to:
   a. Vasoconstrict
   b. Increase HR
   c. Increase BP
   d. Vasodilate

ANSWER: d. Vasodilate. The Nitrate drugs vasodilate smooth muscle, especially in the blood vessels. Nitroglycerine and nitroprusside dilate both arterioles and venous smooth muscle. The two chief effects are to:
   • pool blood in the veins which reduces preload
   • dilation of spastic arteries and arterioles tends to reduce the afterload and drop BP. Nitrates may be so potent a vasodilator as to cause hypotension and headaches. See: Pharm text

17. The chief hemodynamic side effect of IV nitroglycerine is:
   a. Hypercholesterolemia
   b. Hypotension
   c. Tachycardia
   d. Tachypnea

ANSWER: b. Hypotension. The ACLS manual states, "Hypotension sufficient to produce hypoperfusion is the most serious side effect of nitroglycerine . . .. Blood pressure may fall, resulting in nausea, giddiness, faintness, or syncope. . .. " However, headache is the most common side effect.
See: Braunwald, chapter on "Electrocardiography"

Other Medications:

1. ACE inhibitors reduce the production of:
   a. Angiotensin II
   b. Acetylcholine
   c. Adrenalin
   d. Renin

ANSWER: a. Angiotensin II. Angiotensin converting enzyme (ACE) converts angiotensin I into angiotensin II which is a potent vasoconstrictor. The ACE inhibitors reduce this conversion and thus reduce vasoconstriction and hypertension. See: Opie, Drugs for the Heart, "Chapter on ACE inhibitors"

2. A class of drug specifically used to interrupt the "Renin-Angiotensin Aldosterone" system in CHF is:
   a. Ca channel blockers
   b. ACE inhibitors
   c. Beta blockers
   d. Digitalis

ANSWER: b. ACE-inhibitor is an Angiotensin Converting Enzyme inhibitor. It is used extensively in CHF to prevent ventricular remodeling.
BETA BLOCKERS (E.g., Inderal) block the beta-adrenergic receptors.
CA CHANNEL BLOCKERS (E.g., Nifedipine) block the Ca+ fast channels. Slow HR
and vasodilate smooth muscle.
YES: **ACE INHIBITORS** (E.g., Captopril) blocks conversion of Angiotensin I to Angiotensin II. These reduce Renin, Angiotensin II, and Aldosterone blood levels and thus the Na+ retention and vasoconstriction problems.
DIGITALIS, cardiotonic or inotropic drug.
See: Braunwald, chapter on "The Management of Heart Failure."

3. In the acutely dyspneic anaphylactic shock patient what two medical therapies are indicated? (Select two)
   a. IV Fluid administration (200-500 ml IV)
   b. IV Epinephrine (0.5 mg IV)
   c. IV Lidocaine (100 mg IV)
   d. Atropine (.5 mg. IV)

ANSWER: a, b. IV Fluid administration and Epinephrine: IV Fluid administration (200-500 ml. IV). This will replace the fluid lost due to the altered capillary permeability.
IV Epinephrine (.5 mg. IV)
   • NO: IV Lidocaine (100 mg. IV) Although the patient has some PVCs, this is not a life-threatening problem. Anaphylactic shock is.
   • NO: Atropine (.5 mg. IV) This would further speed up the heart rate. The increased HR is an IV infusion & Epinephrine necessary compensation for the low CO
   • In the early stages "Anaphylactic shock" is reversible with administration of large volumes of fluid and/or immediate administration of epinephrine 0.5 - 1.0 mg. IV
See: Braunwald, chapter on "Acute Circulatory Failure (Shock)."

4. For EP lab personnel the priority toward a patient who develops signs of any acute shock is to:
   a. Give chest compressions when BP can no longer be measured
   b. Prepare to administer Epinephrine IV
   c. Administer O2 by nasal cannula
   d. Prepare the defibrillator

ANSWER: c. Administer O2 by nasal cannula. Priorities in shock therapy use the acronym: VIP. V = Ventilation, all shock patients need O2.

V.I.P - Rx - in Shock

- V: Severe hypoxemia patients may need intubation and ventilator support. But first give them O2.
- I: Infusion. All shock patients need an IV line for fluid and drug infusion. All shock patients (except severe Cardiogenic) need volume infusion

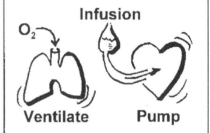

- P: Pump. After ventilation and infusion are taken care of then proceed to improve pump performance and BP. The auscultatory BP may not be measurable in low flow shock states.

Like the ABCs of CPR, get the Airway and ventilation taken care of before proceeding.

Administer fluid, elevate legs, and then treat the MI with inotropic agents. See: Braunwald, chapter on "Acute Circulatory Failure (Shock)."

5. Match each therapy to the allergic reaction it best treats:
   a. **CPR as needed**
   b. **Valium**
   c. **Benadryl, Prednisone, Decadron**
   d. **Epinephrine, Volume Infusion (CPR as needed)**
   e. **Phenergan**

   1. **Rash, nausea, urticaria**
   2. **Dyspnea, wheezing, syncope**
   3. **Seizure, hypotension, bradycardia, dyspnea**
   4. **Seizure, vital signs OK**
   5. **Nausea & vomiting**

CORRECTLY MATCHED ANSWERS ARE:
1. Rash, Urticaria: Benadryl, Prednisone, Decadron
2. Dyspnea, Wheezing, Syncope: Epinephrine, Volume Infusion
3. Seizure, Hypotension, Bradycardia, Dyspnea: CPR as needed
4. Seizure, Vital Signs Ok: Valium
5. Nausea and Vomiting: Phenergan
See: Kern, chapter on "Introduction to cath lab."

6. The initial recommended therapy for bradycardia with hypotension is:
   a. **Dopamine 5-10 mcg/kg/min**
   b. **Transcutaneous pacing**
   c. **Cardioversion 50-100 J**
   d. **Atropine 0.5-1.0 mg**

ANSWER: d. Atropine 0.5-1.0 mg. ACLS says, "If bradycardia produces signs and symptoms of instability, the initial treatment is atropine. If bradycardia is unresponsive to atropine, intravenous (IV) infusion of ß-adrenergic agonists with rate-accelerating effects (dopamine, epinephrine) or transcutaneous pacing (TCP) can be effective while the patient is prepared for emergent transvenous temporary pacing if required." See: ACLS manual

7. Which medication reduces retained water in CHF patients?
   a. **Digitalis (Digoxin)**
   b. **Furosemide (Lasix)**
   c. **Hydralazine (Apresoline)**
   d. **Hydrocortisone (Cortisol)**

ANSWER: b. Furosemide (Lasix) is a loop diuretic used in the treatment of congestive heart failure and edema. All diuretics increase urination and thus provide a means of forced diuresis to eliminate retained water from the body.

8. CHF patients take digoxin (digitalis) or other cardiotonic medication to:
   a. **Slow the heart rate and increase the force of contraction**
   b. **Speed the heart rate and reduce the force of contraction**
   c. **Block the beta-adrenergic system**
   d. **Block the alpha-adrenergic system**
   e. **Block the parasympathetic system**

ANSWER: a. Slow the heart rate and increase the force of contraction. Dig is an inotropic drug that gives the failing LV more contractility. Positive inotropic effect defines this state of "hyped up" chemical contractility. Cardiotonic and catecholamine drugs induce this positive inotropic state. See: Braunwald, chapter on "The Management of Heart Failure"

9. What therapy is indicated for an anaphylactic shock patient who is acutely short of breath?
   a. **IV Fluid administration and Epinephrine**
   b. **IV Fluid administration and Lidocaine**
   c. **IV Dopamine and Epinephrine**
   d. **IV Dopamine and Lidocaine**

ANSWER: a. IV Fluid administration and Epinephrine. In the early stages "Anaphylactic shock" is reversible with administration of large volumes of fluid (200-500 ml. IV) and/or immediate administration of epinephrine .5 mg. IV (or 1.0 mg intratracheal). This fluid will replace the fluid lost due to the altered capillary permeability. IV Epinephrine (.5 mg. -1.0 mg. IV) increases broncho-dilation, peripheral vasoconstriction, blood pressure, and coronary and cerebral perfusion. See: Braunwald, chapter on "Acute Circulatory Failure (Shock)"

10. An exaggerated allergic reaction which may lead to shock is termed:
   a. **Adams-stokes**
   b. **Baroreceptor**
   c. **Anaphylactic**
   d. **Vasovagal**

ANSWER: c. Anaphylactic or anaphylaxis is a manifestation of immediate hypersensitivity resulting in life-threatening respiratory distress, usually followed by vascular collapse, and shock and accompanied by hives, itching, and wheals. Also called "immediate type I hypersensitivity." See: Medical Dictionary

11. Which of the following classes of drugs helps relieve the symptoms of allergy?
   a. Catecholamine
   b. Antihistamine
   c. Barbiturates
   d. Antiemetic

ANSWER: b. Antihistamine drugs block histamine. They prevent increased capillary permeability leading to edema, itching, and smooth muscle contraction, which may lead to bronchospasm. Benadryl is the most common antihistamine. It causes drowsiness and prevents minor allergic reactions. For these reasons it is often used as a premedication for cardiac catheterization, especially in patients predisposed to asthma or allergic reactions. See: Loebl, "Thrombolytic drugs"

12. The use of furosemide in the treatment of severe heart failure is intended to:
   a. Increase contractility
   b. Increase afterload
   c. Decrease preload
   d. Increase CO

ANSWER: c. Decrease preload. Braunwald says: "Furosemide is frequently the diuretic of choice for severe heart failure for three reasons: First it induces a more acute sodium loss than other diuretics; second, it is effective in promoting diuresis even in the presence of a low glomerular filtration rate (GFR); and third, furosemide promotes venodilation and preload reduction." See: Braunwald, chapter on "Pathology of Heart Failure"

13. Administration of furosemide (Lasix) may lead to all the following EXCEPT:
   a. Hypokalemia and subsequent dysrhythmias
   b. Increased preload
   c. Dehydration
   d. Diuresis

ANSWER: b. Increased preload - NO. Its hemodynamic effect is direct venodilation which lowers the preload. Furosemide is a potent fast acting diuretic. Excessive diuresis (urination) may lead to dehydration and reduce the cardiac filling pressures. In patients with CHF this reduces pulmonary congestion, venous pooling, and tissue edema. However, long term use of many diuretics causes excessive potassium excretion and electrolyte imbalance with possible subsequent dysrhythmias. That is why many CHF patients on diuretics must take potassium replacements or are told to eat lots of bananas. As a diuretic, it prevents reabsorption of sodium by the kidney. See: AHA, ACLS Guidelines Chpt. on "Pharmacology II"

14. One common side effect seen in patients who receive diuretic therapy for CHF is:
   a. **Renal failure and pitting edema**
   b. **Difficulty in breathing and cyanosis**
   c. **Hypokalemia and hyponatremia**
   d. **Hyperkalemia and hypernatremia**

ANSWER: c. Hypokalemia and hyponatremia. The prefix "hypo-" indicates reduced. Kalemia indicates potassium in the blood. Remember the chemical symbol for potassium is "K." Normal serum potassium is 3.5-4.5 mEq/L. Naturemia refers to sodium in the blood.
The chemical symbol for sodium is Na. Excessive diuresis (urination) and long-term use of diuretics may lead to excessive potassium excretion and electrolyte imbalance with possible subsequent dysrhythmias. That is why many CHF patients on diuretics must take potassium replacements or are told to eat lots of bananas. See: AHA, ACLS Guidelines Chapter on "Pharmacology II" hyperkalemia, potassium

15. Thiazide diuretics are used in hypertensive patients to:
   a. **Increase circulating blood volume**
   b. **Constrict coronary blood vessels**
   c. **Dilate coronary blood vessels**
   d. **Increase urine production**

ANSWER: d. Increase urine production. Diuretics make you "diurese" or "pee." Diuretics "dry out" patients. Eliminating water from the system reduces blood volume and according to Frank Starling Law reduces the force of cardiac contraction and BP.

Opie says: "In hypertension, to exert an effect, the diuretic must provide enough natriuresis to shrink fluid volume.... Some persistent volume depletion is required to lower the blood pressure. Therefore, once-daily furosemide is usually inadequate because the initial sodium loss is quickly reconstituted throughout the remainder of the day. Thus, a longer acting thiazide-type diuretic is usually chosen for hypertension."
See: Opie, chapter on "Diuretics"

16. Which medication reduces retained water in CHF patients?
   a. **Digitalis (Digoxin)**
   b. **Furosemide (Lasix)**
   c. **Hydralazine (Apresoline)**
   d. **Hydrocortisone (Cortisol)**

ANSWER: b. Furosemide (Lasix) is a loop diuretic used in the treatment of congestive heart failure and edema. All diuretics increase urination and thus provide a means of forced diuresis to eliminate retained water from the body.

17. CHF patients may take digoxin (digitalis) or other cardiotonic medication to:
   a. Slow the heart rate and increase the force of contraction
   b. Speed the heart rate and reduce the force of contraction
   c. Block the beta-adrenergic system
   d. Block the alpha-adrenergic system
   e. Block the parasympathetic system

ANSWER: a. Slow the heart rate and increase the force of contraction. Dig is an inotropic drug that gives the failing LV more contractility. Positive inotropic effect defines this state of "hyped up" chemical contractility. Cardiotonic and catecholamine drugs induce this positive inotropic state. See: Braunwald, chapter on "The Management of Heart Failure"

18. Patients with pacemaker or orthopedic problems may not be able to exercise on a treadmill. All the following medications may be used to simulate exercise in stress testing EXCEPT:

   a. Dopamine infusion
   b. Adenosine infusion
   c. Dobutamine infusion
   d. Dipyridamole infusion

ANSWER: a. Dopamine infusion is not used for stress. After treadmillTalk.com testing. It is primarily a vasoconstrictor, whereas the others are all vasodilators.
Braunwald says: "Dobutamine increases myocardial oxygen demand by increasing myocardial contractility, heart rate, and blood pressure. The increase in coronary flow is comparable to that during physical exercise (twofold to threefold) but less than that with adenosine or dipyridamole. Dobutamine pharmacological stress should be considered a last resort in patients who cannot exercise rather than a substitute for exercise."
See: Braunwald: chapter on "Nuclear Cardiology"

19. Which electrolyte imbalance exacerbates digitalis (Digoxin) toxicity?
   a. Hypokalemia
   b. Hyperkalemia
   c. Hypocalcemia
   d. Metabolic alkalosis

ANSWER: a. Hypokalemia is associated with the diuretics commonly given with digitalis resulting in lower potassium levels that makes dig. toxicity more likely. Opie says, "Diuretics may induce hypokalemia which sensitizes the heart to digoxin toxicity and shuts off the tubular secretion of digoxin when the plasma potassium falls below 2 to 3 mEq/L."   Digitalis which contains cardiac glycosides (sugars) is extracted from the foxglove plant.

Digoxin increases intracellular calcium which gives a positive inotropic (contractility) effect. For this reason, it is used to increase contractility in CHF patients. Digoxin also has a vagal effect on the parasympathetic nervous system, and as such may be used to slow the ventricular rate during atrial fibrillation. Tip: when you see 2 opposite answers (hyper & hypokalemia) one of them is likely to be correct. See: Opie, chapter on "Digitalis..."

20. Your elderly patient comes to the ER with a narrow complex tachycardia with occasional nonconducted beats (2nd degree block). Simple vagal maneuvers fail to convert the rhythm. He also complains of nausea, headache and seeing weird lights and colors. HR is 124. BP is 102/60. He is taking digitalis and diuretics for mild heart failure. All the following are appropriate EXCEPT:
   a. **Draw blood to measure Digitalis and electrolyte levels**
   b. **Administer IV phenytoin or lidocaine**
   c. **Give anesthesia and cardiovert**
   d. **Administer adenosine**

ANSWER: c. Give anesthesia and cardiovert - only as a last resort. Braunwald says, "Digitalis toxicity produces various symptoms and signs, including headache, nausea, and vomiting, altered color perception, halo vision and generalized malaise. More serious than these are digitalis-related arrhythmias, which include bradycardias...and tachyarrhythmias.... The diagnosis can be confirmed by determining the serum digoxin level.... Phenytoin can be used for control of atrial tachyarrhythmias, whereas lidocaine can be successful in treating infranodal tachycardias.... Electrical direct-current cardioversion should be performed only, when necessary, in the digitalis-toxic patient because life-threatening VT or VF can result, which can be very difficult to control." See: Braunwald chapter on "Therapy for Cardiac Arrhythmias"

21. This medication has a profound but fleeting depressive effect on the SA and AV nodes.
   a. **Amiodarone**
   b. **Adenosine**
   c. **Quinidine**
   d. **Sotalol**

ANSWER: b. Adenosine. Intravenous adenosine may be used to convert paroxysmal supraventricular tachycardia (PSVT) to sinus rhythm if the tachycardia is dependent on AV nodal conduction. Adenosine does not convert atrial flutter, atrial fibrillation, or ventricular tachycardia. However, in the presence of atrial flutter or atrial fibrillation, a transient AV block will be observed. This will assist in the diagnosis of the underlying rhythm. The first dose of adenosine is typically 6 mg administered rapidly over 1-3 seconds followed by a 20 ml normal saline bolus. If AV nodal block is not observed, a 12 mg dose may be given in a similar fashion. For more information, see: Understanding EP: A Comprehensive Approach chapter on Antiarrhythmic Medications

22. This medication may be used when attempting to induce atrial fibrillation.
  a. Procainamide
  b. Adenosine
  c. Digitalis
  d. Corvert

ANSWER: b. Adenosine. Adenosine may also be used to induce atrial fibrillation due to the shortening of the atrial action potential duration and atrial refractoriness. This is particularly worth noting in a patient with a history of WPW. Blocking the AV node in a WPW patient may allow for more impulses to travel rapidly to the ventricle via the antegrade conducting pathway. If atrial fibrillation were induced, this could be problematic.

Adenosine may be helpful in the diagnosis of accessory pathways. Once the AV nodal block is observed, ventricular pacing is performed. This may reveal conduction from the ventricle to the atrium over an accessory pathway. The reverse is also true in diagnosing antegrade conducting pathways.
For more information, see: Understanding EP: A Comprehensive Guide chapter on AVRT.

23. This medication should not be given to patients with a history of congestive heart failure.
  a. ACE Inhibitors
  b. Metoprolol
  c. Flecainide
  d. Digoxin

ANSWER: c. Flecainide. Flecainide has a pronounced negative inotropic effect. It should not be given to patients with a history of heart failure of significantly depressed LV ejection fraction.

The inotropic effect is most used in reference to various drugs that affect the strength of contraction of the heart muscle (myocardial contractility). A negative inotropic effect is a weakening in the force of muscle contraction. A depressed LV ejection fraction is when a lower percentage of blood is pumped out of the left ventricle with each contraction. See: Fogoros: Antiarrhythmic Drugs – chapter on Class I antiarrhythmic drugs.

24. This medication is used to reverse severe digoxin toxicity.
  a. Magnesium Sulfate
  b. Diltiazem
  c. Digibind
  d. Tikosyn

ANSWER: c. Digibind. EP Essentials says, "To reverse severe digoxin toxicity, digoxin-specific Fab antibodies (Digibind) should be utilized. Digibind will bond to digoxin in the extracellular spaces, creating a concentration difference that extracts digoxin from the intracellular space.

The bound digoxin is then renally eliminated; therefore, it should not be utilized in a patient with kidney failure."

See: EP Essentials – Understanding EP: A Comprehensive Guide – chapter on antiarrhythmics.

25. This medication is often used in the EP lab to convert atrial fibrillation to sinus rhythm.
   a. **Isoproterenol**
   b. **Amiodarone**
   c. **Adenosine**
   d. **Ibutilide**

ANSWER: d. Ibutilide. Ibutilide is a Class III antiarrhythmic medication. Fogoros says, "Ibutilide is indicated for the elective conversion of atrial fibrillation or atrial flutter. It should be thought of as an alternative to elective direct-current (DC) cardioversion. In clinical studies, the efficacy of ibutilide administration in terminating these arrhythmias (after two 1 mg doses) was 44%."
See: Fogoros: Antiarrhythmic Drugs – chapter on Class III antiarrhythmic drugs.

26. Organ toxicity is related to the iodine atoms in this medication.
   a. **Amiodarone**
   b. **Quinidine**
   c. **Ibutilide**
   d. **Digoxin**

ANSWER: a. Amiodarone. Many side effects of amiodarone are cumulative, but even at low doses side effects are seen in approximately 15% within the first year to over 50% with chronic therapy. "It is widely speculated that much of the unique organ toxicity seen with amiodarone is related to the iodine atoms contained in the drug, a feature not shared by any other antiarrhythmic drug." Thyroid problems are common with this drug. Other side effects include gastrointestinal, hepatitis, and pulmonary complications. See: Fogoros: Antiarrhythmic Drugs – chapter on Class III antiarrhythmic drugs.

27. Junctional rhythm is commonly observed after the administration of this medication.
   a. **Isoproterenol**
   b. **Magnesium**
   c. **Adenosine**
   d. **Atropine**

ANSWER: a. Isoproterenol. Isoproterenol is commonly utilized in the EP lab. When utilizing Isuprel it is common to observe junctional rhythm such as in the following example.

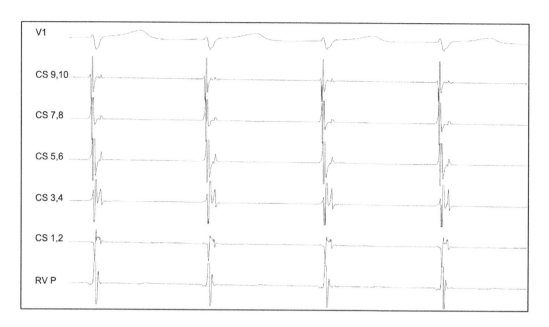

See: EP Essentials – Understanding EP: A Comprehensive Guide – chapter on antiarrhythmics.

28. This food should not be consumed if the patient is taking amiodarone.
   a. Strawberries
   b. Grapefruit
   c. Chocolate
   d. Broccoli

ANSWER: b. Grapefruit. Amiodarone may be taken with or without food but should be taken in the same way each time. Consuming grapefruits and grapefruit juice while taking amiodarone should be avoided. Grapefruit can raise the levels of amiodarone in the body and lead to dangerous side effects.
See: https://www.drugs.com/food-interactions/amiodarone.html

29. What ECG finding may be observed on the patient with digitalis toxicity?
   a. Scooped ST segment
   b. PR lengthening
   c. Peaked T wave
   d. ST elevation

ANSWER: a. Scooped ST segment. EP Essentials says, "Digitalis toxicity may be seen on the ECG, with scooping of the ST segment. Junctional tachycardia, sinus bradycardia, sinus arrest, AV block, or other arrhythmias may be seen. See: EP Essentials – Understanding EP: A Comprehensive Guide – chapter on antiarrhythmics.

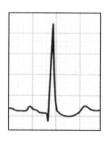

30. Which of the following medications is commonly used to assist with arrhythmia induction in the EP lab?
a. Isoproterenol
b. Magnesium
c. Adenosine
d. Atropine

ANSWER: a. Isoproterenol. EP Essentials says, "Isoproterenol, or Isuprel, is a very commonly used medication in the EP laboratory. Isoproterenol is a synthetic catecholamine, which gives the patient an "adrenaline rush" like epinephrine; however, it acts almost exclusively on beta-receptors. It will enhance cardiac contractility (inotropic) as well as the heart rate (chronotropic). In the EP lab, it will be used to help induce SVT and catecholamine-dependent VT. A bolus of Isuprel followed by continuous IV administration is typically given."
See: EP Essentials – Understanding EP: A Comprehensive Guide – chapter on antiarrhythmics.

31. Defibrillation thresholds may increase with which of the following medications? (Select all that apply)
a. Sotalol
b. Digoxin
c. Metoprolol
d. Amiodarone

ANSWERS: a. Sotalol and d. Amiodarone. See: Abboud, J., & R Ehrlich, J. (2016, August). Antiarrhythmic drug therapy to avoid implantable cardioverter-defibrillator shocks. Retrieved May 17, 2021, from https://www.ncbi.nlm.nih.gov/pmc/articles/PMC5016598/

Contrast:

1. What chemical element in angiographic contrast material makes it radiopaque?
a. Calcium
b. Barium
c. Iodine
d. Lead

ANSWER: c. Iodine. All vascular contrast media are organic compounds including the chemical element Iodine on the benzene ring. It is a heavy metal which absorbs X-rays. This imparts its essential "radiopaque" quality. See: Grossman, chapter on "Angiography: Principles..."

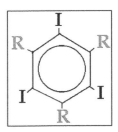

2. For a diabetic patient post-procedure who shows signs of decreased renal function after angiography, expect to administer:
   a. **Mannitol 50 grams IV drip**
   b. **IV saline hydration**
   c. **Lasix 100 mg IVP**
   d. **Hemodialysis**

ANSWER: b. IV saline hydration is indicated in contrast induced nephropathy (CIN). Grossman says, "The main defense against contrast-induced nephropathy is limitation of contrast volume to 3 ml/kg (or 5 mg/kg divided by the creatinine)....Adequate prehydration is also critically important in any patient with impaired baseline renal function....Hydration with ½ normal saline for 12 hours before and after the contrast procedure provided the best protection against creatinine rise (especially with diabetes)." Other treatments include renal dialysis, n-acetyl cysteine (Mucomyst), and using iso-osmolar iodixanol (Visipaque) contrast. See: Grossman chapter on "Complications..."

3. When injected into the blood stream, most contrast draws water into the vascular space. It also causes a sensation of heat. What property of angiographic contrast causes this?
   a. **High ionization constant**
   b. **High Iodine content**
   c. **High osmolarity**
   d. **High viscosity**

ANSWER: c. High osmolarity. The first-generation contrast agents such as Renografin are high osmolarity contrast media (HOCM) compared to blood - about 6 times higher. They cause more hot flashes, more arrhythmias, and take longer to excrete than the newer Low osmolar contrast agents. Like a high salt meal, these agents make you thirsty because they pull water into your vascular space by osmosis. This can cause fluid overload in patients with CHF.
Watson says: "HOCM provokes some discomfort in the patients since the high osmolarity in a vein tends to make the vessel swell (water is attracted from the surrounding tissues), thereby inducing a feeling of heat. When they are injected into arteries, which have fewer flexible walls than veins, they can induce pain." See: Watson Chapter on "Radiography"

4. How is radiographic contrast eliminated from the body?
   a. **Filtered out and excreted through the small intestine**
   b. **It is broken down by the thyroid and metabolized**
   c. **Filtered out by the kidneys and excreted in urine**
   d. **It is broken down by the liver and metabolized**

ANSWER: a. Filtered out by the kidneys and excreted in urine. Watson says, "The large molecular size of the contrast media used in interventional cardiology ensures that very little is passed out though the walls of the vascular system. The same properties also allow the media to be very effectively filtered out of the blood by the kidneys and excreted by the renal system. They are not metabolized." Note, that a KUB Xray film (Kidneys, Ureters, and Bladder) may be taken immediately after angiography to verify excretion of contrast via the kidneys and ureters. If no contrast is seen exiting the kidneys, in the calyces and ureters, it is an indication that contrast is hanging up there and possible renal shutdown. See: Watson, chapter on "Radiography"

5. Osmolality refers to the ability of contrast to:
   a. **Draw water into the vascular space**
   b. **Dissociate into ionic components**
   c. **Eliminate Iodine via the kidneys**
   d. **Excrete water via the kidneys**

ANSWER: a. Draw water into the vascular space through osmosis. Just as eating a high salt diet will make you "put water on" because of its high osmolarity. The human body tries to dilute high concentrations of solutes/salts in tissue, which can lead to hypovolemia. This is important because of the hemodynamic problems contrast agents can cause.

6. During coronary vein angiography your patient develops hypotension and an anaphylactoid reaction. You should administer:
   a. **Epinephrine, Diphenhydramine, Hydrocortisone, and Volume Infusion**
   b. **Epinephrine, Phenylephrine, Neo-Synephrine, and Dopamine**
   c. **Benadryl, Prednisone, Decadron, Theophylline**
   d. **N-Acetyl Cysteine, Ephedrine, Dopamine**

ANSWER: a. Epinephrine, diphenhydramine (Benadryl), hydrocortisone, and volume infusion. Anaphylactic shock is an allergic reaction to an antigen that causes circulatory collapse and suffocation due to bronchial and tracheal swelling.

Kern says, "Allergic Reactions: Hypotension caused by anaphylactoid reaction usually occurs within 20 minutes of exposure to contrast media. Patients at highest risk for anaphylactoid reactions are those with prior anaphylaxis and those with atopy (hypersensitivity) or asthma (who are twice as likely as other patients to have reactions to contrast agents). Recommendations by the Society for Cardiac Angiography and Intervention for treatment of severe anaphylactoid reactions include IV epinephrine with large volumes of normal saline, diphenhydramine, and hydrocortisone.... Patients with bronchospasm should be treated with supplemental oxygen and inhaled beta-agonists such as albuterol. If laryngeal edema develops, the anesthesia service should be called at once, and an intubation tray and a tracheostomy tray should be prepared. IV bolus of epinephrine is most used to treat laryngeal edema. See: Kern chapter on "High Risk Catheterization"

7. If a patient comes for an EP study with a stated allergy to topical iodine, it is most important to:
   a. Use Hibiclens (Chlorhexidine) as the surgical scrub/prep
   b. Use 10% Clorox as the surgical scrub/prep
   c. Use only low-osmolar contrast agents
   d. Not use iodinated contrast agents

ANSWER: a. Use Hibiclens (Chlorhexidine) as the surgical scrub/prep. Chlorhexidine is a chemical antiseptic.

8. The non-ionic contrast agent (Omnipaque) has all these advantages over standard high-osmolar contrast EXCEPT:
   a. Less myocardial depression
   b. Less nausea and hot flash
   c. Less elevation of LV-EDP
   d. Less thrombogenic
   e. Less vasodilation

ANSWER: d. Less thrombogenic. The nonionic agent (Omnipaque) activates platelets and may allow blood mixed with the agent to clot more easily. Peterson says, "...observations would suggest that the nonionic agents, as compared with the ionic agents and irrespective of osmolarity, have a strong propensity to cause platelet activation, the earliest step in arterial thrombotic occlusion.... Patients...were more commonly found to develop new thrombus if a nonionic agent was used..." See: Peterson, chapter on "Radiographic Angiocardiography."
Watson says, "It is a misnomer to classify contrast media reactions as an iodine allergy. Even though patients are questioned regarding an iodine allergy, a true sensitivity to elemental iodine is rare." All contrast agents even low-osmolar contrast contain iodine. See: Watson, chapter on "Radiography"

Chapter 18
Cardiac Implantable Devices

EP Essentials LLC

Device Codes:

1. In the five letter NBG pacemaker code, match each position to its function.
   a. **Chamber sensed**
   b. **Chamber paced**
   c. **Multisite pacing**
   d. **Rate responsiveness**
   e. **Mode of response**

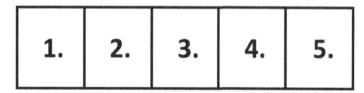

Five Letter Code

CORRECTLY MATCHED ANSWER BELOW:

1.b. Chamber paced: (0, A, V or D) 0-None, A-Atrium, V-Ventricle, D-Dual

2.a. Chamber sensed: (0, A, V or D). Often, the same electrodes sense and pace. E.g., a VVI pacer senses for R waves in the ventricle. If it senses none in the programmed rate zone, it paces in the ventricle.

3.e. Mode of Response: Response to sensing, either none, Triggered, Inhibited, or both. (0, T, I, or D)

4.d. Rate responsiveness: R means it includes motion sensors and that the pacing rate is responsive to exercise. Blank means no motion or exercise sensors.

5.c. Multisite Pacing: The 5th position indicates where multisite pacing occurs, as in a biventricular CRT device - DDDOV.

Here are some mnemonics to help you remember the 5-position pacing code.

I. PACING: These positions go in order of importance and pacemaker history. E.g., the 1st and most important feature, is obviously to pace and stimulate a contraction. The first pacers were dumb, they just paced no matter what. So, #1 is the chamber paced Atrium (A) or Ventricle (V). II. SENSING. The 2nd thing pacers did was to sense the EGM. They sense the EGM to see if the stimulation captured or if an intrinsic beat occurred. Most pacers pace and then sense from each electrode. E.g., If a QRS is sensed it may inhibit the atrial channel.

RESPONSE: After it senses it must decide to inhibit (I) or trigger (T). This is its mode of response. D is for Dual chamber pacers that Trigger from the Atrium into the Ventricle after an AV delay.

RATE Modulation was then added when they developed physiologic sensors in the 1980's. R is rate responsive to exercise.

Multi-chamber pacing. This was added most recently when CRT pacing was developed. V in the 5th position is a CRT device.

You need to learn how to put these 5 letters together to determine the different modes of pacing. See: Ellenbogen: chapter on Pacemaker codes or Journal of Pacing and Clinical EP, NASPE Position Statement, The Revised NASPE/BPEG Generic Code..., 2002, Bernstein, et al.

The Revised NASPE/BPEG Generic Code for Antibradycardia Pacing				
Position: I	II	III	IV	V
Category: Chamber(s) Paced	Chamber(s) Sensed	Response to Sensing	Rate Modulation	Multisite Pacing
O = None	O = None	O = None	O = None	O = None
A = Atrium	A = Atrium	T = Triggered	R = Rate modulation	A = Atrium
V = Ventricle	V = Ventricle	I = Inhibited	*NEW* →	V = Ventricle
D = Dual (A + V)	D = Dual (A + V)	D = Dual (T + I)		D = Dual (A + V)
Manufacturers' designation only: S = Single (A or V)	S = Single (A or V)		PACE. Vol. 25. No. 2 February 2002	

2. Match the pacemaker MODE with the number of its schematic diagram.

    a. **VVI**

    b. **AAI**

    c. **VDD**

    d. **DVI**

Note that a circle in a chamber indicates sensing (like an open ear) and * indicates stimulation (like an electrical spark). The triangle is an amplifier, and the box is pacer processing circuitry. O=Sensing electrode, *=Pacing electrode ▼=ECG amplifier

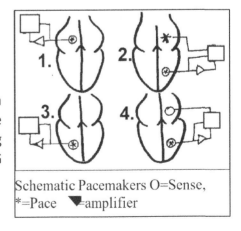

Schematic Pacemakers O=Sense, *=Pace ▼=amplifier

BE ABLE TO MATCH ALL ANSWERS BELOW:
1. b. AAI = Atrial Demand pacemaker
2. d. DVI = AV sequential
3. a. VVI = Ventricular Demand pacemaker.
4. c. VDD = Atrial Synchronous, Ventricular Demand pacemaker

3. The ECG below shows:
   a. **Ventricular bigeminy**
   b. **Atrial bigeminy**
   c. **AAI pacing**
   d. **VVI pacing**

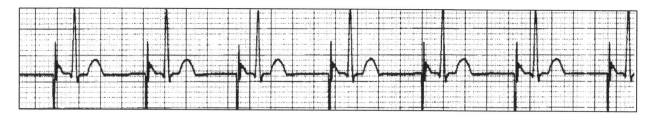

ANSWER: c. AAI pacing. Since pacemaker artifacts (negative spikes) precede each P wave show atrial pacing. In this example we do not see any normal P waves. This could also be AOO mode. since atrial pacing occurs with every beat. We can only be sure that the sensing mode in AAI mode is operational when we see this second diagram. The first complex has a pacemaker spike preceding the atrial complex (a). The second complex is a sinus beat with a normal p wave. The pacemaker sensed it. It inhibits its output. So, no spike is seen in the second beat. In the third beat, no p wave was sensed, so the pacemaker paces the atrium. See: Underhill, chapter on "Pacemakers."

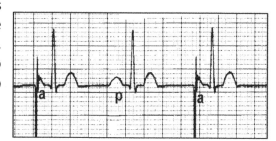

4. This ECG shows:
   a. **Ventricular bigeminy**
   b. **Atrial bigeminy**
   c. **AAI pacing**
   d. **VVI pacing**

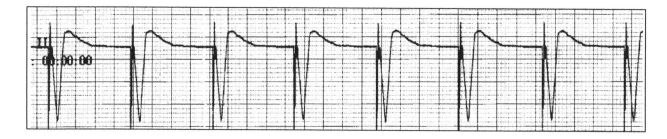

ANSWER: d. VVI pacing. This is ventricular pacing since pacemaker artifacts (negative spikes) precede each QRS complex. This could, however, be VOO, or fixed rate ventricular pacing mode. However, VOO is seldom used. It is a primitive mode and may lead to dangerous pacing on the "T" wave of intrinsic beats. The second tracing shows an intrinsic sinus beat during which the pacemaker output (spike) was inhibited.
See: Underhill, chapter on "Pacemakers."

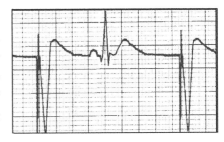

5. An SSI pacemaker is one that:
   a. Has anti-tachycardia features with programmed extrastimuli
   b. Is contraindicated in the presence of atrial fibrillation
   c. Senses and paces and inhibits when a beat is sensed
   d. Senses the atrium and paces the ventricle

ANSWER: c. Senses, paces, and inhibits when a beat is sensed (in either the atrium or ventricle). The S is for single chamber. An SSI may be put in the atrium which paces in AAI mode, or in the ventricle and pace in the VVI mode. VVI mode may be used in patients with intractable atrial fib. But most patients now get dual chamber pacemakers which provide AV synchrony.
See: Moses, chapter on "Types of Pacemakers and Hemodynamics of Pacing"

6. The physician asks you to get a single chamber pacemaker from the shelf.
He can't remember the NBG code for this pacemaker but describes it as follows. It has a sensor that responds to the patient's exercise level. When the pacemaker senses an intrinsic R wave it waits and does not pace. It paces only in the ventricle and only when the rate falls below a set minimum. Which pacemaker does he want?
   a. VAT
   b. DDD
   c. SSIR
   d. VVVR
   e. VDIR

ANSWER: c. SSIR. (VVIR if available, would also be a correct answer.) Pacemakers using the manufacturer's designation "S" in the first 2 positions may be attached to a lead placed either in the atrium or ventricle. Once this SSIR pacing lead is placed in the RV, it will function as a VVIR pacemaker. If it were placed in the RA, it would function as an AAIR pacemaker. The DDD pacemaker does all these things, but it is for dual chamber pacing (RA & RV).

The first letter is the chamber paced. Remember this because pacing is the most important function of a pacemaker. The second letter is the chamber sensed. The third letter is whether it inhibits pacing above the maximum rate. The fourth letter is whether it is rate responsive to a motion sensor." See: Ellenbogen, chapter on Basic Concepts of Pacing.

7. In a pacemaker set to DVI mode, how many chambers are sensed and paced?
   a. **1 chamber sensed, 1 chamber paced**
   b. **1 chamber sensed; 2 chambers paced**
   c. **2 chambers sensed, 1 chamber paced**
   d. **2 chambers sensed; 2 chambers paced**

ANSWER: b. 1 chamber sensed; 2 chambers paced. The D in the first position of the code indicates 2 chambers paced - Atrium and ventricle. The second letter is V, indicating only the ventricle is sensed. The 4th position is now only used for R for rate responsive motion sensors. See: Watson, Chapter on "Cardiac Pacing"

8. A pacemaker that paces both atria and ventricle, but senses only ventricular R wave activity is a _____ pacer.
   a. **VVI**
   b. **VDT**
   c. **DVI**
   d. **DDD**

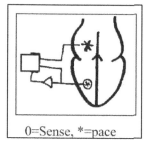

0=Sense, *=pace

ANSWER: c. DVI. This is a dual chamber AV sequential pacemaker. Note the stars for pacing in both atria and ventricle. But it can only sense in the ventricle, and if no R wave is sensed coming down from the AV node after a preset AV delay, it will pace the ventricle. See: Underhill, chapter on "Pacemakers."

9. A 40-year-old man with chronic AF and EF of 55% is unresponsive to rate or rhythm control medications. What type of implanted device will he most likely receive prior to AV node ablation?
   a. **DVI**
   b. **VVIR**
   c. **DDDRV**
   d. **CRT-D**

ANSWER. b. VVIR. An RV pacemaker is adequate because you cannot pace a fibrillating atrium. Since he is young and has a good EF, he will benefit from rate control. The pacemaker is often implanted prior to the ablation to reduce the infection rate and shorten the procedures.

Braunwald says, "In patients with persistent AF, a ventricular pacemaker is implanted, and a dual-chamber pacemaker is appropriate if the AF is paroxysmal. Most patients have a good clinical outcome with right ventricular pacing [VVI]; but in patients with left ventricular dysfunction, biventricular pacing for cardiac resynchronization therapy is appropriate [VVIRV = biventricular]. In patients with an ischemic or nonischemic cardiomyopathy and an ejection fraction =30% to 35%, an ICD may be appropriate for primary prevention of sudden death. However, a simple pacemaker without the ICD often is adequate for patients with a borderline ejection fraction (30% to 35%) and a rapid ventricular rate because the ejection fraction is likely to improve to >35% after the ventricular rate has been controlled by AV node ablation." See Braunwald, chapter on "AF: Nonpharmacologic management"

Ellenbogen says," By implanting the device weeks before the ablation procedure, the problems associated with post implantation pacemaker system malfunction are avoided....
The pacemaker should be set to VVI or VOO mode at 40-50 bpm before ablation." See: Ellenbogen, chapter on AV Node Ablation

10. Identify the NBG pacemaker mode letter labeled at #3 in the box.
   a. **Tachy-arrhythmia functions**
   b. **Programmable functions**
   c. **Mode of Response**
   d. **Chamber sensed**
   e. **Chamber paced**

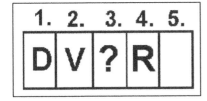

ANSWER: c. Mode of Response, may be either I for inhibited, T for triggered, or D for both.
Chamber paced: "D" indicates Dual chamber pacing (AV sequential)
Chamber sensed: "V" indicates Ventricular sensing (Senses R waves
Mode of Response: "I" indicates Inhibited mode (Inhibits output when it senses an intrinsic R)
Rate responsiveness: "R" includes motion sensors, Blank means no motion sensors
Programmable functions. "R" indicates that the pacing rate is responsive to exercise. (All new pacemakers already have "P" programmability, "M" Multi-programmable, and "T" Telemetry.)
Tachy-arrhythmia functions: "S" shock or "P" for anti-tachycardia pacing. None in this example
See: Braunwald, chapter on "Cardiac Pacemakers and Antiarrhythmic Devices."

11. Identify the NASPE/BPEG pacemaker mode letter labeled at #4 in the box.
   a. **Tachy-arrhythmia functions**
   b. **Programmable functions**
   c. **Mode of Response**
   d. **Chamber sensed**
   e. **Chamber paced**

1.	2.	3.	4.	5.
D	V	I	?	

ANSWER: c. Mode of Response. Rate responsiveness or programmable functions include simple programmability, multi-programmable, telemetry, or rate responsive. This five-letter code was adopted by the NASPE/BPEG as the "generic pacemaker code." In this example, the letters, DVIR signify a common pacing mode with dual chamber pacing, Ventricular sensing, in Inhibition mode. If the 4th letter is R, this would indicate a Rate responsive pacemaker (responsive to exercise). See: Braunwald, chapter on "Cardiac Pacemakers and Antiarrhythmic Devices."

12. In emergency temporary pacing the designation for asynchronous pacing is:
- a. VOO
- b. VDT
- c. VVIR
- d. DDD
- e. AAI

ANSWER: a. VOO pacers pace the ventricle continuously without regard to what the heart is doing. It is asynchronous because it does not synchronize it's pacing to the patient's rhythm. It is only used in emergencies because it can compete with the ventricle and even fire on a T wave. However, if the rate is set faster than the intrinsic rate it will capture the ventricular rhythm and pace rapidly. This mode might be used if a pacemaker dependent patient undergoes surgery where cautery would interfere with pacemaker sensing. Moses says, "Electrocautery should not be used within six inches of an implanted pulse generator." In most models, placing a magnet over the pacemaker will turn it into this VOO asynchronous mode. See: Moses, ch. on "Follow up..."

13. This ECG is from a patient with a ___ pacemaker.
- a. VOO
- b. DVO
- c. DAT
- d. DDD

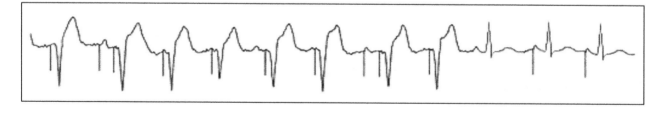

ANSWER: d. DDD pacemaker. In this ECG, the first beat shows a ventricular pacer spike, VVI mode. The second beat shows dual chamber pacing - DVI. The fifth beat shows VAT mode, with a normally conducted p wave. The ninth beat is a normally conducted sinus beat. The last two beats are AAI mode with atrial pacing. You should be able to recognize all these common pacing modes. See: Moses, chapter on "Types of Pacemakers and Hemodynamics of Pacing"

14. What mode of pacing senses both atrium and ventricle, but only paces the ventricle when needed?

    a. DVI

    b. DDD

    c. VVI

    d. VDD

ANSWER: d. VDD Paces ventricle only, but senses atrium and ventricle. This is known as P wave or atrial synchronous pacing. It can inhibit a ventricular pace event if it senses an R wave. If no R wave is sensed, it can trigger (after an appropriate AV interval) from the atrium into the ventricle. So, the last letter is D for both I and T.

The diagram below shows the sensors are an O and pace electrode as *. Note how the atrial sensor triggers the ventricular pacer to fire, only when needed (No A sensed). The ventricular electrode can sense the V and will inhibit if needed. The grid at right shows
how A + V = D, and T + I = D. See: Moses, chapter on "Types of Pacemakers"

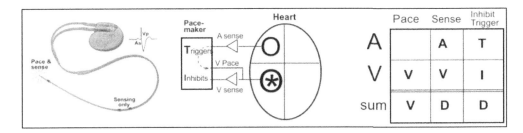

15. Match the mode with its number on the ECG.

    a. VVI

    b. AAI

    c. DDD

    d. DVI

    e. VOO

    f. VDD

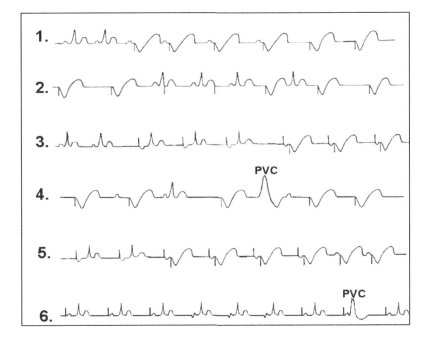

CORRECTLY MATCHED ANSWERS:

1. f. VDD, Atrial synchronous pacing, Paces Ventricle after an AV delay or Low-rate limit
2. e. VOO, Asynchronous ventricular
3. d. DVI, AV sequential, committed, when no QRS is sensed, it fires both atrial and ventricular pacers
4. a. VVI, Ventricular demand, senses PVCs, not P waves
5. c. DDD, fully automatic
6. b. AAI, Atrial demand, does not sense PVCs

See: Moses, chapter on "Types of Pacemakers and Hemodynamics of Pacing"

16. What mode of pacing best reduces the risk of AF from starting in patients with sinus node dysfunction?

    a. ICD with backup pacing
    b. AAI pacemaker
    c. VVI pacemaker
    d. CRT pacemaker

ANSWER: b. AAI pacemaker. Zipes says, "In patients with persistent or chronic atrial fibrillation, permanent pacemakers have traditionally been used to treat patients with slow ventricular rates. There is also evidence that permanent pacing might prevent atrial fibrillation in this population. Several large randomized clinical trials conclusively demonstrated that permanent pacing, especially dual-chamber pacing, reduces atrial fibrillation in patients with sinus node dysfunction. The benefit appears largest in patients with atrial pacing alone compared with dual-chamber pacing." See: Zipes, chapter on Newer Applications of Pacemakers. Because of these adverse hemodynamic effects of RV pacing, permanent pacemakers in the RV may predispose patients to atrial fibrillation.

17. What would be the code for ventricular inhibitory pacing with rate modulation and multisite ventricular pacing?

    a. DDDBiV
    b. DDDRV
    c. VVDBiV
    d. VVIRV

ANSWER: d. VVIRV: "Ventricular inhibitory pacing with rate modulation and multisite ventricular pacing (i.e., biventricular pacing or more than one pacing site in one ventricle). This mode is often used in patients with heart failure, chronic atrial fibrillation, and intraventricular conduction delay; assessed by atrial fibrillation group in MUSTIC study."

18. Which implantable device, used long term, increases the patient's risk of developing AF the most?

    a. AAI
    b. DDD
    c. VVI
    d. OOO

ANSWER: c. VVI. RV pacing alone leads to unsynchronized ventricular contraction and atrial enlargement. Atrial enlargement is associated with AF. Beside potential AF, VVI pacing is also associated with pacemaker syndrome and reduced cardiac output because of loss of atrial synchronization. See: Medtronic.com

19. Percutaneously implanted leadless pacemakers typically:
   a. **Are inserted via jugular vein**
   b. **May be retrieved acutely**
   c. **Require special leads**
   d. **Require atrial pacing**

ANSWER: b. May be retrieved acutely. The following are key points to remember about leadless pacemakers at the time of publication.
   1. The leadless pacemaker, which is 90% smaller than a transvenous pacemaker, is a self-contained generator and electrode system implanted directly into the right ventricle. The device is implanted via a femoral vein transcatheter approach; it requires no chest incision or subcutaneous generator pocket.
   2. The primary advantage of a leadless pacemaker is the elimination of several complications associated with transvenous pacemakers and leads pocket infections, hematoma, lead dislodgment, and lead fracture. The leadless pacemaker also has cosmetic appeal because there is no chest incision or visible pacemaker pocket.
   3. Leadless pacemakers provide only single-chamber ventricular pacing and lack defibrillation capacity. Leadless pacemakers may be suitable for patients with permanent atrial fibrillation with bradycardia or bradycardia-tachycardia syndrome or those who infrequently require pacing Leadless pacemakers are inappropriate for patients who require dual-chamber pacing, such as patients with certain forms of heart block or sinus node dysfunction...
   4. The future of leadless device technology is promising and might eventually lead to expanded pacing capabilities. One beneficial application for leadless devices may be postoperatively following transcatheter aortic valve replacement. According to one study, 28% of patients require pacemaker about 5 days after transcatheter aortic valve replacement."

20. What kind of device/leads may cause pocket stimulation?
   a. **Integrated Bipolar**
   b. **CS lead (CRT)**
   c. **True Bipolar**
   d. **Unipolar**

ANSWER: d. Unipolar. Pacemaker-induced extracardiac stimulation may involve the diaphragm, the pectoral or the intercostal muscles. The common causes are unipolar lead, electrode insulation defects, lead displacement, and connector problems. The most common cause for pocket stimulation is unipolar pacing but may also be seen with an insulation defect on the pacemaker lead. See: Kalaycı, B., Kalaycı, S., Akgün, T., & Karabag, T. (2017, July 02). A case of twitching on the pacemaker pocket.

Retrieved 5/12/21, from https://www.sciencedirect.com/science/article/pii/S2405818117300302

21. What does it mean when the lead impedance is significantly lower than the last device checked on this 5-year-old system?
   a. Lead fracture
   b. Micro dislodgement
   c. Macro dislodgement
   d. Lead insulation break

ANSWER: d. Lead insulation break. If the impedance is lower it is related to an insulation problem, if the impedance is significantly higher it is related to a lead fracture. A dislodgment is unlikely since the system is 5 years old.

22. A patient had a pacemaker implanted 3 months prior and has complaints of dyspnea, facial swelling, cough, and distorted vision. What is the most likely cause?
   a. Diaphragmatic Stimulation
   b. Pacemaker Syndrome
   c. SVC Syndrome
   d. RV Perforation

ANSWER: c. SVC Syndrome. "Dyspnea is the most common symptom, observed in 63% of patients with SVCS. Other symptoms include facial swelling, head fullness, cough, arm swelling, chest pain, dysphagia, orthopnea, distorted vision, hoarseness, stridor, headache, nasal stuffiness, nausea, pleural effusions, and light-headedness," according to Medscape. "The mechanical stress associated with pacemaker wires may lead to vessel wall inflammation, thrombus formation, and ultimately to venous obstruction and occlusion. This usually occurs early after implantation but can even occur after many years. Pacemaker induced superior vena cava syndrome is an unusual complication of pacemaker implantation. Endothelial damage caused by repeated trauma from the lead is thought to be responsible for stenosis. Malignancy has been historically the most common etiology. However, the increase in use of indwelling venous catheters and cardiac pacemaker has resulted in more patients with superior vena cava syndrome of benign etiology."
See: Senthilvel, E., Papadakis, A., Jain, V., & Bruner, J. (2009, July 29). Pacemaker induced superior vena cava syndrome: A case report. https://www.ncbi.nlm.nih.gov/pmc/articles/PMC2740218/

Indications:

1. When a patient receives an ICD because he was previously resuscitated from cardiac arrest due to VF or VT it is termed:
   a. Secondary intervention
   b. Secondary prevention
   c. Primary intervention
   d. Primary prevention

ANSWER: b. Secondary prevention. In secondary prevention, an ICD is placed to prevent a second incidence of VF/VT. Here, the first incidence of SCD was resuscitated and is likely to return. The second incidence may be fatal unless an ICD is implanted.

Cardiology Advisor says, "There are patient with a history of dangerous sustained ventricular tachyarrhythmias or sudden death who may be considered for an ICD for secondary prevention of sudden cardiac death, and there are patients who are at increased risk for dangerous sustained ventricular tachyarrhythmias or sudden cardiac arrest who may be considered for an ICD for primary prevention of sudden cardiac arrest." See: Samii, https://www.thecardiologyadvisor.com

When a patient receives an ICD for "primary prevention" of SCD it means he or she has not yet experienced an episode of SCD but is at great risk. Such patients show sustained VT or VF induced at EP study or have low EF (30%-40%) due to prior MI or other structural heart disease.

17. The decision to implant a permanent pacemaker for bradycardia is usually based on:
   a. Patient symptoms and ambulatory monitoring ECG
   b. Stress test and Signal-averaged ECG
   c. Patient symptoms and EP study
   d. Stress test and echocardiogram

ANSWER: c. Patient symptoms and ambulatory monitoring ECG. Fogoros says: "In most cases the decision as to whether to implant a permanent pacemaker for SA nodal dysfunction should be made on clinical grounds and not on the results of an electrophysiology study." Symptoms must be correlated with documented bradycardia on the ECG using event recorders and/or ambulatory (Holter) monitoring. See: Fogoros chapter on EP Testing for Bradyarrhythmias

18. Most authorities recommend a pacemaker for asymptomatic patients in 1st degree block if the:
   a. HV >100 ms
   b. HV <100 ms
   c. AH >100 ms
   d. AH <100 ms
   e. Never recommend pacers in these patients

ANSWER: a. HV >100 ms. Fogoros says: "The treatment of asymptomatic 1st degree block is somewhat controversial, but most authorities recommend placing a permanent pacemaker in patients with HV intervals greater than 100 ms, because this reflects a significantly diseased distal conduction system." Remember normal HV interval is 35-55 ms, so 100 is way out of the normal range. Normal AH interval is 55-125 ms. So, the distracters in the 100 range could be normal.
See: Fogoros chapter on EP Testing for Bradyarrhythmia

19. The most common bradyarrhythmias are caused by:
   a. **Changes in patient position (E.g., sudden standing)**
   b. **Beta-adrenergic hypersensitivity (E.g., Adrenalin)**
   c. **AV node disease (heart block)**
   d. **SA node disease**

ANSWER: d. SA node disease. Fogoros says: "Disease of the SA node is the most common cause of bradyarrhythmias. SA nodal disease, when accompanied by symptoms, is commonly called sick sinus syndrome . . . Idiopathic SA nodal disease is a degenerative disease. Anatomic studies in idiopathic SA nodal disease have revealed destruction of the SA node, accompanied by fibrous and fatty infiltration and a decrease in the number of functional nodal cells. Typically advancing age is associated with fewer functional SA nodal cells."
See: Fogoros chapter on "Principles of the Electrophysiology Study"

20. These acronyms relate to pacemaker replacement & battery depletion.
Match each pacemaker state with its acronym.

1. **EOL**	a.	**Pacemaker fails to function or dies**
2. **ERI**	b.	**Original settings when pacer new from factory**
3. **BOL**	c.	**Consider replacement, pacemaker will die soon (low battery)**
4. **POR**	d.	**Near death, loss of volatile memory and default backup pacing begins**

CORRECTLY MATCHED ANSWERS ARE:
   1. EOL a. End of Life: Pacemaker fails to function or dies
   2. ERI c. Elective Replacement Indicators: Consider replacement, low battery
   3. BOL b. Beginning of life: Original settings when pacemaker is new from factory.
   4. POR d. Power on reset: Near death with loss of volatile memory, default backup pacing starts.

Ellenbogen says: "The behavior of pacemakers approaching battery depletion is highly variable among different manufacturers...It is important to distinguish end of life (EOL) from ERI. The former connotes gross pacemaker malfunction or lack of function; the latter strives to indicate a time when the generator replacement should be considered within a period of a few weeks or months. ERIs should be reached in the absence of patient symptoms or electrocardiographically demonstrated abnormalities in free-running pacer function. With all manufacturers, rate response... [will be] disabled at ERI. With all devices the pacing rate in response to magnet application is altered at ERI." "As the lithium-iodide battery discharges, the internal impedance of the battery to current flow increases. At or near EOL, transient high-current drain from the battery may further reduce the output voltage . . . True ERI or EOL behavior must be distinguished from 'Power on reset' (POR) mode that results from loss or corruption of the pacemaker's volatile electronic memory. POR mode is a simple backup pacing mode (typically VVI or VOO) that is stored in non-volatile, read only memory and allows the device to function after loss of programmable memory." See: Ellenbogen chapter on "Follow-up of the pacemaker patient"

21. What is the most common reason to implant a permanent pacemaker in patients with symptomatic supraventricular bradycardia?
   a. **Hypersensitive carotid sinus syndrome**
   b. **Complete heart block**
   c. **Sick sinus syndrome**
   d. **Sinus rhythm**

ANSWER: c. Sick sinus syndrome. Moses says: "The sick sinus syndrome is the condition most treated by pacemaker placement. This disorder includes a variety of cardiac arrhythmias, all characterized by SA arrest or SA exit block. The result of both is sinus bradycardia. The junctional escape mechanism may be inappropriately slow in patients with sick sinus syndrome. Patients with SA node dysfunction often has alternating supraventricular tachycardias and bradycardias. This paradoxical juxtaposition of rapid and slow heart rhythms has resulted in the term tachy-brady syndrome (or sick sinus syndrome)." See: Moses, Ch. "Indication for Pacing"

22. Pacemaker syndrome is caused by:
   a. **The patient's emotional dependency on the pacemaker**
   b. **The patient's fear of electrical device interference**
   c. **Malfunctioning activity sensors on DDDR pacers**
   d. **Non physiologic VVI pacing**

ANSWER: d. Non physiologic VVI pacing. Moses says: "With VVI, the possibility exists of poorly timed atrial contraction in relation to ventricular contraction. If the atria contract while the ventricles contract, mitral and tricuspid valve regurgitation may result, with subsequent low cardiac output and pulmonary congestion. Another manifestation associated with absent AV synchrony is the pacemaker syndrome. It is caused by single-chamber ventricular pacing and may have a variety of symptoms. Most of these symptoms are due to the lower blood pressure and cardiac output that often exist during VVI pacing. It is usually alleviated by an upgrade to a DDD device."
See: Moses, chapter on "Types of Pacemakers and Hemodynamics of Pacing"

23. When putting in a VVI pacemaker, how should you check to avoid future diaphragmatic stimulation?
   a. Take PSA (analyzer) measurements
   b. Check the ECG to confirm capture
   c. Vagal nerve stimulation
   d. Pace with 10 V

ANSWER: d. Pace with 10 V. Ellenbogen says, "When a reasonable position [for RV lead] is obtained, preliminary measurements of the electrical parameters are made . . . Threshold parameters tested with a PSA [Pacemaker System Analyzer] define the electrical adequacy of the lead position . . . If satisfactory parameters are not obtained, alternative lead positions should be sought. It is important to confirm that diaphragmatic pacing does not occur by temporarily testing the lead at high output energy (10V)." If pacing at high voltage causes hiccups, you should move the lead. It is the phrenic nerve that stimulates the diaphragm. See: Ellenbogen, chapter on "Techniques of pacemaker implantation"

24. During implantation of a new dual chamber PPM, after the RV lead is positioned and reasonable parameters established, the next step is to:
   a. Proceed to insert and position the RA lead
   b. Check patient comfort and vital signs
   c. Check the ECG to confirm capture
   d. Suture the RV lead

ANSWER: d. Suture the RV lead to the suture sleeve and fascia. "When a reasonable position [for RV lead] is obtained, preliminary measurements of the electrical parameters are made . . . The lead stylet is then removed, and the lead secured to the pectoral fascia with 2-0 or 0 nonabsorbable suture (silk or equivalent). These sutures should be placed around a suture sleeve, and never directly to the lead insulation, which may fracture under this chronic stress . . ." After this, the RA lead is placed and assessed. "The RA appendage has become the preferred implant site for atrial leads because of its trabeculated nature." See: Ellenbogen, chapter on "Techniques of pacemaker implantation

25. Two months after PPM implant the patient loses ventricular capture. The measured RV lead threshold has risen from 0.6 V at implant to 5.0 V. This is most probably due to:
   a. Normal rise due to fibrous tissue buildup at electrode tip (will come down with time)
   b. Lead perforation of RV wall (May lead to tamponade or diaphragmatic stimulation)
   c. Insulation or conductor break (may be seen on impedance testing)
   d. Lead dislodgement (may or may not be seen on comparison Xray)

ANSWER: d. Lead dislodgement (may or may not be seen on comparison Xray). Moses says, "A pacemaker wire usually has its lowest threshold (acute threshold) at the time of implantation. Over the period of 2-6 weeks the threshold rises to its highest level at approximately three or four times the acute level and then falls to a chronic threshold that is usually stable at approximately two or

three times the acute level." This threshold rise is eight times the acute threshold, more than expected from maturation. So, it is not a conductor or insulation problem, because Ellenbogen says, "acute lead conductor or insulation failure very soon after implant is rare."
See: Moses, chapter on "Electrophysiology of Pacing"

26. Temporary disabling of a pacemakers sensing amplifiers after the delivery of an output pulse to prevent it from sensing its own its own discharge, usually from a different chamber is termed:
   a. **Far field Check-out period**
   b. **Noise sampling period**
   c. **Refractory period**
   d. **Inhibition period**
   e. **Blanking period**

ANSWER: e. Blanking period. "The temporary disabling of pacemaker sensing amplifiers after delivery of an output pulse. The blanking period prevents inappropriate sensing of residual energy from the pacemaker output pulse and dual-chamber pacemakers output pulses or intrinsic events in the chamber other than that in which the event occurred. For example, in dual chamber pacing, blanking prevents sensing in the ventricle of an output pulse delivered to the atrium. The duration of the blanking period is usually programmable." This helps prevent crosstalk between chambers and PMT. See: Hayes, Dictionary of Cardiac Pacing..."

27. This diagram shows paced atrial and ventricular electrograms.
Match the name of each refractory period to its number.
   1. **Follows V pace, prevents QRS and T wave sensing in atrium _____**
   2. **Follows A pace, Limits the maximum upper rate _____**
   3. **Follows A pace, prevents inappropriate inhibition of the ventricular system by the atrial system _____**
   4. **Follows V pace, prevents T wave sensing in ventricle _____**

   a. **Post Ventricular Atrial Refractory Period (PVARP)**
   b. **Ventricular Refractory Period (VRP)**
   c. **Ventricular Blanking Period (VBP)**
   d. **Total Atrial Refractory Period (TARP)**

CORRECTLY MATCHED ANSWERS
1. Follows V pace, prevents QRS and T wave sensing in atrium (extending may prevent pacer mediated tachycardia) This is the atrial equivalent to the ventricular blanking period.
a. Post Ventricular Atrial Refractory Period (PVARP)
2. Follows A pace, Limits the maximum upper rate. Atrial events cannot be sensed by the atrial channel. It is the sum of the AV interval and the PVARP.
d. Total Atrial Refractory Period (TARP)
3. Follows A pace, prevents inappropriate inhibition of the ventricular system by the atrial system
c. Ventricular Blanking Period (VBP)

4. Follows V pace, Prevents T wave sensing in ventricle
b. Ventricular Refractory Period (VRP)

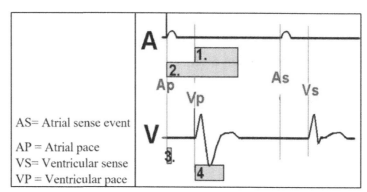

See: Moses, chapter on "Types of Pacemakers and Hemodynamics of Pacing"

28. A 65-year-old man's heart rate was 53 bpm while exercising and 46 bpm when resting? The diagnosis is:
   a. Chronotropic incompetence
   b. Exercise induced ischemia
   c. Chronic fatigue syndrome
   d. Sick Sinus Syndrome

ANSWER: a. Chronotropic Incompetence. When a patient's HR does not increase, they may be chronotropic incompetent. These patients may benefit from a rate responsive pacemaker. This way when they require a faster heart rate, the device will sense this from various sensors (minute ventilation, accelerometer....) and increase the patients HR to an appropriate level.
"Chronotropic incompetence (CI), broadly defined as the inability of the heart to increase its rate commensurate with increased activity or demand, is common in patients with cardiovascular disease, produces exercise intolerance that impairs quality of life, and is an independent predictor of major adverse cardiovascular events and overall mortality."
See: Contemporary Reviews in Cardiovascular Medicine, Chronotropic Incompetence, by Brubaker..., Circulation 2011: 123

29. Select the most appropriate ACC/AHA classification of indications for permanent pacing in children and adolescents with congenital heart disease. A child with sinus node dysfunction with symptomatic bradycardia is classified as:
   a. Class I
   b. Class II
   c. Class III
   d. Class IV

ANSWER: a. Class I. Symptomatic sinus node dysfunction with documented symptoms due to age-inappropriate bradycardia is a class I indication for a permanent pacemaker. The ACC/AHA guidelines currently use a grading schema based on level of evidence and indicate the strength of recommendation for a therapy or treatment. It also makes a valuable judgment about the relative importance of the risks and benefits. Class I therapies are agreed as good, class III as bad and class II is in between. There is no class IV.

Definitions of the classes of recommendation are as follows:
- Class I: there is evidence and/or general agreement that a given procedure or treatment is useful and effective.
- Class II: there is conflicting evidence about the usefulness/efficacy of a procedure or treatment.
- Class III: there is evidence and/or general agreement that the procedure/treatment is NOT useful/effective and in some cases may be harmful. There is no Class IV.

Recommendations for Permanent Pacing in Children, Adolescents, & Patients with CHD 2010

CLASS I (PPM implant is Indicated) in the following:
- Permanent pacemaker implantation is indicated for advanced second- or third-degree AV block associated with symptomatic bradycardia, ventricular dysfunction, or low cardiac output. (Level of Evidence: C)
- Permanent pacemaker implantation is indicated for SND with correlation of symptoms during age-inappropriate bradycardia. The definition of bradycardia varies with the patient's age and expected heart rate. (Level of Evidence: B)
- Permanent pacemaker implantation is indicated for postoperative advanced second- or third-degree AV block that is not expected to resolve or that persists at least 7 days after cardiac surgery. (Level of Evidence: B)
- Permanent pacemaker implantation is indicated for congenital third-degree AV block with a wide QRS escape rhythm, complex ventricular ectopy, or ventricular dysfunction. (Level of Evidence: B)
- Permanent pacemaker implantation is indicated for congenital third-degree AV block in the infant with a ventricular rate less than 55 bpm or with congenital heart disease and a ventricular rate less than 70 bpm. (Level of Evidence: C)

http://guidelines.gov/content.aspx?id=12590
http://jama.jamanetwork.com/article.aspx?articleid=183453

30. A teenager has transient postoperative third-degree AV block with return to normal AV conduction in seven days. In the ACC/AHA evidence-based guidelines, which classification most closely fits this adolescent's indication for a permanent pacemaker?
   a. Class I
   b. Class II
   c. Class III
   d. Class IV

ANSWER: c. Class III. In a young patient with transient postoperative 3rd degree AV block, a permanent pacemaker is not indicated (class III). See: ACC/AHA indications for pacing in youth. Class I is always indicated. Class II may be indicated in specific conditions. Class III is not indicated. There is no Class IV. http://jama.jamanetwork.com/article.aspx?articleid=183453

31. Most older pacemakers and ICDs can be severely affected by some types of electromagnetic interference (EMI). All the following types of EMI are NOT recommended around PPM patients unless necessary, EXCEPT? (E.g., Which is the safest?)
   a. Radiation therapy
   b. Electrocautery
   c. Cardioversion
   d. Arc welding
   e. Diathermy
   f. MRI

ANSWER: c. Cardioversion. "These problems can be prevented by placing the paddles or patches at least 15 cm away from the generator or using an anterior-posterior approach. (Another study recommends >8 cm from a device.) The pacemaker should always be interrogated before and after the attempt of cardioversion."

"Electrocautery should be bipolar, if possible and not be used in the vicinity of the PM. The orientation of current flow should be perpendicular to the lead of the PM system. Electrocautery application should be limited to a few seconds. The PM should be programmed to asynchronous VOO mode and/ or a temporary PM should be inserted as back-up in case of dependency. Instead of electrocautery use of an ultrasonic scalpel reduces EMI. Minimal power settings should be used for electrocautery. The heart rhythm should be monitored, and the PM checked after the surgery."
"Currently, most heart devices are not considered safe in an MRI environment because the MRI could change the settings and/or temporarily affect the normal operation of the heart device." Medtronic.com. If essential, reprogram to 000 (all off) and image the head only.
"Radiation therapy: Direct irradiation of the PM must be avoided and if this is not possible, the PM should be explanted and moved to another suitable site. Careful monitoring of the patient and temporary PM availability should be assured."

Arc welding is especially dangerous, especially currents above 130 amps.

Diathermy is also dangerous. It is used in physical therapy to deliver heat directly to deeper tissues of the body. Several companies now have PPM purported to be unaffected by EMI.

"This is the first study to prospectively demonstrate that ECV [elective cardioversion] can be safely performed in patients with implanted pacemaker, ICD, and cardiac resynchronization therapy (CRT) systems using an anterior–posterior shock electrode orientation with a distance to the implanted device >=8 cm." http://eurheartj.oxfordjournals.org/content/early/2007/06/14/eurheartj.ehm211 See: Medtronic ppt on "Questions on implantable Cardiac Devices" and Indian Pacing Electrophysiology J. 2002 Jul-Sep; 2(3): 74–78., Electromagnetic Interference on Pacemakers, by Okan Erdogan, MD

32. Which of the following would be most likely to stop function of modern demand pacemakers?
   a. **High power radio-antennas or microwaves**
   b. **Microwave oven and Metal detectors**
   c. **Arc welding and Electro-cautery**
   d. **X-ray machines and CT scanners**

ANSWERS: c. Arc welding and Electrocautery. These both induce huge electric currents in the body. If these currents are sensed as P or QRS complexes they will inhibit the pacemaker output, with possible disastrous bradycardia consequences. Lesser amounts of electrocautery are usually tolerated without reprogramming modern pacemakers. However, if the cautery is used within about 6 inches of the battery pack it may inhibit the pacer. Touching the cautery to the pacer may permanently damage it. See: Moses, chapter on "Electrophysiology of pacing"

33. A patient comes to the EP lab with a left bundle branch block (LBBB) ECG pattern. While passing an RV lead, the patient develops an additional right bundle branch block. The ECG would show:
   a. **Right fascicular block pattern**
   b. **Bifascicular block with PVCs**
   c. **Second degree heart block**
   d. **Complete heart block**

ANSWER: d. Complete heart block occurs when both left sided fascicles and the right fascicle are blocked. The heart's normal sinus pacemaker impulse cannot pass through the bundle branches into the ventricle. Complete heart block results in junctional or ventricular escape bradycardia taking over. Patients coming to the EP lab with LBBB are at risk of going to complete heart block as you place the electrodes. In such cases it is best to put in the RV catheter first so backup pacing will be available. See: Kern, chapter on "Electrophysiology."

34. What type of device would generate this ECG?
   a. **Transcutaneous pacer**
   b. **ATP burst pacer**
   c. **DDD pacer**
   d. **CRT**
   e. **ICD**

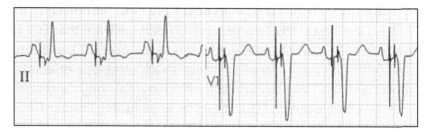

ANSWER: d. CRT (Cardiac Resynchronization Therapy) otherwise known as biventricular pacing. The unusual feature are the two spikes preceding the QRS indicating biventricular pacing. Usually, these patients have LBBB and pacing the LV 1st before the RV results in synchronization of the two ventricular contractions. You may not see the 2 ventricular spikes on ECG like you do here, as they often fire almost simultaneously. The timing of the RV & LV spikes is adjustable on modern CRT pacers. Although the V spikes shown are more widely separated than normal, it indicates biventricular pacing as found in a CRT pacer - 5th letter of the code is V.

35. Pacemaker implant packs include these standard surgical instruments.
Match each surgical instrument to its name.
   a. **Needle holder**
   b. **Mayo scissors**
   c. **Curved Kelly clamp**
   d. **Metzenbaum scissors**
   e. **Curved mosquito clamp**
   f. **Goulet retractor**
   g. **Weitlaner retractor**
   h. **Army-Navy retractor**
   i. **Senn retractor**

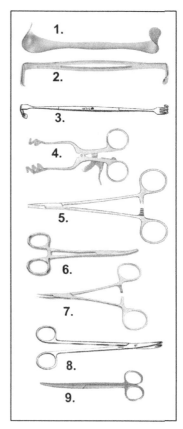

ANSWER:

1. f. Goulet retractor

2. h. Army-Navy retractor

3. I. Senn retractor

4. g. Weitlaner retractor

5. a. Needle holder

6. c. Curved Kelly clamp

7. e. Curved mosquito clamp

8. d. Metzenbaum scissors

9. b. Mayo scissors

Besides the above, other commonly used instruments are: Scalpel #10 blade, Towel clips, Suture material (absorbable and non-absorbable), Eye needle (3F or 4F), Forceps (adson, debakey, mouse-tooth, & smooth)

36. Current Rate adaptive pacemakers may utilize one of the following exercise sensors EXCEPT:
   a. **Piezoelectric Accelerometer (motion detector)**
   b. **Intracardiac impedance (Stroke Volume)**
   c. **Respiration (Transthoracic Impedance)**
   d. **Velocity of ventricular shortening**
   e. **Blood pH or O2 Saturation**
   f. **Evoked QT Interval**

ANSWER: e. Blood pH or O2 Saturation sensors are too complicated because they require intravascular blood sampling techniques (pH electrode or O2 saturation) and thus are not used in currently available pacemakers. Evoked QT Interval (Vitatron) senses shorter QT with exercise, responds by pacing faster.

Minute ventilation/respiration sensing pacers employed by Boston Scientific and Medtronic are available.

Piezoelectric Accelerometer motion sensing pacers are most common (shaker can). -d. Intracardiac impedance (Stroke Volume) sensing pacers employed by Biotronik. This is a closed loop sensor (CLS) which provides physiologic feedback. Because on exercise, as the pacer senses the increasing ventricular stroke volume it responds by pacing faster. This allows it to respond to the body's metabolic demands, even emotional stress. -f. Velocity of ventricular shortening sensing pacers employed by Sorin Best-Living Systems. This is a closed loop sensor (CLS), because with exercise, as the velocity of RV shortening increases, it responds by pacing faster. It adjusts to metabolic demands.

Ellenbogen says, "Over the years, many of these sensors have been implemented in implantable devices.... However, only activity, MV, and CLS sensors [Stroke Volume & Velocity of Shortening] are currently used for rate response. The activity sensor has the advantage of reliability and ease of implementation; its lack of proportionality to exercise workload has not been a major clinical disadvantage for most patients.... VVIR pacing has been shown to improve most aspects of QOL [Quality of Life] over fixed-rate pacing." See: Ellenbogen chapter on Implantable sensors for Rate Adaptation

37. In rate adaptive pacemakers all the following are problems associated with using piezoelectric activity sensors to monitor exercise level EXCEPT: (Which one below is an advantage?)
   a. **Motion sensors respond very rapidly to small amounts of exercise**
   b. **Motion sensors respond proportionally to high work levels**
   c. **Motion vibration is directly related to physiologic demand**
   d. **Motion sensors only sense motion in the AP direction**

ANSWER: d. They only sense motion in the AP direction – this is GOOD. Motion sensors are usually mounted in the can to only respond to forward AP motion. This is better than having it respond to motion in any plane, because vertical or side-ways vibrations, like bumpy card rides, could have an adverse effect.

Motion vibration does not equate to physiologic demand on exercise like QT interval or minute ventilation do. A bumpy card ride may be interpreted as exercise. BAD.

Motion sensors are not proportional at high workloads. BAD. That is why most motion sensing pacers have slope adjustments at higher heart rates.

Motion sensors respond too rapidly early in exercise and too slowly at high exercise levels. BAD. Note how your heart rate does not normally accelerate immediately on exercise. It goes up slowly. This is a normal delay that uses up your aerobic reserve.

Physiologic sensors (SV, QT, MV) are better at evaluating metabolic demand.

Watson says, "Generally, sensors that respond to body motion have a fast response, while physiologic sensors tend to have accuracy. Emphasis has recently been focused on combining two different sensor technologies." See, Watson chapter on Cardiac Pacing Ellenbogen says, "Experience with sensors has suggested that rapidly responding sensors (e.g., activity) are not proportional at higher levels of cardiac workload, whereas proportional sensors are usually slow in response. As a result, an activity sensor over paces at low activity levels but under paces at higher exertional levels. Furthermore, single sensors may be limited by insensitivity to non-exercise stress and are prone to interference by nonphysiologic causes. Thus, it is logical to enhance their rate-response profile by combining two or more sensors." See: Ellenbogen chapter on Implantable sensors for Rate

38. An advantage of bipolar leads in pacemakers is:
   a. **The pacer spike is easier to see on the surface ECG**
   b. **They are less susceptible to EMI noise**
   c. **Smaller generators and battery packs**
   d. **The lead diameter may be smaller**

ANSWER: b. They are less susceptible to EMI noise. Since both electrodes are within the heart, they tend to sense less EMI noise and muscle tremor. Because of this and the redundancy of an extra wire, most leads currently implanted are bipolar. See: Moses, chapter on "Pacemaker Technology"

39. Compared to bipolar pacemakers the unipolar electrode configuration is more prone to: (select two)
   a. **Oversensing of EMI and muscle artifacts**
   b. **Pectoralis muscle stimulation**
   c. **Higher polarization resistance**
   d. **Pacemaker syndrome**

ANSWER: a & b. Pectoralis muscle stimulation, and oversensing of EMI and muscle artifacts. Since the pacer can is near the pectoralis muscle, it may cause it to twitch during pacing - especially if the conducting side of the can faces out and touches the pectoralis muscle. Since the measuring electrodes are far apart (apex to shoulder), it tends to sense everything in the thorax including muscle tremor and electromagnetic interference. The signal to noise ratio is lower (poorer) than for bipolar electrodes. That is why bipolar electrodes are used in all ICDs for sensing small waves, like fibrillation or flutter. A unipolar electrode has a longer distance between electrodes From RV to shoulder. See: Moses, chapter on "Pacemaker Technology"

40. The ring electrode (proximal wire) of a patient's temporary pacer lead has broken. To convert this bipolar external lead system into a unipolar system, the good distal electrode should be connected to the negative battery terminal. What should be used as the positive pole?
   a. **The external pacemaker box**
   b. **Some metal on the procedure table**
   c. **A clip attached to the skin or wound**
   d. **What remains of the distal pacer wire**

ANSWER: c. A clip attached to the skin or wound. Moses says, "The temporary unipolar system may confuse someone unfamiliar with pacemakers but is analogous to the permanent unipolar system. A single electrode is passed to the heart and (usually) connected to the negative electrode. Electrons pass through the wire and the heart; then, to complete the circuit, they must pass to the skin, where a metal clamp, needle, or wire suture has been attached to a wire connected to the positive terminal of the generator." See: Moses, chapter on Pacemaker Technology

41. A porous-tip steroid-emitting tip on a pacemaker lead is beneficial because they reduce the acute: (Select two)
   a. **Stimulation threshold**
   b. **Sensing threshold**
   c. **Fixation force**
   d. **Lead resistance**
   e. **Inflammation**

ANSWER: a & e. Stimulation threshold and Inflammation reaction. Inflammation is a normal reaction to the electrode tip. Normally this tissue becomes acutely inflamed in the first weeks after implantation. This pushes the electrode tip away from the myocardium. This causes a slight increase in tissue resistance, (not the lead resistance) making it harder to capture the ventricle during this acute phase. A porous and steroid emitting tip reduces this acute tissue inflammation. It also increases the tip surface area, increases current density and reduces the stimulation threshold. See: Moses, chapter on "Pacemaker Technology"

42. Which numbers below are typical and adequate in an acute ventricular pacemaker implant? (All measured at 0.5 ms pulse width)
   a. **Threshold 0.5 V, sensed R wave 10 mV**
   b. **Threshold 1.8 V, sensed R wave 20 mV**
   c. **Threshold 0.5 V, sensed R wave 0.5 mV**
   d. **Threshold 1.8 V, sensed R wave 20 mV**

ANSWER: a. Threshold 0.5 V, sensed R wave 10 mV. You want the stimulation threshold to be as low as possible, at least under 1 volt, so 0.5 V is adequate. 1.5 V is too high. And you want the sensed R wave to be as high as possible, at least over 4 mv so 10 is adequate. Note that chronic measurements (usually taken at the time of battery replacement) are almost double those found at implant, because the lead tip area has matured and is more fibrotic. Here are the acceptable implant measurements from Watson.

Acceptable Implant Values	Atrium	Ventricle
Acute Stimulation Threshold	<=1.5 V	<=1.5 V @ 0.5 ms duration
Chronic Stimulation Threshold	<=2.5 V	<=2.5 V @ 0.5 ms duration
Sensed P wave or R wave	>=2.0 mV	>=5.0 mV
Lead impedance	300-1500 Ohms	300-1500 Ohms

These numbers differ slightly depending on the author. I have selected the easiest to remember values. See: Boston Scientific

43. Which of the following pacemaker electrodes use active fixation?
   a. **Ring Electrode**
   b. **Helical screw**
   c. **Porous tip**
   d. **Tined tip**

ANSWER: b. Helical screw. These are lead wires imbedded in the myocardial surface. One type of active lead is a tiny metal helix that screws into the muscle. If the screw is on the end of a lead, it is an active transvenous lead. Some are retractable to allow safe passage through the vein. Others have a soluble dextrose coating over the sharp helix. If the screw goes on the outside of the heart, it is termed an epicardial active lead. Passive leads usually have fins or tines to anchor them into the trabeculations. See: Moses, chapter on "Pacemaker Technology"

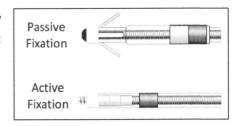

44. The tined J lead pacemaker wire/lead shown is recommended for what chamber of the heart?
  a. **LV Trabeculations**
  b. **Coronary Sinus**
  c. **RA appendage**
  d. **RV apex**

ANSWER: c. RA appendage. The J lead curve helps guide it into the right atrial appendage and the tines help embed and hold it into the trabeculations. A stiff wire stylus helps guide it through the subclavian vein and RA. When the wire is removed it forms this J shape which can be hooked into the RA appendage. Pacemaker RA electrodes are shorter than RV electrodes. CS/LV electrodes are longest. See: Moses, chapter on "Pacemaker Technology"

Interrogation & Programming

1. This ECG, taken immediately after a temporary pacer was placed in your patient shows intermittent_____, which could be improved by _____.
  a. **Loss of capture, increase the sensitivity**
  b. **Loss of capture, repositioning the lead**
  c. **PVCs, increase the output voltage**
  d. **PVCs, repositioning the lead**

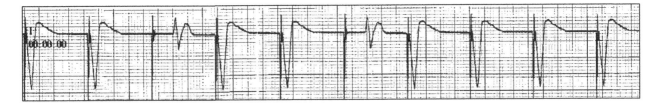

ANSWER: b. Loss of capture, repositioning the lead. The pacemaker artifacts (negative spikes) precede most QRS complexes indicating ventricular pacing. But the 3rd and 6th pacer artifacts do not capture the ventricle (No QRS immediately follows). The heart responds to the pause with a ventricular escape beat. Since the pacer was just placed, the lead is not yet adherent to the RV wall, this is an RV lead positioning problem. Increasing the pacer output voltage is a temporary solution.

The solution is to increase the pacer mA or reposition the electrode to get better contact in the RV. See: Watson, Chapter on "Cardiac pacing"

2. This ECG may be described as:
   a. **VOO pacing with occasional - Loss of capture**
   b. **AAI pacing with occasional - Loss of capture**
   c. **Ventricular bigeminy**
   d. **Atrial bigeminy**

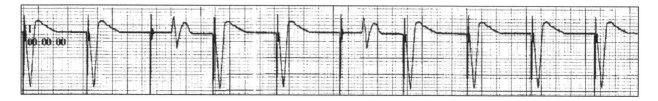

ANSWER: a. VOO or VVI pacing with occasional Loss of capture. The pacemaker artifacts (negative spikes) precede most QRS complexes indicating ventricular pacing. But the 3rd and 6th pacer artifacts do not capture the ventricle (No QRS immediately follows). The heart responds to the pause with a broad complex ventricular escape beat. The blood pressure will increase with this escape beat. This increase is due to longer filling time following the ineffective pacer spike. It is analogous to the large arterial pressure seen in post-PVC beats. The solution is to increase the pacer voltage or reposition the electrode to get better contact in the RV. See: Underhill, chapter on "Pacemakers."

3. This ventricular pacemaker ECG shows what problem?
   a. **Anti-tachycardia pacemaker with severe over sensing**
   b. **3rd degree block with rapid atrial response**
   c. **Second degree block with 5:1 conduction**
   d. **Runaway pacemaker with non-capture**

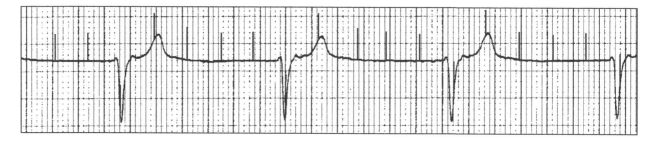

ANSWER: d. Runaway pacemaker and non-capture. This pacer is firing at over 200/minute. This rate is not physiologic and may trigger a ventricular arrhythmia. Neither are the pacer spikes capturing the ventricle. This pacemaker had a system failure and was dangerously out of control. Shut off pacer, explant, and replace. See: Underhill, chapter on "Pacemakers."

4. Pacemaker spikes may often be seen on the surface ECG.
Match each pacer related ECG in the box with its name.
  a. **Intrinsic beat**
  b. **Unipolar paced beat**
  c. **Bipolar paced beat**
  d. **Fusion beat**
  e. **Pseudo-fusion beat**
  f. **AV Sequential paced beat**

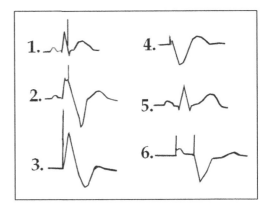

BE ABLE TO MATCH ALL ANSWERS BELOW:
1. e. Pseudo-fusion beat
2. d. Fusion beat
3. b. Unipolar paced beat
4. c. Bipolar paced beat
5. a. Intrinsic beat
6. f. AV Sequential paced beat

Beats #1 & 2 show fusion. These occur when a pacer spike falls in an intrinsic narrow QRS complex. #1 is pseudo-fusion and is too late to have any hemodynamic effect. #2 is a fusion beat where the pacer spike may fall early enough in the QRS that the remainder of the QRS is broad and paced. #3 & 4 show paced beats with spikes preceding the broad QRS. Spike #3 unipolar is usually taller than a bipolar pacer spike. #5. The intrinsic complex is the patient's own normal configuration, usually a narrow QR. #6. AV sequential pacing has 2 spikes, one preceding the P wave and a second preceding the QRS complex. In pacer lingo the beats following an atrial artifact are termed A (instead of P wave), and those following ventricular pacing spikes are termed V (instead of QRS). See: Moses, Chapter on "Follow-up of the pacemaker patient"

5. How should the polarity of bipolar ventricular pacemaker leads be set up?
  a. **The cathode (-) is in the heart and the anode (+) is in a remote location.**
  b. **The anode (+) is in the heart and the cathode (-) is in a remote location.**
  c. **Both the anode (+) and the cathode (-) are in the heart.**
  d. **Neither the anode nor the cathode is in the heart.**

ANSWER: c. Both the anode (+) and the cathode (-) are in the heart. Current flows between the electrodes in the RV. So, it senses locally and gives a very localized response. The voltage threshold tends to be slightly higher in bipolar compared to unipolar electrodes. See: Moses, chapter on Pacemaker Technology

6. During a pacemaker implant when connecting a pacing lead, the negative terminal of the pacer should be connected to the:
   a. **Subcutaneous tissue, via some clip**
   b. **Pacemaker generator**
   c. **Proximal electrode**
   d. **Distal electrode**

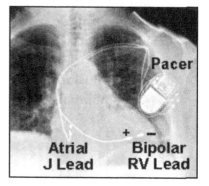

ANSWER: d. Distal electrode. Slightly lower thresholds result when the distal electrode is the negative pole. Moses says: "The distal electrode is usually attached to the negative terminal (cathode) because the heart is generally more easily stimulated if electrons travel from the distal electrode, which usually has the best myocardial contact...." Exceptions exist.
See: Moses, chapter on "Pacemaker Technology"

7. In properly set up unipolar pacers, electrons are emitted from the cathode which is the:
   a. **+ polarity tip electrode**
   b. **- polarity tip electrode**
   c. **+ polarity pacer can**
   d. **- polarity pacer can**

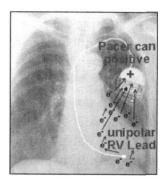

ANSWER: b. - polarity tip electrode. In a unipolar pacer the metal wall of the pacemaker can is attached to the positive pole of the battery. Electrons exit the distal electrode tip in the RV and travel up though the chest and return to the can which has a positive polarity. In a unipolar pacer, when if you pull the pacer can out of the chest, pacing stops. There is no more + pole. If your patient is pacer dependent beware of unipolar. Inform the physician and program to bipolar, if possible, to avoid this problem.

Watson says: "In all pacing systems, regardless of the polarity of the lead, the distal electrode is the negative (cathode), or active pole. . ... Original lead designs were unipolar. Unipolar leads have only one conductor within the lead body. The conductor forms the cathode ... The anode is formed by an area of the pulse generator casing that is not covered with insulating material. Thus, the current of energy travels to the active pole (cathode), then to the myocardium, and completes its circuit by returning via the indifferent pole (anode). One advantage to pacing in a unipolar mode is the resultant large deflection of the pacer output seen on tracings. However, this mode of pacing and sensing also has disadvantages. If the pulse generator's electrode surface is implanted toward the muscle, twitching may occur with each pacing output as the current travels from the tip electrode to the pacemaker generator. Even when implanted away from the muscle, there is the possibility that the pectoral muscle, or other muscle masses, may be stimulated enroute." The large antenna created between the can and tip, makes unipolar configuration more prone to inhibition from over-sensing of EMI and muscle artifact noise. See: Watson, chapter on "Pacemaker Technology"

8. You are assisting with a DDDR pacemaker generator change on a pacemaker dependent patient. The doctor attaches the new generator to the leads, but no pacing occurs until the generator is placed in the pocket. This happened because:
   a. **The leads are reversed in the header**
   b. **The pacing threshold is high**
   c. **It is a unipolar electrode**
   d. **It is a bipolar generator**

ANSWER: c. It is a unipolar electrode, meaning the positive pole was not connected until the pacer generator makes moist contact with extra-cardiac tissue. Just like with your car battery, you can't start until both + and - terminals are connected. In unipolar pacers, the "can" is the + indifferent electrode and completes the circuit. A bipolar unit would start as soon as the leads are connected because both terminals will be in the heart. See: Ellenbogen, chapter on "Basic Concepts of Pacing"

9. Before the output of a permanent pacemaker is set, the patient's stimulation threshold must be determined. This is the:
   a. **Safety margin necessary to safely maintain myocardial capture**
   b. **Minimum voltage required to stimulate a purkinje cell**
   c. **Sensitivity of a demand pacer to sense intrinsic beats**
   d. **Minimum voltage necessary to capture the heart**

ANSWER: d. Minimum voltage necessary to capture the heart and trigger cardiac contractions. Moses says: "The threshold in cardiac pacing is the minimal electrical stimulus required to cause cardiac muscle contraction." This important number can be measured in mA (current) or voltage (pulse width remains fixed usually at 0.6 ms) and tells you how reactive that area of the RV endocardium is to stimulation. For example, if the electrode tip touches an infarcted area of myocardium the threshold may be too high to pace effectively or may not pace at all. See: Moses, chapter on "Electrophysiology of pacing"

10. In a temporary pacemaker, the RV pacing threshold is:
   a. **The number of joules necessary to "overdrive" the NSR**
   b. **The maximum amount of mA necessary to block the NSR**
   c. **The maximum HR necessary to capture the ventricular rhythm**
   d. **The minimum amount of mA required to elicit regular cardiac contractions**

ANSWER: d. The minimum amount of mA required to elicit rhythmic ventricular responses. The minimum electrical stimulation (pacemaker output pulse) required to consistently initiate atrial or ventricular depolarization and cardiac contraction. The voltage required to obtain capture usually is greater than the value at which capture is lost. Pacing thresholds are usually expressed in volts and mA at a specified pulse duration. But temporary pacers are usually measured in mA while permanent pacers use volts. See: Hayes, Dictionary of Cardiac Pacing.

11. Where should the pacemaker rate be set during acute stimulation threshold measurement?
   a. **60 bpm**
   b. **120 bpm**
   c. **Just faster than the patient's HR**
   d. **Just slower than the patient's HR**

ANSWER: c. Just faster than the patient's HR. You want to overdrive the patient's intrinsic HR. If you set it lower than the patient's rate, it will sense the patient's intrinsic rate and inhibit its output (stop firing). After determining the threshold, the rate is usually set to demand mode at a rate just below the patient's normal heart rate. That way, if he becomes bradycardic the pacer will begin firing at its programmed rate, and avoid a sudden drop in CO. In demand mode, the pacer only fires when needed. See: Moses, chapter on "Electrophysiology of pacing"

12. From this recording of a pacemaker threshold measurement determine the stimulation threshold.
   a. **2 V**
   b. **2.5 V**
   c. **3 V**
   d. **3.5 V**

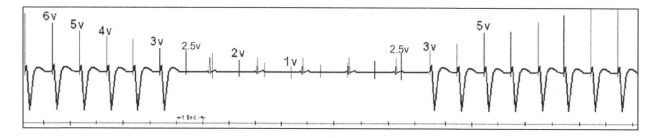

ANSWER: c. 3 V is the threshold. As you turn down the pacer amplitude below 3 volts, you lose pacing, and the patient returns to his intrinsic rhythm - sinus bradycardia. Then as you increase the pacer output it captures the rhythm again at 3. volts. In this example to capture the patient's rhythm consistently you must program the pacemaker voltage over 3 volts, preferably double that, around 6 volts.

This tracing shows the same voltage threshold when lowering the voltage as when increasing it. However, it may vary slightly, depending on whether you are increasing or decreasing the voltage. Normally the threshold is slightly lower (0.1-0.2 V) when increasing from sub-threshold. So, the right side of the tracing should start capturing around 2.8 V instead of 3.0 Volts. However, this slight difference termed the Wedensky effect, is usually clinically insignificant. See: Moses, chapter on "Electrophysiology of pacing"

13. When measuring a patient's ventricular pacing stimulation threshold, it is 5 volts when decreasing the voltage, but 6 volts when increasing the voltage. This is termed the:
   a. **Electrode polarity effect**
   b. **Wedensky hysteresis effect**
   c. **Rebound or incremental effect**
   d. **Polarizing or afterpotential effect**

ANSWER: b. Wedensky hysteresis effect. When pacing the heart rapidly the stimulation threshold may vary depending on whether you turn up the voltage to reach threshold or turn down the voltage. When measuring stimulation threshold, it may vary depending on the cycle length and stimulation strength. Normally you turn down the voltage until you lose capture, instead of raising the voltage until you gain capture. The Wedensky hysteresis effect says that the threshold may be slightly higher when turning down the voltage or mA, because the heart gets conditioned to the rapid pacemaker stimulation.

Here hysteresis means the threshold may be different when turning up the mA or voltage, than when turning down the mA or voltage. A similar use of the term "hysteresis" in a pacemaker means it is programmed to not begin firing until the patient's heart rate falls below a certain rate; but when the pacemaker begins firing, it fires at a rate that is faster than the escape rate. i.e., escape rate is different when rate increases than when it decreases.

Ellenbogen says, of "Capture Hysteresis (Wedensky effect): The threshold stimulus amplitude measured by decreasing the voltage or current until loss of capture occurs is sometimes less than that determined by increasing the stimulus intensity from below threshold until gain of capture occurs. This hysteresis-like phenomenon is the Wedensky effect, the effect of subthreshold stimulation on the subsequent suprathreshold stimulation when the stimulus amplitude is increased. Langberg et al. observed no demonstrable capture hysteresis at pacing cycles longer than 400 ms. They concluded that the Wedensky effect was related to asynchronous pacing in the relative refractory period when incrementing the stimulus intensity, versus the synchronous late-diastolic stimulation when decrementing the stimulus amplitude until loss of capture." See Ellenbogen chapter on Clinical Cardiac Pacing, Defibrillation and CRT.

14. A pacemaker with a bipolar ventricular lead is set to a sensitivity of 5 mV. Some intrinsic R-waves are not sensed. You should:
   a. **Increase sensing by lowering sensitivity to 2.5mV**
   b. **Move the sensitivity control to asynchronous**
   c. **Increase the sensing to 10 mV**
   d. **Decrease the sensing to 1 mV**

ANSWER: a. Increase sensing by lowering sensitivity to 2.5mV. Remember you are setting a trigger. When an R-wave exceeds this trigger level it will be sensed. Lowering the sensitivity setting makes the pacer MORE sensitive. If you went too low, it might even sense P or T waves. Sensitivity is usually set at ½ of the maximum R wave amplitude. This diagram shows how lowering the sensitivity level to 2.5 mV allows sensing of all the R waves. Remember, sensitivity is a fence you look over to see the intrinsic waves. When the lead is correctly positioned on viable myocardium, the sensed R wave should exceed 4 mV. See: Medtronic.com

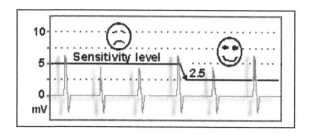

15. What adjustment changes a temporary pacemaker from the demand mode to asynchronous mode?
    a. Increase pacer sensitivity
    b. Decrease pacer sensitivity
    c. Increase refractory period
    d. Decrease refractory period

ANSWER: b. Decrease pacer sensitivity. To go asynchronous (fixed rate) turn off the sensing by decreasing pacer sensitivity to incoming signals by turning the knob to the right. If this is a ventricular pacemaker this puts it into VOO mode. This is the simplest of all pacemaker modes and results in fixed rate pacing at the programmed rate. In many pacemakers, applying a magnet may also result in fixed rate pacing. See: Moses, chapter on "Types of Pacemakers and Hemodynamics of Pacing"

16. Which one of the following BEST describes the primary mechanism by which a DDDR pacemaker increases cardiac output, as compared to a VVIR pacemaker?
    a. Inhibits output on PVCs
    b. Increasing heart rate on exercise
    c. Appropriate AV synchrony at all heart rates
    d. Appropriate biventricular synchrony for BBB

ANSWER: c. Appropriate AV synchrony at all heart rates. Assuming the same HR, the DDDR gives a more appropriately timed atrial kick which simulates normal AV conduction. This should increase SV and CO around 25% over VVI pacing. DDDR pacers track the patients SA node intrinsic rate for physiologic heart rate. In case the patient has a sick sinus node, the DDDR can sense a patient's exercise level and increase HR accordingly. VVI pacers cannot sense the atrial rate and when the HR drops, they simply pace at a fixed rate to prevent bradycardia. VVI is the simplest and cheapest type of permanent pacemaker available. DDDR is the most complex, most physiologic, and most expensive pacemaker. Of course, for more money defibrillators can also be added, making it an ICD.

VVIR patients may develop "pacemaker syndrome" due to loss of AV synchrony. Post-implantation, an increased percentage of ventricular paced beats is the only variable that significantly predicts development of pacemaker syndrome. Both DDDR & VVIR pacers inhibit when they sense a PVC, and both increase their heart rate when they sense the patient is exercising. See: Braunwald, chapter on "Cardiac Pacemakers and Defibrillators"

17. Which one of the following statements is true of a rate-responsive ventricular pacemaker with a motion sensor?
   a. **Retrograde conduction is a potential problem with this pacing mode**
   b. **They are useful in patients with atrial tachy-arrhythmias**
   c. **They are useful in sinus node dysfunction**
   d. **They maintain AV synchrony**

ANSWER: c. They are useful in treating sinus node dysfunction such as sick sinus syndrome. Rate responsiveness makes the heart rate increase with increased motion or respiratory minute volume mimicking the normal response to exercise. Moses says: "Rate modulation is the ability of pacemakers to increase the pacing rate in response to physical activity or metabolic demand. Rate-modulated pacemakers use some type of sensor other than sensing intrinsic atrial depolarization. Also known as rate-responsive or rate-adaptive." However, they do nothing for AV synchrony or preventing retrograde conduction. And rate responsiveness is not helpful in atrial fibrillation - the atrial rate is already too fast. See: Moses, Glossary

18. Which of the following complications is MOST common early following a transvenous pacemaker implant?
   a. **Generator deprogramming**
   b. **Lead dislodgement**
   c. **Pneumothorax**
   d. **Battery failure**
   e. **Lead failure**

ANSWER: b. Lead dislodgement. Ellenbogen says, "The most common complication of lead placement is its subsequent dislodgement. This may be obvious on fluoroscopy or radiography or accompanied by no obvious change in position and usually occurs early before clot and fibrosis act to anchor the device further.... A unique cause of lead dislodgement is known as twiddler's syndrome. In these cases, the patient unwittingly twists the pacemaker generator in the pocket, turning it in such a way that the leads are wound around it and are withdrawn from the heart.... The incidence of lead dislodgement has been reduced with refinement of both active- and passive fixation devices; it is now <2-3%." Battery failure occurs about every 5 years. It is expected and not really a complication. See: Ellenbogen, chapter on "Techniques of pacemaker implantation and removal" http://ats.ctsnetjournals.org/cgi/content/full/70/4/1426

19. What happens during normal maturation of a transvenous endocardial pacer lead?
   a. **Decrease in stimulation threshold to a level below that found at implant**
   b. **Thrombosis builds up and calcification around electrode tip**
   c. **Encapsulation of lead with endothelial tissue**
   d. **Lead and electrode surface deterioration**

ANSWER: c. Encapsulation of lead with endothelial tissue. Just like stents, pacemaker wires and electrodes become coated with endothelium which makes them less thrombogenic and less likely to be rejected by the body. After several years, these electrodes grow into the myocardial wall and may be difficult to remove. Active fixation leads do not have porous tips and are much easier to remove. At the time of implant the stimulation threshold is the lowest it will ever be. The threshold rises for several weeks then falls, but not to the level found at implant. See diagram in next question.

Candinas says that Autopsies reveal, "Extensive encapsulation is present in most long-term pacemaker leads, which may complicate lead removal. The site and thickness of encapsulation are highly variable. Tricuspid valve adhesion, which is usually underestimated, may be severe." See, Postmortem Analysis of Encapsulation Around Long-Term Ventricular Endocardial Pacing Leads," Candinas, et.al., Mayo Clinic Proceedings, Feb 1999

Ellenbogen says "The typical course of events following implantation of a nonsteroid eluting endocardial pacing lead starts with an acute rise in threshold that begins within the first 24 hr. The threshold usually continues to rise over the next several days, usually peaking at approximately 1 week. The typical stimulation threshold then gradually declines over the next several weeks. By 6 weeks, the myocardial stimulation threshold has usually stabilized at a value that is significantly greater than that measured at implantation of the lead, but less than the acute peak."
See: Ellenbogen, Basic concepts of pacing.

20. All the following symptomatic patients should receive synchronized cardioversion EXCEPT:
   a. **Rapid ventricular tachycardias**
   b. **Slow ventricular tachycardias**
   c. **Rapid supraventricular tachycardias**
   d. **Slow supraventricular tachycardias**

ANSWER: a. Rapid ventricular tachycardias such as ventricular flutter or fibrillation should not be cardioverted, because there is no distinct QRS for the synchronizing circuit to trigger from. Fibrillation and flutter waves are typically broad low amplitude waves. Braunwald says: "A synchronized shock (i.e., one delivered during the QRS complex) is used for all cardioversions except for very rapid ventricular tachyarrhythmias, such as ventricular flutter or VF. " See: Braunwald chapter on "Electrotherapy for Cardiac Arrhythmias"

21. Match the measurement of lead impedance found on the pacemakers below with the problem listed.

1. **Broken lead**
2. **Eroded insulation**
3. **Normal value for lead impedance**

a. **80 ohms**
b. **500 ohms**
c. **2500 ohms**

CORRECTLY MATCHED ANSWERS
1. Broken lead (open) c. 2500 ohms
2. Eroded insulation (short) a. 80 ohms
3. Normal lead impedance: b. 500 ohms

Normal lead impedance varies from 300 to 1200. When the lead resistance suddenly rises either 200 ohms or significantly above normal, suspect a broken lead. When the lead impedance drops over 200 ohms - suspect an insulation break. In the upper diagram note that the insulation is good, but there is a break in the conducting wire. This would yield a high resistance measurement. In the lower diagram there is a low resistance electrical path through an insulation break and back to the positive pole. This would yield a low resistance measurement.
See: Moses, chapter on "Electrophysiology of pacing"

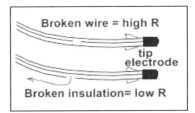

22. You see pacer artifacts on a patient's ECG but loss of capture. The lead impedance has dropped from 600 to 100 ohms. This suggests:

a. **Lead dislodgement**
b. **Insulation break**
c. **Failure to sense**
d. **Lead fracture**

ANSWER: b. Insulation break. Acceptable levels of lead impedance are 300-1200 ohms. Impedance of 100 ohms is exceptionally low, suggesting a short in the lead insulation. Like in a garden hose, if the hose springs a leak (insulation break), less water (current) will exit the tip. Current leakage reduces the delivered mA which may be below threshold. The opposite, high impedance, would suggest lead fracture, which would also reduce or eliminate the delivered current. See: Watson chapter on Pacing

23. In a patient with an RV transvenous pacemaker, the QRS following the pacing artifact has what morphology?
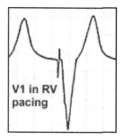
V1 in RV pacing
   a. **Right axis deviation**
   b. **RR' in lead V1**
   c. **RBBB**
   d. **LBBB**

ANSWER d. LBBB. Since the ectopic paced beat starts in the RV and moves leftward, it has the same pattern as a LBBB - a Leftward and posterior axis with a long often notched QRS complex. In lead V1 it shows the negative QS pattern shown with opposite T wave.

24. Patients with DDDR pacemakers who exhibit retrograde VA conduction are prone to develop:
   a. **Competition between pacemaker and SA node**
   b. **Pacer mediated endless-loop tachycardia**
   c. **Atrial fibrillation or flutter**
   d. **Sick sinus syndrome**

ANSWER: b. Pacer mediated endless-loop tachycardia. The negative T waves indicate VA conduction backwards into the atrium. With DDD pacers this is a setup for a pacemaker mediated tachycardia (PMT), where the atrial pacer triggers from the retrograde/re-entrant "P" waves and paces the ventricle after an AV delay. These retrograde P waves are inverted and fall in the ST segment. Watson says: "In the presence of ventricular pacing, the surface ECG is observed for P waves falling within ST segments or T waves. the presence of retrograde conduction may subject the patient to pacemaker-mediated tachycardia. This form of reentry is initiated if a retrograde P wave is sensed, triggering ventricular pacing output, and the scenario is perpetuated... Therefore, when a dual chamber pacemaker is implanted and RAVC (Retrograde AV Conduction) is present, it is important to measure the RAVC time. . .." See: Watson, Chapter on "Cardiac pacing"

25. In pacemaker strength duration curves *chronaxie* is defined as:
   a. **2 x stimulation threshold**
   b. **½ sensing threshold**
   c. **2 x rheobase**
   d. **½ rheobase**

ANSWER: c. 2 x rheobase. In pacemakers this is the approximate lowest energy level to capture the ventricle. Note in the diagram how it is near the lowest energy to capture and preserve battery life. In this curve pacemaker chronaxie is 2.2 V which is the minimum voltage stimulation threshold at 0.2 ms pulse width. Chronaxie would be the most efficient energy use, but it is too near the steep left-hand side of the curve, where energy rises sharply. So, 0.5 ms is a good compromise, with a threshold of 1.5 V. However, you would want to set the pacemaker at about twice this or 3 volts for a safety margin.

In the graph, the dotted line curve shows all the different voltages and pulse widths that can capture the ventricle. It's like plotting 25 thresholds, each at a different pulse width, not done clinically. Which setting is best; usually the one that requires minimal energy near chronaxie? Braunwald says, "The plot of stimulus or shock strength as a function of pulse duration is known as a strength-duration curve, in which the effect on threshold of equivalent change in duration is much greater at short durations than at long

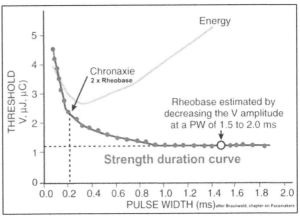

durations [of pulse width]. The long-duration asymptote (the lowest value) is referred to as the rheobase. The chronaxie is defined as the threshold duration at twice the rheobase amplitude.... The shock strength for defibrillation typically is programmed near the ICD's maximum output of 700 to 800 V or 30 to 40 J with pulse durations of 3.5 to 6 milliseconds for the first phase of biphasic waveforms, longer than the defibrillation chronaxie of about 3 milliseconds but toward the short end of the range of shock-waveform time constants of 4 to 8 milliseconds." See: Braunwald chapter on Pacemakers

Ellenbogen says: "In a timesaving, useful, and reasonable clinical sense, one may empirically set the stimulus duration at a value determined from experience, such as 0.4 to 0.5 ms and then determine the current and voltage thresholds. Safety factor allowances of current and voltage are then added or subtracted based on the patient's current and projected clinical status... The goal is to find the combination of pacing threshold stimulus current, voltage, and pulse width that results in minimal charge drain from the pulse generator battery at normal pulse rates. See: Ellenbogen chapter 1 on Artificial Electrical Stimulation"

26. What class of antiarrhythmic drugs can significantly raise a patient's stimulation threshold and cause loss of capture?
   a. 1a
   b. 1b
   c. 1c
   d. III

ANSWER: c. 1C drugs, Flecainide, Propafenone, Amiodarone, & Sotalol are the Na channel blockers. Braunwald says, "Various drugs and metabolic effects can alter pacing and defibrillation thresholds. The most clinically important metabolic abnormalities include any marked acidosis or alkalosis and marked electrolyte abnormalities, especially hyperkalemia. The most clinically important drug effects are the alterations in pacing and sensing thresholds that can be seen with class IC drugs (e.g., flecainide) and the effect of amiodarone on defibrillation thresholds." See: Ellenbogen chapter 1 on Artificial Electrical Stimulation"

27. This table shows pacemaker program settings and measurements on four different patients. Which patient's pacemaker has the least battery drain, and will remain functioning the longest?

	Pulse Amplitude (volts)	Low-Rate bpm	Resistance (ohms)	Pulse Width (ms)	% Paced
a. Patient 1	3.0 v	90	500	0.5	100 %
b. Patient 2	2.0 v	60	300	0.5	100 %
c. Patient 3	2.5 v	60	300	0.5	50 %
d. Patient 4	2.5 v	60	500	0.5	50 %

ANSWER: d. Patient #4 has the lowest pulse amplitude (the most critical #), a higher resistance which will reduce current flow, the lowest rate, and the lowest % paced. Power consumption increases as the square of voltage. Watts = E2 /R See: Medtronic.com

28. A patient with an endocardial unipolar VVI pacemaker faints in the shower whenever he scrubs his back or whenever he presses his arms together in isometric exercise. What is the most probable cause and remedy?
   a. Pacemaker syndrome with loss of AV synchrony - put in DDD
   b. Movement of electrode - loss of capture - reposition lead
   c. Broken lead - intermittent with motion - replace lead
   d. Myopotential inhibition of pacer - switch to bipolar
   e. Battery is at end of life (EOL) - replace generator

ANSWER: d. Myopotential inhibition of pacer - switch to bipolar. The sensing amplifier may sense muscle potentials as QRS complexes. This is most likely in unipolar configuration because of the pectoral muscles overlying the positive electrode (can). See: Moses, chapter on "Electrophysiology of pacing"

29. A patient with a DDD pacer develops symptomatic SVT. The physician decides to reprogram the pacer to DDI mode, because DDI mode:
   a. Has adjustable max tracking rate
   b. Will switch to Wenckebach mode
   c. Cannot trigger from the atrium
   d. Slows the atrial rate

ANSWER: c. Cannot trigger from the atrium. This excludes physiological VAT pacing. Without a T or D in the 3rd position this pacer cannot trigger from the atrium into the ventricle. Fast supraventricular rates will not be tracked and triggered into the ventricle. VVI pacing will remain the dominant mode when needed. See: http://www.ncbi.nlm.nih.gov/pubmed/15807297

30. In this ECG, what does the notched T waves (shown at the ?) indicate?
   a. **Bigeminal PVCs with R on T**
   b. **Retrograde P waves**
   c. **Hyperkalemia**
   d. **Hypocalcemia**

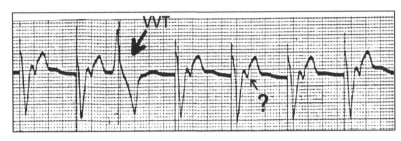

ANSWER: b. Retrograde P waves. The negative "T" waves in lead II indicate VA conduction backwards into the atrium. If a DDD pacer were in place, this could lead to a disastrous pacemaker mediated tachycardia (PMT), where the pacer might trigger from the retrograde/reentrant "P" waves.

The beat marked with an arrow shows VVT mode. In VVT mode a sensed QRS triggers the pacer. The pacer spike falls directly on the QRS complex. This wastes battery energy, but it may be useful in faster intrinsic rates as a marker to indicate that the pacemaker is sensing properly. See: Underhill, chapter on "Pacemakers."

31. This ECG is a lead II ECG strip from a patient with a DDD pacemaker. Post implant he has complained of tachycardia. What reprogramming would reduce the potential for a pacemaker mediated tachycardia? Reprogram to:
   a. **Atrial Refractory Period 200 ms**
   b. **AV Delay 200 ms**
   c. **PVARP 300 ms**
   d. **VRP 250 ms**

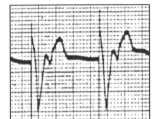

ANSWER: c. PVARP 300 ms. The negative "T" waves indicate VA conduction backwards into the atrium. With DDD pacers this is a setup for a pacemaker mediated tachycardia (PMT), where the atrial pacer triggers from the retrograde/re-entrant "P" waves and paces the ventricle after an AV delay. The retrograde P waves occur from 200 to 300 ms after the pacer spike need to be blocked with ablation or the atrial sensor must be made refractory during this period.

Extend the Post Ventricular Atrial Refractory Period (PVARP).

Retrograde atrial conduction as shown may subject the patient to pacemaker mediated tachycardia. It may be necessary to program the pacemaker's post ventricular atrial refractory period (PVARP) to avoid sensing retrograde P waves. See: Watson, Chapter on "Cardiac pacing"

32. A patient in extreme bradycardia who has passed out frequently is scheduled for a DDD pacemaker. He receives two target tip steroid emitting bipolar pacing electrodes. At the time of implant, the patient's ventricle had a 1.2-volt threshold at 0.6 ms. However, after one week the patient develops intermittent loss of capture. The threshold is now 4 volts at 1.0 ms. The pacer has been reprogrammed to its maximum output = 5 volts at 1.5 ms. What should be done to allow a greater safety margin?

    a. **Reduce the lead resistance to increase pacemaker current**
    b. **Wait another month for threshold to come down**
    c. **Return to EP lab and replace the generator**
    d. **Return to EP lab and reposition the lead**

ANSWER: d. Return to EP lab and reposition the lead. Screw in leads may be removed by counterclockwise rotation. And it is usually possible to reposition a lead that has only been recently implanted, as the endothelialization process at the electrode tip takes several months. But chronic tined leads are often impossible to remove. If it cannot be removed it may be left in the body, capped, and a new second lead placed alongside it. By increasing the output to 5 volts you may retain capture for a brief time but will have inadequate safety margin during the acute phase. The patient's surgical site will have to be reopened and the catheter repositioned under fluoroscopy. New thresholds should be below 1 volt.
See: Moses, chapter on "Types of Pacemakers and Hemodynamics of Pacing"

33. This patient's AAI pacemaker is firing too slowly at 50 bpm. Atrial pacer measurements and settings are: Atrial threshold = 1V, Pulse amplitude = 3V, P-wave = 3 mV, sensitivity = 0.1 mV, Atrial refractory period is 200 ms, atrial escape rate set at = 60 bpm (1000 ms). Which parameter would you reprogram to increase the rate to 60 bpm?

    a. **Program escape interval 800 ms**
    b. **Program escape interval 1200 ms**
    c. **Program refractory period to 100 ms**
    d. **Program refractory period to 500 ms**

ANSWER: d. Refractory period to 500 ms. The escape interval of 1000 ms should yield a heart rate of 60 bpm. The problem here is the sensing amplifier senses the QRS, as an A wave. This resets the timing circuit to start its 1000 ms countdown until it fires again. The pacer is working correctly for the settings. When the refractory period is reset to 500 ms, the QRS is not sensed because it is in the refractory period of the pacemaker. The sensing begins after the T wave. If there is a premature beat after the T it will be sensed, inhibit the pacemaker, and reset the timing circuit. In the last half of the strip atrial pacing spikes will occur every 1000 ms for an atrial and ventricular rate of 60 bpm as shown. See: Moses, chapter on "Electrophysiology of pacing"

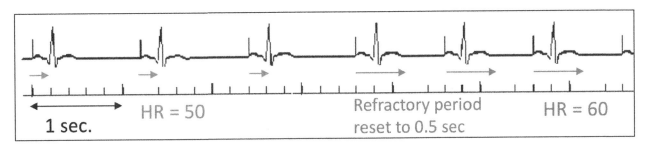

1 sec. | HR = 50 | Refractory period reset to 0.5 sec | HR = 60

34. In patients with debilitating atrial fibrillation that is unsatisfactorily treated with medications or ablation, the electrophysiologist may decide to "ablate and pace." This involves:
   a. **Ablating the AV node and placing a AAIR pacer**
   b. **Ablating the AV node and placing a DDDR pacer**
   c. **Ablating the SA node and placing a AAIR pacer**
   d. **Ablating the SA node and placing a DDDR pacer**

ANSWER: b. Ablating the AV node and placing a DDDR pacer. Atrial fibrillation that is conducted down the AV node often causes a rapid irregular ventricular rhythm. If the AF cannot be controlled the AV node may be ablated via RF catheter energy, which blocks the AV node and leaves the patient with a slow idioventricular rhythm. A DDDR pacer can then be used to speed the ventricular rate and give AV synchrony. Motion sensors can make the ventricular rhythm responsive to exercise. Complete AV node ablation is often avoided by ablating small areas of the AV node, which may slow the conduction time adequately so a pacemaker implant may be avoided. See: Braunwald, Chapter on "Electrical Therapy of Arrhythmias" and Fogoros, chapter on "Transcatheter Ablation"

35. In DDDR pacemakers the maximum tracking rate is the fastest rate the ventricle can be paced in response to:
   a. **Sensed ventricular events**
   b. **Paced ventricular events**
   c. **Sensed atrial events**
   d. **Paced atrial events**
   e. **The rate sensor**

ANSWER: c. Sensed atrial events. When a DDD pacemaker senses intrinsic activity in the atrium, it will try to match the sensed atrial events with ventricular events in a way that preserves 1:1 AV synchrony. Tracking refers to pacing the ventricle in response to sensed atrial activity. E.g., The pacer will track atrial rate rises to about 100-120 bpm. But the patient may be uncomfortable with rates (tachycardias) beyond this point, so a maximum tracking rate is programmed in. Above this rate there will be Wenckebach or fixed ratio block, and there will be more P waves than V waves. See: sjmprofessional.com presentation "Dual-Chamber-Upper-Rate-Behavior"

The "maximum sensor rate" is the other common programmable maximum rate. Ellenbogen says, "In dual-chamber devices programmed in the DDDR mode, rate-adaptive pacing might result from ventricular tracking of the atrial rhythm or be sensor driven (atrial or AV sequential pacing). When rate adaptation is activated, a sensor driven rate is recorded, if the sensor-driven rate exceeds both the intrinsic atrial rate and the lower rate limit, rate-adaptive pacing occurs. A programmed maximum sensor rate determines the fastest rate at which pacing can occur." See: Ellenbogen, Hemodynamics of cardiac pacing

36. Considering the entire history of a permanent pacemaker, from implant to end of life, at what time is the stimulation threshold usually LOWEST?
   a. **During chronic stabilization phase**
   b. **During acute rejection phase**
   c. **At time of initial implant**
   d. **End of life (EOL)**

ANSWER: c. At the time of initial implant threshold is lowest. After that, inflammation and scarring increase and raise the threshold. Moses says: "Time produces a clinically ... important change in threshold. A pacemaker wire usually has its lowest threshold (acute threshold) at the time of implant. Over a period of 2-6 weeks, the threshold rises to its highest level at approximately three or four times the acute level and then falls to a chronic threshold that is usually stable at approximately two or three times the implant level." See: Moses, chapter on "Electrophysiology of pacing"

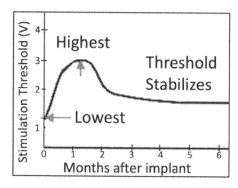

37. What best reduces the acute rise in thresholds within the first two months after initial permanent pacer implant?
   a. **Keeping a narrow safety margin to prevent irritation at the tip.**
   b. **Good analyzer measurements at time of implant**
   c. **IV steroids or steroid eluting electrode tip**
   d. **IV epinephrine or other catecholamine**

ANSWER: c. IV steroids or steroid eluting electrode tip. Most modern pacemaker leads have steroids imbedded in the tip. This prevents excessive inflammation in the acute phase and reduces the 4-to-6-fold acute threshold rise in the first two months after implant. IV steroids are given rarely, but also can reduce the acute threshold rise. Note in the diagram how much lower the stimulation threshold is with steroids. See: Moses, chapter on "Electrophysiology of Pacing"

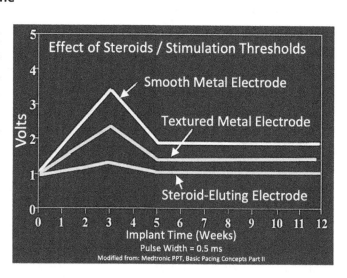

38. Considering the entire history of a permanent pacemaker, from implant to end of life, at what time is the HIGHEST stimulation threshold usually measured?
   a. **During chronic stabilization phase (1 year)**
   b. **During acute rejection phase (1 month)**
   c. **At time of initial implant (time 0)**
   d. **End of life (EOL - 5-10 years)**

ANSWER: b. During acute rejection phase (1 month), is when the acute threshold is greatest due to acute inflammation. Moses says: "Over a period of 2-6 weeks, the threshold rises to its highest level at approximately three or four times the acute level and then falls to a chronic threshold that is usually stable at approximately two or three times the implant level."
See: Moses, chapter on "Electrophysiology of pacing"

39. Your patient has just received a replacement VVI pacemaker generator. What sensitivity measurement should be made with your invasive pacemaker system analyzer (PSA) post implant?
   a. **R wave voltage more than the programmed sensitivity**
   b. **Ventricular tachycardia stimulation threshold**
   c. **R wave peak-to-peak voltage and slew rate**
   d. **Ventricular DFT**

ANSWER: c. R wave peak-to-peak voltage and slew rate. Watson says: "MEASUREMENTS: Sensing: Intrinsic P (atrial) and R (ventricular) waves are measured in their respective chambers to ensure sensing of intrinsic activity . . . peak to peak values of the intrinsic signal is recorded, ... It is vital that the intrinsic amplitude be large enough to allow for adequate sensing. If the intrinsic deflection is not of sufficient amplitude the pacemaker will not sense or see the intrinsic activity. This may lead to inappropriate pacing. Delivery of a pacing stimulus during the relative refractory period may induce ventricular arrhythmias. . . The slew rate is the measure of the voltage over time of the peak slope of the intracardiac signal. Pacemakers also use it to assist in sensing intrinsic activity. It is measured in volts per second (V/sec)." However, slew rate is rarely helpful and is seldom measured. Stimulation threshold is not a sensitivity measurement. DFT is defibrillation threshold, not taken with a pacemaker implant. See: Watson, Chapter on "Cardiac pacing"

40. Following a recent PPI, a patient comes to clinic for pacemaker interrogation. The following EGM event was retrieved as happening one week ago.
What should be your next step as a clinician?
   a. **Check EGM with various positions and exercises - Possible muscle tremor**
   b. **Manipulate the pocket - Possible loose header screw or broken lead**
   c. **Check x-ray of pacemaker - possible leads switched in the header**
   d. **Obtain relevant patient history - possible EMI**

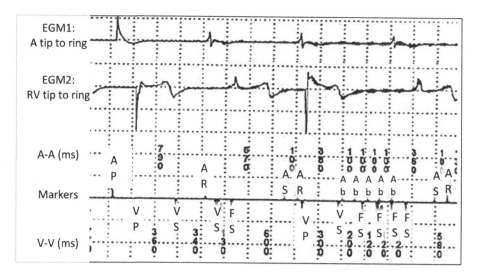

ANSWER: d. Obtain relevant patient history - possible EMI. In this example there is noise on both the atrial (first line) and ventricular (second line) tracings. Manipulating the pocket may be helpful if they lead integrity was the issue or the set screw was loose; however, this example affects both channels. Upon obtaining a detailed patient history the patient recalled having a tingling feeling while working on his car engine a week earlier. Without this information, the patient might have gone through an additional, unnecessary procedure.

41. If the acute sensed R wave of a patient peaks at 3 mV, where should the pacemaker sensitivity be set to provide a 2:1 safety margin?
   a. 1.5 mV
   b. 3.0 mV
   c. 6.0 mV
   d. 12.0 mV

ANSWER: a. 1.5 mV. Remember that the sensitivity is the threshold above which the R wave will be sensed. If the sensing level is set correctly, it allows the upper 50% of the R wave to be detected as shown. Low frequency waves (T waves) and high frequency waves (EMI noise) are filtered out. While bandpass filters filter out much high frequency EMI noise, refractory periods and blanking periods do most of the work of eliminating far-field noise.

Watson says: "When programming sensitivity it is important to remember that the higher the value programmed (in millivolts) the less sensitive the system is. In other words, a high value is less sensitive, and a low value is highly sensitive, or less = more. An analogy may also be made with a brick wall. The higher the wall is raised, the less one will be able to see. If the wall is lowered, more will be seen (sensed)." See: Watson, Chapter on "Cardiac Pacing"

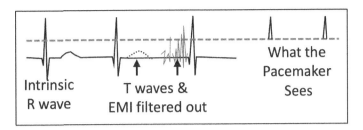

42. This patient with a DDD pacemaker occasionally feels very tired. Judging from the ECG strip with annotations what could be wrong with the pacer?

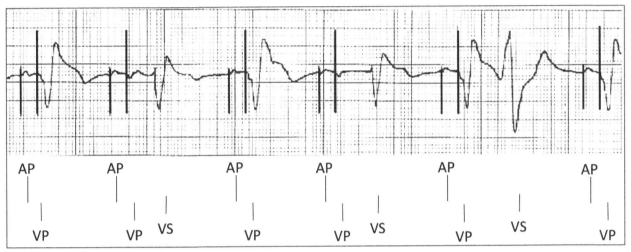

a. **Ventricular oversensing**
b. **Ventricular undersensing**
c. **Magnet mode AV sequential pacing**
d. **Occasional loss of ventricular capture**

ANSWER: d. Occasional loss of ventricular capture. Complex #2 and #5 show ventricular pacing spikes (VP), with no resulting QRS complex. This indicates occasional loss of capture. The atrial spikes capture the atrium each time as noted by the p waves following the atrial pacer spikes (AP). Complexes 3, 6 and 8 indicate ventricular sensing of the patients intrinsic QRS (VS). Try increasing the ventricular pacer output or pulse width, suggesting insulation break.
See: Medtronic, The ECG Workbook

43. What are the main reasons patients with ICDs get inappropriate shocks?
   Select two answers below.
   a. **Lead oversensing**
   b. **Muscle tremor**
   c. **Unrecognized SVT**
   d. **ICD component failure**
   e. **Electromagnetic interference**

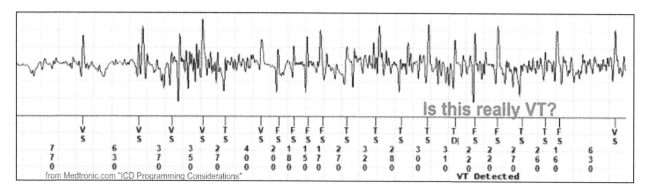

from Medtronic.com "ICD Programming Considerations"

ANSWERS: a. Lead oversensing and c. Unrecognized SVT. A noisy lead, just like a noisy ECG may look like VF or VT. This may be due to a broken lead or ventricular oversensing. SVT morphology may be misinterpreted as VT.

Unrecognized SVT in the VT rate zone accounts for 20% of all inappropriate shocks & lead oversensing with worn and noisy leads accounts for 12% of all shocks. To avoid inappropriate shocks program the ICD to more frequent ATP. The EGM at right could be interpreted by an ICD as VT but is really a broken lead. These topics can be reviewed by watching the Medtronic.com online video "ICD Programming Considerations"

44. During initial implant of a permanent DDD pacemaker what are the suggested PSA measurements for properly placed leads, according to Ellenbogen? Match the ideal measurements below for a PPM implant.

1.	V capture threshold	a.	> 1.5 mV
2.	A capture threshold	b.	> 4 mV
3.	V wave sensing	c.	< 1.5 mV
4.	A wave sensing	d.	< 1 V

CORRECTLY MATCHED ANSWERS ARE:

1.	V capture threshold	<1 V (preferably less than 0.5 V)
2.	A capture threshold	<1.5 V
3.	V wave sensing	> 4 mV
4.	A wave sensing	> 1.5 mV

Obviously, the R wave is a larger voltage than the P wave voltage due to larger tissue mass. Thus, the sensed R wave of >4 mV is expected to be much higher than sensed A wave voltage >1.5 mV. The capture voltage raises in both chambers as the electrodes age and develop fibrous capsules over their tips. So, when pacemakers are replaced the acceptable capture voltage is expected to be less than <3 volts (about twice the initial threshold). With aging the sensed voltages do not change much.

Ellenbogen says, "Threshold parameters tested with a PSA [Pacemaker System Analyzer] define the electrical adequacy of lead position.... If satisfactory parameters are not obtained, alternative lead positions should be sought.... On occasion, optimal parameters may not be achieved, and acceptance of the best available position is necessary. However, because the short and long-term success of the pacing system is related to the initial lead position, effort should be expended to obtain the best possible initial location in terms of both stability and electrical performance...." See, Ellenbogen, Cardiac Pacing & ICDs, chapter on "Techniques of Pacemaker implantation and removal"

45. How does sensing effect pacing? In general, with temporary VVI pacing, oversensing causes _____ and undersensing causes _____.
    a. **Underpacing, Underpacing**
    b. **Underpacing, Overpacing**
    c. **Overpacing, Underpacing**
    d. **Overpacing, Overpacing**

ANSWER: b. Underpacing, Overpacing. Oversensing will inhibit the pacemaker from firing when it shouldn't. It will sense a T wave thinking it is a QRS and not fire. Undersensing will miss QRS complexes and will fire anyway (overpacing), dangerously on a T wave, putting in too many unneeded pacer spikes. See: Medtronic.com

46. This ECG strip from a pacemaker interrogator shows:
    a. **Overpacing due to oversensing**
    b. **Overpacing due to undersensing**
    c. **Underpacing due to oversensing**
    d. **Underpacing due to undersensing**

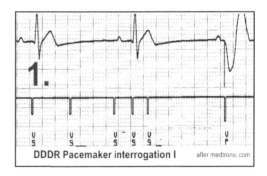

DDDR Pacemaker interrogation I   after medtronic.com

ANSWER: c. Underpacing due to oversensing. Note the second P and T are sensed inappropriately, which inhibits the pacer, resulting in underpacing. HR is only 40 bpm.
This pacemaker is sensing too much, making it think the heart rate is adequate.
In general, oversensing causes underpacing, and undersensing causes overpacing. This pacemaker is sensing too much (note it is sensing P, R and T waves), making it think the heart rate is adequate, so it doesn't pace even though it is needed.

Zipes says, "Oversensing is caused by the sensing of signals [wrongly] interpreted as the atria or ventricles deflecting in their respective channels. Sensing signals originating in the opposite chamber is called crosstalk. For example, ventricular deflection may be sensed on the atrial channel. More seriously, atrial stimulus may be detected on the ventricular channel, resulting in ventricular inhibition and asystole.

Artifact might also give the appearance of oversensing. True undersensing is mostly caused by lead dislodgment or inadequate intrinsic amplitude. Sensing abnormalities are commonly seen secondary to insulation defects and lead fracture." See: Zipes, chapter on Implantable Pacemakers

47. This ECG strip from a pacemaker interrogation shows:

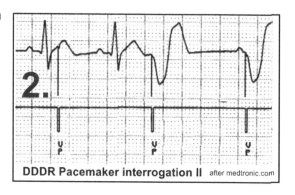

   a. **Overpacing due to oversensing**
   b. **Overpacing due to undersensing**
   c. **Underpacing due to oversensing**
   d. **Underpacing due to undersensing**

ANSWER: b. Overpacing, due to undersensing. Note the 1st pacer spike dangerously falls on a T wave. The pacer is firing asynchronously at 60 ppm with no apparent sensing. It shows competitive pacing between SA node and pacemaker.

Zipes says, "True abnormalities including undersensing, which is a failure to recognize normal intrinsic cardiac activity, and oversensing, which is unexpected sensing of an intrinsic or extrinsic electrical signal... lead fracture can also result in undersensing"

See: Zipes, chapter on Implantable Pacemakers

48. This patient has a DDDR pacemaker. This ECG suggests probable:
   a. **Pacemaker Wenckebach**
   b. **Pacemaker mediated tachycardia**
   c. **Pacemaker atrial oversensing- lead insulation break**
   d. **Pacemaker ventricular overpacing due to sinus arrest**

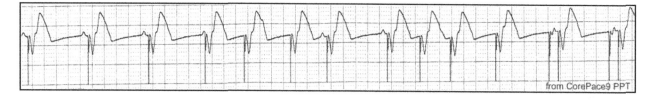

ANSWER: c. Pacemaker atrial oversensing- lead insulation break. Note the ECG marker strip shows several atrial sense events with no visible P wave, followed by premature ventricular paced events. Since the atrial channel is oversensing noise, it triggers excessive ventricular pacing. This shows atrial underpacing due to atrial oversensing. This may be due to unseen artifacts from a lead insulation problem. (Note: VS is Ventricular sensing, VP is Ventricular Pacing, AR is Atrial refractory)

See:http://www.xpowerpoint.com/CorePace-Module-9--Pacemaker-Troubleshooting--PPT.html

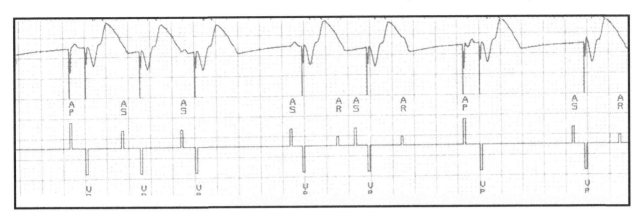

49. On performing a device interrogation on a follow up appointment for an ICD placement, the following report was printed. What happened after the "Burst"?

a. Unsuccessful Cardioversion

b. Unsuccessful defibrillation

c. Successful defibrillation

d. Successful ATP attempt

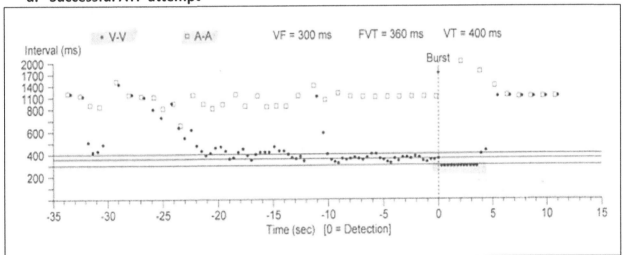

ANSWER: d. Successful ATP attempt. Notice that there appears to be a lot more Vs sensed by the device than As. Also, the atrial rate is approximately 60 bpm while the ventricular rate is approximately 350 ms or 170 bpm and very irregular. This is VT / Ventricular fibrillation. On the last 1/3 of the strip, notice where burst pacing was performed, otherwise known as ATP (antitachycardia pacing). Many physicians program the device to perform ATP while charging. ATP is at a rate of 300 which successfully breaks the tachycardia as noticed by the following plot. After the ATP (burst) conduction appears to be 1:1 at a rate of approximately 60bpm.

50. On device interrogations on this dual chamber pacemaker patient, what is the rhythm observed?
    a. **Atrial Fibrillation with RVR (rapid ventricular response)**
    b. **Ventricular Tachycardia**
    c. **AVNRT**
    d. **AVRT**

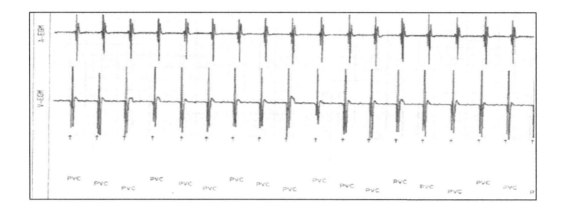

ANSWER: c. AVNRT. This is the typical look of AVNRT as shown on a pacemaker programmer. Notice the 1:1 conduction and very regular rhythm. Ventricular tachycardia can have retrograde P waves, but it is uncommon to have 1:1 conduction at this rate. Atrial Fibrillation would not have been as regular as this rhythm, it would be more chaotic on the atrial channel. Also, AVRT is unlikely since the VA interval is extremely short. With a VA interval less the 60 ms, AVNRT is the most likely answer. In AVRT, the VA interval is longer since the impulse must travel through the ventricular muscle.

51. A patient has a single chamber pacemaker implanted. The next day upon device interrogation the following EGM is recorded. What is the most likely explanation?
    a. **Loose set screw**
    b. **Lead fracture**
    c. **VF**
    d. **AF**

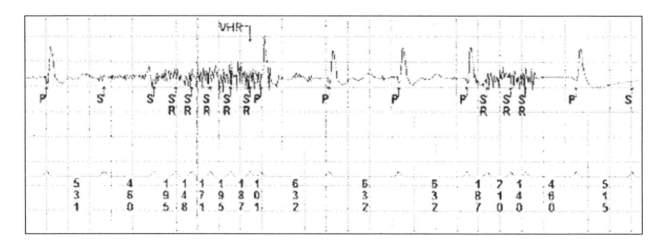

ANSWER: a. Loose set screw. Notice the SR (Sensed R response) markings on the ventricular channel showing a sensed ventricular event. Therefore, the device is oversensing something. It is not sensing VF because the interference goes in and out, and the underlying ventricular beats look nothing like the sensed events. All device companies have different markings on their EGMs, so one must familiarize themselves before diving in. This is not AF as noted by the sensed event appearing on the ventricular channel since this is a single chamber device. Lead fracture may have this appearance but is extremely unlikely the day after implant. The most logical explanation is a loose set screw causing the interference. The patient would need to be brought back to the lab and have the pocket reopened to repair this.

52. You have measured stimulation threshold using a temporary pacemaker/or stimulator connected to a patient's bipolar lead in the RV. Now the Dr. tells you to measure the ventricular sensing threshold. You set the pacing output to minimum. You are watching the sense and pace indicator lights while turning up the sensitivity control (E.g., from 10 to 0.1 mV). The sensing threshold is where:

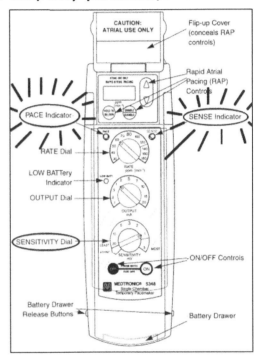

   a. **Both indicators start flashing**
   b. **Both indicators stop flashing**
   c. **The sense indicator starts flashing, and pace indicator stops flashing**
   d. **The pace indicator starts flashing, and sense indicator stops flashing**

ANSWER: c. The sense indicator starts flashing, and pace indicator stops flashing. The sense light flashes when a V is sensed. When nothing is sensed, pacing will occur, and the pace light flashes. When the sensitivity knob is turned to the left (Async.) It is very insensitive and cannot sense V waves, so it paces continuously. As you turn the knob to the right, making it more sensitive, it begins to sense V waves and pacing stops. That's a good thing. A normal QRS is more physiologic than a paced QRS. Only when the heart rate is too low is a paced beat a better thing.

Since you only want to measure sensitivity now and not stimulation threshold, first turn down the pacing output (minimum mA) and down the heart rate (10 bpm below intrinsic), so it's sure not to pace as you do this. It is best to first start with a sensitivity knob to the far right (very sensitive) where you are not pacing. Turn the sensitivity knob left to where you lose sensing and begin pacing.

Note that voltage because it will be close to the threshold. Then slowly turn the knob back up, to where you lose pacing and gain sensing. That point, going up slowly, is the sensing threshold. Where the lights switch is the threshold.

You are essentially seeking to measure the peak V wave voltage (sensing threshold) so you can sense it on every cardiac contraction and inhibit pacing during sinus rhythm.

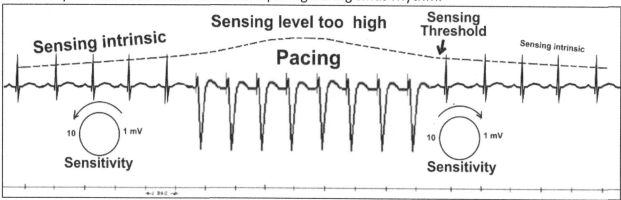

If the peak R wave is 5 mV, you want to set the sensing at about 2.5 mV so you will sense/trigger for every V. The first odd thing to note is that the sensitivity knob is backwards. It is most sensitive at lower numbers. Turning the knob to the left (less sensitive) has higher voltage readings. This ECG shows how it might look on the monitor if you could see the sensing level (dotted line). It's like a fence you look over. The sensing circuits only see what is above the fence. When the fence is too high to see the V, it paces (middle of diagram). Thus, as you turn the sensitivity knob up (right) it starts sensing and stops pacing as shown.

Medtronic temporary pacemaker instructions say:
- Set rate at least 10 ppm below patient intrinsic rate
- Adjust output to 0.1 mA
- Decrease SENSITIVITY: Slowly turn dial counterclockwise until pace indicator flashes continuously.
- Increase SENSITIVITY: Slowly turn dial clockwise until sense indicator flashes and pace indicator stops flashing. This value is the sensing threshold.
- Set SENSITIVITY to half (or less) the threshold value. This provides at least a 2:1 safety margin.
- Restore RATE and OUTPUT to previous values.

53. An MI patient has an intrinsic rate of 60-80 bpm with a stimulation threshold of 2 mA. With the external pacemaker shown, when the switch is turned to "on" with the settings shown, what will occur?

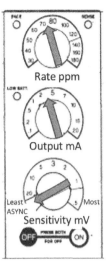

   a. **No pacing will occur**
   b. **Demand pacing (fires if HR exceeds 75)**
   c. **Demand pacing (fires if HR falls below 75)**
   d. **Fixed rate pacing at 75 bpm with competition**

ANSWER d. Fixed rate pacing at 75 bpm with competition. Since the pacer output exceeds the stimulation threshold it will capture the ventricle at a rate of 75. Since it is set to asynchronous mode, it will fire at a fixed rate. If the patient's intrinsic SA rate exceeds 75 the two pacers will compete to capture the ventricle. This is dangerous since the pacer spike may fire into the T wave and lead to ventricular arrhythmias. The sensitivity switch should be turned up until it is sensitive enough to detect the patient's QRS. This will cause the pacer to inhibit (stop pacing) when the patient's intrinsic rate exceeds 75 bpm. See: Moses, chapter on "Types of Pacemakers and Hemodynamics of Pacing"

ICDs:

1. When a patient receives an ICD with indications of only low EF and increased risk of sudden cardiac death, it is termed:
   a. **Lifestyle modification**
   b. **Secondary prevention**
   c. **Primary prevention**
   d. **Risk modification**

ANSWER: c. Primary prevention. ACC guidelines say: "Primary prevention refers to the prevention of SCD in individuals without a history of cardiac arrest or sustained VT.... It refers to use of ICDs in individuals who are at risk for but have not yet had an episode of sustained VT, VF, or resuscitated cardiac arrest."

ACC guidelines say: "Primary prevention refers to the prevention of SCD in individuals without a history of cardiac arrest or sustained VT.... It refers to use of ICDs in individuals who are at risk for but have not yet had an episode of sustained VT, VF, or resuscitated cardiac arrest." (ACC/AHA/HRS 2013 Guidelines) Most patients with structural heart disease and low EF

(<35%) qualify for an ICD without having experienced SCD. Just remember that primary prevention is given first, before any SCD happens. See: http://circ.ahajournals.org/content/117/21/2820.full

2. When a patient receives an ICD for secondary prevention of sudden cardiac death (SCD) it means he or she:
   a. Has failed optimal antiarrhythmic medications
   b. Has been resuscitated from an episode of SCD
   c. Has a cardiomyopathy with ejection fraction of <35%
   d. Has a cardiomyopathy with ejection fractions less than 30% and QRS width greater than 120ms

ANSWER: b. Has been resuscitated from an episode of SCD. ACC guidelines say, "Secondary prevention refers to the prevention of SCD in those patients who have survived a prior cardiac arrest or sustained VT. Primary prevention refers to the prevention of SCD in individuals without a history of cardiac arrest or sustained VT. Patients with cardiac conditions associated with a high risk of sudden death who have unexplained syncope that is likely to be due to ventricular arrhythmias are considered to have a secondary prevention indication."

Just remember that "secondary prevention" gives the patient a "second chance" to survive SCD. See: ACC... Guidelines: Appropriate Use Criteria for Implantable Cardioverter-Defibrillators and Cardiac Resynchronization Therapy, 2013

3. The most important intervention to revive patients in cardiac arrest is:
   a. Prompt response by EMS
   b. Prompt IV epinephrine
   c. Prompt defibrillation
   d. Uninterrupted CPR

ANSWER: c. Prompt defibrillation. The most important intervention in adult emergency cardiac care (ACLS) is defibrillation. The keyword is revive. CPR doesn't revive patients in arrest - defibrillation does. AHA current guidelines say, "Early defibrillation is critical to survival from sudden cardiac arrest (SCA) for several reasons:
   a. The most frequent initial rhythm in out-of-hospital witnessed SCA is ventricular fibrillation (VF)
   b. The treatment for ventricular fibrillation is defibrillation
   c. The probability of successful defibrillation diminishes rapidly over time
   d. VF tends to deteriorate to asystole over time. "
AHA says: "If bystanders provide immediate CPR, many adults in VF can survive with intact neurologic function, especially if defibrillation is performed within 5 to 10 minutes after SCA. CPR prolongs VF, delays the onset of asystole, and extends the window of time during which defibrillation can occur. Basic CPR alone, however, is unlikely to terminate VF and restore a perfusing rhythm." See: AHA Guidelines for CPR and ECC Science Part 6: Electrical Therapies

4. During EP study a patient goes into VF. You give several shocks through the R2 defibrillation pads. They are ineffective at converting the VF. While other members begin ACLS resuscitation, you should:
   a. Apply precordial thumps
   b. Use 2nd defibrillator to shock in different paddle positions
   c. Try to break the VF with programmed electrical stimulation
   d. Continue shocking at maximum J. after medication and CPR trials

ANSWER: b. Use 2nd defibrillator (or hand paddles) to shock along different axes. If the 1st defibrillation with R2 pads fails to convert VF, use a 2nd defibrillator placed in different areas around the heart. There should always be a backup defibrillator for every EP study. Try to pass the current through as much ventricular tissue as possible. In large people or very dilated hearts it may be difficult to find an optimal shocking position. One alternative paddle position is shown. Try several different paddle positions, especially the AP position. Note: You cannot covert VF with pacing or programmed stimulation - it must be shocked. Of course, do not hesitate to give CPR if initial shocks fail. Watson says: "defibrillator (and a backup device in case the first one fails)" See: Watson, Chapter on "Electrophysiology"

5. When defibrillating a patient in VF, what is your LAST step just before you discharge the defibrillator?
   a. Recheck pulse and ECG rhythm
   b. Be sure the defibrillator is fully charged to the appropriate energy level
   c. Ensure that no one is in contact with the patient or stretcher ("clear the victim")
   d. Press with 25 lb. of pressure and press the discharge button on the apex paddle

ANSWER: c. Ensure that no one is in contact with the patient or stretcher ("clear the victim"). Although all the listed answers are important, it is most important to not create a second victim by shocking someone on your own team. ACLS current guidelines say: "The person who presses the SHOCK button is responsible for ensuring that no one is touching the patient when a shock is delivered . . . state in forceful voice before each shock, for example, 'I'm going to shock on three. One, I am clear . . . Two, you are clear . . . Three, everybody is clear.'" You must press BOTH buttons, one on each paddle. See: AHA, ACLS Provider Manual, chapter on "VF treated with CPR and AED"

6. Synchronized cardioversion (countershock):
   a. Is triggered from the patients P wave
   b. Is the primary treatment for all forms of cardiac arrest
   c. Delivers a shock a few milliseconds after the peak R wave
   d. Is used only for rhythms with ventricular responses of < 60/min

ANSWER: c. Delivers a shock a few milliseconds after the peak R wave - within the QRS. Some machines show you exactly where in the QRS the pulse will fire. You don't want to fire during the vulnerable relative refractory period, on the downslope of the T wave. Emergent high energy defibrillation is used in VF and pulseless VT cardiac arrest. We cardiovert arrhythmias with reentry loops (like AF) which only need to be interrupted. This can be done with low energy pulses. But in the automatic ventricular rhythms (like VF) the defibrillation pulses must be large enough to depolarize the entire ventricle - RV & LV. See: AHA, ACLS Provider Manual, chapter on "Advanced Skills"

7. Most defibrillators are constructed such that you CANNOT cardiovert when monitoring the patient's ECG through the:
   a. **Quick look paddles**
   b. **Limb leads (4 wire)**
   c. **Monitor leads (3 wire)**
   d. **Disposable defibrillation pads**

ANSWER: a. Quick look paddles. ACLS guidelines say: "cardioverters synchronize only to the signal from the monitor electrodes and never through the hand-held quick-look paddles. An unwary practitioner may try to synchronize - unsuccessfully in that the machine will not discharge - and may not recognize the problem." Quick look paddles are for emergency use only.
See: AHA, ACLS Provider Manual, chapter on "Stable Tachycardias"

8. Your physician decides to cardiovert a patient with SVT. After placing the cardioverter/defibrillator in synchronization mode and administering a sedative and analgesic to the patient, the patient suddenly becomes unresponsive and pulseless. The ECG rhythm is as shown. The physician says, "SHOCK HER NOW!" But when you hold down the discharge buttons on the defibrillator - nothing happens. Why?
   a. **The defibrillator battery is low**
   b. **The SYNC switch is not functioning properly**
   c. **Fibrillation waves won't trigger the synchronizer**
   d. **Low energy shocks are inadequate to convert VF**

ANSWER: c. Fibrillation waves won't trigger the synchronizer circuit. In VF the fibrillation waves are usually rounded and low in amplitude. A synchronized defibrillator waits until it senses an adequate R wave, then fires. The R waves must be high enough in voltage and have steep enough slope to trigger the monitors threshold. Many defibrillators automatically start in "defib." mode to prevent this problem.

There is no evidence that the battery or SYNC switch have failed. It is true that cardioversion normally starts at lower energy (50-100J) because cardioversion is designed to break up a small reentry loop in the atrium with a low energy pulse. In VF the defibrillation pulses must be large enough to depolarize the entire ventricle, both RV & LV. SEE: AHA, ACLS Provider Manual, chapter on "Unstable Tachycardia"

9. What is the effect of placing a magnet over all models of ICDs?
   a. **Disables shocks**
   b. **Disables pacing**
   c. **Varies with ICD manufacturer**
   d. **Disables sensing, pacing, and shocks**
   e. **Places ICD into asynchronous mode**

ANSWER: c. Varies with ICD manufacturer. The key here is ALL models. Some literature states that placing a magnet over a patient's ICD disables it. Medscape says, "These false recommendations are repeated in some medical review articles in a categorical manner, ... The reality is quite different. Only devices manufactured by Medtronic, Biotronik, and MicroPort (Sorin/ELA) respond in this way (turn off the ICD). Those produced by Abbott and Boston Scientific behave according to the way in which they have been programmed to respond to the application of the magnet. Nominally, the programming is normal and on, respectively, but it can be modified at the discretion of the physician in such a way that the device does not modify its mode of functioning in the presence of a magnetic field." See: "Application of a Clinical Magnet over ICD: Is It Safe and Useful? Discussion"
See: http://www.medscape.com/viewarticle/585151_2

10. Which clinical trial showed that EP study was not necessary for ICD therapy to be effective in patients with low EF and prior MI?
   a. **MADIT-I**
   b. **MADIT-II**
   c. **DEFINITE**
   d. **COMPANION**

ANSWER: b. MADIT-II. "MADIT-I (Multicenter Automatic Defibrillator Implantation Trial) was a small study designed in 1991 to place an ICD in patients with a prior MI, asymptomatic NSVT, an LVEF < 35%, and inducible VT or VF that are not suppressible during EPS. In those early days, ICD placement required a thoracotomy. The study was stopped early because of significantly improved survival."
"The MADIT-II was a much larger study started in 1997 that did not require an EP study to prove inducibility and used percutaneous catheter insertion instead of thoracotomy. In MADIT II, the inclusion criteria for implantation of an ICD were expanded, requiring only those patients had a prior MI at least 30 days before implantation, and that they have an EF of 0.30 or less. The trial, supported entirely by Guidant, was also stopped early due to significantly improved survival. As a result of MADIT II, patients no longer must undergo invasive EP testing to receive the ICD therapy. This has led to criticism that some ICDs may now be implanted without sufficient evidence."

"MADIT-CRT showed that cardiac resynchronization therapy (CRT) that includes defibrillation (CRT-D) reduced all-cause mortality or heart-failure events in patients with mild heart failure when compared with implantable cardioverter defibrillation (ICD) therapy alone. CRT combined with ICD decreased the risk of heart-failure events in asymptomatic patients with a low ejection fraction and wide QRS complex. This trial was also stopped early because of improved survivability."

"In COMPANION, CRT pacing with or without ICD capability was associated with a significant one-year relative-risk reduction of about 20% for all-cause death or hospitalization when added to optimal medical therapy in patients with ischemic or nonischemic NYHA class 3-4 HF, an LVEF <35%, and a QRS interval of >120 ms. The benefit emerged for both CRT and CRT/ICD therapy.... COMPANION and DEFINITE could be turning points in the acceptance of electrical-device therapy for patients with cardiomyopathy and HF." See: http://www.theheart.org/article/142485.do

11. ACC, AHA, HRS guidelines have a Class I recommendation for implanting ICDs in patients who have EF <40% and:
   a. **EP study showing inducible VF or sustained VT**
   b. **Atrial tachyarrhythmias associated with the WPW syndrome**
   c. **Drug-refractory CHF and not candidates for cardiac transplantation**
   d. **RV or LV outflow tract VT or idiopathic VT without structural heart disease for NYHA Class IV**

ANSWER: a. EP study showing inducible VF or sustained VT.
Guidelines say: "Class I: ICD therapy is indicated in patients with nonsustained VT due to prior MI, LVEF less than 40%, and inducible VF or sustained VT at electrophysiological study. (Level of Evidence: B)" The other indications listed are only class III recommendations for ICD, meaning that an ICD is NOT recommended. See: HRS gridlines

12. A relatively healthy 76-year-old obese female was implanted with an ICD after witnessed VT. One year later there is no longer capture on the ventricular lead. A chest x-ray revealed the ventricular lead was dislodged and twisted around the ICD generator. What is the most probable cause?
   a. **Excessive arm movement during exercise**
   b. **Timothy's Syndrome**
   c. **Twiddler's Syndrome**
   d. **Tricuspid Regurgitation**

ANSWER: c. Twiddler's syndrome is when a patient manipulates and rotates the pulse generator in the pocket so many turns that it resulted in lead dislodgment, diaphragmatic stimulation, or loss of capture. This happens with pacemakers too. This is not always due to conscious rotation. It may be seen in obese women with large defibrillator pockets, sometimes attributed to weight loss with manipulation and rotation of the generator, or a generator that was not sutured down. Arm movement and early TR may cause dislodgement, but not twisting. Timothy's Syndrome is a form of long QT syndrome.

13. The energy ranges available for ICD shocks range from:
   a. **0.001 to 2 joules**
   b. **0.1 to 40 joules**
   c. **5 to 100 joules**
   d. **20 to 360 joules**

ANSWER b. 0.1 to 40 joules. High efficiency ICD devices may need as little as 0.1 joules to cardiovert VT but may need to go as high as 40 joules in refractory VF. See: Watson, Chapter on "Implantable Cardioverter Defibrillator"

14. Current ICDs use high efficiency cardioversion and defibrillation. The most efficient shock waveforms are:
   a. **Biphasic**
   b. **Sinusoidal**
   c. **Monophasic**
   d. **Square waves**

ANSWER a. Biphasic waveforms convert patients with less energy than the traditional monophasic waveform. In the biphasic defibrillation current goes from cathode to anode then reverses and returns in a push-pull manner. Watson says: "Much investigation has gone into developing the optimal shock waveform. As a result, the shape of the defibrillation waveform has changed and become more efficient. The biphasic or bidirectional waveform has proven to be more efficient than the unidirectional or monophasic waveform, thus providing lower defibrillation thresholds." In defibrillators 200 joules biphasic is equivalent to 360 joules monophasic. See: Watson, Chapter on "Implantable Cardioverter Defibrillator"

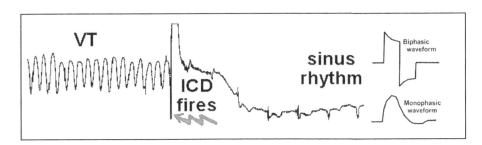

15. ICDs have different zones which classify arrhythmias by rate and duration to:
   a. **Treat arrhythmias by site of origin (RA, RV, LV...)**
   b. **Classify arrhythmias according to its origin (SVT, VT...)**
   c. **Treat different arrhythmias differently (Slow VT, VF...)**
   d. **Classify arrhythmias according to severity (3 being worst)**

ANSWER c. Treat different arrhythmias differently (Slow VT, VF...). For example, slow VT is typically best treated with anti-tachy pacing. Here is an example of how zones may be programmed to deliver different therapies at different rates:

Zone	Tachycardia Rate (bpm)	Therapy Delivered
1	126-160	ATP-1, ATP-2, 1J, 5J, 34J
2	161-200	ATP, 10J, 34J
3	>200	34J

In this example tachy rates in zone 1, between 126 and 160 bpm get initial ATP-1 therapy, then if that is unsuccessful ATP-2 therapy, then cardioversion at 1, 5 and 34 joules. Fast VT in zone 2 in the 161 to 200 bpm range will start with another ATP protocol, then if that is unsuccessful cardioversion at 10 and 34 joules. These ATP protocols were assessed during the prior EP study. Zone 3: VT or VF in the range >200 bpm would get immediate defibrillation at 34 joules. Note that the rates of these zones do not overlap.

Watson says: "Tachycardia is based on rate and duration of rate as programmed by the practitioner. Most devices allow for the definition of two or three different tachycardia zones, based on rate. A maximal duration for the heart rate to be in that zone may also be programmed. If rate and duration criteria are met, therapy is initiated. For example, ventricular tachycardia may be defined as a heart rate between 150 and 180 bpm for 16 consecutive beats to meet detection criteria. Ventricular fibrillation may be defined as a heart rate above 180 bpm. However, the criteria for the duration of ventricular fibrillation are typically less stringent. Instead of requiring 16 beats in a row, any 12 of 16 beats may need to be classified as VF to meet detection." See: Watson, Chapter on "ICDs"

16. In tiered ICD therapy with three ventricular rate zones, the fastest zone (E.g., cl of 280 to 240 ms) is termed the _____ zone. The primary therapy in this zone uses _____.
   a. **VT, ATP**
   b. **VF, ATP**
   c. **VF, Low energy cardioversion**
   d. **VF, High energy defibrillation**
   e. **VT, Low energy cardioversion**

ANSWER: d. VF, High energy defibrillation. There may be several rate zones in an ICD, zones for slow VT, Fast VT, and VF. Of course, VF is the fastest rate and cannot be converted with pacing maneuvers (ATP). Just as in ACLS emergency defibrillation is the primary therapy.

17. Which of the following poses the greatest risk to an ICD patient?
   a. **Electric Blanket**
   b. **Microwave Oven**
   c. **Kitchen Appliances**
   d. **Airport metal detector**
   e. **Gasoline Powered chainsaw**

ANSWER: e. Gasoline Powered chainsaw. Medtronic says, "Maintain at least a 12-inch distance between the components of the ignition system of a gas-powered chainsaw and your heart device. Also, it is better to use one that is built with the spark plug located away from the hand grips. Immediately stop cutting and turn off your chainsaw if you start feeling lightheaded, dizzy, or you believe your implantable defibrillator has delivered a shock. Do not work on the engine while it is running. Do not touch the coil, distributor, or spark plug cables of a running engine.... a running chainsaw may present a higher risk of injury to you than other power tools."

"Given the short duration of security screening, it is unlikely that your Medtronic heart device will be affected by metal detectors (walk-through archways and hand-held wands) or full-body imaging scanners (also called millimeter wave scanners and 3D imaging scanners) such as those found in airports, courthouses, and jails."

"No Known Risk if used as intended and in good working condition: Microwave Oven, Kitchen Appliances – small and large (blender, can opener, refrigerator, stove, toaster), Metal detectors, Electric Blanket...."

www.Medtronic.com, Questions about Implantable Cardiac Devices, Electromagnetic Compatibility Guide

18. Your team has just put in an ICD and are about to test it. The key role of the circulator or other ACLS certified staff in DFT testing is to:
   a. **Remotely initiate VF**
   b. **Be ready to perform CPR**
   c. **Stand by the external defibrillator**
   d. **Administer antiarrhythmic medications**

ANSWER: c. Stand by the external defibrillator. If the ICD fails to convert the patient 2 times after inducing VF, the physician will want immediate external defibrillation, because the patient is in cardiac arrest. Some ACLS person must be immediately available, usually the circulating nurse, to operate the external defibrillator. Before shocking, that person is responsible to "clear" the patient. ACLS recommends saying "I'm Clear, you're clear, we're all clear" before administering external defibrillation. However, in the EP lab we shock so much, a simple "clear" is usually sufficient. After successful DFT testing the circulating nurse should check the pulse and BP to be sure the defibrillation is not only on ECG.

19. After a patient's ICD is implanted and the DFT measured, what power level is usually set to provide adequate safety margin for subsequent defibrillations?
   a. **At the DFT**
   b. **2 times the DFT**
   c. **½ of measured DFT**
   d. **10 Joules higher than DFT**

ANSWER: d. 10 Joules higher than DFT. Ellenbogen says, "Historically, an implantation safety margin of at least 10 joules between the measured DFT and the maximum output of the pulse generator is considered adequate.... This has led to the customary practice of programming shock strength to at least 10 J greater than the DFTs measured at implantation." But the LESS study suggested that a 5 J safety margin may be adequate with modern ICD systems. See: Ellenbogen chapter on ICDs

20. During an ICD generator change it is important to be sure its sensing circuits are turned off because:
   a. **It may stop brady-pacing**
   b. **It may pace asynchronously**
   c. **Cautery can cause the device to defibrillate**
   d. **Cautery may damage the ICD sensing circuits**

ANSWER: c. Cautery can cause the device to defibrillate because the high frequency cautery can mimic VF. This has happened. Either place a magnet over the ICD or have the pacer rep program the device to "off." It is most desirable to have the ICD sensing detectors turned off, thereby preventing defibrillation. But, if necessary, a STERILE magnet can be placed to do this. Be aware that in most devices the magnet will not affect brady pacing. See: Ellenbogen chapter on ICDs

21. Which ICD patient would be best suited to add an array (or additional coil– depending on device company)?
   a. **Low DFT**
   b. **Enlarged LV**
   c. **Small heart**
   d. **Advanced age**

ANSWER: b. Enlarged LV. Patients with a large LV may have an exceedingly high DFT requiring modification of the defibrillation waveform, shock vector or coil position. The typical RV coil / SV coil ICD configuration may not capture/defibrillate the LV. The physician wants a 10J safety margin on the DFT testing to assure that the patient will be defibrillated. Subcutaneous coils may provide more efficient distribution of the defibrillation current.

"Inadequate defibrillation efficacy (DE) requiring device modification is a small, but significant problem in patients undergoing placement of an implantable cardioverter-defibrillator (ICD). Management options for a patient with inadequate DE includes repositioning of the right ventricular (RV) ICD lead, reversal of the shock polarity, removal of the superior vena cava (SVC) coil from the shock vector, and modification of the biphasic waveform tilt and/or pulse width. If these or other maneuvers fail to achieve adequate DE, a subcutaneous defibrillation (SQ) array is often placed." GANESH VENKATARAMAN, MD and S. ADAM STRICKBERGER, MD Washington Electrophysiology and Cardiovascular Research Institute, Washington Hospital Center, 1381.

22. What type of device is shown on this Xray and post-implant test?
   a. Subcutaneous ICD, successful defibrillation
   b. Subcutaneous ICD, unsuccessful defibrillation
   c. Implantable Rhythm Recorder, recording of VF and external defibrillation
   d. Implantable loop recorder, recording of VT with spontaneous conversion

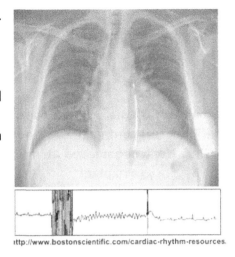

ANSWER: a. Subcutaneous ICD, successful defibrillation. Note the single electrode alongside the sternum, and the successful defibrillation test printout.

Boston Scientific says: "Like transvenous ICDs, the S-ICD System utilizes a pulse generator capable of delivering life-saving high-energy shocks to convert VT/VF. Unlike transvenous ICDs, the S-ICD System is implanted in the lateral thoracic region of the body and utilizes a subcutaneous electrode instead of transvenous leads to both sense and deliver therapy."

This is the Boston Scientific SQ-RX® Pulse Generator which can deliver an 80J biphasic defibrillation shock between the electrode and can. The single subcutaneous electrode is tunneled subcutaneously next to the sternum. See video of implant at.
http://www.bostonscientific.com/cardiac-rhythm-resources/cameron-health/sicd-implant .html

23. This Xray shows a _____. After implantation, this Boston Scientific device is programmed to shock at _____ joules.
   a. S-ICD, 65 J.
   b. S-ICD, 80 J.
   c. T-ICD, 65 J.
   d. T-ICD, 80 J.

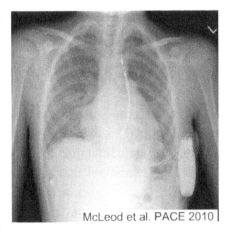

McLeod et al. PACE 2010

ANSWER: b. S-ICD, 80 J. This is an Xray of a boy with a subcutaneous ICD (S-ICD). A single coil and sensing lead are implanted under the skin just above the left side of the sternum. This lead is implanted by tunneling the lead under the skin and never enters the vasculature. This avoids vascular complications due to implanted leads and is one of the best features of S-ICDs. The S-ICD is tested at 65 Joules and if successful, it is then set to a fixed shock level of 80 J. S-ICDs are also simpler to program, with only 4 parameters to set post-implant, as compared to the dozens of parameters on a Transvenous ICD. For these reasons

subcutaneous ICDs are expected to be used on younger patients and those with risks associated with transvenous leads.
See:http://www.bostonscientific.com/cardiac-rhythm-resources/cameron-health/sicd-components.html

24. Which of the following are advantages of SICDs (Subcutaneous implantable cardioverter-defibrillator) compared to standard implantable transvenous ICDs? (Select 3 answers)
   a. **No fluoro needed at implant**
   b. **Easy to explant**
   c. **Utilizes ATP for VT**
   d. **No risk of vascular injury**
   e. **Greater system longevity**
   f. **Utilizes backup Brady pacing**
   g. **Weight less than thoracic ICD**

ANSWER: a, b, & d. Hauser says, "The subcutaneous implantable cardioverter-defibrillator is a novel device that does not require insertion of a transvenous lead; rather, it delivers 80-J transthoracic shocks via a subcutaneous pulse generator....Compared with S-ICDs, single chamber T-ICDs weigh approximately one-half as much, have a longer battery life, and they defibrillate transvenously with =40 J [lower energy DFT]. Unlike the S-ICD, the tiered therapy T-ICD provides 3 functions, namely defibrillation, ATP, and bradycardia pacing. A large proportion of ICD patients have VT that can be terminated painlessly by ATP."

It can be explanted easily by simply pulling out the lead from under the skin. Since all landmarks are external, no fluoro is needed. And, since it is completely subcutaneous, no vessel needs be punctured. It doesn't have ATP like most ICDs. It paces for up to 30 seconds after defibrillation but does not sense or pace bradycardias. Since its output is twice that of a transvenous implantable defibrillator, the can is larger and heavier. See: Hauser, "The Subcutaneous Implantable Cardioverter-Defibrillator" JACC, Jan 2013

25. Where is the SICD (Subcutaneous implantable cardioverter-defibrillator) lead-electrode tunnel placed?
   a. **Left subclavian vein**
   b. **Left subclavicular area to LV apex**
   c. **Left subclavicular area to inferior sternum**
   d. **Left parasternal border from Xiphoid to angle of Louis**

ANSWER: d. Left parasternal border from Xiphoid to angle of Louis. Angle of Louis is at the junction of manubrium & sternum, where the 2nd rib joins the sternum.

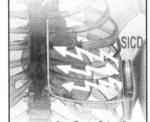

Hauser says, "The subcutaneous implantable cardioverter-defibrillator is a novel device that does not require insertion of a transvenous lead; rather, it delivers 80-J transthoracic shocks via a subcutaneous pulse generator implanted in the left lateral chest via a subcutaneous left parasternal lead-electrode." online JACC, Hauser, "The Subcutaneous Implantable Cardioverter-Defibrillator" Jan 2013

26. You need to implant a CRT-D in a man with LBBB. He had a large anterior MI three years ago and was recently resuscitated from cardiac arrest. During the CRTD implant you cannot get an adequate DFT. All the following are recommended options EXCEPT:
   a. **Changing shock vector**
   b. **Reversing shock polarity**
   c. **Repositioning the CS lead**
   d. **Implanting a high output device**

ANSWER: c. Repositioning the CS lead. The CS lead is used in CRT to pace the LV. CS leads are too small to function as defibrillation electrodes, so repositioning it won't help.
NIH says: "Inadequate defibrillation efficacy (DE) requiring device modification is a small, but a significant problem in patients undergoing placement of an implantable cardioverter-defibrillator (ICD). Management options for a patient with inadequate DE includes repositioning of the right ventricular (RV) ICD lead, reversal of the shock polarity, removal of the superior vena cava (SVC) coil from the shock vector, and modification of the biphasic waveform tilt and/or pulse width. If these or other maneuvers fail to achieve adequate DE, a subcutaneous defibrillation (SQ) array is often placed." See:
http://www.innovationsincrm.com/cardiac-rhythm-management/2012/april/256-azygou   s-vein-coil-defibrillation-efficacy" ://www.ncbi.nlm.nih.gov/pubmed/7479175

27. When programming a patient's ICD, if you do not do a defibrillation threshold (DFT) measurement, it is most common to set the ICD output for VF at:
   a. **Optimum ATP pacing protocol**
   b. **10 joules below maximum output of ICD**
   c. **10 joules on 1st shock, then maximum thereafter**
   d. **2 times estimated DFT threshold (for patient's height and weight)**

ANSWER b. 10 joules below maximum output of ICD is necessary - on two successive defibrillation attempts. You always want a wide safety margin to be sure that the first shock will succeed when VF occurs. This margin is generally agreed to be 10 joules below the maximum output of the ICD. Since measuring DFT consumes time and battery power, many physicians do not measure DFT. Instead, they set the output level at 10 joules below maximum ICD output level. For a 30 J device, this would be 20 J. Pacing may break VT but not VF.

Abedin says of DFT, "VF is induced, and a progressively lower amount of energy is delivered. The lowest amount of energy that successfully defibrillates is called the DFT. This may necessitate repeated induction of VF. Alternatively, two consecutive successful defibrillations using energy with a 10J margin has been shown to provide success rate of 98% during follow-up." Although he also says, "Using biphasic shock a margin of twice the
DFT provides 95%probability of successful defibrillation" Abedin, chapter on Electrical Therapy for Cardiac Arrhythmias"

Kanjwall & Mainigi, say, "Early studies in defibrillation revealed that a tested and confirmed safety margin at implantation of >10 J (i.e., 10 J below the maximum output of the device) was adequate to ensure success in the event of a "real-life" arrhythmic episode.... Presently it is more common to ensure a repeated successful defibrillation 10 J or more below the maximum output of the device or at least once 15–20 J or more below the maximum output of the device. This testing protocol does not determine the actual
defibrillation threshold but does establish defibrillation efficacy"
http://www.innovationsincrm.com/cardiac-rhythm-management/2012/special-fellows-edition-supplement/251-defibrillation-threshold-testing-a-primer

28. You have just finished implanting an ICD in a patient. Testing found the defibrillation threshold (DFT) to be 5 joules. For an appropriate safety margin, it is conventional to set the defibrillator output level at:
   a. **7 joules**
   b. **10 joules**
   c. **15 joules**
   d. **20 joules**

ANSWER: c. 15 joules. Ellenbogen says, "In practice, the simple convention of programming output to 10 J greater than the DFT is widely accepted and usually provides reliable defibrillation. This method is expedient at implant, but lesser energy margins may be satisfactory as well if more thorough testing is performed." See: Ellenbogen, chapter on "Implantable Cardioverter Defibrillator"

29. During ICD testing after implant, how is VF induced?
   a. **2000 Hz pulse trains at different rates**
   b. **50 Hz pacing burst or shock on T wave**
   c. **It is not. Only VT is induced and tested**
   d. **Low voltage pulse trains at different rates**

ANSWER b. 50 Hz burst pacing or pulses on T wave. Some ICDs use a 50 Hz fibrillation, much like those used in open heart surgery. Holding a button down generates 50 Hz sine wave electrical signal in the heart. This lethal frequency induces VF. Other companies' protocols use DC energy or shock the patient on the T wave vulnerable period to induce VF or use rapid ventricular burst pacing. Testing of the ICD after implant is less common today.

See: Watson, Chapter on "Implantable Cardioverter Defibrillator"

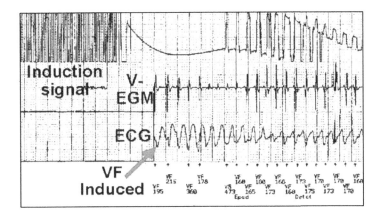

30. During ICD testing when VF is induced and the ICD fails to fire, all the following are true EXCEPT:
   a. **Defibrillating over the ICD may damage the device**
   b. **If your initial shocks fail, try different paddle positions (E.g., AP)**
   c. **Delay ACLS for up to 1 minute to allow the ICD to detect and treat the VF**
   d. **Epicardial ICD patches may insulate the heart against anterior-lateral shocks**

ANSWER: c. Delay ACLS for up to 1 minute to allow the ICD to detect and treat the VF is TOO LONG a delay. Remember in cardiac arrest you only have 4 minutes until brain death begins, less in sick patients. Watson says: "Should an arrhythmia occur; the device will usually detect and start therapy in less than 30 seconds. During emergency situations, however, care of the patient should be based on BCLS and ACLS protocols. Standard treatment should not be delayed. . .. If external defibrillation is required, avoid placing the paddles directly over the implanted device. Should the standard anterior-lateral paddle placement fail to convert the rhythm, consider changing the paddle placement to anterior-posterior. Epicardial patches may tend to insulate the heart from external shocks, thus reducing their effectiveness." See: Watson, Chapter on "Implantable Cardioverter Defibrillator"

31. In two coil ICDs the shocking electrodes are usually configured to shock between the:
   a. **SVC & RV**
   b. **SVC & LV**
   c. **Can & RV**
   d. **Can & LV**

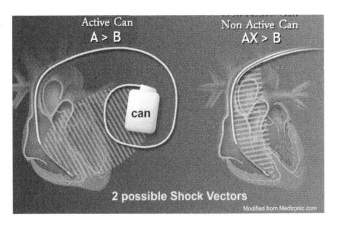

ANSWER: a. SVC & RV. Zipes says, [In the two-coil design] "The proximal coil is often located in the superior vena cava or subclavian vein.... Invariably, [ICDs] have a high-energy coil located near the distal end and lie within the right ventricular cavity.... The development of smaller ICD generators has allowed pectoral implantation, which has enabled the use of the outer generator casing as the second electrode (hot can)." See: Zipes, chapter on ICDs

Between these 3 large defibrillation electrodes (RV, IVC and Can) there are many possible programable configurations for the defibrillation vector, such as RV -> Can, RV -> IVC, etc. See: Medtronic.com, Core ICD Concepts, Module #3

32. You are implanting an ICD on a 12-year-old female patient with genetic cardiomyopathy. During an initial EP study, she is both VT and VF inducible. But, during the ICD implant procedure the implanted leads fail to provide an adequate DFT. You recommend:
   a. **Implanting a CS lead**
   b. **Implanting an LV lead**
   c. **Implanting a high output device**
   d. **Implanting a subcutaneous lead array**

ANSWER: d. Implanting a subcutaneous lead array. With inadequate defibrillation safety margin, a SQ array may be her best option. Stephenson says: "Despite the benefits of transvenous implantable cardioverter defibrillators (ICDs), concern exists that patients with high defibrillation thresholds (DFTs) have an inadequate safety margin between the DFT and the maximum defibrillator energy. A new transvenous ICD lead adjunct, a subcutaneous lead array (SQ Array), was developed to increase safety margins by lowering DFTs. Composed of three lead elements joined in a common yoke, the SQ Array is tunneled subcutaneously in the left lateral chest." See: Electrophysiological Interventions for Inherited Arrhythmia Syndromes, Stephenson, Circulation, Aug. 2012

The minimally invasive implantable cardioverter-defibrillator (ICD) is termed a Subcutaneous Implantable Defibrillator (S-ICD). This approach avoids implanting transvenous leads into the heart, which has been the usual procedure for cardiac devices. Instead, the ICD is entirely implanted outside the thoracic wall.

Cardiac Resynchronization Therapy:

1. ACC, AHA, HRS guidelines recommend CRT for patients who have CHF with functional class III or IV on optimal medical therapy with an EF < _____ and QRS duration >_____.
   a. **35%, 0.12 sec**
   b. **35%, 0.16 sec**
   c. **50%, 0.12 sec**
   d. **50%, 0.16 sec**

ANSWER: a. 35%, 0.12 sec. "(Class I) Recommendations for Cardiac Resynchronization Therapy in Patients with Severe Systolic Heart Failure 1. For patients who have LVEF less than or equal to 35%, a QRS duration greater than or equal to 0.12 seconds, and sinus rhythm, CRT with or without an ICD is indicated for the treatment of NYHA functional Class III or ambulatory Class IV heart failure symptoms with optimal recommended medical therapy." Although an EF > 50% is normal, heart failure does not normally appear until the heart is dilated and EF is much reduced.

See: ACC/AHA/HRS 2008 Guidelines for Device-Based Therapy of Cardiac Rhythm Abnormalities

2. What the type of pacemaker is shown in this Xray?
   a. **(S-ICD) Subcutaneous ICD**
   b. **(DCP) Dual chamber pacing**
   c. **(MLTP) Multi-lead Transvenous pacing**
   d. **(CRT) Cardiac Resynchronization Therapy**

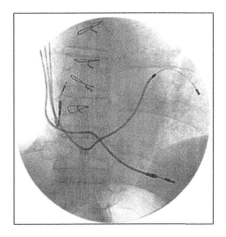

ANSWER: d. (CRT) Cardiac Resynchronization Therapy is also termed biventricular pacing (may hear it called BiV pacing). A biventricular pacemaker, also known as CRT (cardiac resynchronization therapy) is a type of pacemaker that can pace both RV and LV to coordinate ventricular contraction. LV pacing comes through a lead in the coronary sinus and posterolateral coronary vein. Poor asynchronous ventricular contraction occurs when one ventricular chamber beats before the other resulting in inefficient ejection of blood. This is usually due to bundle branch block. If the side that is blocked receives a pacemaker stimulus timed appropriately early, it may resynchronize contraction of the two ventricles, so they beat at the same time. This helps remodel the dilated heart in CHF patients. In the Xray image, note the three leads: RA, RV and LV (Cor. vein in upper right paces LV).

3. What are the expected benefits of CRT implantation in appropriately responding patients? (Select 3 answers)
   a. **Reduced EF**
   b. **Improved quality of life**
   c. **Elimination of drug therapy**
   d. **Reduced mortality from CHF**
   e. **Reduced hospitalizations form CHF**

ANSWER: b, d, e. It will increase the EF by 5-10% (not decrease it), and CRT does not eliminate drug therapy in heart failure patients. The purpose of CRT (Cardiac Resynchronization Therapy) is to get the RV and the LV to pump together. This is accomplished by placing a lead in the RV and in the branch of the CS which captures the LV. When the LV and the RV are pumping in synchrony it is more efficient and can improve the patient's ejection fraction.

Medtronic says, "It is not a replacement for drug therapy, and it is recommended that cardiac resynchronization therapy patients also continue taking medication as determined by their physician....After receiving a CRT device, you will have limitations with respect to magnetic and electromagnetic radiation, electric or gas-powered appliances, and tools with which you are allowed to be in contact"
See: http://www.medtronic.com/patients/heart-failure/device/benefits-risks/index.htm

4. Biventricular pacemakers / CRT devices are often used to treat patients with:
  a. **CHF**
  b. **WPW**
  c. **Brugada Syndrome**
  d. **Sick Sinus Syndrome**

ANSWER: a. CHF. Cardiac Resynchronization Therapy (CRT) is for severe CHF patients with a wide QRS. Instead of just one ventricular wire, there are two, one for each ventricle. Both ventricular pacing wires fire almost simultaneously and resynchronize the activity of the right and left ventricular contractions in patients with BBB.

Cardiac resynchronization therapy involves placing one atrial lead and two ventricular leads. The RA and RV leads are standard leads placed in the right heart chambers. The new third lead for the left ventricular is placed in a left sided cardiac vein via the coronary sinus. This wire assures that the LV can be paced separately from the RV. It uses atrial- synchronized, simultaneous bi-ventricular pacing. This therapy may reduce paradoxical septal wall motion, improve LV diastolic filling time, reduce pre-systolic mitral regurgitation, and improve LV dP/dt.

Many CHF patients have a bundle branch block or interventricular conduction delay, resulting in a diminished LV preload. When ventricular contraction occurs the LV contracts late and may be displaced to the left as the RV septum displaces it. The result is inefficient and asynchronous ventricular contractions.

Before Implant: Asynchrony

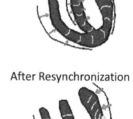

With atrial- synchronized bi-ventricular pacing, both ventricles are activated simultaneously. This allows the LV to complete contraction and begin relaxation earlier, which increases filling time. Bi-ventricular pacing is indicated for heart failure patients who remain symptomatic despite stable, optimal medical therapy with a QRS width ≥ 130ms, LV systolic dysfunction with an ejection fraction (LVEF) of ≤ 35 %, and moderate to severe heart failure (NYHA Class III/IV). Some of these patients respond immediately with decreased heart failure symptoms. See: Medtronic.com

After Resynchronization

5. CRT pacemakers are usually programmed to:
  a.   **Pace 100% of the time**
  b.   **Pace when CHF is detected**
  c.   **Pace during tachycardia (ATP)**
  d.   **Pace whenever BBB is detected**
  e.   **Synchronize atrial & ventricular pacing**

ANSWER: a. Pace 100% of the time. Fogoros says, "CRT pacemakers have three pacing leads instead of two: A right atrial lead, a right ventricular lead, and a left ventricular lead. They work similarly to DDD pacemakers except for two things. First, with CRT pacing both ventricles are paced instead of just the right ventricle. Second, bi-ventricular pacing itself, rather than rate support, is the primary desired therapy – CRT pacemakers are thus programmed to pace virtually 100% of the time, under all conditions." See: Fogoros chapter on Cardiac Resynchronization

6. The main long-term benefit of CRT on the left ventricle is:
  a.   **Reduce end-diastolic size and BP**
  b.   **Reduce end-diastolic size and LV mass**
  c.   **Reduce systolic blood pressure and LV mass**
  d.   **Reduce diastolic and systolic blood pressure**

ANSWER: b. Reduce end-diastolic size and LV mass. CRT increases EF, not decreases it.
Fogoros says, "CRT has been demonstrated to reverse left ventricular remodeling. Specifically, it has been shown to reduce the end-systolic and end-diastolic dimensions of the left ventricle, as well as reducing the left ventricular mass. This reverse remodeling is thought to reflect a fundamental improvement in ventricular systolic function." See: Fogoros chapter on Cardiac Resynchronization

7. In resynchronization therapy, after the LV lead is properly placed and tested the next thing to do is:
  a.   **The guider sheath is sliced and removed**
  b.   **Confirm placement of LV lead with fluoroscopy**
  c.   **The guider sheath is pulled out over the CS lead**
  d.   **Confirm placement of LV lead with a CS venogram**

ANSWER: a. The guide sheath is sliced and removed. Ellenbogen says, "A delivery guide helps insert a lead that is appropriately sized and positioned in the vein and is less likely to be displaced. When used, a delivery guide provides better support than a wire alone to advance the LV lead more securely into the vein. With large veins, a 9F delivery guide allows larger (6F-7F), more stable leads to be placed, versus the smaller, 6F to 7F delivery guides (4F-5F leads).....Cutting a braided CS access catheter and/or delivery guide requires a hemostatic hub designed to be either sliced or removed after the lead is placed.....Before peeling, the assistant stabilizes the lead distally by pinching the walls of the sheath against the lead where the sheath exits the body. With the lead secure, the hub is cracked, and the sheath peeled down to the fingers of the assistant. The cycle of withdraw, pinch, and peel is repeated until the sheath clears the body, and the assistant secures the lead."

See: Ellenbogen, chapter on LV Lead Implantation

8. In resynchronization therapy, after the LV lead is placed it should be tested for: (Select best 2 answers)
   a. **Adequate pacing threshold**
   b. **Retrograde VA conduction**
   c. **Absence of diaphragmatic pacing**
   d. **Placement stability with a tug test**
   e. **Absence of coronary vein occlusion**

ANSWER: a. Adequate pacing threshold and c. Absence of diaphragmatic pacing. Once the LV pacing lead is in place with satisfactory pacing thresholds and no phrenic or diaphragmatic pacing, the delivery guide (if used), CS access catheter, and stylet must be removed without dislodging the lead. All the delivery guides available (BSC, St. Jude, Medtronic, Pressure Products) must be sliced to be removed." See: Ellenbogen chapter on "LV Lead Implantation"

9. Most patients that receive a biventricular pacemaker, also get a/an:
   a. **Implantable defibrillator**
   b. **AV node ablation**
   c. **DVIR pacemaker**
   d. **S-ICD**

ANSWER: a. Implantable defibrillator. Fogoros says, "It ought to be noted further that the vast majority of patients with an indication for CRT therapy also have an indication for an implantable defibrillator; so the great majority of patients with heart failure who are candidates for CRT should receive CRT devices that also provide ICD therapy (referred to as CRT-D devices)" Several studies show CRT-Ds extend patients' lives. See: Fogoros chapter on Cardiac Resynchronization

10. The only significant difference between implanting an ICD and a CRT-D device is a:
   a. **Retrograde LV lead**
   b. **Coil RV lead**
   c. **CS lead**
   d. **LA lead**

ANSWER: c. CS lead. Fogoros says, "The only significant difference between implanting a CRT device and a pacemaker (or between implanting a CRT-D device and an ICD) is the need to place an additional lead for left ventricular pacing." This additional LV lead is placed in a lateral coronary vein via the coronary sinus. See: Fogoros chapter on Cardiac Resynchronization

11. The most common problem associated with pacing the LV from the coronary veins is:
   a. **Inability to capture the ventricle**
   b. **Diaphragmatic stimulation**
   c. **Coronary sinus perforation**
   d. **Coronary vein thrombosis**
   e. **Coronary ischemia**

ANSWER: b. Diaphragmatic stimulation. Fogoros says, "In testing the left-sided lead, the operator looks not only for adequate R wave voltage, pacing threshold, and impedance measurements, but also for evidence of diaphragmatic stimulation – the most common problem with pacing from the coronary veins." Remember to pace with high voltage to check for diaphragmatic stimulation. See: Fogoros chapter on Cardiac Resynchronization

12. A minority of patients treated with biventricular pacing do NOT improve clinically. Most of the following are characteristics of "non-responder patients." Which characteristic below suggests a patient is more likely to be a "good responder" to CRT?
   a. **LBBB (verses RBBB)**
   b. **Transmural MI scar (verses epicardial scar)**
   c. **Ischemic heart disease (verses non-ischemic)**
   d. **Anterior coronary vein lead placement (verses Posterior-lateral)**

ANSWER: a. LBBB (verses RBBB). Ellenbogen clinical characteristics of cardiac resynchronization therapy responders and non-responders. See: Ellenbogen chapter on Cardiac Resynchronization Therapy

	Good Response more likely	**Response less likely**
QRS duration	>150 ms	<150 ms
Heart disease	Non-ischemic	Ischemic
LV contractility	asynchronous	synchronous
Bundle branch block	LBBB	RBBB
Scar burden	Non-transmural scar	Transmural scar
Severity of mitral regurgitation.	Mild-moderate MR	Severe MR
Lead position	Posterior-lateral	Anterior or inferior

13. In placing the LV lead in small diameter coronary veins, which type of resynchronization LV lead design has the smallest diameter?
   a. **Unipolar OTW**
   b. **Unipolar stylet**
   c. **Bipolar OTW**
   d. **Bipolar stylet**

ANSWER: a. Unipolar OTW. Zipes says, "Several factors figure unpredictably into this lead selection, including coronary venous anatomy, extracardiac stimulation, and LV epicardial pacing thresholds. Currently available transvenous LV pacing leads may be either stylet-driven or over-the-wire (OTW). In general, the smallest diameter leads are unipolar and OTW. Larger-diameter leads may be delivered using stylets or OTW (hybrids). Some leads have multiple electrodes that can be used individually or in combinations. Most lead designs rely on passive wedging the lead tip into the target vein for fixation. Reversible self-retaining cants, S- or pigtail-shaped curves, and deployable retention lobes can increase the effective diameter of smaller leads for mechanical stability without degrading maneuverability, but they may be difficult or impossible to extract." See: Zipes, chapter on CRT

14. Three reasons to use multipolar CS/LV leads in resynchronization therapy are: (Select best 3 answers)
   a. **Stimulate the LV in the area of lowest threshold**
   b. **Stimulate the LV in the area of highest threshold**
   c. **Stimulate the LV in the area of least asynchrony**
   d. **Stimulate the LV in the area of greatest asynchrony**
   e. **Prevent vagal nerve stimulation by changing the LV pacing vector**
   f. **Prevent phrenic nerve stimulation by changing the LV pacing vector**

ANSWER: a. lowest threshold, d. greatest asynchrony, & f. Prevent phrenic nerve stimulation by changing the LV pacing vector. The phrenic nerves run down between the lung and heart to innervate the diaphragm. It contains motor, sensory, and sympathetic nerve fibers and is important for breathing. These nerves provide the only motor supply to the diaphragm. If a coronary vein lead is close to the phrenic nerve a coronary vein pacemaker lead can stimulate it and cause diaphragmatic twitching like hiccups. Any of the 4 electrodes can be programmed for LV pacing without moving the lead and changing the pacing vector.
Ellenbogen says, "The important clinical advantage of multiple electrode LV pacing leads and independent output circuits with programmable polarity options is the much better chance of finding a cardiac venous site that offers a low stimulation threshold while minimizing the chances of phrenic nerve stimulation." See: Ellenbogen, chapter on CRT

15. In patients with CHF and LBBB that are severely symptomatic, properly performed CRT-P (without defibrillator) reduces sudden death and mortality by:
   a. **5-15%**
   b. **20-30 %**
   c. **40-50%**
   d. **Symptomatic relief only, no reduction in mortality**

ANSWER: c. 40-50%. Zipes says, "In patients with heart failure, DCM and ventricular conduction delay CRT pacing is an effective adjunctive treatment for moderately severely symptomatic heart failure associated with DCM [Dilated Cardiomyopathy] and ventricular conduction delay. Randomized, controlled trials involving more than 5000 patients have demonstrated modest, concordant improvements in functional class, exercise tolerance, and quality of life. Heart failure hospitalizations are reduced by 29% to 52%, heart failure death by 51%, sudden cardiac death by 46%, and total mortality by 40%....CRT-pacing (CRTP) unaccompanied by back-up defibrillation reduces sudden death and total mortality by 46% and 40%, respectively, effects which exceed the relative mortality benefits of ICDs in overlapping patient populations and which presumably relate to improved pump function and remodeling." See: Zipes chapter on CRT

16. Patient hiccups after placing the LV lead of a BiV pacer, most suggests:
   a. **Atrio-esophageal irritation**
   b. **Competitive ventricular pacing**
   c. **Vagal nerve stimulation of the lung**
   d. **Phrenic nerve stimulation of diaphragm**
   e. **Parasympathetic mediated vasovagal effect**

ANSWER: d. Phrenic nerve stimulation of diaphragm. Medscape says, "Phrenic nerve injury occurred in 0.48% of cases, with right phrenic nerve affected more frequently than the left. Right phrenic nerve injury usually was associated with the electrical disconnection of the right superior pulmonary vein or of the superior vena cava. ... Left phrenic nerve injury occurred instead after ablation of the left atrial appendage. Phrenic nerve palsy is usually associated with dyspnea, cough, or hiccups; diagnosis is usually made with evidence of diaphragmatic elevation at the chest X-ray. Prognosis of phrenic nerve injury is usually particularly good: complete recovery has been described in a report by Bai et al. after an average follow-up of about 9 months...." See: http://www.medscape.com/viewarticle/752625_7

17. In a CRT procedure, where should the LV lead be placed? Select the two best answers:
   a. **LV apical vein**
   b. **Great cardiac vein**
   c. **Posterior cardiac vein**
   d. **Lateral marginal vein**
   e. **Great cardiac vein**
   f. **Little cardiac vein**

ANSWER: c. Posterior Cardiac vein or d. Lateral marginal (or posterolateral) veins.
In the diagram the two veins on the left lateral wall are the usual targets for LV pacing. Ellenbogen says: "Careful studies of retrograde coronary venography have revealed that the anterior interventricular vein is present in 99% of patients and the middle cardiac vein is present in 100%. Those veins are undesirable for LV pre-excitation because they do not reach the late activated portion of the LV free wall. Unfortunately, approximately 50% of patients have only a single vein serving the LV free wall.

Anatomically, this is a lateral marginal vein in slightly more than 75% and a true posterior vein that ascends the free wall in approximately 50% of patients. Thus, as many as 20% of patients may not have a vein that reaches the optimal LV free wall site for delivery of CRT. In some instances, target veins are present but too small for cannulation with existing lead systems, or paradoxically too large to achieve mechanical fixation." Like the coronary arteries there are two major veins the run down the interventricular groves: Great vein and Middle vein. Target veins will be between these two marker veins. See: Ellenbogen, chapter on CRT

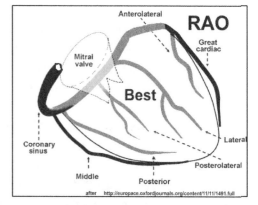

18. During CRT procedures, what is the most common complication of LV lead placement?
   a. **Coronary artery occlusion &/or Myocardial infarction**
   b. **Coronary sinus rupture with cardiac tamponade**
   c. **Coronary vein dissection &/or perforation**
   d. **Ventricular irritability with VT or VF**
   e. **TIA or stroke**

ANSWER: c. Coronary vein dissection &/or perforation of the thin-walled veins where the left sided pacing electrode is placed. Ellenbogen says, "Acute Complications of LV Lead Placement in the Coronary Veins: Endothelial dissection of the CS is the most common complication (~6%-8%); is usually caused by guidewires, catheters, and balloons; and can force premature termination of the procedure. Endothelial dissection is easily recognized during venography as staining of the CS wall, which can track retrogradely to the ostium and pericardial space. However, pericardial tamponade virtually never occurs, unless it is accompanied by a true perforation or rupture of the vessel wall. Intimal flaps heal completely within 2 to 3 months without residual structural damage or venous remodeling. Coronary venous laceration or perforation tends to occur during lead and guidewire manipulations in small-caliber veins, is recognized by sudden free movement of the guidewire within the pericardial space, typically results in tamponade, and often requires cardiac surgery for oversewing of the culprit vessel.... [However,] unlike RV perforation, coronary venous perforation rarely causes tamponade." See: Ellenbogen, chapter on LV lead placement

"Complications Related to the Left Ventricular Lead: CRT trials used CRTs with transvenous implanted leads. The most common complications included coronary vein dissection (1.3%) and coronary vein perforation (1.3%)." See: van Rees, Implantation-Related Complications of Implantable Cardioverter-Defibrillators and Cardiac Resynchronization Therapy Devices: A Systematic Review of Randomized Clinical Trials, JACC 2011

Multisite Pacing: The 5th position indicates where multisite pacing occurs, as in a biventricular CRT device - DDDOV. This update to the code occurred in 2001 with the introduction of CRT pacing. Older codes reserved this for anti-tachycardia functions, now only commonly found in ICDs.

E.g., VVIRV = Ventricular inhibitory pacing with rate modulation and multisite ventricular pacing (i.e., biventricular pacing or more than one pacing site in one ventricle). CRT pacemakers are often used in patients with heart failure, chronic atrial fibrillation, broad QRS and intraventricular conduction delay. See: Ellenbogen: chapter on Pacemaker codes

Lead Extraction:

1. What is the most common reason for cardiac implanted lead removal?
    a. **Lead failure**
    b. **Recalled leads**
    c. **Device infection**
    d. **Replacement with newer device and/or lead**

ANSWER: c. Device infection. Burch, et.al. Say, "Although they are designed to be implanted permanently in the body, occasionally these leads must be removed, or extracted. The most common reason for lead extraction is device infection. If any part of the system becomes infected, it is usually impossible to cure the infection without completely removing all hardware from the body. This requires removal of the pulse generator from the chest wall, as well as removal of all leads from the veins and heart." 60%-80% of these infections are from staphylococcus (CoNS). See: http://www.circ.ahajournals.org/content/123/11/e378.full

2. What is the most common organism causing implanted device infection?
    a. **Streptococci**
    b. **Enterococcus**
    c. **Pseudomonas**
    d. **Staphylococcus**

ANSWER: d. Staphylococcus. Ellenbogen says, "Bacteriology: Staphylococcus species cause most implant infections, with some series reporting 80%.... Organisms such as Pseudomonas, Klebsiella, Proteus, and Enterococcus are seen less frequently (8%). See: Ellenbogen, on "Techniques and Devices for Lead Extraction"

3. In a patient with an implanted ICD, complete removal of both the leads and device is recommended in all the following EXCEPT:
    a. **Occult gram-positive bacteremia**
    b. **Non-functional leads in very old patients**
    c. **Pocket abscess without involvement of leads**
    d. **Symptomatic SVC stenosis or occlusion with lead sepsis**
    e. **Valvular endocarditis without involvement of the device**

ANSWER: b. Non-functional leads in patients with life expectancy less than 1 year. If there is infection of leads or device, everything should be removed.

"Class III: 1. Lead removal is not indicated in patients with non-functional leads if patients have a life expectancy of less than one year. (Level of evidence C)" See: 2009-HRS_LeadExtraction.pdf

4. In patients with implanted cardiac devices when infection is present, when is complete extraction NOT required and medications (antibiotics/antivirals) may be used alone? (Select 2 best answers)
   a. **Incision infection only**
   b. **Viral infection of device only**
   c. **Small vegetation attached to lead**
   d. **Streptococcal infection of leads only**
   e. **If the bacteremia is not due to the device or leads**

ANSWER: a, e. If there is infection of leads or device, everything should be removed.

"Class III: 1. Lead removal is not indicated in patients with non-functional leads if patients have a life expectancy of less than one year. (Level of evidence C)" See: 2009-HRS_LeadExtraction.pdf

5. All the following are "Power Sheaths" used in device extraction EXCEPT:
   a. **RF sheath**
   b. **Laser sheath**
   c. **Flexcath sheath**
   d. **Mechanical sheath**

ANSWER: c. Flexcath sheath. Burch, et.al. Say, "The latest technologies for lead extraction deliver various forms of energy to the tip of the sheath. These are called power sheaths. As the sheath is pushed over the lead and comes to an area of attachment, the operator can turn on the sheath's energy source to heat or vaporize scar tissue. This has the effect of cutting the lead from its attachments, allowing the lead to be removed with much less force. Once the entire lead is freed from scar tissue, it can be pulled out of the body safely. One of these specialized sheaths uses electrocautery, like what is used to cut through tissue in surgery. Another commonly used sheath has a ring of tiny lasers at its tip. When activated, the lasers vaporize water molecules in scar tissue within 1 mm, which allows the sheath to be passed slowly over the entire lead until it can be removed.... There is also a mechanical cutting tool for breaking through dense or calcified scar." See:
http://www.circ.ahajournals.org/content/123/11/e378.full

HRS Lead Extraction.pdf lists 7 extraction tools: Traction Devices, Mechanical Sheaths, Laser Sheaths, Rotating Threaded Tip Sheath, Telescoping Sheaths.
See: 2009-HRS_LeadExtraction.pdf

6. For patients that have had an implanted pacemaker for several years, which method has been shown most successful at complete lead extraction?
   a. **Mechanical rotating threaded tip sheath**
   b. **Traction with locking lead**
   c. **Laser sheath**
   d. **RF sheath**

ANSWER: c. Laser sheath. Hauser, et.al., say: "The multicenter randomized pacing lead extraction with the excimer sheath (PLEXES) trial found that laser-assisted extraction was more efficacious than non-laser techniques in 301 patients. Laser-assisted extraction resulted in a significantly higher proportion of complete lead removals than non-laser methods (94 vs. 64%; $P < 0.001$) ...." See: Medscape: Deaths and Cardiovascular Injuries Due to Device-assisted
Implantable Cardioverter–Defibrillator and Pacemaker Lead Extraction by Hauser, Europace, 2010: at www.medscape.com/viewarticle

7. According to the 2009 Expert Consensus, pacemaker lead extraction should only be done with:
   a. **A pacemaker representative present**
   b. **An electrophysiologist operator**
   c. **Cardiac surgery standby**
   d. **Backup pacing in place**

ANSWER: c. Cardiac surgical standby. The guidelines state the operator may be either an electrophysiologist or cardiothoracic surgeon with adequate extraction experience (~30 cases). Because of the elevated risk of these procedures, they should be done in the surgical suite of a hospital with a high volume of extraction procedures. Note in the diagram how simple traction can tear tissue from the heart resulting in tamponade.

Hauser, et.al. Say: "In conclusion, device-assisted chronic pacemaker and ICD lead extractions have resulted in deaths and cardiovascular injuries due to catastrophic venous tears and myocardial perforations. Many of the deaths occurred despite emergency surgical intervention. However, immediate surgery was often successful, and competent standby cardiothoracic surgery is essential when performing pacemaker and ICD lead extraction with or without device assistance.... These findings suggest that device-assisted lead extraction should be performed only in specialized centers by experienced physicians and their teams."
See: Medscape: Deaths and Cardiovascular Injuries Due to
Device-assisted Implantable Cardioverter–Defibrillator and Pacemaker Lead Extraction by Hauser, Europace, 2010: at www.medscape.com/viewarticle/719558_4

8. Considering the major complication of pacemaker lead extraction, what equipment is most important to have available?
   a. External pacemaker
   b. Embolectomy device
   c. Pericardiocentesis tray
   d. Emergency thoracotomy tray

ANSWER: c. Pericardiocentesis tray. Ellenbogen quotes a 1.4% risk of pericardial tamponade, 0.4% hemothorax and a 0.8% of death. Because of this, he recommends performing extractions in the OR and only when essential. He says, "The operator should have on hand all the tools that may be needed in a complex case, whether their use is anticipated or not. A pericardiocentesis tray, a chest tube kit and an emergency thoracotomy tray should be readily available, and an echocardiography machine should be accessible [to image pericardial effusion] .... When unmodified traction is applied to the lead, the heart wall may invaginate and tear the myocardium around the lead tip. Using countertraction, the outer sheath holds the myocardium in place, thus minimizing deformity and tearing of the myocardium." Push on the sheath, pull on the lead to give counter-traction as shown. Have ICE available in case of tamponade. Passive leads and chronically implanted leads are more difficult to extract." See, Ellenbogen chapter on "Techniques of pacemaker implantation and removal"

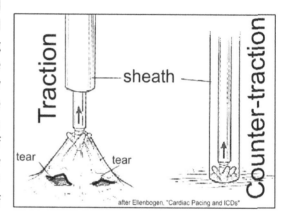

after Ellenbogen, "Cardiac Pacing and ICDs"

Chapter 19
Complications & Post Procedure

1. Complications (pg. 757)
2. Mechanical Circulatory Support Devices (pg. 775)
3. Post Procedure (pg. 781)

EP Essentials LLC

Complications:

1. During the procedure, the RV was punctured with a catheter. The patient becomes hypertensive and groggy. The physician attempts to explain the seriousness of the situation to the patient, and that emergency pericardiocentesis or surgery is needed, but the patient is unresponsive.
The standard informed consent form was signed and is on the chart. Without verbal informed consent of the patient to puncture his chest with a pericardiocentesis needle you should:
   a. **Proceed with lifesaving Pericardiocentesis anyway.**
   b. **Proceed with non-interventional life support maneuvers. E.g., Transcutaneous pacemaker, CPR...**
   c. **Defer the procedure until more specific informed consent can be obtained.**
   d. **Call a consulting physician and/or surgeon into the lab to get a second opinion.**

ANSWER: a. Proceed with lifesaving Pericardiocentesis anyway. Even if the consent form does not mention the possibility of these emergency maneuvers (most do), you should proceed with Pericardiocentesis on the basis that this is a lifesaving emergency procedure. In this groggy state the patient is not competent to decide. This is "implied consent." It is analogous to the decision to do CPR on an unconscious patient. YOU DO IT unless you know of specific "Do Not Resuscitate" (DNR) orders. As a professional, it would be negligent to do otherwise. See: Pepine, Chapter on "Cath Techniques..."

2. An apprehensive elderly patient experiences pain during femoral vein catheter insertion. After the catheters were advanced to begin the electrophysiology study, the patient feels nauseous, with pale cool skin. Her BP is 80/50 mmHg and falling. The HR remains at 65/min. What complication is developing?
   a. **Cardiogenic shock**
   b. **Vasovagal reaction**
   c. **Anaphylaxis**
   d. **Allergic reaction**

ANSWER: b. Vasovagal reactions are usually characterized by bradycardia. However, in older patients (as here) hypotension may be the only sign. Fear and anxiety are a setup for vasovagal reactions. Add a little pain and the vagus nerve goes wild. The overstimulated parasympathetic system depresses all cardiac functions: HR, BP, contractility, EF... And the patient is in trouble.

Vasovagal reactions need to be identified and treated quickly. If allowed to persist, irreversible shock may develop. These vagal discharges can usually be quickly counteracted with .5-1 mg. Atropine IV, elevation of the legs, and fluid administration. Pressor drugs may be used if hypotension persists. See: Grossman, Chapter on "Complications"

3. Within minutes after coronary sinus angiography the patient develops wheezing and becomes short of breath. The BP falls to 90/50 mmHg The pulse raises to 120. Frequent PVCs are seen. He becomes pale and diaphoretic. How should the patient be positioned?
   a. **Supine, Elevate the legs 6 - 12 inches**
   b. **Sit the patient up 30-45 degrees**
   c. **Turn in left lateral position - legs flexed**
   d. **Reverse Trendelenburg position**

ANSWER: a. Supine, Elevate the legs 6 - 12 inches or Trendelenburg, not reverse Trendelenburg. These are classic signs and symptoms of anaphylactic shock. It is due to loss of plasma volume with an increase in hematocrit. These are the same characteristics of hypovolemic shock. Both are treated by administration of IV fluid. Raising the patient's legs provides an immediate "transfusion" of lower limb blood into the thorax. See: Braunwald, chapter on "Acute Circulatory Failure."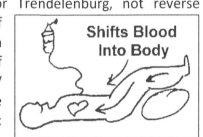

4. Neurological complications may be associated with emboli from this area.
   a. **Femoral arterial access site**
   b. **Femoral vein access site**
   c. **Right atrium/ventricle**
   d. **Left atrium/ventricle**

ANSWER: d. Left atrium/ventricle. Emboli from the left ventricle, aortic valve or aorta may cause neurological complications during a VT ablation whereas emboli form the left atrium may cause this complication during left atrial procedures. This risk may be mitigated with careful anticoagulation, the use of ICE for the detection of thrombus formation. This may be treated with thrombolytic therapy.
2019 HRS/EHRA/APHRS/LAHRS expert consensus statement on catheter ablation of ventricular arrhythmias Journal of Arrhythmia, 2020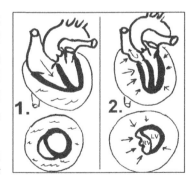

5. Non-cancerous SVC obstruction is usually caused by:
   a. **Right pulmonary vein isolation**
   b. **Atherosclerosis**
   c. **Deep vein thrombosis**
   d. **Indwelling pacer leads**

ANSWER: d. Indwelling pacer leads. Braunwald says, "In the developed world, SVC syndrome of nonmalignant cause (benign SVC syndrome) is usually iatrogenic in origin, and most frequently caused by indwelling intravenous catheters and pacing leads. Complications of pacemaker lead placement, such as venous thrombosis and Stenosis, occur in up to 30 percent of patients. Only a few patients become symptomatic, however, but the presence of multiple leads, retention of severed lead(s), and pervious lead infection may increase risk for

SVC syndrome.... Ideally, interventional treatment should also include removal of the inciting lead or catheter. ...In patients with SVC syndrome of nonmalignant cause, based on mid-term follow-up results, stenting is the treatment of choice." In this example the SVC developed small collateral circulation. See: Braunwald, chapter on "Endovascular Treatment of Noncoronary Obstructive Vascular Disease"

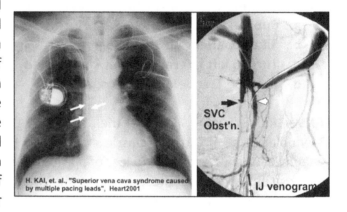

6. SVC obstruction is best treated with:
   a. **Surgical venoplasty**
   b. **Thrombolytic drugs**
   c. **Angioplasty**
   d. **Stent**

ANSWER: d. Stent. Braunwald says, "superior vena-cava stenting is a low-risk procedure that provides fast and long-lasting symptomatic relief in malignant caval obstruction.... In patients with SVC syndrome of nonmalignant cause, based on mid-term follow-up results, stenting is the treatment of choice. Surgical therapy should be reserved for patients with benign SVC syndrome refractory to percutaneous therapy." See: Braunwald, chapter on "Endovascular Treatment of Noncoronary Obstructive Vascular Disease"

7. An abrupt fall in blood pressure during cardiac ablation may be indicative of this complication.
   a. **Cardiac Tamponade**
   b. **Valvular Injury**
   c. **AV Fistula**
   d. **Stroke**

ANSWER: a. Cardiac Tamponade. This may be caused by catheter manipulation, RF delivery, or epicardial perforation. An arterial line is recommended to monitor pressure during complex ablations. Contact force sensing catheters may be useful in monitoring the amount of force that is being applied to the cardiac tissue to help prevent perforation. Pericardiocentesis may need to be utilized if this complication occurs.

2019 HRS/EHRA/APHRS/LAHRS expert consensus statement on catheter ablation of ventricular arrhythmias Journal of Arrhythmia, 2020

8. When does pericardial effusion become pericardial tamponade?
   a. **When blood enters pericardium (hemorrhagic)**
   b. **When the effusion is over 200 ml**
   c. **When cardiac compression begins**
   d. **When the effusion becomes loculated**

ANSWER c. When cardiac compression begins. Effusion continues until pericardial pressure equals the RA and RV diastolic filling pressures. At this point RA and RV collapse begins, RV preload falls, and hence LV preload and SV fall. BP drops and death is imminent if the rate of pericardial pressure increase is greater than the rate of filling pressure increases. Pericardiocentesis is required.

The left diagram (#1.) shows the chronic effusive pericardium filling. This is effusion, not tamponade, and sometimes 2000 ml of fluid may accumulate slowly as the pericardium stretches, without tamponade. However, in the right diagram (#2.), the RA effusion leads to tamponade and RV collapse because the effusion occurs faster than the pericardium can stretch and pressure builds up, exceeding the cardiac filling pressures. This is tamponade. It is easily seen on echo by collapse of the RA & RV in diastole as shown. In the EP lab a puncture of the heart may cause a rapid accumulation of blood in the pericardium requiring pericardiocentesis. See: Braunwald, chapter on "Pericardial Diseases."

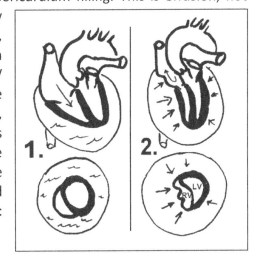

9. How should the patient be positioned for a pericardiocentesis procedure?
   a. **Propped up at 20-30 degrees**
   b. **Propped up to about 45 degrees**
   c. **Trendelenburg position**
   d. **Reverse Trendelenburg position**

ANSWER: b. Propped up to about 45 degrees with a wedge or bolster. This brings the heart closer to the anterior wall and allows the pericardial fluid to pool into the anterior/inferior pericardium to be more easily "tapped" by the pericardiocentesis needle. Grossman says, "The patient torso is propped to a level of about 45° using a bolster or other mechanism, and the transducers are zeroed to the level of the

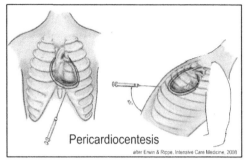
Pericardiocentesis
after Erwin & Rippe, Intensive Care Medicine, 2008

heart position. The subxiphoid approach is classic: Removal of as little as 50 mL is often sufficient to relieve frank tamponade and improve hemodynamics. After removal of 100 to 200 mL of fluid, it is informative to remeasure the pericardial and right atrial pressure before resuming aspiration." See Grossman, chapter on Pericardial Disease.

10. **Two common puncture sites used in pericardiocentesis are:**
    a. **Angle of Louis or point of maximum intensity (PMI)**
    b. **High parasternal and suprasternal**
    c. **Internal jugular and subclavian**
    d. **Subxiphoid and intercostal**
    e. **Axillary and subcostal**

ANSWER: d. Subxiphoid and intercostal. Kern shows several areas of access for pericardiocentesis, all on the lower part of the rib cage or sternum. Grossman says, "The patient's torso is propped up to a level of about 45 degrees.... The subxiphoid approach is classic: a skin nick is made 1 to 2 cm below the costal margin just to the left of the xiphoid process, to allow the needle to miss the ribs.... entering the pericardial space overlying the right ventricle. Echocardiography from the subxiphoid window is thus especially useful...apical or low parasternal intercostal puncture sites are potential alternatives..." See: Grossman, chapter on "Pericardial Disease"

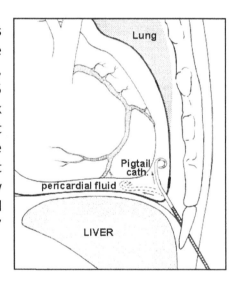
Lung
Pigtail cath.
pericardial fluid
LIVER

11. **During pericardiocentesis, continue to aspirate fluid from the pericardial space until:**
    a. **Until pericardial pressure equals RA pressure**
    b. **The cardiac silhouette stops bouncing**
    c. **You can no longer aspirate fluid**
    d. **About 50 ml remains**

ANSWER: c. You can no longer aspirate fluid. Grossman says, "Removal of as little as 50 ml. is often sufficient to relive frank tamponade and improve hemodynamics. After removal of 100 to 200 ml. of fluid, it is informative to remeasure the pericardial and right atrial pressure before resuming aspiration. When fluid can no longer be aspirated, fluoroscopy should show that the previously immobile cardiac silhouette now exhibits a normal pulsation pattern, and a repeat echocardiogram should show only minimal posterior effusion…. Tamponade physiology is relieved when the right atrial pressure falls and intrapericardial pressure is restored to a level at or below zero." See, Grossman, chapter on "Pericardial Disease"

12. The classic signs of acute pericardial tamponade (Beck's triad) are:
   a. **Drop in O2 saturation, tachycardia, and space between coronary arteries & LV wall on fluoro.**
   b. **Low arterial blood pressure, distended neck veins, and distant heart sounds.**
   c. **Low arterial blood pressure, mental confusion, and tachycardia.**
   d. **Nausea, chest pain, and sense of impending doom.**
   e. **Anxiety, chest pain, and distended neck veins.**

ANSWER: b. Low arterial blood pressure, distended neck veins, and distant heart sounds. Beck's triad is a collection of three medical signs associated with acute cardiac tamponade, an emergency condition wherein fluid accumulates around the heart and impairs its ability to pump blood. The signs are low arterial blood pressure, distended neck veins, and distant, muffled heart sounds. Remember the difference between signs and symptoms. Signs can be measured. The symptoms are what the patient feels. Only the last two answers are signs.

13. After several unsuccessful transseptal punctures the physician begins to worry. What is one of the earliest symptoms of acute pericardial tamponade?
   a. **Sense of Euphoria**
   b. **Pulsus paradoxus**
   c. **Hypotension**
   d. **Bradycardia**
   e. **Chest pain**

ANSWER: e. Chest pain. Holmes says, "The occurrence of myocardial perforation and subsequent fluid accumulation within the pericardium should be suspected clinically during the time of catheterization if the patient begins to complain of chest pain. The typical pain of a new pericardial irritation is that of substernal discomfort sometimes radiating up into the neck and jaw. Acute pericardial irritation can also present with atypical symptoms such as shoulder discomfort, abdominal discomfort, or even nausea. In some instances, the patient may describe a sense of doom even before hemodynamic changes are observed."

"Central aortic pressure and RA pressures can provide excellent indirect evidence of perforation and subsequent tamponade. In the initial stages, the blood pressure response is variable: although hypotension is a hallmark of tamponade, systemic aortic pressure may

increase initially along with an increase in heart rate due to a sympathetic response to the initial pericardial irritation. On occasion, the earliest finding is acute bradycardia and hypotension, reflecting a vasovagal reaction to sudden pericardial stretch. Other symptoms may include nausea or chest discomfort. As tamponade begins to develop, systemic pressure may be sustained transiently by increased adrenergic stimulation and peripheral vasoconstriction. However, pulse pressure will decrease and pulsus paradoxus develops, reflecting an exaggerated decrease in pulse pressure during inspiration. At this time, RV filling pressures will begin to elevate." Remember that symptoms are what the patient feels.
See: Holmes, "Iatrogenic Pericardial Effusion and Tamponade in the Percutaneous Intracardiac Intervention Era", Holmes, et al, JACC, Aug. 2009

14. Following several unsuccessful transeptal needle puncture attempts, a patient's BP is falling, and his neck veins are distended. The associated complication is:
   a. **Bradycardia associated with hemopericardium**
   b. **Aortic puncture with pericardial tamponade**
   c. **LV puncture with myocardial infarction**
   d. **TIA or stroke from dislodged thrombus**

ANSWER: b. Aortic puncture with pericardial tamponade. The aortic root lies close to the fossa Ovalis where the transeptal puncture is made. Any slight deviation in anatomy or needle location can puncture the aorta. This may seal because the needle is small. Or it may bleed into the pericardium, compressing the heart so much that it cannot fill properly. Cardiac tamponade can be a fatal complication if not recognized and treated promptly.

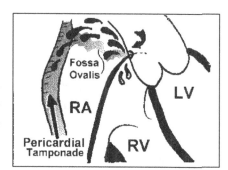

Pressure monitoring at the needle tip would tell you immediately if you punctured the aorta. If bleeding occurs around the needle, the Brockenbrough catheter can be used to plug the puncture site while the patient is taken to surgery. Pericardiocentesis in the lab may be lifesaving.
See: Grossman, chapter on "Percutaneous Approach."

15. In the EP lab, pericardiocentesis is usually done with two kinds of guidance/imaging?
   a. **Fluoro & 2-dimensional echocardiogram**
   b. **ECG & 2-dimensional echocardiogram**
   c. **Fluoro & Intracardiac echocardiogram**
   d. **ECG & Intracardiac echocardiogram**

ANSWER: a. Fluoro & 2-dimensional echocardiogram. Grossman says, "At most centers, pericardiocentesis is performed in the cardiac catheterization laboratory using a combination of echocardiographic and fluoroscopic guidance." ECG may be used but is not really guidance or imaging. A unipolar needle ECG lead will show ST elevation if you accidentally touch or puncture myocardium with the needle. See: Grossman

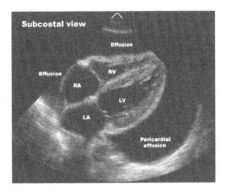

16. Echocardiography is brought to the EP lab to assist with pericardiocentesis. The echo tech says the effusion is "loculated." This means the effusion is:
   a. **Filled with strands of tissue**
   b. **In small compartments**
   c. **Bloody with clots**
   d. **Clear fluid**

ANSWER: b. In small compartments. Loculation means "divided into small cavities or compartments." If the two pericardial walls adhere together with scar tissue, effusion fluid cannot fill that part of the pericardial sack. So, the effusion is not concentric, but localized in certain areas around the heart. Of course, you direct the needle at the pericardial space holding the loculated effusion. Grossman says, "It is helpful to obtain a two-dimensional echo just prior to the procedure to document the presence, location, and size of the effusion; to determine the presence of loculation or significant stranding; and to determine the location on the body surface where the effusion lies closest to the surface at which the fluid depth overlying the heart is maximal. Once an entry location

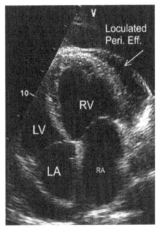

is selected, the echo can indicate the optimal direction for needle passage and the approximate depth of needle insertion that will be required." Watch a dramatic animation of pericardial rupture with bloody pericardial tamponade resulting in cardiac constriction. See: medical dictionary http://www.youtube.com/watch?v=QwgfuDegC5Y&NR=1

17. A major complication of pericardiocentesis is the needle puncturing the heart, and its vessels. The LEAST likely and LEAST dangerous complication is needle puncture of the:

    a. RA
    b. RV
    c. LV
    d. Coronary veins

ANSWER: c. LV is least dangerous, because it is tough and thick, whereas the right heart structures are thin and easily punctured. Coronary arteries and veins are also thin and being on the epicardial surface are easily punctured. Braunwald says: "Injuries to the coronary veins, the right atrium, and the right ventricle are most dangerous; these are thinned walls and likely to bleed briskly. "Simple" perforation of the myocardium, particularly the left ventricle, without laceration is not rare but is well tolerated." See: Braunwald, Chapter on "Pericardial Disease"

18. Retroperitoneal hematoma is a complication to a HIGH femoral artery puncture. It's signs and symptoms are:

    a. The appearance of blood on the surgical dressing
    b. Complaints of chills, fever, and chest pain
    c. Slowing of the pulse and swelling at the puncture site
    d. Pallor, fall in blood pressure, tachycardia, and abdominal pain

ANSWER: d. Pallor, fall in blood pressure, tachycardia and abdominal or back pain. There may be right lower quadrant swelling and tenderness. This rare complication is important because it can be lethal. If the puncture site is high and pressure is held too low, arterial blood may leak from the femoral artery and extravasate superiorly into the pelvis or the peritoneal cavity. This amounts to a loss of blood due to an unseen hematoma, as it is masked by the soft abdomen.

Steeram says: "Early recognition is essential and should be prompted by a falling hematocrit, lower abdominal pain, or neurological changes in the lower extremity. There should be a low threshold for performing abdominopelvic CT scans in such patients. Management of RPH must be individualized:

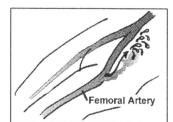

    1. patients with neurological deficits in the ipsilateral extremity require urgent decompression of the hematoma
    2. anticoagulation should be stopped or minimized, 3) hematoma progression by serial CT necessitates surgical evacuation and repair of the arterial puncture site." See: http://www.ncbi.nlm.nih.gov/pubmed/8476149

This is a form of hypovolemic shock caused by insufficient circulating volume. Signs and symptoms of hypovolemic shock include ↓BP, ↓RA, ↓LA filling pressures, ↓CO. vasoconstriction, ↑HR, Lactic acidosis, pallor, and cool skin. Fluid administration can be lifesaving. See: Braunwald, chapter on "Shock."

19. Your overweight patient has undergone right and left heart catheterization. The physician had a challenging time gaining vascular access. He ended up puncturing the left Femoral artery superior to the head of the femur. You are ready to pull the femoral sheath when the patient complains of severe back pain with tenderness in the right inguinal area. ACT is 310, Hgb is 10, O2 sat is 94%. Suspect:
   a. Aortic transseptal perforation with pericardial tamponade
   b. Retroperitoneal hemorrhage
   c. Pseudoaneurysm of LFA
   d. Aortic dissection

ANSWER: b. Retroperitoneal hemorrhage or bleeding into the belly. This complication may occur with high femoral artery punctures. Freed says: "Effective compression may be impossible since the arterial structures area retroperitoneal and hemorrhage from the puncture site may accumulate posteriorly rather than in the inguinal region. . .."
"Abdominal pain occurs in approximately 60% of patients with retroperitoneal
hematomas, with back and flank pain in approximately 25%. . .. Often the diagnosis is suspected from an asymptomatic drop in hemoglobin." See: Freed, chapter on "Medical and Peripheral Complications"

20. All the following are therapy options for retroperitoneal bleed EXCEPT:
   a. Continued pressure over puncture site
   b. Protamine administration
   c. Surgical arterioplasty
   d. Blood transfusion
   e. Thoracentesis

ANSWER: e. Thoracentesis is not indicated since the bleeding is in the abdomen, not the thorax. Freed says: "After confirmation of retroperitoneal hematoma, cessation of heparin and removal of arterial catheters with prolonged compression of the involved vessel is mandatory. Most retroperitoneal bleeds will stop spontaneously. Although many patients may require a blood transfusion, most are hemodynamically stable. However, continued decline in hematocrit, signs of volume depletion, or hemodynamic instability despite reversal of anticoagulants indicate that hematoma expansion is likely and surgical exploration may be warranted." See: Freed, chapter on "Medical and Peripheral Complications"

21. After a long EP case, your patient develops back pain post venous sheath removal. A simple comfort measure specific to this complaint is:
   a. Rolling on contralateral side
   b. Pillow under knees
   c. Added Fentanyl
   d. Sitting upright
   e. Hot blankets

ANSWER: b. Pillow under knees. It is best to treat pain simply and without drugs if possible, depending on the level of pain. You do not want to sit the patient up or roll him during the hemostasis time. Hematoma may result. See: EP Nurse recommendation

22. Following femoral artery catheterization, a patient's leg becomes pulseless, cool, pale, mottled, and painful from acute femoral artery occlusion. Initial therapy should include:
   a. Cooling or icing the extremity
   b. Elevating the extremity
   c. Vasodilator infusion
   d. Heparin infusion

ANSWER: d. Heparin infusion. Initial therapy is to anticoagulate the patient to prevent further embolization and clot extension. The definitive treatment is surgical removal of the clot, usually with Fogarty catheters. Other therapies are bypass graft surgery, Endarterectomy, and thrombolytic medications. See: Hurst and Logue, chapter on "vascular disease." Also, See: Underhill chapter on "vascular diseases." also see study guide B7f4 Arterial occlusion.

23. Acute femoral arterial occlusion following catheterization may be treated with all the following EXCEPT:
   a. Thrombolytic medication
   b. Endarterectomy
   c. Fogarty catheter
   d. Arterial stent
   e. Bypass graft

ANSWER: d. Stents NO. They are excellent to keep a vessel open. But it will not prevent a clot from lodging in a patent vessel.
Other emergency therapy includes:
   • Pain control with narcotics. Keep the patient very warm to relieve arterial spasm. A room warmed to 80-85 degrees helps. Wrap the involved extremity loosely in cotton to preserve body heat and protect it from trauma.
See: Hurst and Logue, chapter on "vascular disease." Also, See Braunwald, chapter on "Diseases of the Aorta." also study guide B7f Arterial occlusion.

24. Acute femoral arterial occlusion following catheterization presents with of all the following clinical signs and symptoms EXCEPT?
   a. Pale or mottled leg color
   b. Warm sweaty leg
   c. Leg Numbness
   d. Leg paralysis
   e. Pulseless leg
   f. Leg pain

ANSWER: b. Warm sweaty leg. Below the occlusion the leg is cool to the touch due to poor capillary flow. This is sometimes termed "Polar" coldness - like the "North Pole." Note they all have words starting with P.

The 6 Ps of acute arterial occlusion are:

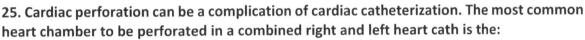

- PAIN
- PARALYSIS
- PARAESTHESIA (Numbness),
- PALLOR
- POLAR (coldness)SS
- PULSELESS

6 Ps of Arterial Occlusion

See: Underhill, chapter on "Abnormalities of coagulation, bleeding and clotting."

25. Cardiac perforation can be a complication of cardiac catheterization. The most common heart chamber to be perforated in a combined right and left heart cath is the:
  a. RA
  b. RV
  c. PA
  d. LA
  e. AO

ANSWER: b. RV. 0.6% of bilateral heart cath patients experience cardiac perforation. The RV is the chamber most often accidentally punctured. It is a thin-walled chamber in which the catheter is often severely torqued and manipulated. RV perforation happens most commonly in elderly female patients and when the RV outflow track is aggressively probed. Most of these perforations in low pressure chambers seal themselves. However, some lead to dangerous pericardial tamponade. In high-risk patients, soft catheters should be

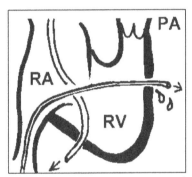

used and carefully manipulated only by experienced physicians. Naturally, in transeptal catheterization the RA is the chamber most often perforated. See: Grossman, Chapter on "Complications..."

26. Twelve hours following angiography a patient develops a painful pulsatile mass just below the skin at the femoral artery puncture site. A femoral artery bruit can be heard with a stethoscope. What is the most likely complication?
  a. **False aneurysm (FA)**
  b. **True aneurysm (TA)**
  c. **AV fistula (FA-FV)**
  d. **Hematoma (FA)**

ANSWER: b. False aneurysms (or pseudoaneurysms) are pulsating encapsulated hematomas in communication with a ruptured artery. Blood swishes back-and-forth between the femoral artery (FA) and the false aneurysmal chamber, through a narrow neck.

These aneurysms frequently enlarge and rupture, although the rupture may not occur for several days post-cath. The causes include enlarged puncture site and inadequate groin compression when the sheath is pulled. Surgical intervention may be necessary. Some practitioners attempt to close the false lumen with additional groin compression while observing Doppler flow through the aneurysm's "Neck." A compressor clamp may be used to close the neck and allow it to clot off. Grossman says, "Blood flowing in and out of the arterial puncture expands the hematoma cavity during systole and allows it to decompress back into the arterial lumen in diastole. Since the hematoma cavity contains no normal arterial wall structures (i.e., media or adventia), this condition is referred to as false or pseudoaneurysm." See: Grossman, chapter on "Complications..."

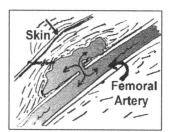

27. To rule out pneumothorax prior to discharge following PPI, it is most important to order:
    a. **ECG telemetry and 12-lead ECGs**
    b. **Pulmonary function tests**
    c. **PA & lateral chest x-rays**
    d. **Echocardiography**

ANSWER: c. PA & lateral chest x-rays. Edwards says, "An undisputed indication for chest radiography after pacemaker insertion is to confirm the presence of clinically significant pneumothorax. Chest radiography will in this situation guide subsequent management, in terms of the decision to observe, aspirate or insert an intercostal drain...." See: Journal of Postgraduate Medicine, 2005, NC Edwards, et. al.

28. Your patient has a history of chronic AF, anterior MI, renal dialysis, and CHF.
What is the complication to watch for when ablating with an irrigated tip ablation catheter on long cases?
    a. **Stroke**
    b. **AV block**
    c. **Hypertension**
    d. **Hypervolemia**
    e. **Pericardial tamponade**

ANSWER: d. Hypervolemia with volume overload and exacerbation of CHF resulting in pulmonary edema. Excessive fluid administration through the irrigated catheter can overload these patients and push them into edema and congestive heart failure.

Shah, says, "A 17 or 30 ml/min saline infusion rate, depending on the type of procedure, is required to achieve effective control of coagulum and char on the ablation electrode resulting in the potential for significant volume loads to the patient during complex and lengthy procedures. Some patients have co-morbidities that reduce their ability to manage a large volume load, making them susceptible to developing pulmonary edema or heart failure during or after the ablation procedure. Patients with left ventricular dysfunction and/or renal failure are particularly susceptible and would benefit from a lower volume load." See: http://www.biosensewebster.com/docs/Shah.pdf

29. To best reduce the risk of PV stenosis after RF induced PVI, reduce target ablation temperature, energy output and:
   a. **Monitor esophageal temperature**
   b. **Ablate the antrum, not the in the PV**
   c. **Use RF not irrigated RF energy**
   d. **Monitor PA pressure**

ANSWER: b. Ablate the antrum, not in the PV. Issa says, "The best way to manage PV stenosis is to avoid it [pulmonary vein]. PV stenosis is independently related to RF lesion location, size, and distribution, and to baseline PV diameter. The prevalence of this complication has decreased because of various factors, including abandonment of in-vein ablation at the site of the AF focus, limiting ablation to the extra ostial portion of the PV or PV antrum, use of advanced imaging techniques to guide catheter placement and RF application, reduction in target ablation temperature and energy output, and increased operator experience." Pacemaker perforation of the ventricle can also cause this if the pacing electrode touches the diaphragm. See: Issa, chapter on "Complications of Catheter Ablation of AF"

30. To prevent atrio-esophageal fistula during PVI ablation, any of the following methods may be recommended EXCEPT:
   a. **Marking the esophagus with electroanatomical mapping systems**
   b. **Monitoring esophageal internal temperature**
   c. **Marking the esophagus with a contrast**
   d. **Esophageal balloon inflation**

ANSWER: d. Esophageal balloon inflation. No, it may increase contact with the LA and increase the chance of burning through. Sorgente says, "the strict anatomic relationship between the left atrium and the esophagus together with the delivery of radiofrequency energy on the posterior wall of the left atrium are the principal causes leading to the occurrence of atrio-esophageal fistula.... it is strongly advisable to avoid delivery of elevated levels of radiofrequency energy on the posterior wall of the left atrium or on the posterior aspect of the PV antra, usually areas of presumable contact with the esophagus.... It's customary practice in many centers to monitor the esophageal temperature with an esophageal probe to titrate the radiofrequency energy application on the areas at potential risk of esophageal injury and to stop radiofrequency energy delivery when a rapid elevation of the esophageal internal temperature is recorded. In centers which do not perform cardiac computed tomography or cardiac magnetic resonance before the procedure, the use of an esophagram with water soluble contrast may represent a valid trick to avoid ablation on portions of the left atrium in close vicinity of the esophagus"

"Localization of the region of contact between left atrium and esophagus can be obtained before the procedure itself by means of computed tomography after a barium swallow or magnetic resonance after a barium plus gadolinium glutamate swallow or during the ablation procedure with intracardiac echocardiography. Electroanatomical mapping systems... allow the superimposition of the esophageal imaging obtained... with the real-time electroanatomical map of the left atrium"

"Questionable is also the clinical utility of a cooled saline-irrigated balloon inside the esophageal lumen during AF catheter ablation. Indeed, if on the one hand cooling of the internal lumen of the esophagus should limit the transmural rise of the temperature, on the other hand inflation of a balloon device inside the esophagus could increase the area of contact with the left atrium, enhancing paradoxically the heat transfer and the chances of thermal injury." See: Sorgente, et al., Europace. 2011, on Medscape.com, "Complications of Atrial Fibrillation Ablation"

31. What are the two most common major complications in PVI procedures?
   a. **Atrioesophageal fistula and cardiac tamponade**
   b. **Atrioesophageal fistula and complete AV block**
   c. **PV stenosis and cardiac tamponade**
   d. **PV stenosis and complete AV block**

ANSWER: c. PV stenosis and cardiac tamponade. Braunwald says, "The risk of a major complication from radiofrequency catheter ablation of AF is reported to be 5% to 6%. In a large international survey, the most common major complications were cardiac tamponade (1.2%), pulmonary vein stenosis (1.3%), and cerebral thromboembolism (0.94%). The risk of vascular injury is reported to be 1% to 2%. " See: Braunwald chapter on AF

32. The three most common lethal complications of PVI are: (select best three answers)
   a. **Atrioesophageal fistula**
   b. **Phrenic nerve ablation**
   c. **Myocardial infarction**
   d. **VF or intractable VT**
   e. **Cardiac Tamponade**
   f. **Complete AV block**
   g. **PV stenosis**
   h. **Stroke**

ANSWER: a. Atrioesophageal fistula, e. Cardiac Tamponade, h. Stroke. Braunwald says, "The risk of atrioesophageal fistula is less than 0.1%; however, this complication is of great concern because it often is lethal. Large international surveys have reported the risk of a fatal complication to be in the range of 0.05% to 0.1%. In a survey of 32,569 patients who underwent catheter ablation of AF, the mortality rate was 0.1%, and the most common causes of death were cardiac tamponade (25% of deaths), stroke (16%), atrioesophageal fistula (16%), and pneumonia" See: Braunwald chapter on AF.

33. The chief sign of phrenic nerve damage is:
   a. **Apnea**
   b. **Nausea**
   c. **Dyspnea**
   d. **Chronic cough**

ANSWER: c. Dyspnea. In phrenic nerve damage "The most frequent symptom is dyspnea, which is present in all symptomatic patients. Other symptoms or clinical findings are cough or hiccup during ablation and the development of post ablation pneumonia or pleural effusion." See Issa, chapter on "Complications of Catheter Ablation of AF"

34. To detect and prevent phrenic nerve damage during PVI procedures, observe diaphragmatic motion by pacing the phrenic nerve or:
   a. **Monitoring patterns of abdominal muscular spasm**
   b. **Observing the minute ventilation**
   c. **Observing inhalation on fluoro**
   d. **Monitoring O2 saturation**

ANSWER: c. Observing inhalation on fluoro. If one side of the diaphragm stops its normal motion, that phrenic nerve is damaged. Medtronic says: "Phrenic nerve impairment – Stop ablation immediately if phrenic nerve impairment is observed. Use continuous phrenic nerve pacing throughout each cryoablation application in the right pulmonary veins. To avoid nerve injury, place a hand on the abdomen in the location of the diaphragm to assess for changes in the strength of the diaphragmatic contraction or loss of capture. In case of no phrenic nerve capture, frequently monitor diaphragmatic movement using fluoroscopy.... New onset hemi-diaphragmatic movement disorder, detected by radiologic assessment, was observed in 11.2% (29/259) of all cryoablation procedures." SEE: Medtronic.com, ARCTIC FRONT®, 2AF232, 2AF282 Cardiac Cryoablation Catheter Technical Manual.

35. What is the usual long-term consequence of phrenic nerve injury during PVI?
   a. **Most patients recover over time**
   b. **Decreased exercise tolerance**
   c. **Chronic dyspnea**
   d. **Chronic cough**

ANSWER: a. Most patients recover over time. Issa says, "Fortunately, phrenic nerve injury has been an infrequent complication of AF catheter ablation. Complete (66%) or partial (17%) recovery of diaphragmatic function was observed in most patients." See Issa, chapter on "Complications of Catheter Ablation of AF"

36. Asymptomatic phrenic nerve damage may be diagnosed after the case with:
   a. Pulmonary effusion on Xray
   b. Pulmonary function testing
   c. Nerve stimulation testing
   d. Hemidiaphragm on Xray

ANSWER: d. Hemidiaphragm on Xray. (Hemidiaphragm is a condition in which half of a patient's diaphragm appears to be raised or elevated.) Some patients with phrenic nerve damage are asymptomatic except for paradoxical diaphragm motion or ipsilateral diaphragmatic elevation on Xray.

"Phrenic nerve injury can be asymptomatic in 31% of cases.... In asymptomatic patients, the diagnosis is made on the routine chest x-ray with hemidiaphragm paresis or paralysis (hemidiaphragm elevation with paradoxical movement)." See Issa, chapter on "Complications of Catheter Ablation of AF"

37. All the following increase the risk of CARDIAC PERFORATION during cardiac catheterization EXCEPT:
   a. Transseptal or endomyocardial biopsy procedure
   b. Temporary pacing catheter placement
   c. Pulmonary or systemic hypertension
   d. Elderly women over 65 years of age

ANSWER: c. Pulmonary or systemic hypertension results in ventricular hypertrophy, which strengthens the ventricle. Because the female RV is thinner, it is more susceptible to perforation, especially in the elderly female. Stiff catheters of any kind also increase the incidence of cardiac perforation and of tamponade. Hypertrophied hearts are more difficult to perforate, because of increased thickness. See: Grossman and Peterson, Chapters on "Complications..."

38. During PVI procedures phrenic nerve damage is most common when ablating the:
   a. Right superior PV
   b. Left superior PV
   c. Posterior LA
   d. Lateral LA

ANSWER: a. Right superior PV. Issa says, "Right phrenic nerve injury has been described during ablation in and around the right superior PV and electrical isolation of the SVC.... Although it is much less common, left phrenic nerve injury can also occur during RF delivery at the proximal LA appendage roof.... The intracardiac course of the right phrenic nerve, especially as it approximates the SVC and RA (and not infrequently the right superior PV), is the principal reason for susceptibility to nerve damage from endocardial ablation." Some labs do RSPV ablation last to avoid this problem early in the case. See Issa, chapter on "Complications of Catheter Ablation of AF"

39. A fall in the patient's hemoglobin may be seen with this complication.
   a. Pseudoaneurysm
   b. Valvular Injury
   c. Heart Failure
   d. TIA

ANSWER: a. Pseudoaneurysm. A fall in the patient's hemoglobin, as well as groin or low back pain may be seen with vascular injury, hematomas, pseudoaneurysm, and AV fistulae. This complication may be mitigated with the use of ultrasound-guided access. Access site complications may be treated with ultrasound-guided compression, thrombin injections, and surgical closure.
2019 HRS/EHRA/APHRS/LAHRS expert consensus statement on catheter ablation of ventricular arrhythmias Journal of Arrhythmia, 2020

40. Two days after successful atrial fibrillation ablation, the patient presented with palpitations, cough and shortness of breath. This complication associated with right superior pulmonary vein isolation with cryoablation is:
   a. Pericardial tamponade
   b. Phrenic nerve damage
   c. Congestive heart failure
   d. Pulmonary vein rupture

ANSWER: b. Phrenic nerve damage. "The right phrenic nerve descends vertically from its origin and continues along the right anterolateral surface of the superior vena cava. Descending down the anterolateral wall of the superior vena cava, it approaches the superior cavo-atrial junction and follows in close proximity to the right-sided pulmonary veins. At this level, the distance between the right superior pulmonary vein and the right phrenic nerve is between 0.0 mm and 2.3 mm. Therefore, the right phrenic nerve is particularly at risk when ablations are carried out in the superior vena cava and the right superior pulmonary vein." Abbadessa, et al, right phrenic nerve palsy following transcatheter radiofrequency current atrial fibrillation ablation: Case report SAFGE Journals, 2019.

41. Which of the following may be a complication of performing a CS venogram? (Select all that apply)
   a. Venous trauma
   b. Vein dissection
   c. Decreased BUN
   d. Contrast-induced nephropathy

ANSWERS: a, b, d. Preprocedural hydration is often utilized to help limit the possibility of contrast-induced nephropathy. "CS venography is generally safe with a compliant occlusive balloon and when the tip of the balloon is observed during a test injection before initial balloon inflation. Contrary to conventional wisdom, it is not safe to inflate a balloon advanced over a wire before a test injection. When the balloon is advanced over a wire into a small branch and inflated before a test injection, it will rupture the vein resulting in extravasation. During balloon inflation, the increased venous pressure distal to the balloon forces contrast into the damaged area, leading to aneurysm formation. If the aneurysm ruptures, blood, and contrast escape into the pericardial space resulting in hemodynamic compromise." Zou, F., Brar, V., & Worley, S. (2021, February). Interventional device implantation, part i: Basic techniques to avoid complications: A hands-on approach. Retrieved May 17, 2021, from https://www.ncbi.nlm.nih.gov/pmc/articles/PMC7894320/

Mechanical Circulatory Support Devices:

1. Which two of the following may pose as a challenge for ablation with a patient that has an LV assist device?
   a. Ablation is not possible and is a Class III indication
   b. Limitations in preprocedural imaging
   c. Inability to use heparin
   d. Electromagnetic noise

ANSWER: b & d. An LV assist device may pose as a challenge during cardiac ablation, but the presence of the device is not a contraindication. Preprocedural imaging is limited as well as an increase in electromagnetic noise making it challenging to observe the required small, fractionated signals in a VT ablation for example.
See: 2019 HRS/EHRA/APHRS/LAHRS expert consensus statement on catheter ablation of ventricular arrhythmias Journal of Arrhythmia, 2020

2. This is a benefit of using a mechanical circulatory support device during an ischemic VT ablation.
   a. Increase in intra-cardiac filling pressures
   b. Decreased likelihood of VT termination
   c. Shorter duration of mapping available
   d. Maintenance of vital organ perfusion

ANSWER: d. Maintenance of vital organ perfusion. Other advantages include a reduction of intra-cardiac filing pressures, LV volume, wall stress, and myocardial O2 consumption. There is also an improvement in cardiac perfusion during prolonged periods of mapping. By maintaining the patient's hemodynamic stability, the physician can map for a longer duration which will increase the likelihood of VT termination without an increase in procedural mortality.

Virk, et al, Mechanical Circulatory Support During Catheter Ablation of Ventricular Tachycardia: Indications and Options. Heart, Lung, and Circulation, 2019

3. Which of the following is not an example of a mechanical circulatory support device?
   a. Impella
   b. ECMO
   c. IVUS
   d. IABP

ANSWER: c. IVUS. IVUS stands for Intravascular Ultrasound. This is a catheter-based ultrasound system used to visualize the circulatory system vasculature. Mechanical circulatory support devices include the IABP (Intra-Aortic Balloon Pump), ECMO (Extracorporeal Membrane Oxygenation), Impella, TandemHeart, and LVAD (Left Ventricular Assist Device).

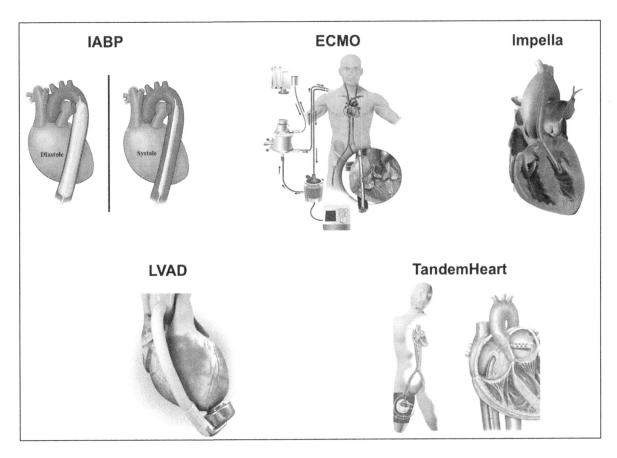

Virk, et al, Mechanical Circulatory Support During Catheter Ablation of Ventricular Tachycardia: Indications and Options. Heart, Lung, and Circulation, 2019

4. Which mechanical circulatory support device would be preferred for an ischemic VT ablation on a patient that may become hemodynamically unstable?
   a. Impella
   b. ECMO
   c. LVAD
   d. IABP

ANSWER: a. Impella. The Impella is the most utilized support device for use during cardiac ablations that may require hemodynamic support. The Impella is a heart pump that is intended for temporary use. It is inserted through a sheath and guided over a wire into the left ventricle. Once in position, and turned on, blood is drawn into the Impella from the left ventricle and expelled into the ascending aorta, taking over the pumping function of the patient's heart. See: Impella Heart Pump https://www.impella.com

5. This is a possible procedural challenge and/or complication often seen with the LVAD during cardiac ablation.
   a. **Cardiac ablation is unable to be performed when an LVAD is utilized.**
   b. **Recording system interference**
   c. **Access site hematoma**
   d. **AV fistula**

ANSWER: b. Recording system interference. The LVAD is not for temporary use and does not utilize the standard access site of the femoral artery. Therefore, access site hematoma and AV fistulas may be seen during cardiac ablation procedures but are unrelated to the use of the LVAD.

Cardiac ablation can be performed on a patient that has an LVAD, but interference (or noise) may be observed on the electrograms.
Virk, et al, Mechanical Circulatory Support During Catheter Ablation of Ventricular Tachycardia: Indications and Options. Heart, Lung, and Circulation, 2019

6. A VT ablation on a hemodynamically unstable patient without a mechanical circulatory support device may require this to be performed. (Pick two)
   a. **Late potential mapping**
   b. **Entrainment mapping**
   c. **Activation mapping**
   d. **Extensive ablations**

ANSWER: a & d. A mechanical circulatory support device makes it possible for the physician to perform a more detailed mapping of the reentrant circuit in a patient that would otherwise be hemodynamically unstable. To perform either activation (timing) or entrainment mapping, the patient must be in tachycardia. With a combination of these mapping strategies, the VT circuit and critical isthmus may be identified. This will lead to a more precise ablation target of the reentrant circuit. If ablation is performed during tachycardia there is a clear endpoint when the tachycardia terminates with ablation and is unable to be reinduced. Without inducing the rhythm, the physician will need to perform more extensive ablations along the scar border to eliminate all reentry channels.

Late potential mapping may be performed while the patient is in sinus rhythm with a 3D mapping system. A detailed substrate (voltage) map be performed at the same time. Channels within the low voltage areas as well as late potentials, or diastolic potentials, will be targeted with ablation. The example displayed is a late activation map with white as all signals acquired before or during the QRS complex and all other colors after the end of the QRS with purple being the latest activation.

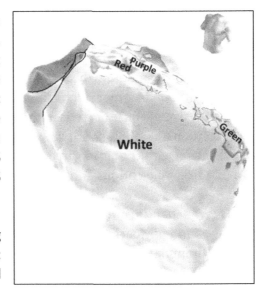

Virk, et al, Mechanical Circulatory Support During Catheter Ablation of Ventricular Tachycardia: Indications and Options. Heart, Lung, and Circulation, 2019

7. Brief episodes of VT during substrate mapping without a myocardial support device may be associated with this post-procedure complication. (Select all that apply)
   a. **Detrimental effects on end-organ perfusion**
   b. **Release of catecholamines**
   c. **Increased inotropy**
   d. **Lactic Acidosis**

ANSWER: a, b, & d. "Even a substrate mapping strategy can be complicated by recurrent VT events during catheter manipulation and require multiple cardioversions. Such repetitive brief episodes of unstable VT can have cumulative detrimental effects on end-organ perfusion, lactic acidosis, the release of catecholamines and neurohormones and activation of systemic inflammatory cytokines. This may lead to depression of myocardial contractility and worsening end-organ perfusion. A major sequela is post-procedural decompensated heart failure, which is associated with increased mortality in follow-up. Acute hemodynamic instability in the peri-procedural setting of VT ablation occurred in 11% of patients with structural heart disease undergoing VT ablation in one study and was associated with an approximately five-fold increased risk of mortality in follow-up." Inotropy relates to contractility, in this example, there would be a depression of myocardial contractility.
Virk, et al, Mechanical Circulatory Support During Catheter Ablation of Ventricular Tachycardia: Indications and Options. Heart, Lung, and Circulation, 2019

8. This mechanical circulatory support system utilizes ECG-based triggers.
   a. **TandemHeart**
   b. **Impella**
   c. **ECMO**
   d. **IABP**

ANSWER: d. IABP. The intra-aortic balloon pump is dependent on ECG-based triggers. This may work well in a stable and regular rhythm, but the use is limited during rapid VT. The IABP is a balloon catheter that is inserted through the femoral artery. The balloon is placed in the descending aorta below the left subclavian artery and above the renal arteries. The balloon inflates during diastole which increases blood flow to the coronary arteries. It then deflates during systole, which decreases the ventricular afterload. The augmentation of the cardiac output with an IABP is approximately 0.5 L/min.

Virk, et al, Mechanical Circulatory Support During Catheter Ablation of Ventricular Tachycardia: Indications and Options. Heart, Lung, and Circulation, 2019

9. This mechanical circulatory support system utilizes an external centrifugal pump.
   a. **TandemHeart**
   b. **Impella**
   c. **ECMO**
   d. **IABP**

ANSWER: a. TandemHeart. The TandemHeart is a percutaneous left atrial-to-femoral artery bypass system that uses an external centrifugal pump. This system uses a 21Fr venous cannula placed transseptal into the left atrium. A 17Fr. Arterial cannula in the femoral artery is also utilized. These ports are connected to the external centrifugal pump the withdraws oxygenated blood from the left atrium and delivers it to the arterial circulation at up to 5L/min.

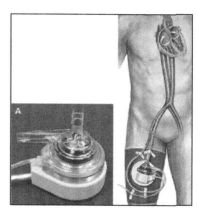

Virk, et al, Mechanical Circulatory Support During Catheter Ablation of Ventricular Tachycardia: Indications and Options. Heart, Lung, and Circulation, 2019

10. The Impella is placed in this location.
   a. **Inlet in the RV / Outlet in the pulmonary artery**
   b. **Inlet in the LV / Outlet in above the aortic root**
   c. **Inlet in the RA / Outlet in the femoral artery**
   d. **Inlet in the LA / Outlet in the femoral artery**

ANSWER: b. Inlet in the LV / Outlet in the aortic root. The Impella has a 2.5Fr axial blood flow pump on the distal end of the catheter. This pump is positioned approximately 4 cm below the aortic valve annulus. The outlet for this system is just above the aortic root, pumping the blood out to the ascending aorta. This system produces an output of up to 2.5 L/min, but the augmentation of cardiac output can be increased to 3.5 L/min (with Impella CP) or 5 L/min (with Impella 5.0).

Virk, et al, Mechanical Circulatory Support During Catheter Ablation of Ventricular Tachycardia: Indications and Options. Heart, Lung, and Circulation, 2019

11. This mechanical circulatory support system may utilize the jugular vein as an access site.
   a. TandemHeart
   b. Impella
   c. ECMO
   d. IABP

ANSWER: c. ECMO. "The venoarterial ECMO involves a 19–25 Fr venous cannula inserted in the right atrium via the femoral venous system and a 17–21 Fr arterial cannula placed in the aorta. Blood is extracted from the venous system (right atrium) using a centrifugal pump and is passed through an external mem-brane oxygenator system and then its return into the arterial system. It can be performed percutaneously at the bedside using femoral or jugular vessels. Alternatively, surgical techniques can be used to facilitate direct cannulation of the right atrium and aorta. ECMO provides biventricular circulatory support and oxygenation thereby alleviating concerns about the potentially deleterious impact of prolonged VT on ventricular function, coronary perfusion, pulmonary perfusion, and reducing the need for additional vasopressor support. It is the MCS of choice in patients with severe right ventricular (RV) dysfunction as none of the other MCS address RV output."
Virk, et al, Mechanical Circulatory Support During Catheter Ablation of Ventricular Tachycardia: Indications and Options. Heart, Lung, and Circulation, 2019

12. Match the following mechanical circulatory support device to the correct mechanism.
   a. TandemHeart
   b. Impella
   c. ECMO
   d. IABP

   1. Diastolic support & systolic unloading via deflation and inflation of balloon within aorta.
   2. Peripheral cardiopulmonary bypass using an external membrane oxygenator system.
   3. Percutaneous left atrial-to-femoral artery bypass using external centrifugal pump.
   4. Percutaneous left ventricle-to-ascending aorta axial pump.

ANSWER: a. 3, b. 4, c. 2, d. 1
Virk, et al, Mechanical Circulatory Support During Catheter Ablation of Ventricular Tachycardia: Indications and Options. Heart, Lung, and Circulation, 2019

13. Aortic Insufficiency is not a contraindication with the use of this system.
   a. TandemHeart
   b. Impella
   c. ECMO
   d. IABP

ANSWER: c. ECMO. Contraindications for the ECMO include severe PVD and uncontrolled bleeding diathesis.

Virk, et al, Mechanical Circulatory Support During Catheter Ablation of Ventricular Tachycardia: Indications and Options. Heart, Lung, and Circulation, 2019

Post Procedure:

1. The recommended way to pull the venous sheath and hold manual pressure while establishing hemostasis post-catheterization is to hold pressure _____ the skin puncture site, with _____ pressure.
   a. Just above, 2-3 fingers digital
   b. Just above, heel of the hand
   c. On, 2-3 fingers digital
   d. On, heel of the hand

ANSWER: c. on, 2-3 fingers digital "when removing venous sheaths, you can hold pressure right on the puncture site (compared to above the site for arterial sheath removals) and you need little pressure because of the low pressures of the venous system. You also do not want to totally occlude the vein, which could lead to

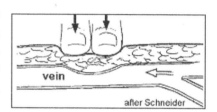

small clot formation." See: Todd Ginapp, Cath Lab Digest 11/5/09

2. The recommended way to pull an arterial sheath and hold manual pressure while establishing hemostasis on the femoral artery post-cath is to hold pressure _____ the skin puncture site, with _____ pressure.
   a. Just above, 2-3 fingers digital
   b. Just above, heel of the hand
   c. Just below, 2-3 fingers digital
   d. Just below, 2-3 fingers digital

ANSWER: a. Just above the skin puncture site with 2-3 fingers digital pressure., Most authors recommend that pressure be held with the 2-3 left middle fingers, with the index finger just superior to the skin puncture site. The index finger compresses the arterial puncture, while the middle (and ring) fingers compress the artery upstream

Holding pressure above ARTERIAL puncture site to occlude the artery. This requires a strong left hand and fingers. Finger pressure is more focused than the heel of the hand and makes it easier to see any bleeding. Notice that the needle track starts at the skin but travels at an angle superiorly down to the artery. If you push directly on the skin puncture you will not see bleeding; if you press below the skin puncture site, you will not compress the needle track.

Ragosta says, "With the sheath still in place, the arterial pulse is palpated above the sheath insertion site using the middle and index fingers of the left hand. The sheath is slowly removed with compression applied above the site using the left hand.... [but not excessive pressure which might strip a clot from the sheath]. Compression

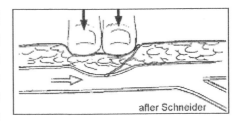

after Schneider

should be applied with enough force to prevent bleeding; initially, this usually obliterates the distal pulse. Pressure should be slowly relieved to allow the palpation of the distal pulse [feel with the right hand on a foot artery] yet still maintain hemostasis. Usually, 10 to 20 minutes of compression is required to achieve hemostasis in a patient with a 6 to 8 Fr sheath that has not been anticoagulated. In patients who received anticoagulation with heparin, an activated coagulation time [ACT] of less than 180 seconds is required before manual compression is performed."
See: Ragosta, chapter on Vascular Access and Hemostasis

3. When pulling an arterial sheath, how much pressure should be exerted on the femoral artery, after initial bleeding has been stopped (according to Grossman)?
   a. **Just enough to obliterate the pulse - so no pulse is felt in the foot for 10 min, then taper off**
   b. **Just enough so a faint pulse is felt in the foot for 5 min, then taper off**
   c. **As hard as you can push for 5 min then taper off**
   d. **As hard as you can push the entire time**

ANSWER: b. After the initial bleeding has stopped press simply hard enough so a faint pulse is felt. Kern recommends that a 20-minute arterial pressure hold be divided into four five-minute periods - each held with diminishing pressure.
0-5 MIN: HOLD firm steady pressure with the middle three fingers of your left hand. Compress the artery firmly but ease up enough so you can just barely feel faint pedal pulses with your right hand. Grossman also recommends this method. However, Watson recommends occlusive pressure for the first 5 minutes. So, it depends on local practice.
   • 5-10 MIN: HOLD with 75% force used in the first 5 minutes. The pedal pulse should be stronger.
   • 10-15 MIN: HOLD with 50% force.
   • 15-20 MIN: HOLD with 25% force. Full pedal pulses.
Finally, slowly lift your index and other fingers. Peek at the wound for bleeding or swelling (hematoma). If any is seen continue holding pressure for 5-10 more minutes longer if there are bleeding problems or larger sheaths are used.

Sometimes, full compression (occlusion) of the artery is necessary to control bleeding. If the pulse MUST be temporarily cut off completely, allow distal circulation periodically by easing up for a few seconds. Give the ischemic leg a drink of fresh blood every few minutes.
The best pressure is steady. Never remove pressure suddenly or disturb the deep tissues until the initial thrombus plug has developed in the artery.

Grossman says, "procedures using larger arterial sheaths or with thrombolytic agents, or IIb/IIIa receptor blockers, more prolonged (30 - to 45 minute) compression is typically required." See: Kern, chapter on "Vascular Access." and Watson, chapter on "Hemostasis"

4. A patient has just finished having an ablation in which arterial and venous access were utilized and the sheaths remain in the right groin. The safest method to establish hemostasis for both vessels is to first pull the _____ sheath and apply pressure to that site for _____, and then pull the other sheath and hold pressure on _____ .

    a. Arterial, for 15 min, the vein for 10 min
    b. Arterial, for 10 min, both for 5 min
    c. Arterial, for 1 min, both for 15 min
    d. Venous, for 5 min, artery for 15 min
    e. Venous, for 10 min, the artery for 10 min
    f. Venous, for 15 min, both for 5 min

ANSWER: a. Kern recommends first controlling each puncture separately. First remove the arterial sheath. Pull and hold it for 15 min. Then pull the venous sheath and hold pressure on it for 5-10 min. This keeps venous access longer, should the patient need emergency medications. It also reduces the chance of AV fistula and allows one hand to be free to check pedal pulses. This is certainly the safest method, but total hold time is long (20-25 min).

Grossman mentions a method of holding both simultaneously with different hands. He recommends positioning your left hand over both puncture sites. First pull the arterial sheath then after 5 minutes, if there are no complications, pull the venous sheath and apply gentle pressure with your right hand positioned directly over the venous puncture site. Since venous blood flows in the opposite direction, you need to hold pressure below the venous puncture site. Remember that venous pressure is much less than arterial, so compression pressure is much less. Continue to hold both together for another 10 minutes. This makes a total hold time of 15 minutes. Proper sheath removal and pressure is vital to prevent hematomas.

See: Kern, chapter on "Vascular Access." and Grossman, chapter on "Percutaneous Approach."

5. To avoid excessive bleeding when it is safest to pull the sheaths after a venous and arterial access procedure. The ACT should be less than:

    a. 160 seconds
    b. 220 seconds
    c. 260 seconds
    d. 300 seconds

ANSWER: a. 160 seconds. The ACT must be low enough to allow clotting of the needle track and vessel wall. If no heparin is given sheaths may be pulled immediately after the study. "Results from a retrospective chart audit of 44 patients indicated that 3 hours after the last dose of heparin, only 7% of the patients met the criteria of ACT < 150 seconds to have their femoral sheaths removed, and 21% of patients had an ACT of < 160 seconds. It is recommended that current standard orders be changed to begin drawing ACT levels at 3 hours post last heparin dose and removing sheaths when ACT is < 160 seconds." Ragosta suggests an ACT of <180 sec. J Nurse Care Qual. 2004 Jan-Mar;19(1):34-8."

6. When palpating distal pulses during arterial hemostasis, the posterior tibial artery is located _____ malleolus ankle bone.
   a. **Behind the lateral**
   b. **In front of the lateral**
   c. **Behind the medial**
   d. **In front of the medial**

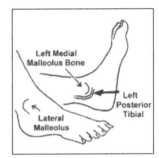

ANSWER: c. Behind or posterior to the medial malleolus ankle bone. It is sometimes called the "medial malleolar branch" of the posterior tibial artery. This artery arises from the popliteal artery behind the knee, which arises from the femoral artery. If the femoral becomes partially occluded, these pedal pulses will be diminished. There are four locations commonly palpated in the lower extremity:
   • Femoral artery (above the femoral head in each groin)
   • Popliteal artery (posterior aspect of leg behind each knee)
   • Dorsalis pedis artery (on the anterior Posterior Tibial Artery aspect of the foot, between the first and second metatarsal.)
   • Posterior tibial artery (behind or posterior to the medial malleolus ankle bone.) See: Snopek, chapter on "Femoral Angiography."

7. After an EP study with irrigated ablation, when the patient is given to the recovery nurse all the following information should be conveyed, EXCEPT:
   a. **Description of the ablation procedure details**
   b. **Recently administered medications**
   c. **Arrhythmias induced**
   d. **Foley Urine Output**
   e. **Baseline vitals**

ANSWER: a. Description of the ablation procedure. The follow-up nurses only need to know the essentials that can affect this patient care, not what is "nice" to know. Understanding irrigated ablation is not important to the patients post catheterization care.

8. Education should be given to pacemaker implant patients post pectoral implant. All the following are typical instructions to the patient in the immediate post procedure period EXCEPT:
   a. **Don't raise your ipsilateral arm above your shoulder**
   b. **Don't raise the head of the bed (lay flat)**
   c. **Don't get the incision site wet**
   d. **Don't lift heavy objects**

ANSWER: b. Don't raise the head of the bed. Watson says, "Bed rest may be maintained for the first three hours, or up to 24 hours. The head of the bed should be maintained at 30 deg. (pectoral implants) to avoid edema in the head and neck region. A sling may be used to immobilize the ipsilateral arm overnight.... The patient and/or caretakers should observe the site for a reference for comparison when at home. Any redness, swelling, discharge, increased bruising or pain, or a persistent temperature greater than 100 deg F should be reported to the physician. For pectoral implants, it should be emphasized that the ipsilateral arm (usually left arm) should not be raised above shoulder height for the first few days, postoperatively. Activity such as sweeping or lifting heavy objects (more than 510 lbs.) objects should be avoided for 3-4 weeks. This is to protect the surgical site and to allow endothelialization of the lead tip within the heart." See Watson, chapter on Cardiac Pacing

Ellenbogen lists the following patient education essentials post-implantation:
- Carrying pacemaker ID card
- Refrain from vigorous arm activity for 4 weeks
- Keep the incision site dry for 5-7 days
- Temporary driving restrictions (if syncope was present)
- Report any fever, infections, pain, redness, swelling or incision drainage

See: Ellenbogen chapter on "Follow-up"

9. In teaching a patient to care for his femoral artery puncture site after a catheterization procedure, which instruction below is correct?
   a. **"Occasionally raise your head to look down at your groin to see if it's bleeding. If it is, call the nurse."**
   b. **"Don't sit up by yourself. But the nurse may elevate your bed to a slight sit up position."**
   c. **"Keep your hand on the bandage to feel for wetness or bleeding."**
   d. **"Try to cough up any fluid in your lungs"**

ANSWER: b. "Don't sit up by yourself. But the nurse may elevate your bed to a slight sit up position." Kern says, the patient should be given the following instructions:
- Keep your head down
- Hold the groin site when coughing
- Keep punctured leg straight
- Stay in bed
- Drink fluids
- Call a nurse for assistance if there is bleeding, leg numbness or pain, or chest pain.

See: Kern, chapter on "Arterial and Venous Access"

10. Your patient had a post-MI VT ablation with 6F catheters. When giving instructions after holding arterial pressure post-ablation, teach the patient all the following EXCEPT?
- a. "Don't cough. If you must cough, hold pressure on the puncture site."
- b. "If after 1 hour you still can't urinate, sit up and try."
- c. "Keep your leg straight. Don't bend it."
- d. "Don't lift your head off the pillow."
- e. "Drink lots of fluids."

ANSWER: d. "If after 1 hour you still can't urinate, sit up and try" - no. Don't sit up and don't force urination with a Valsalva. This increases abdominal and intravascular pressure that could break open a puncture site. Of course, arterial access sites are more prone to hematoma because of their higher blood pressure. Kern says, "Depending on the catheter and sheath size, the patient is kept at bed rest for 2 to 6 hours after puncture. With small diameter catheters (i.e., <5F) shorter times (<2 hrs.) can be used.
See: Kern, chapter on "Arterial and Venous Access"

11. Your patient is noncompliant in taking his medications for systemic hypertension. He should be taught that a common complication of uncontrolled hypertension is:
- a. Don't presume to teach the patient. Only the physician should do his.
- b. Pulmonary fibrosis with pulmonary hypertension
- c. Congestive Heart Failure
- d. Cerebral hemorrhage
- e. Arterial calcification

ANSWER: d. Cerebral hemorrhage leading to stroke. Hemorrhaging and occlusion of blood vessels in the body are common complications of uncontrolled hypertension. This complication can occur in the brain (stroke), the eyes, the heart (myocardial infarction) and the kidneys. It is our professional duty to educate such patients and alert them to the risks of not taking their medication. See: Lippincott's State Board Review for NCLEX-PN.

12. You have just completed an EPS and the physician has left the room. Your patient asks you to interpret the results of his study. Your response as a healthcare professional should be to:
- a. Explain that the physician will interpret it and report the results
- b. Honestly interpret it to the best of your ability
- c. Say you don't know how to interpret results
- d. Explain that the results are inconclusive

ANSWER: a. Explain that the physician will interpret it and report the results. One of the ten principles of professional conduct adopted by the ARRT is "Radiologic Technologists shall not diagnose, but in recognition of their responsibility to the patient, they shall provide the physician with all information they have relative to radiologic diagnosis for patient management." We do not possess all the information or training necessary to diagnose the patient. Diagnosis, pathology, and treatment are the physician's final responsibility. We can often reinforce his comments, clarify things, and respond to our patient's questions, but always with the qualification that the physician has the final say.

See: Torres, chapter on "The Radiologic Technologist and professionalism"

13. Where should pressure be applied when removing a femoral arterial sheath?
   a. **At puncture site**
   b. **>1 in cranial to the site**
   c. **>1 in caudal to the site**
   d. **Both above and below the puncture site**

ANSWER: b. >1 in cranial to the site. "To remove the sheath, the operator places left-hand fingers over the femoral artery, an inch more cranial (toward the patient's head) than the skin incision." Kern, M. (2013, October 01). Back to basics: Femoral artery access and hemostasis. Retrieved May 08, 2021, from https://www.cathlabdigest.com/articles/Back-Basics-Femoral-Artery-Access-Hemostasis

Chapter 20
Research & Miscellaneous

1. Research Methods & Statistics (pg. 789)
2. Miscellaneous Procedure & Lab Information (pg. 799)

EP Essentials LLC

Research Methods & Statistics:

*Not needed for the RCES

1. A frequency diagram of data grouped into cells (as shown) is termed a:
   a. **Cumulative block diagram**
   b. **Frequency block diagram**
   c. **Scatter diagram**
   d. **Histogram**

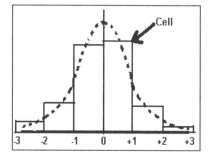

ANSWER: d. Histogram. Statistical data is usually distribution curve/cells presented in a histogram. Here, the horizontal axis is divided into cells. The height of each cell increases as the frequency of samples within it increases. All measurements between 1 and 2 (in this example) accumulate in the 5th cell. When the top of a histogram is smoothed out it becomes a frequency distribution curve (dashed line). The most common frequency distribution curve is this bell shaped "normal distribution curve." See: Duncan, Knapp & Miller, chapter on "Descriptive Statistics."

2. Match the following terms and descriptions:

a. Mean	1. The most frequently occurring sample value
b. Mode	2. Middle number of a ranked series
c. Median	3. Arithmetic average (center of gravity)

CORRECTLY MATCHED ANSWERS ARE:

MEAN: the average or center of gravity. If you use scissors to cut out a histogram or distribution curve, the balance point is the mean (center of gravity). It is calculated by taking the sum of all measured values and dividing them by the number of measurements taken.

- Mean = (1/n) $\sum Y$ or the sum ($\sum$) of all the sample values (Y) divided by the total number in the sample (n).

Mode: the most frequently occurring sample value.

Median: is a peak in the histogram or frequency curve.

The mode of (1, 2, 2, 3, 4) is 2, because the #2 occurs more frequently than any other number. Remember that MODE = MOST (both have 4 letters).

MEDIAN = middle number of a ranked series. The sample numbers must be ranked in order of increasing value. Then find the middle number. It's easy if there are an odd number in the sample size. For example, in the sample 1, 3 & 9 the number 3 is in the middle. Just count the numbers and find the one in the middle. But here is an even number in the sample. You must find the middle 2 numbers and take their average. E.g., In the set 1, 2, 3, 6 the median is 2.5.

Remember that the "MEDIAN" is in the MIDDLE of the road (same number of letters too). It is the center of the data by count.

See: Duncan, Knapp & Miller, chapter on "Descriptive Statistics."

3. A statistical sample of 6 numbers is 2, 4, 4, 5, 6, & 7.
Calculate and match the mean, mode and median of this list.

1. **MEAN**	a. **4**
2. **MODE**	b. **4.5**
3. **MEDIAN**	c. **4.67**

CORRECTLY MATCHED ANSWERS ARE:

1. MEAN = c. 4.67 = [$\sum$ (2+4+4+5+6+7)] / 6 = The average.
2. MODE = a. 4 the MOST frequently occurring number.
3. MEDIAN =b. 4.5 = halfway between the middle two numbers (4 and 5).

The Median should be selected so an equal number of values are above and below it. It is the center of the data by count. For an odd number of values in the sample, the median is the middle number. For an even number of observations, as shown here, the median is the average of the two middle values.

Remember, mean is average, Median is the Middle, and MODE is the MOST.

See: Duncan, Knapp & Miller, chapter on "Descriptive Statistics."

4. The most commonly occurring value in an array of values is known as the:
   a. Mean
   b. Mode
   c. Median
   d. Kurtosis

ANSWER: b. Mode is the MOST frequently occurring number in a statistical sample or population. Note MODE and MOST both start with "MO" and both have 4 letters. Thus, in the series [1,2,3,4,7,9,9,11,15] the number 9 occurs MOST - twice, MORE often than any other number. Thus, 9 is the MODE. Median is the number which divides the group into 2 equal halves. In the group above, the number 7 has 4 numbers below it and 4 above it = median.
See: Duncan, Knapp & Miller, chapter on "Descriptive Statistics."

5. Statistical methods used to evaluate "variability" within a sample are listed in the box. Match each term to its definition?
   a. Difference between largest and smallest values
   b. Average of the deviations from the mean squared
   c. Square root of the sum of the squared deviations over the number of samples taken

   1. Range
   2. Variance
   3. Standard Deviation

CORRECTLY MATCHED ANSWERS ARE:
1. RANGE: a. Difference between the maximum and minimum numbers. (Max. - min.)

2. VARIANCE: b. Average of the squared deviations. Take each number in the sample and subtract it from the sample mean. Square each difference. Add all these squared numbers together. Divide that sum by the number in the sample minus one. It can also be calculated by squaring the standard deviation below.

$$\frac{\sum (Y_i - Avg.)^2}{n-1}$$

3. STANDARD DEVIATION: c. square root of the variance above. Or take each number in the sample and subtract it from the sample mean. Square each difference. Add all these squared numbers together. Divide that sum by the number in the sample minus one. Take the square root of that quotient. Standard deviation is the most common and most important measure of dispersion. Once you have calculated the mean and standard deviation, the shape and location of the bell curve is defined.

$$\sqrt{\frac{\sum (Y_i - Avg.)^2}{n-1}}$$

See: Duncan, Knapp & Miller, chapter on "Descriptive Statistics."

6. A statistical sample of numbers is 2, 4, & 7. Using the formulas given above, calculate these three statistical values and match each to its term.

    a. **2.54**   **1. Range**

    b. **5.0**   **2. Variance**

    c. **6.34**   **3. Standard Deviation**

CORRECTLY MATCHED ANSWERS ARE:

    1. Range = 5 = 7-2 = (max. - min.) values in the sample

    2. Variance = [(4.33-2) 2 + (4.33-4)2 + (7-4.33)2]/ (3-1) = [5.44 + 0.11 + 7.13]/2 = 12.68/2 = 6.34

    3. Standard Deviation = Square root of {[(4.33-2) 2 + (4.33-4)2 + (7-4.33)2]/ (3-1)} = Square root of {[5.44 + 0.11 + 7.13]/2} = Square root of {12.68/2} =square root of 6.34 = 2.54

Note that it could also be found by taking the square root of the variance √6.34 = 2.54.

See: Duncan, Knapp & Miller, chapter on "Descriptive Statistics."

7. With a normal distribution curve, what percent of the population sampled will be within +/- one standard deviation of the mean?

    a. **34.3%**

    b. **68.3%**

    c. **95.4%**

    d. **99.7%**

ANSWER: b. 68.3%.   This curve is the most important distribution curve in medicine. Here a 2-tailed cut-off at plus and minus one standard deviation (z score of +-1) includes 68% of the central curve area. For example, 68% of a series of normally distributed test scores will fall within +-1 SD. Most medical work requires +-2 Standard deviations to be statistically significant because it includes 95% of the population. These percentages are worth memorizing because they are fixed numbers determined by the shape of the normal distribution curve. See: Duncan, Knapp & Miller, chapter on "Descriptive Statistics."

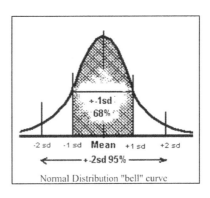

Normal Distribution "bell" curve

8. What is the most common statistical measure of variability or dispersion within a sample?

    a. **Standard deviation**

    b. **Mean**

    c. **r value**

    d. **Range**

ANSWER: a. Standard deviation commonly used to measure how tightly points are clustered around the mean. It is the sum of all the differences from the mean, squared (Yi mean)2; divided by n-1; all taken to the 0.5 power (square root). See: Braunwald chapter "Electrocardiography"

$$\sqrt{\frac{\sum (Y_i - Avg.)^2}{n-1}}$$

9. What is the most common statistical measure of central tendency or average of a sample?
   a. Mode
   b. Mean
   c. Median
   d. Meridian

ANSWER: b. Mean is the average. It is the sum of all (Y) values divided by the total number in the series (n). Average = Mean = (Y1 + Y2 + Y3 .... Yn) / n
See: Braunwald chapter "Electrocardiography"

10. In discriminating between 2 statistical samples, which "p value" is most significant and would almost never occur because of chance?
   a. -99.0
   b. 0.005
   c. 0.50
   d. 0.999

ANSWER: b. 0.005. P value stands for PROBABILITY OF CERTAINTY, and can be found in almost any medical statistical journal article. P values range from 0 (total certainty) to 1.0 (total uncertainty). So, the smaller the p the more certain that this result could NOT occur by chance. Thus, a p value of .005 indicates that a result would occur only 0.5% of the time by random chance. Saying it another way p=.005 indicates a 5/1000 chance that the populations in question are the same. This is "near certainty." P values smaller than .01 or 1% are usually adequate for medical statistical probability. See: Duncan, Knapp & Miller, chapter on "Descriptive Statistics."

11. Which of the following occurs as the amount of variation (scatter) around a linear regression line increase?
   a. Correlation coefficient ® increases
   b. Correlation coefficient ® decreases
   c. Slope of linear regression line (m) increases
   d. Slope of linear regression line (m) decreases

ANSWER: b. Correlation coefficient ® decreases. Correlation coefficient measures the strength of the relationship between variables. The tighter the correlation, the closer "r" approaches 1.0 and a 45-degree straight line. The first diagram shows how LV-EDV measured by quantitative angiography correlates with true volume. This scatter diagram correlation of 0.70 shows a good correlation. However, when LV-EDV by Fast CT scanner is correlated with true EDV, the correlation is even better at 0.95. The dashed line is the "Line of best fit" to the scattered points. This line is termed the "regression" line. Note how there is less

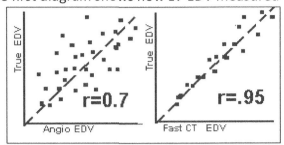

scatter around the "fast CT" dashed regression line. See: Duncan, Knapp & Miller, chapter on "Descriptive Statistics."

12. Which of the following r values (correlation coefficients) is reasonable and shows the strongest correlation between two variables?
   a. - 0.59
   b. +0.90
   c. +1.25
   d. +99.0

ANSWER: b. +.90.   R stands for regression coefficient. It correlates direct relationships between variables. For example, BSA correlates well with resting CO (r=.86), as one would expect but poorly with LVEDP (r=.07). The larger the person the larger the CO, but everyone has the same normal EDP. The closer the R value to 1.0 the closer the values correlate, and the more one can directly predict the other.
See: Duncan, Knapp & Miller, chapter on "Descriptive Statistics."

13. The difference between the value of a sample means and the hypothesized total population mean is evaluated by the:
   a. **Standard deviation of the population**
   b. **Standard deviation of the mean**
   c. **Range of the sample medians**
   d. **Range of the sample modes**

ANSWER: b. Standard deviation of the mean. When you take a small statistical sample, you cannot be sure that the mean of your sample is the true mean of the population from which you are sampling. The total population has a mean μ and standard deviation σ. The larger your sample the surer you can be that the sample mean Y is close to accurate. When many small samples (size n) are taken, the collection of means from these many samples will have a normal distribution, have mean   y⁻ (mean of the means), and standard deviation s = (σ/√n). The special distribution of sample means is a small bell curve with the same mean and a standard deviation of (σ/√n.)   This new s =σ/√n is called the "standard deviation of the mean." It is used to adjust the passing score for CCI exams from year to year. The more people take the exam (larger sample size), the more likely the passing score will be 72%. See: Duncan, Knapp & Miller, chapter on "Descriptive Statistics."

14. When patients with proven CAD have a normal treadmill test, it is termed a ___ result:
   a. **True-positive**
   b. **True-negative**
   c. **False-positive**
   d. **False-negative**

ANSWER: d. False negative. When NO False-negative results on treadmill test significant ST depression is found at high workloads, the treadmill test result is termed
"Negative." The absence of ST depression is usually, but not always, a "positive" indicator of normality. Diagnostic tests often miss people with significant disease.

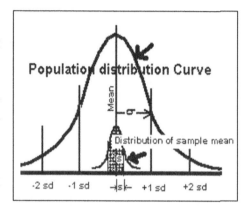

These people are termed "false negatives." Sensitivity is a statistical reflection of the potential error caused by these false-negative results of a test. A test with a sensitivity of 1.0 would have NO false negatives. Treadmill test sensitivity is around 0.68 (68%) indicating 32% false negatives. See: Selzer, Chapter on "Approach to Diagnosis."

15. Statistics are used to evaluate the accuracy of a diagnostic test. Match each term to its definition.
   a. **Reflects the reliability of a test against a certain "yardstick"**
   b. **Reflects the potential error caused by false negative test results in patients with disease**
   c. **Reflects the potential error caused by false positive test results in normal people**

   1. **Sensitivity**
   2. **Specificity**
   3. **Predictive Accuracy**

CORRECTLY MATCHED ANSWERS ARE:
SENSITIVITY: b. Sensitivity measures how "sensitive" a test is to detect a disease in diseased people. It is the probability that a person having a disease will be correctly identified by a positive diagnostic test. Note that sensitivity deals with diseased patients. In a good diagnostic test most, diseased patients will be true positives (TP). The patients that mess this up are the people with false-negative tests, the people who have normal ECGs on treadmill, but do in fact have CAD (see previous question). The falser negatives the lower the sensitivity.

Thus, sensitivity is a statistical reflection of the potential error caused by false-negative results of a test. Mathematically Sensitivity = (TP)/ (TP + FN).

SPECIFICITY: c. Specificity measures how "specific" a test is at avoiding normal people. Treadmill tests may falsely pick up people who hyperventilate, take digitalis, have bundle branch block, or are in fact "normal." These are termed false positives (FP). A very specific test will have no false positives. Specificity is the probability that a normal person will be correctly identified as normal (negative) by a clinical test. Note that specificity deals with normal people having normal diagnostic tests (true negatives = TN). The people that mess this up are the normal people with false-positive results, the normal people who have significant ST depression on treadmill (as shown). The falser positives the lower the specificity. Thus, specificity is a statistical reflection of the potential error caused by false-positive results of a test. Mathematically Specificity = TN / (TN + FP)
Sensitivity reflects error due to false negatives (missed sick people)
Specificity reflects error due to false positives found in (falsely diagnosed normal people).
One way to remember these is that both seNsitivity and false-Negatives contain "N," while both sPecificity and false-Positives contain "P."

3. PREDICTIVE ACCURACY: a. reflects the reliability of a test against a certain
"Yardstick." It is the probability that positive clinical test correctly identifies a patient as HAVING a disease, or the % of the time a diagnostic test correctly diagnoses a disease. For example, the predictive accuracy of angio to diagnose coronary lesions is 95%. Because, of those who go to autopsy, 95% of those lesions could be documented.
See: Duncan, Knapp & Miller, chapter on "Descriptive Statistics" and Selzer, chapter on "Approach to diagnosis."

16. Statistically, the more NORMAL PATIENTS that have a "positive" treadmill test (false positive), the lower that test's:
   a. **Sensitivity**
   b. **Specificity**
   c. **Prognosis**
   d. **Predictive accuracy**

ANSWER: b. Specificity. When significant ST depression is found at low workloads, the treadmill test result is termed "positive." ST False-positive results on treadmill test depression is usually, but not always, a "positive" indicator of CAD. Diagnostic tests often falsely diagnose normal people. These people are termed "false positives." Specificity is a statistical reflection of the potential error caused by these false-positive results of a test. A test with a specificity of 1.0 would have NO false positives. Treadmill test specificity is around 0.77 (77%) indicating 23% false positives. Hopefully, referral to more specific tests such as thallium, echo, and angiography prevent most of these misdiagnosed cases.
See: Selzer, Chapter on "Approach to Diagnosis."

17. Match each statistical term to how it is calculated below.
   a. **Many true Positive (↑TP) and few False Negatives (↓FN)**
   b. **Few true Positives (↓TP) and many False Negatives (↑FN)**
   c. **Many true Negatives (↑TN) and few False positives (↓FP)**
   d. **Few true Negatives (↓TN) and many False positives (↑FP)**

   1. **High Sensitivity**
   2. **High Specificity**
   3. **Low Sensitivity**
   4. **Low Specificity**

CORRECTLY MATCHED ANSWERS ARE:
- High sensitivity= a. Many true Positives (↑TP) and few False Negatives (↓FN) are found in a very sensitive diagnostic test. Mathematically Sensitivity = (TP)/ (TP + FN). Since true positives is the numerator, as TP increases, so does the sensitivity. In evaluating people with a disease, this test correctly diagnoses the disease most of the time (↑TP) and only misdiagnosis it a few times (↓FN). E.g., You perform a treadmill test on 100 people with proven CAD and only 80 of them show >1 mm ST depression. The remaining 20 have < 1 mmHg. This treadmill test is 80% sensitive to detecting CAD. Sensitivity = [TP/ (TP + FN) = 80/100 = 80%]. Remember the TP add, "Sensitive Toilet Paper is Friction Negative" (Sensitivity ≈ TP/FN.)
- Low sensitivity= b. Few true Positive and Many False Negatives
- High specificity = c. Many true Negatives and few False positives
- Low specificity = d. Few true Negatives and many False positives

You probably won't be asked to calculate these numerically, only understand them. See: Braunwald chapter "Electrocardiography" also, Todd, Vol. II, Chapter on "ECG"

18. During a series of exercise tolerance tests on normal individuals 5 out of 100 patients were misdiagnosed with CAD. What is the predictive accuracy of this treadmill test?
   a. **Sensitivity = 5%**
   b. **Sensitivity = 95%**
   c. **Specificity = 5%**
   d. **Specificity = 95%**

ANSWER: d. Specificity = 95%. Note that mathematically, Specificity = TN / (TN + FP). Since true negatives is the numerator, the truer negatives (and the fewer false positives) the higher the specificity. Or conversely the falser positives the lower the specificity. If your treadmill 100 normal people and 95 of them show <1 mm ST depression. The remaining 5 are mis-diagnosed with > 1 mm ST depression. This treadmill test is then 95% specific for CAD. Specificity = TN/ (TN + FP) = 95/100 = 95%. Ideally, we would like a test to be 100% sensitive (no false negatives among diseased individuals) and 100% specific (no false positives among normal individuals). But not even gold standards are that accurate. See: Braunwald chapter "Electrocardiography"

19. While carrying out a blood gas quality control program, the technologist notices that the value of the control sample has been slowly drifting downward for a week as shown below. The most likely cause of this drift is:
   a. Electronic malfunction of the analyzer
   b. Inadequate mixing of the control sample
   c. Contamination of the reference standards
   d. Deterioration of reagent as a result of aging

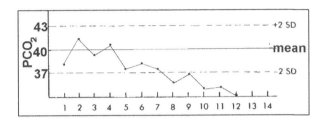

ANSWER: d. Deterioration of reagent because of aging. This type of slow change could only result from slow changes such as deterioration. Note that beginning with value #9 the analyzer is "out of control" which is the acceptable band 2 standard deviations. After that you can see a trend towards being out of control. Understand Trends, shifts, drift. See: Ruppel, Manual of Pulmonary Function Testing, Chapter on "Quality Assurance."

20. While carrying out a quality control program, the technologist notices that the value of one control sample is outside of the +2 standard deviation control limit as shown below. What proportion of the controls can be outside of the ±2 standard deviation limit, and your system still be considered "in control?"
   a. None
   b. 1/100
   c. 1/50
   d. 1/20

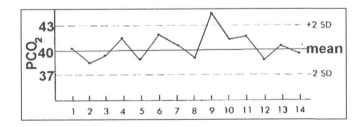

ANSWER: d. 1/20 or 5%. Note value number 9 is above the +2 standard deviation limit. These are termed "outliers." An "outlier" should alert you. Is this analyzer "out of control" here? Not necessarily. Remember in statistics the 95%confidence interval is ±2 standard deviations. So, we normally expect 95% of the numbers will be within these limits, and only 5% of the control samples will be outside of that limit. So, this high reading is probably a random error, since 1/20 of the normal values randomly fall outside the ±2 standard deviations limits. Run your known control sample again. If it falls outside of these limits again, then something needs "fixing," because you are "out of control." See: Ruppel, Chapter on Quality Assurance."

21. Survival curves like this showing % of patients surviving a treatment over time are termed:
   a. **Stewhart-Hamilton curves**
   b. **Kaplan–Meier curves**
   c. **Levey-Jennings curves**
   d. **Frank-Starling curves**

ANSWER: b. Kaplan–Meier curves. Graphs like these make it easy to compare survival rates of different treatments. They are commonly used in medical literature. Treatment #1 is obviously best because some patients survive longer than 70 months.
"In analyzing survival data, ... The survival function S(t) is defined as the probability of surviving at least to time M (months). The graph of S(t) against t is called the survival curve. The Kaplan–Meier method can be used to estimate this curve from the observed survival times without the assumption of an underlying probability distribution. The method is based on the basic idea that the probability of surviving k or more periods from entering the study is a product of the k observed survival rates for each period (i.e., the cumulative proportion surviving). Here, p1 is the proportion surviving the first period, p2 is the proportion surviving beyond the second period conditional on having survived up to the second period, and so on." http://www.ncbi.nlm.nih.gov/pmc/articles/PMC1065034/

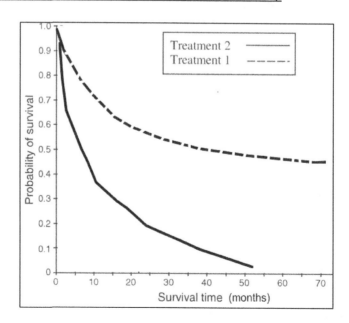

Miscellaneous Procedure & Lab Information:

1. According to the ACC/AHA recommendation system, which classification is given when the risk of a procedure exceeds the benefit and should not be performed?
   a. Class I
   b. Class IIa
   c. Class IIb
   d. Class III

ANSWER: d. Class III. This recommendation system is based on the assessment of the estimated benefits and risks.

Class I: The benefit of an intervention/procedure far exceeds its risk.

Class IIa: The benefit of an intervention/procedure moderately exceeds its risk.

Class IIb: The benefit of an intervention/procedure may not exceed its risk.

Class III: The benefit of an intervention/procedure is equivalent to or is exceeded by the risk.

2019 HRS/EHRA/APHRS/LAHRS expert consensus statement on catheter ablation of ventricular arrhythmias. *Journal of Arrhythmia*

2. According to the ACC/AHA recommendations system, a treatment is reasonable and can be useful, effective, or beneficial (benefit moderately exceeds risk) is given this class recommendation.
   a. Class I
   b. Class IIa
   c. Class IIb
   d. Class III

ANSWER: b. Class IIa.

CLASS I
- Is recommended
- Is indicated/useful/effective/beneficial
- Should be performed/administered/other

CLASS IIa (Moderate)
- Is reasonable
- Can be useful/effective/beneficial

Class III: No Benefit
- Is not recommended
- Is not indicated/useful/effective/beneficial
- Should not be performed

CLASS IIb (Weak)	Class III: Harm
• May/might be reasonable • May/might be considered • Usefulness/effectiveness is unknown/unclear/uncertain or not well established	• Potentially harmful • Causes Harm • Associated with excess morbidity/mortality • Should not be performed/administered/other

2019 HRS/EHRA/APHRS/LAHRS expert consensus statement on catheter ablation of ventricular arrhythmias. *Journal of Arrhythmia*

3. Data is sent from the amplifier of the 3D mapping system to the CPU via which cable?
   a. SC fiber optic cable
   b. LC fiber optic cable
   c. Ethernet cable
   d. Copper wire

ANSWER: a. SC fiber optic cable. "In EP we often see gray, and orange fiber-optic cables and they are usually duplex cables or two lines. Without getting into the weeds about the difference between the gray SD cables and the orange LC, know that the orange cables typically transmit to the display monitors such as from the mapping system to the screen input for the physician to view as well as from the live and review displays from the recording system.

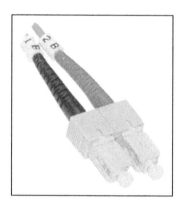

The gray SC cables are typically used for data in the EP lab, such as from the recording system amplifier to CPU (newer systems), the 3D mapping system amplifier to the CPU, and various other components of the 3D mapping system." See: EP Essential's 8/21/20 blog post "The Delicate Lifeline of EP" www.ep-essentials.com/blog

4. The monitor displays of the recording system and mapping system are sent to a display monitor for the physician to view at tableside via which cable?
   a. SC fiber-optic cable
   b. LC fiber-optic cable
   c. Ethernet cable
   d. Copper wire

ANSWER: b. LC fiber-optic cable. "The orange LC fiber-optic cable typically transmits to the display monitors such as from the mapping system to the screen input for the physician to view as well as from the live and review displays from the recording system. In the following image, the orange LC connector utilizes a latch as opposed to the SC (gray cable) locking tab. Having half the footprint of the SC connector gives it huge popularity in datacoms and other high-density patch applications, as its combination of small size and latch feature make it ideal for densely populated racks/panels."

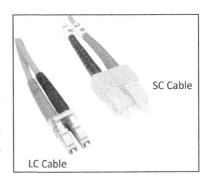

See: EP Essential's 8/21/20 blog post "The Delicate Lifeline of EP" www.ep-essentials.com/blog

5. What is a disadvantage of fiber-optic cables in the EP lab vs. copper wires?
   a. **Lower resistance to electromagnetic noise**
   b. **Slower bandwidth**
   c. **Easier to fracture**
   d. **Slower speed**
   e. **Expense**

ANSWER: c. Easier to fracture. "Fiber optic cables are particularly delicate; they can be cracked from too much tension during cable pulling. More frequently, a fracture is seen in the EP lab due to improper care. In the ideal setting, cables will be run through conduits in the floor or ceiling/boom; however, not all labs are set up permanently. In a mobile EP lab setting, cables are continually connected

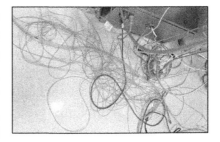

and disconnect. Each of these connections put all the cables at risk of failure due to wear and tear. Cables that are laid on the floor are often stepped on, tripped over, tangled in other equipment, or even run over by equipment and carts. When putting away for storage, if they are wound too tightly or pulled, this may lead to failure as well."

Notice the improper care of these display monitor fiber-optic cables.

The benefits of fiber-optic cables:
• **SPEED:** Fiber optic networks operate at high speeds
• **BANDWIDTH:** large carrying capacity
• **DISTANCE:** Signals can be transmitted further without needing to be "refreshed" or strengthened.
• **RESISTANCE:** Greater resistance to electromagnetic noise such as radios, motors, or other nearby cables.
• **MAINTENANCE:** Fiber optic cables cost much less to maintain.

See: EP Essential's 8/21/20 blog post "The Delicate Lifeline of EP" www.ep-essentials.com/blog

6. How is signal transmitted from the amplifier to the CPU for 3D mapping systems and newer recording systems?
a. **LAN or WAN networks**
b. **Electric pulses**
c. **Analog signals**
d. **Light pulses**

ANSWER: d. Light pulses. "At one end of the system is a transmitter. This is the place of origin for information coming on to fiber-optic lines. The transmitter accepts coded electronic pulse information coming from copper wire. It then processes and translates that information into equivalently coded light pulses. A light-emitting diode (LED) or an injection-laser diode (ILD) can be used for generating light pulses. Using a lens, the light pulses are funneled into the fiber-optic medium where they travel down the cable.

Think of a fiber cable in terms of an exceptionally long cardboard roll (from the inside roll of paper towel) that is coated with a mirror on the inside. If you shine a flashlight in one end you can see light come out at the far end - even if it's been bent around a corner.

Light pulses move easily down the fiber-optic line because of a principle known as total internal reflection. This principle of total internal reflection states that when the angle of incidence exceeds a critical value, light cannot get out of the glass; instead, the light bounces back in. When this principle is applied to the construction of the fiber-optic strand, it is possible to transmit information down fiber lines in the form of light pulses."

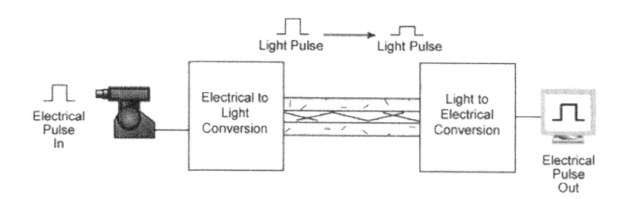

See: EP Essential's 8/21/20 blog post "The Delicate Lifeline of EP" www.ep-essentials.com/blog

Practice Tests

1. Practice Test #1 (pg. 805)
2. Practice Test #2 (pg. 814)
3. Practice Test #3 (pg. 827)

These are geared for the RCES examination. If you are taking the CEPS/IBHRE examination, please review more of the complex concepts and medications. Answers are listed at the end of each exam.

Practice Test #1: (30 questions)

1. What is the most anterior heart chamber?
   a. **Right Atrium**
   b. **Right Ventricle**
   c. **Left Atrium**
   d. **Left Ventricle**

2. Which of the following demonstrates poor sterile technique?
(select all that apply)
   a. **Circulator reaching over the sterile field to pour fluids onto the table**
   b. **Scrub personnel's back to the sterile field**
   c. **Scrub personnel's hands resting near chest level**
   d. **Circulator walking in between sterile fields**

3. Which can describe the direction of the atrial depolarization in this Lead II example?
   a. **High to Low**
   b. **Low to High**
   c. **Right to Left**
   d. **Left to Right**

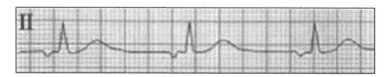

4. What is the view in the x-ray image?
   a. **AP**
   b. **PA**
   c. **RAO**
   d. **LAO**

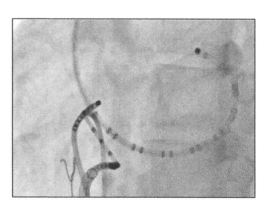

5. Which of the following identifies the distal RV electrodes?

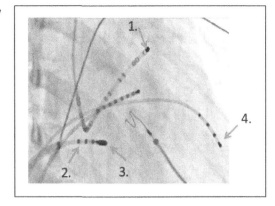

    a. 1
    b. 2
    c. 3
    d. 4

6. Which waveform is identified with the arrow?

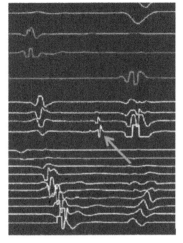

    a. A
    b. H
    c. V
    d. T

7. LAO is the view used to help differentiate the right from left side of the heart.
    a. True
    b. False

8. In the image below with a standard catheter positioning, which CS electrode pair records the furthest left lateral atrial signal?

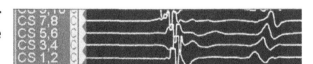

    a. CS 7,8
    b. CS 5,6
    c. CS 3,4
    d. CS 1,2

9. Which of the following are possible during baseline measurements if the patient has an antegrade conducting accessory pathway?
(select all that apply)
    a. Short HV interval
    b. Negative HV interval
    c. Normal HV interval
    d. Short PR interval

10. Which catheter is being utilized for pacing in the following example?
   a. HRA
   b. HIS
   c. CS
   d. RV

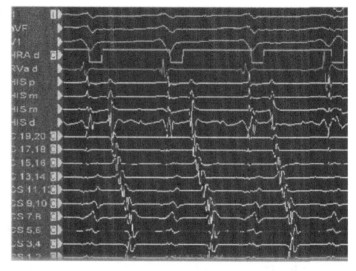

11. What is observed with the extra-stimulus testing displayed (600/290)?
   a. AVNERP
   b. AERP
   c. VAERP
   d. VERP

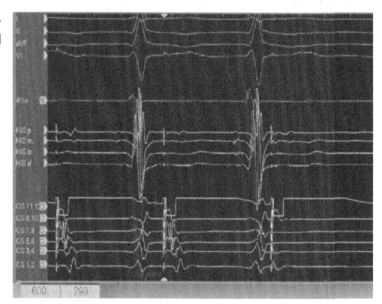

12. What is observed with decremental pacing in the electrogram?
   a. AVNERP
   b. Wenckebach
   c. AH Jump
   d. AVNRT

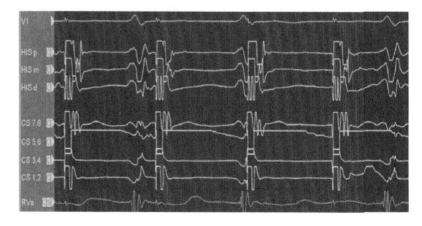

13. The following electrogram displays an entrainment attempt in the CTI via the ablation catheter. What is observed?

    a. Not entrained

    b. Ablation catheter is in the circuit

    c. Ablation catheter is not in the circuit

    d. Concealed entrainment

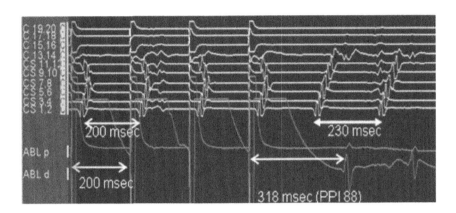

14. What is observed with the extrastimulus testing displayed in the example below?

    a. AVNERP

    b. VAERP

    c. Induction of AVNRT

    d. Induction of Atrial Flutter

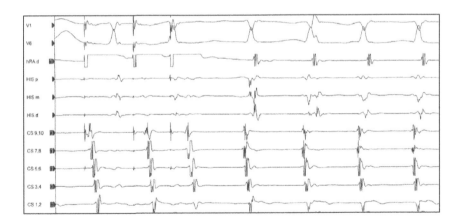

15. What is observed in the following example of a 360 ms pacing cycle length entrainment attempt?

    a. Termination of tachycardia

    b. VAAV response

    c. VAV response

    d. Not entrained

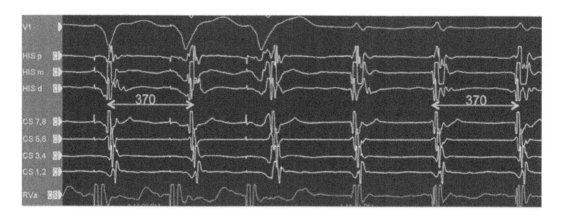

16. What is the most likely rhythm induced in the electrogram below?

    a. Atrial Fibrillation

    b. Atrial Flutter

    c. AVRT

    d. AVNRT

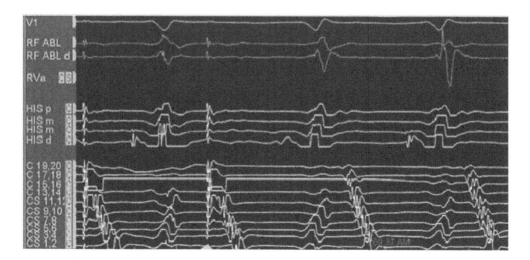

17. What is the rhythm displayed in the electrogram?
    a. Atrial Fibrillation
    b. Atrial Flutter
    c. Atrial Tachycardia
    d. AVRT
    e. AVNRT

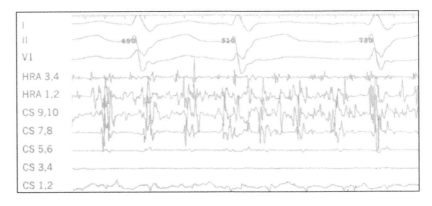

18. What is the most likely rhythm induced in the electrogram?
    a. Atrial Fibrillation
    b. Atrial Flutter
    c. Atrial Tachycardia
    d. AVRT
    e. AVNRT

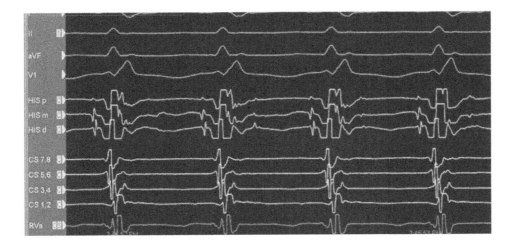

19. **What is the most likely rhythm in the displayed electrogram?**
    a. Atrial Fibrillation
    b. Atrial Flutter
    c. Atrial Tachycardia
    d. AVRT
    e. AVNRT

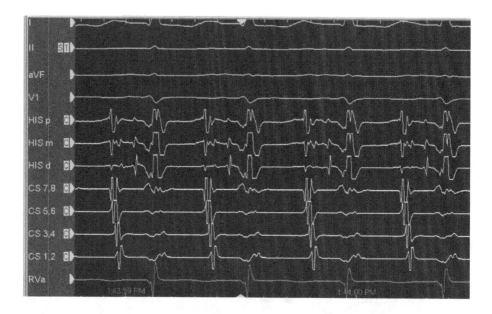

20. **What is observed with the extrastimulus testing displayed (600/420)?**
    a. AVNERP
    b. VAERP
    c. AH Jump
    d. AV Nodal Echo Beat

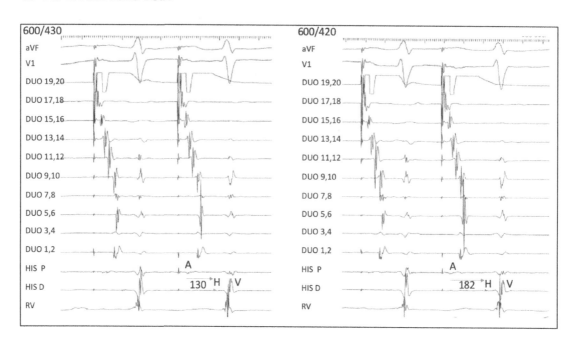

21. Where is the approximate location of the accessory pathway in the electrogram?
    a. Right Lateral
    b. Left Lateral
    c. Anterior Septal
    d. Posterior Septal

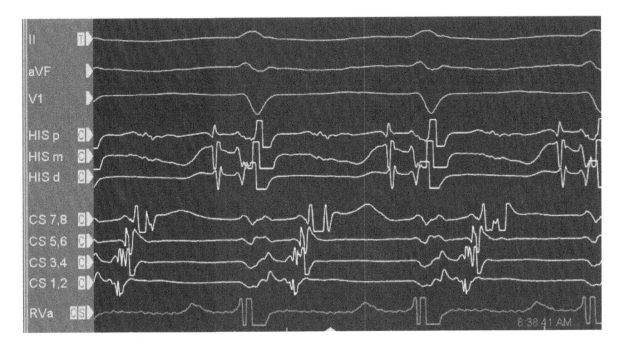

22. This rhythm was observed during an RF ablation for AVNRT. What do you recommend?
    a. Come off ablation - damage to the fast pathway
    b. Come off ablation as tachycardia continues
    c. Continue ablation - damage to the fast pathway
    d. Continue ablation - possible successful site

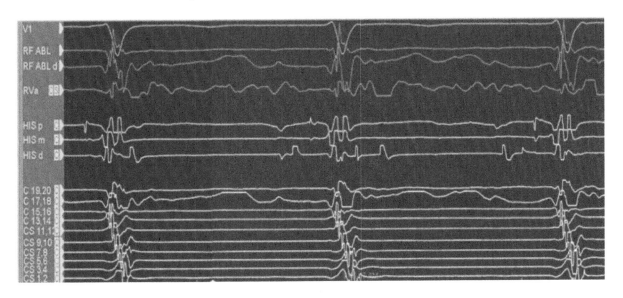

23. Where is the most likely origin of the VT in the 12-Lead ECG below?
    a. Right ventricular outflow tract
    b. Left ventricular outflow tract
    c. Right ventricular apex
    d. Left ventricular apex

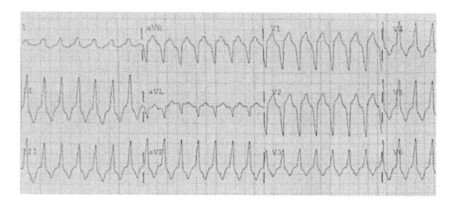

24. Which of the following is responsible for the majority of the lesion size during RF ablation?
    a. Restrictive heating
    b. Conductive heating
    c. Resistive heating
    d. Convection heating

25. Which class of antiarrhythmic medications primarily acts on the sodium channels?
    a. Class I
    b. Class II
    c. Class III
    d. Class IV

26. Blood would appear _____ on an intracardiac echo image.
    a. White
    b. Black
    c. Red
    d. Blue

27. What are appropriate high filter settings for ECG and intracardiac electrograms?
    a. 0.05 Hz, 30 Hz
    b. 0.5 Hz, 3 Hz
    c. 5 Hz, 300 Hz
    d. 50 Hz, 300 Hz

28. A patient has an HCO3 of 28, which of the following is the most appropriate diagnosis
    a. Respiratory Acidosis
    b. Respiratory Alkalosis
    c. Metabolic Acidosis
    d. Metabolic Alkalosis

29. Prior to bringing the patient back to the EP lab, the labs were reviewed. Which of the following would be an appropriate potassium level?
    a. 0.5 mEq/L
    b. 2.5 mEq/L
    c. 3.5 mEq/L
    d. 5.8 mEq/L

30. What is the longest coupling interval (S1, S2) that fails to capture the tissue?
    a. Effective refractory period
    b. Relative refractory period
    c. Functional refractory period
    d. Absolute refractory period

ANSWERS:

1. b.	11. b	21. b
2. a,b,c,d	12. b	22. d
3. b	13. c	23. a
4. d	14. c	24. b
5. d	15. d	25. a
6. b	16. c	26. b
7. a	17. a	27. a
8. d	18. e	28. d
9. a,b,c,d	19. c	29. c
10. a	20. c	30. a

Practice Test #2: (50 questions)

1. What equipment is commonly in a pericardiocentesis kit? (select all that apply)
   a. Ultrasound
   b. Pigtail Catheter
   c. 18-gauge needle
   d. Dilators

2. The following is an example of an arterial line blood pressure recorded during the procedure. What is recommended?

   a. Reposition the arterial line
   b. Give an IV fluid bolus
   c. Aspirate / Flush the transducer
   d. Replace the transducer

3. Which of the following is a Class Ia medication?
   a. Ibutilide
   b. Flecainide
   c. Quinidine
   d. Lidocaine

4. Which of the following pieces of equipment may be utilized to perform the actual transseptal puncture?
   a. Catheter
   b. Bing Stylet
   c. BRK
   d. Steerable Sheath

5. Which of the following methods is most commonly utilized to induce focal atrial tachycardia?
   a. Burst Pacing
   b. Decremental Pacing
   c. Parahisian Pacing
   d. Extrastimulus Testing

6. What is the most common complication with LAA closure procedures?
   a. Stroke
   b. Pericardial Effusion
   c. Air Embolism
   d. Vascular Complications

7. If the transseptal puncture is made to anterior, what may be accidentally punctured?
   a. Pulmonary Artery
   b. Left Atrial back wall
   c. Left Atrial Appendage
   d. Aorta

8. The transseptal sheath was inserted into the ascending aorta, what should be the next step?
   a. Give 2000 U heparin
   b. Withdraw the sheath and reengage the fossa
   c. Contact cardiac surgery
   d. Advance the ablation catheter

9. Which X-ray view is used to position the CS catheter from the IJ?
   a. Left Lateral
   b. RAO
   c. LAO
   d. AP

10. After starting a patient on Warfarin, the patient should be informed about_____.
(select the best 3)
   a. INR monitoring
   b. PTT monitoring
   c. Avoid excessive alcohol
   d. Avoid beta carotene

11. What core body temperature is when the patient is considered to be hypothermia? (the highest temperature that is considered to be hypothermia)
   a. 34° C
   b. 35° C
   c. 36° C
   d. 37° C

12. Match the following garden hose illustration to the impedance change it would represent if it was an implantable device lead.
   a. Low Impedance
   b. High Impedance
   c. Normal Impedance

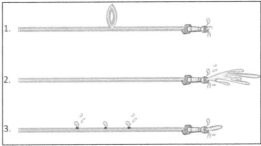

13. Benzodiazepines may be reversed with _____.
    a. Vitamin K
    b. Flumazenil
    c. Naloxone
    d. Protamine

14. What is an appropriate ACT level for performing an LAA closure?
    a. 300 to 400 seconds
    b. <100 seconds
    c. 100 to 200 seconds
    d. >400 seconds
    e. 200 to 300 seconds

15. If the RA electrogram was disconnected, which electrograms would be affected?
    a. Leads II, III, aVF
    b. Leads II & III
    c. Leads I, II, aVR
    d. Leads II, III, aVR

16. Which tachycardia may be ruled out in this recorded electrogram?

    a. Atrial Tachycardia
    b. AVNRT
    c. AVRT
    d. Atrial Flutter

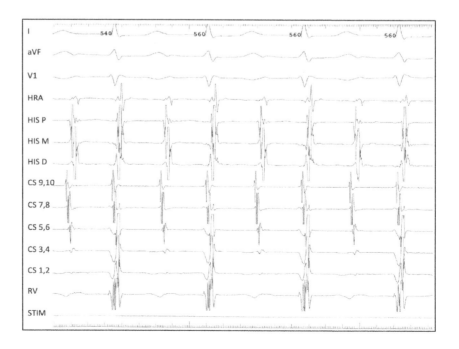

17. A VA interval of < 70ms during tachycardia is characteristic of which rhythm?
  a. Atrial Tachycardia
  b. AVRT
  c. Atrial Flutter
  d. AVNRT

18. While mapping atrial tachycardia, what would the unipolar signal look like at the best area for ablation?
  a. RS wave
  b. R wave
  c. QR wave
  d. QS wave

19. What is observed in the following electrogram recorded midway through a typical AFL ablation? The Duo catheter is placed within the right atrium and the distal tip was advanced into the CS. The ablation catheter is being utilized for pacing on the lateral RA near Duo 7,8.
  a. Medial to Lateral Block
  b. Bidirectional Block
  c. Intermittent Capture
  d. Manifest Entrainment
  e. Concealed Entrainment
  f. No Capture

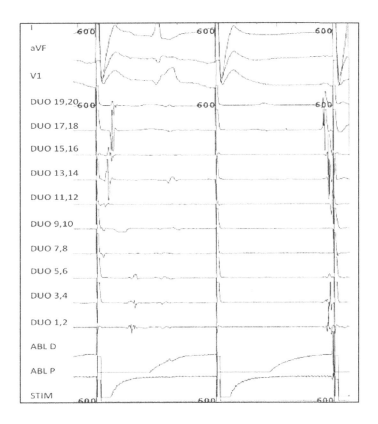

20. How would you describe tachycardia in the displayed ECG?
(displayed leads – III, V1, II, V5)

    a. CW AFL
    b. Atrial Fibrillation
    c. Atypical AFL
    d. CCW AFL

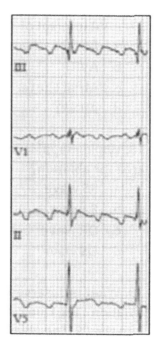

21. Which of the following BEST describes the following electrogram?
    a. Retrograde AP ERP
    b. VERP
    c. AERP
    d. Retrograde AVNERP
    e. AP ERP
    f. AVNERP

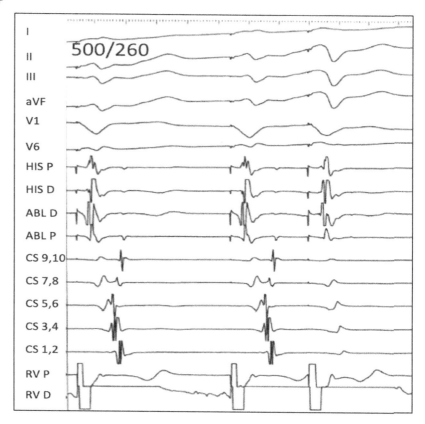

22. What is observed in the following ECG?
    a. RBBB
    b. Manifest AP
    c. LBBB
    d. Concealed AP
    e. 2nd degree type II HB
    f. 2nd degree type I HB

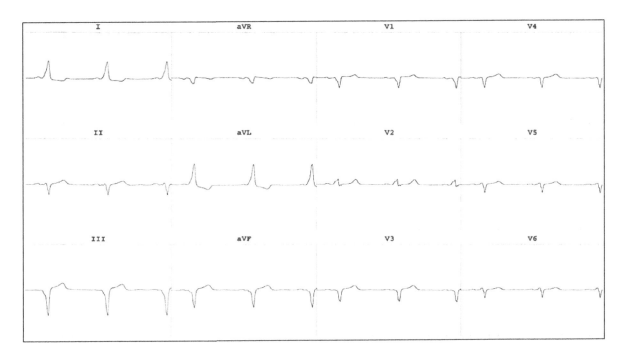

23. Match the following:
    a. Sodium
    b. Calcium
    c. Potassium
    d. Chloride
    e. Phosphate
    f. Bicarbonate

    1. Bone and teeth bind up 85%
    2. Predominant extracellular anion
    3. Major cation of the extracellular fluid
    4. Major intracellular cation
    5. ½ of blood this is bound to proteins, the rest is in its ionized form
    6. Second most abundant anion in the blood

24. What does the PR interval represent?
    a. SA node to AV node
    b. Atrial and ventricular depolarization
    c. AV node to ventricular myocardium
    d. Time within the AV node

25. What is observed in the following ICE image?
    a. Home View
    b. Clot
    c. Transseptal Puncture
    d. Pericardial Effusion

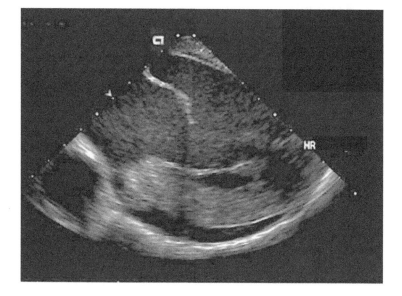

26. Convert 260ms to bpm.
    a. 200 bpm
    b. 192 bpm
    c. 304 bpm
    d. 230 bpm

27. What is the typical pulse width set on the pacing stimulator for an EP study?
    a. 2.0 sec
    b. 2.0 ms
    c. 0.20 ms
    d. 0.20 sec

28. How would you assess conduction while the patient is in junctional rhythm observed during RF slow pathway ablation?
    a. Pace the atrium
    b. Perform parahisian pacing
    c. Come off ablation
    d. Pace the ventricle

29. How many defibrillators should be in the EP lab?
    a. One available in the department
    b. If the patient has a defibrillator, one additional is needed.
    c. One available in each lab
    d. Two defibrillators in the lab

30. While obtaining right femoral venous access, pulsatile blood is observed. What should be the next step?

    a.   Remove and attempt more medial

    b.   Remove and attempt more lateral

    c.   Abandon site and attempt left femoral venous access

    d.   Insert the venous sheath

31. What is observed in the following electrogram?

    a.   VA Block

    b.   Left Lateral AP

    c.   AV Block

    d.   Posterior Septal AP

    e.   Right Lateral AP

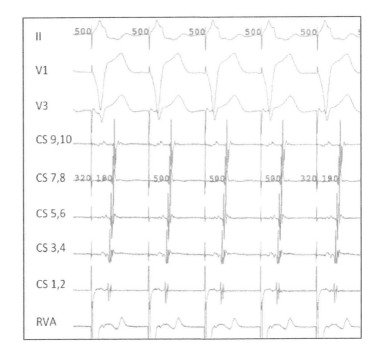

32. After ablation of a left posterior accessory pathway, the following ECG was recorded. What is observed?

    a.   Cardiac Memory

    b.   Myocardial Infarction

    c.   Hyperkalemia

    d.   Cardiac Ischemia

    e.   Pericardial Effusion

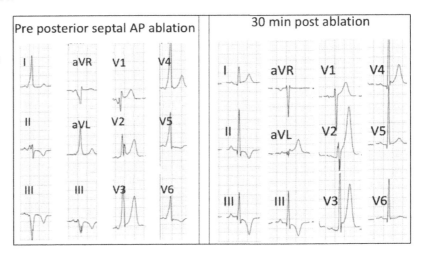

33. A patient had a pacemaker implanted 3 months prior and has complaints of dyspnea, facial swelling, cough, and distorted vision. What is the most likely cause?
   a. SVC Syndrome
   b. Diaphragmatic Stimulation
   c. RV Perforation
   d. Pacemaker Syndrome

34. What is a normal atrial pacemaker lead impedance?
   a. 1400 Ohms
   b. 500 Ohms
   c. 200 Ohms
   d. 1200 Ohms

35. Which of the following is a Class Ic medication?
   a. Quinidine
   b. Flecainide
   c. Ibutilide
   d. Lidocaine

36. During hemostasis, the patient's heart rate begins to drop; what is the most likely cause?
   a. Venous Occlusion
   b. Retroperitoneal hemorrhage
   c. Vasovagal reaction
   d. AV Fistula

37. Match the automatic rate of each of the following areas.
   a. < 40 bpm
   b. 40 to 60 bpm
   c. 60 to 100 bpm

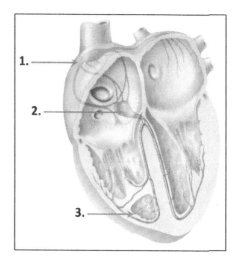

38. Where would the target of ablation be on the following 3D image?
(1. white, 2. orange, 3. blue, 4. green)
   a. Site 1
   b. Site 2
   c. Site 4
   d. Site 3

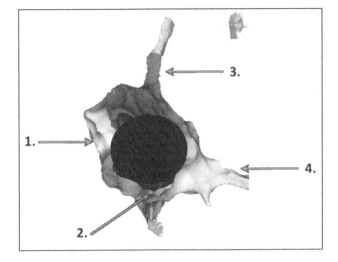

39. What is the function of the heart that allows the cardiac cells to respond to electrical stimulus?
   a. Automaticity
   b. Conductivity
   c. Contractility
   d. Excitability

40. What is the first step when utilizing a temporary pacemaker?
   a. Set the rate faster than the patient's ventricular rate
   b. Check sensing by setting the pacemaker rate at 10-20 bpm/min < spontaneous ventricular rate and check ECG and pulse generator for pacing inhibition
   c. Set a pulse of 3 V or > and asynchronous (sensitivity) to assure capture
   d. Check battery status
   e. Determine the threshold by gradually turning down the voltage until capture is lost

41. What structure is a circuit boundary for a typical atrial flutter on the lateral aspect?
   a. Cavo Tricuspid Isthmus
   b. Coronary Sinus Ostium
   c. Foramen Ovalis
   d. Crista Terminalis

42. While utilizing a laser sheath for lead removal, how is counter traction applied?
   a. Suture tied to the lead body
   b. Lead Locking Stylet
   c. Mechanical Dilator Sheath
   d. Manufacture J-tipped stylet

43. Match the following surgical instruments to the correct name.
   a. Metzenbaum Scissors
   b. Army Navy Retractor
   c. Senn Retractor
   d. Needle Holder
   e. Debakey Forceps
   f. Weitlaner Retractor
   g. Adson Pickups
   h. Hemostat
   i. Right Angle Forceps
   j. Mayo Scissors

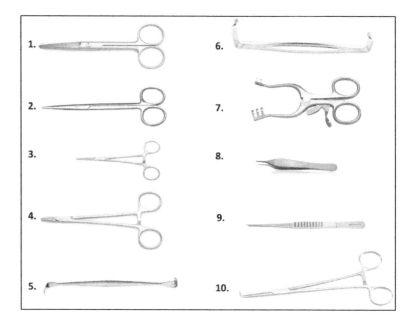

44. While holding pressure on the femoral artery to acquire hemostasis, pulses should be checked at which site?
   a. Pedal
   b. Popliteal
   c. Brachial
   d. Ulnar

45. Why should the operator and EP staff continue to observe the electrogram/ECG after RF energy is stopped?
Monitor for:
   a. Coagulum Buildup
   b. Tissue Adhesion
   c. Thermal Latency
   d. Steam Pop

46. Which of the following has the greatest impact on lesion size?
   a. Convection Heating
   b. Conductive Heating
   c. Recurrent Heating
   d. Resistive Heating

47. **Which is the most appropriate reason for the removal of old pacemaker leads?**
    a. Lead Fracture
    b. Infection
    c. Insulation Break
    d. Lead Recall

48. **What is a contraindication for an S-ICD implantation?**
    a. Previous endocarditis
    b. Patient with no venous access
    c. Symptomatic Bradycardia
    d. Patient with a high risk of infection

49. **What is the frame rate setting that would lead to the lowest dosage to the operator?**
    a. 30 FPS
    b. 7.5 FPS
    c. 10 FPS
    d. 15 FPS

50. **Which X-ray view is used to determine if a catheter or lead is in the RVOT?**
    a. RAO
    b. RAO Caudal
    c. LAO
    d. LAO Caudal

ANSWERS:

1. b,c,d	15. c	28. a	42. b
2. c	16. c	29. d	43. 1. j, 2. A, 3.h,
3. c	17. d	30. a	4.d, 5.c, 6.b,
4. c	18. d	31. b	7.f, 8.g, 9.e,
5. a	19. c	32. a	10.i
6. d	20. d	33. a	44. a
7. d	21. a	34. b	45. c
8. c	22. b	35. b	46. b
9. c	23. a.3, b.5, c.4,	36. c	47. b
10. a, b, c	d.2, e.1, f.6	37. 1.c, 2.b, 3.c	48. c
11. b	24. b	38. b	49. b
12: 1.b, 2.c, 3.a	25. d	39. d	50. a
13. b	26. d	40. d	
14. e	27. b	41. d	

Practice Test #3: (50 questions):

1. Which fluoroscopic view is the most commonly utilized to visualize the LAA for a closure procedure?
    a. LAO caudal
    b. RAO cranial
    c. RAO caudal
    d. LAO cranial

2. What is the NBG code for a pacemaker that can sense both the atrium and the ventricle, but only paces in the ventricle when needed?
    a. VVI
    b. VDD
    c. VAD
    d. DDD

3. Where should pressure be applied when removing a femoral artery sheath?
    a. > 1 in caudal to the site
    b. > 1 in cranial to the site
    c. At puncture site
    d. Both above and below the puncture site

4. Match the following blade to the correct label.
    a. # 10 blade
    b. # 11 blade
    c. # 15 blade

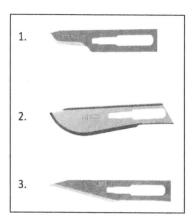

5. The next day check on a new PPM insertion reveals loss of capture on the RV lead. The patient receives a portable chest x-ray, and no change is observed. What is the most likely cause?
    a. Loose screw in the header
    b. Micro dislodgement
    c. Insulation breach
    d. Macro dislodgement

6. At procedure completion, the patient has significant low back pain, and their blood pressure is decreasing. What should be done next?
   a. Place a pillow under the patient's knees
   b. Order an ultrasound of the groin site
   c. Have the patient bend their left leg to help relieve the pressure
   d. Administer fentanyl for sheath removal
   e. Remove the arterial line 1st, after hemostasis, remove the venous

7. After the procedure, the patient begins experiencing weakness, confusion, dizziness, and difficulty speaking. What is the most likely cause?
   a. Stroke
   b. Vasovagal Reaction
   c. Myocardial Infarction
   d. Tamponade

8. Which of the following is not a good indicator for successful transseptal access into the LA (differentiate between LA/RA)?
   a. Pressure Recording
   b. Contrast Injection
   c. ICE Visualization
   d. O2 Saturation
   e. Electrogram

9. The "on-face" view of the atrioventricular valves may be observed in which view?
   a. LAO
   b. AP
   c. RAO
   d. PA

10. There is noise on the distal channels of the displayed catheter. Which troubleshooting strategy should be performed last?
    a. Check pin connections
    b. Replace catheter
    c. Disconnect/Reconnect catheter
    d. Replace cable

11. On 3D maps, the latest electrical activity is typically represented by which color?
   a. Purple
   b. Blue
   c. Red
   d. Green

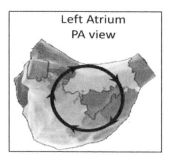

12. This valve may be found in front of the coronary sinus and may make entry more challenging.
   a. Thebesian
   b. Portal
   c. Vieussens
   d. Eustachian

13. What is the primary ion exiting the cell during phase 3 of a ventricular myocardial cell?
   a. Chloride
   b. Calcium
   c. Potassium
   d. Sodium

14. This electrogram was recorded during baseline testing. Which of the following may essentially be ruled out with this finding?
   a. Atrial Tachycardia
   b. Atrial Flutter
   c. AVRT
   d. AVNRT

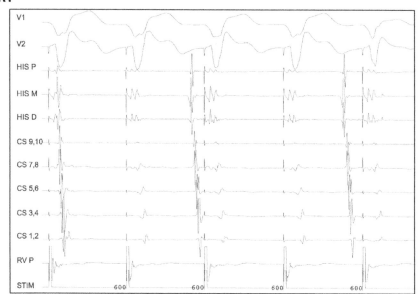

15. How often does the Hemochron point of care testing for ACTs need to be quality control tested?
    a. Every 8 hours (during patient care)
    b. Every 24 hours (during patient care)
    c. Once a week
    d. Once a month

16. A substrate map is often utilized to assess the _____.
    a. Reentrant circuit
    b. Activation of the tachycardia
    c. Voltage of the tissue
    d. Pacing morphology map

17. Match the ECG to the correct label.
    1. Atypical Flutter
    2. Atrial Fibrillation
    3. Counterclockwise typical flutter
    4. Atrial Flutter 1:1
    5. Clockwise typical flutter – CW AFL

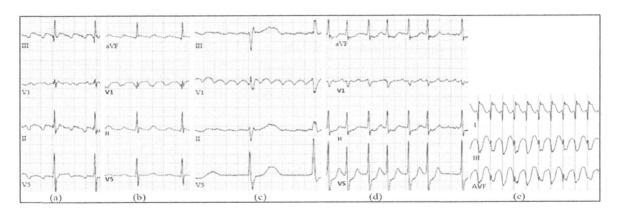

18. What is observed in the following electrogram?
    a. Retrograde AP ERP
    b. VERP
    c. AVNERP
    d. Retrograde AVNERP
    e. AERP
    f. AP ERP

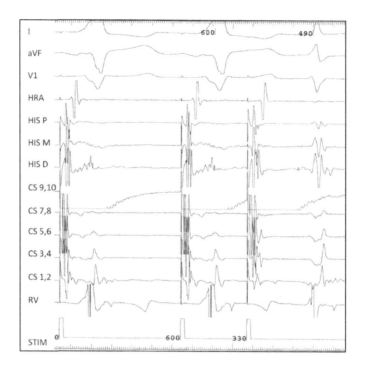

19. What is observed in the following electrogram?
    a. Long AH
    b. Long His bundle duration and HV interval
    c. Long HV
    d. Long His bundle duration and HV interval

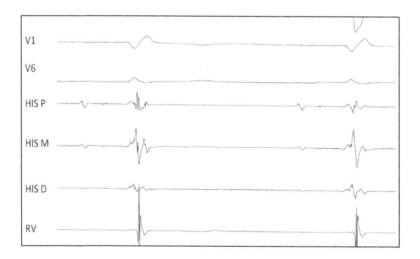

20. An HV interval of 72ms represents _____.
    a. Distal conduction disease
    b. AV nodal disease
    c. SA nodal disease
    d. Accessory pathway presence
    e. Interatrial disease

21. Which class of medications affect the Na⁺ channels?
    a. Class I
    b. Class II
    c. Class III
    d. Class IV

22. Why might doppler be utilized with ICE during PVI?
    a. Monitor for pericardial effusion
    b. Check for pulmonary vein stenosis
    c. Observe lesion formation
    d. Guide transseptal access

23. What kind of device/leads may cause pocket stimulation?
    a. True Bipolar
    b. CS lead (CRT)
    c. Integrated Bipolar
    d. Unipolar

24. What does it mean when the lead impedance is significantly lower than the last device check on this 5-year-old system?
    a. Micro dislodgement
    b. Lead fracture
    c. Lead insulation break
    d. Macro dislodgement

25. Which area is considered sterile on the gown?
    a. The complete front of the gown and sleeves
    b. Font and back of the gown and the arms up to two inches below the elbows
    c. Only the chest and the arms up to two inches above the elbows
    d. Entire gown

26. Which of the following locations identifies an accessory pathway potential?
    a. 3
    b. 1
    c. 2
    d. 4

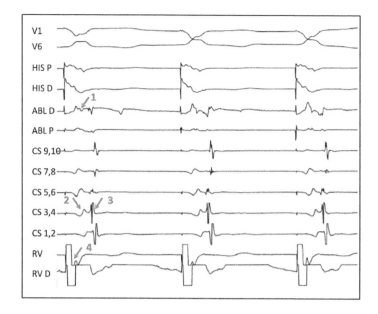

27. Which of the following is a Class Ib medication?
    a. Lidocaine
    b. Ibutilide
    c. Flecainide
    d. Quinidine

28. There is noise on all 12 ECG leads. Which electrode is most likely the problem?
    a. V1
    b. Right Arm
    c. Left Leg
    d. Left Arm
    e. Right Leg

29. What is expected when a successful RF lesion has been created?
    a. Impedance increase of 10%
    b. Impedance decrease of 10%
    c. Power increase of 5%
    d. Power decrease of 5%

30. What is the most reliable landmark for femoral arterial access?
    a. Femoral Head
    b. Pubic Symphysis
    c. Inguinal Crease
    d. Femoral Pulse

31. Which of the following sites is most utilized for pericardiocentesis?
    a. Short Axis
    b. Suprasternal
    c. Basal
    d. Subxiphoid

32. What does a patient's ABG that came back with a pCO2 of 47 indicate?
    a. Respiratory Acidosis
    b. Metabolic Alkalosis
    c. Respiratory Alkalosis
    d. Metabolic Acidosis

33. Which is the best x-ray view to visualize the CS veins for CRT LV lead placement?
    a. RAO
    b. LAO
    c. AP
    d. LL

34. What is the lower limit (cutoff) for the administration of beta-blockers?
    a. Diastolic BP < 60 mmHg
    b. Diastolic BP < 70 mmHg
    c. Systolic BP < 90 mmHg
    d. Systolic BP < 120 mmHg

35. What is the clotting test used to measure the effect of warfarin?
    a. PTT
    b. PT
    c. INR
    d. ACT

36. Which x-ray angulation is utilized for a venogram prior to a ppm insertion?
    a. LAO
    b. AP
    c. RAO
    d. LL

37. The esophageal temperature is commonly monitored during RF ablation of which area?
    a. LA anterior wall
    b. LA posterior wall
    c. RA anterior wall
    d. RA posterior wall

38. Defibrillation thresholds may increase with which of the following medications?
(select all that apply)
   a. Sotalol
   b. Amiodarone
   c. Digoxin
   d. Metoprolol

39. Where is the CS ostium located in reference to the tricuspid valve?
   a. Superior
   b. Anterior
   c. Inferior
   d. Posterior

40. Which electrode does Lead I and Lead III have in common?
   a. Left Leg
   b. Left Arm
   c. Right Leg
   d. Right Arm

41. Which of the following medications are opioids?
(select all that apply)
   a. Fentanyl
   b. Versed
   c. Flumazenil
   d. Valium
   e. Naloxone
   f. Benadryl
   g. Meperidine

42. What is the measurement for the absorbed x-ray dose?
   a. Seifert
   b. Gray
   c. REM
   d. RAD

43. What is observed in the following electrogram?
   a. AERP
   b. Slow Pathway ERP
   c. Fast Pathway ERP
   d. AVNERP

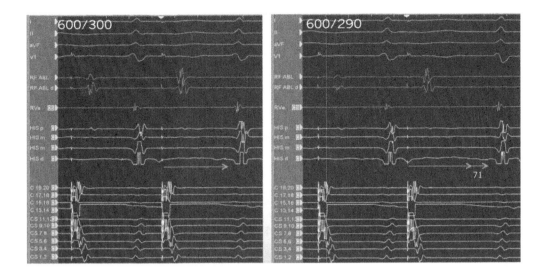

44. Which of the following may be a complication of performing a CS venogram? (select all that apply)
    a. Decreased BUN
    b. Venous trauma
    c. Contrast-induced nephropathy
    d. Vein dissection

45. Where would be the best location for an IV on a right-handed patient that is coming to the lab for a permanent pacemaker?
    a. Left volar
    b. Left dorsal
    c. Right dorsal
    d. Left antecubital
    e. Right volar
    f. Right antecubital

46. Convert 150 bpm to ms.
    a. 350 ms
    b. 115 ms
    c. 400 ms
    d. 450 ms

47. Which ECG lead is the most useful in determining RV vs. LV pacing?
    a. V1
    b. Lead III
    c. Lead I
    d. Lead II

48. Which of the following are characteristics of bundle branch reentry VT?
(select all that apply)
    a. **RBBB Morphology**
    b. **LBBB Morphology**
    c. **V-to-V drives the H-to-H**
    d. **Monomorphic**
    e. **Polymorphic**
    f. **H-to-H drives the V-to-V**

49. When attempting transseptal access, the following pressure was recorded. Where is the most likely location?
    a. **Aorta**
    b. **Pulmonary artery**
    c. **Left atrium**
    d. **Right atrium**

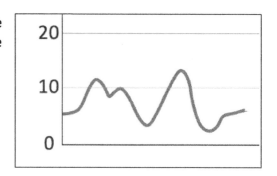

50. Which of the following will increase the patient's x-ray exposure?
(select all that apply)
    a. **Raising the table**
    b. **Steep angulation**
    c. **Using collimators**
    d. **Increasing the frame rate**

ANSWERS:

1. c	14. c	26. b	39. d
2. b	15. a	27. a	40. b
3. b	16. c	28. e	41. a, g
4. 1.c, 2.a, 3. B	17. 1.c, 2.d, 3.a,	29. b	42. d
5. b	4. 3, 5. B	30. d	43. c
6. b	18. f	31. d	44. b, c, d
7. a	19. c	32. a	45. d
8. e	20. a	33. b	46. c
9. a	21. a	34. c	47. a
10. b	22. b	35. b	48. b, d, f
11. a	23. d	36. b	49. c
12. a	24. c	37. b	50. b, d
13. c	25. c	38. a, b	

References:

- 300th Cryoballoon Ablation At Our Unit. (2016, Feb 17) Image retrieved from http://www.capetownafcentre.co.za/news/300th-cryoballoon-ablation
- Abedin, Z, Essential Cardiac Electrophysiology: The Self-Assessment Approach, Blackwell Publishing, 2013
- Aibolita (Retrieved July 2018) Bundle Branch Reentrant VT. Retrieved from http://aibolita.com/heart-and-vessels/50757-bundle-branch-reentrant-vt.html
- Allmers, Nancy M., and Verderame, Joan A., Appleton, and Lange's Review for Surgical Tech. Exam, Appleton and Lange, Fourth Edition, 1996
- American Heart Association, Textbook of ADVANCED CARDIAC LIFE SUPPORT, 2010
- American Heart Association. Atrial Fibrillation. Watch, Live and Learn. Video retrieved from http://watchlearnlive.heart.org
- American Heart Association. Ventricular Fibrillation. Watch, learn and live. Animation retrieved from http://watchlearnlive.heart.org
- Anand, R. (Nov 2011) EP Lab Digest, Volume 11, Issue 11. Key Consideration for Designing an Electrophysiology Laboratory in a Community Hospital.
- Antzelevitch, C. & Burashnikov, A. (2011, Mar 1) Overview of Basic Mechanisms of Cardiac Arrhythmia. Retrieved from https://www.ncbi.nlm.nih.gov/pmc/articles/PMC3164530/
- Asirvatham, S. J., Mayo Clinic Electrophysiology Manual, Mayo Clinic Scientific Press, 1dst Edition, 2014
- Baim, D. S and Grossman W.., Cardiac Catheterization, Angiography, and Intervention, 7th Ed., Lea and Febiger, 2006
- Basicmedical Key: Fastest Basicmedical Insight Engine. AV Nodal Reentrant Tachycardia: Atypical. (2017, Mar 25) Retrieved from https://basicmedicalkey.com/av-nodal-reentrant-tachycardia-atypical/
- Berne, R. M. and Levy, M. N., Cardiovascular Physiology, 8th Ed., Mosby Yearbook, 2001
- Biosense Webster, http://www.biosensewebster.com/
- Braun, Nemcek, and Vogelzang, Interventional Radiology Procedure Manual, Churchill Livingstone, 1997
- Braunwald, Eugene, Ed., HEART DISEASE A Textbook of Cardiovascular Medicine, 9th Ed., W. B. Saunders Co., 2012
- Browning, T. (2013, Nov 19) Class II antiarrhythmics. Retrieved from https://www.youtube.com/watch?v=2uUj05KaVyo
- Burns, E., (2018) Life in the Fastlane: Brugada Syndrome. Retrieved from https://lifeinthefastlane.com/ecg-library/brugada-syndrome/
- Burns, E., (2018) Life in the Fastlane: VT versus SVT. Retrieved from https://litfl.com/vt-versus-svt-ecg-library/
- Chinitz, J., Michaud, G. Stephenson, K. (Oct 2017) The Journal of Innovations in Cardiac Rhythm Management. Impedance-guided Radiofrequency Ablation: Using Impedance to Improve Ablation Outcomes. Retrieved from

http://www.innovationsincrm.com/cardiac-rhythm-management/articles-2017/october/1100-impedance-guided-radiofrequency-ablation

- Cleveland Clinic (2011, Oct 5) Catheter Ablation For Atrial Fibrillation. Animation retrieved from https://youtu.be/SZ_ulfj-hIQ
- Cleveland Clinic (2019, Apr 23) Arrhythmogenic Right Ventricular Dysplasia (ARVD) Retrieved from https://my.clevelandclinic.org/health/diseases/16752-arrhythmogenic-right-ventricular-dysplasia-arvd (2019, Oct 3)
- Cohen, Todd, Practical Electrophysiology, HMP Publications, 2005
- Craig, Gloria P., Clinical Calculations Made Easy, Solving Problems Using Dimensional Analysis, 2nd Ed., Lippincott, 2001 Curry, Dowdey, and Murry, Christensen's Introduction to the Physics of Diagnostic Radiology, 3rd Ed., Lea & Febiger Publishers
- Crawford, M. & DiMarco, J. (2003, Dec 1) Cardiology
- Daily, E. K., and Schroeder, J. S., Techniques in Bedside Hemodynamic Monitoring, 4th Edition
- Dave Droll, Cath Lab Digest, Clipping versus Shaving: Who Wins in the End? Infection Risk and Hair Removal Guidelines, Sept 2005
- Deisenhofer, I., Zrenner, B., Yin, Y., Pitschner, H., Kuniss, M., GroBmann, G., Stiller, S., Luik, A., Veltmann, C., Frank, J., Linner, J., Estner, H., Pflaumer, A., Wu, J., Von Bary, C., Ucer, E., Reents, T., Tzeis, S., Fichtner, S., Kathan, S., Karch, M., Jilek, C., Ammar, S., Kolb, C., Liu, Z., Haller, B., Schmitt, C., & Hessling, G., (2010, Nov 15) Cryoablation Versus Radiofrequency Energy for the Ablation of Atrioventricular Nodal Reentrant Tachycardia (the CYRANO Study) Results From a Large Multicenter Prospective Randomized Trial. Retrieved from http://circ.ahajournals.org/content/122/22/2239
- DiMario, et. al., "Clinical application and image interpretation in intracoronary ultrasound" in European Heart Journal, 1998
- Dubin, Dale, RAPID INTERPRETATION of EKG's, 3rd Ed., Cover Publishing Co., 1982
- ECGPedia contributors. (2013, May 22) Brugada Syndrome. In ECGPedia, Part of Cardionetworks.org. Retrieved from http://en.ecgpedia.org/wiki/Brugada_Syndrome
- Ellenbogen, K, A, and Wood, Cardiac Pacing and ICDs, Blackwell Publishing, 5th Edition, 2008
- Ellenbogen, Kay, Lau, Wilkof, Clinical Cardiac Pacing, Defibrillation, and Resynchronization Therapy, 4th Edition, 2011
- Endosonics Company Literature and Web Site (Endosonics.com), 1999
- EP Europace Vol. 7, Issue 6 (2005, Nov 1) Electroanatomic mapping characteristics of ventricular tachycardia in patients with arrhythmogenic right ventricular cardiomyopathy/dysplasia.
- Fernandez-Armenta, J. & Berruezo, A. (May 2014) How to Recognize Epicardial Origin of Ventricular Tachycardias. Retrieved from https://www.researchgate.net/publication/262339568_How_to_Recognize_Epicardial_Origin_of_Ventricular_Tachycardias
- Fogoros, R. (2012, Sept 17) Electrophysiology Testing
- Fogoros, R., MD, Practical Cardiac Diagnosis, Electrophysiologic Testing, Blackwell Scientific Pub.,4th Edition, 2006

- Function of the Atrioventricular and Semilunar Valves. Retrieved from http://antranik.org/function-of-the-atrioventricular-and-semilunar-valves-and-fibrous-skeleton/
- Garcia and Holtz, 12-Lead EKG, The Art of Interpretation, Jones, and Bartlett Publishers, 2001
- Gardner, D. and Anderson-Manz E. (2001, May 1) How to Perform Surgical Hand Scrubs. Retrieved from http://www.infectioncontroltoday.com/articles/2001/05/how-to-perform-surgical-hand-scrubs.aspx
- Gruendemann and Meeker, Alexander's Care of the Patient in Surgery, CV Mosby Co., 1987
- Highlights of the 2010 American Heart Association Guidelines for CPR and ECC, http://static.heart.org/eccguidelines/pdf/ucm_317350.pdf
- Ho, R. (2008, Aug 18) Electrophysiology of Arrhythmias: Practical Images for Diagnosis and Ablation.
- Ho, R.T., Electrophysiology of Arrhythmias: Practical Images for Diagnosis and Ablation, Published by Lippincott, 1st Edition, 2010
- https://ghr.nlm.nih.gov/condition/brugada-syndrome#synonyms
- https://ghr.nlm.nih.gov/condition/jervell-and-lange-nielsen-syndrome#resources
- Huang, S.K. and Wood, M. A., Catheter Ablation of Cardiac Arrhythmias, Saunders Elsevier, 2nd Edition, 2011
- Huen, M. (2018) 10 Fact About Retroperitoneal Hematoma. Retrieved from http://www.thrombocyte.com/retroperitoneal-hematoma/
- Images retrieved from https://www.sjm.com and https://www.sjm.com/en/professionals/disease-state-management/cardiac-arrhythmias/integrated-lab
- Intravascular Ultrasound, An interactive Learning Tool With CME Credit, J.M. Hodgson, Senior Editor, Technology Solutions Group, Ltd., Ed. Div.
- Isa, Miller and Zipes, Clinical Arrhythmology and Electrophysiology, A Companion to Braunwald's Heart Disease, Saunders/Elsevier Publishers, 2009
- Issa, Z.F., Miller, J.M., & Zipes, D.P., (Philadelphia: Saunders Elsevier, 2009) Clinical Arrhythmology and Electrophysiology
- J.B. Lippincott Co., 1989
- Joseph, J.P. & Rajappan, K. (2011, Nov 12) Radiofrequency ablation of cardiac arrhythmias: past, present, and future. Retrieved from http://qjmed.oxfordjournals.org/content/105/4/303
- Kern, M. J., Ed., The Cardiac Catheterization Handbook, 4th Ed., Mosby-Yearbook, Inc., 2003
- King, & Yeung, Interventional Cardiology, McGraw-Hill Co., 2007
- Kirkorian, G., Moncada, E., Chevalier, P., Canu, G., Claudel, JP., Bellon, C., Lyon, L. & Touboul, P. (1994, Dec 1) Radiofrequency ablation of atrial flutter. Efficacy of an anatomically guided approach. Circulation: Vol. 90, No. 6 Retrieved from https://www.ahajournals.org/doi/abs/10.1161/01.cir.90.6.2804

- Kiser, A., Wimmer-Greinecker, G., Kapelak, B., Bartus, K., Sadowski, J. (Image modified on July 2018) Paracardioscopic Ex-Maze Procedure for Atrial Fibrillation. Image retrieved from http://ismics.org/abstracts/2008/V13.cgi
- Klabunde, R. (2008, Dec 13) Cardiovascular Physiology Concepts: Sinoatrial Node Action Potentials. Retrieved from http://www.cvphysiology.com/Arrhythmias/A004
- Kusukmoto, F., Understanding Intracardiac EGMs and ECGs, Wiley-Blackwell Publishers, 1st Edition 2010
- Loebl, Suzanne, and Spratto, George, and Heckheimer, Estelle, The Nurses Drug Handbook, 2nd Ed., Wiley Medical Pub., 1980 Ed., Lippincott Williams & Wilkins, 2002
- Makhija, A., Thachil, A., Sridevi, C., Rao, B., Jaishankar, S. & Narasimhan, C. (2009) Indian Pacing and Electrophysiology Journal. Substrate Based Ablation of Ventricular Tachycardia Through an Epicardial Approach.
- Mann, Roger, Edwards, and Scott, Electrophysiology Board Review (Board Review for Electrophysiology Book 1), Published by Knowledge Testing. Com
- Marriott, Henry J., and Conover, Mary H., Advanced Concepts in Arrhythmias, The C.V. Mosby Co., 1983
- Matthews, R. (Retrieved July 2018) Cardiology Explained and Presented by Robert Matthews, MD. The Wolff-Parkinson_White Syndrome. Retrieved from http://www.rjmatthewsmd.com/Definitions/wolff_parkinson_white_syndrome.htm
- McGowan, A. (2004, Dec 14) Iatrogenic Arteriovenous Fistula. Retrieved from http://www.medscape.com/viewarticle/494434
- Medical Expo. The Online Medical Device Exhibition. (2018) Ultrasound Catheter / Vascular. Retrieved from http://www.medicalexpo.com/prod/st-jude-medical/product-70886-446852.html
- Medical Expo. The Online Medical Device Exhibition. (2018) Vascular Access Sheath / Steerable. Retrieved from http://www.medicalexpo.com/prod/st-jude-medical/product-70886-518094.html
- Medical Multimedia Laboratories. Heart Sounds and Cardiac Arrhythmias. SVT Tutorial. Retrieved from www.Blaufuss.org
- Medtronic, The ECG Workbook, Medtronic Inc.1996, Medtronic.com
- Michaud, GF., Tada, H., Chough, S., et al. (2001) Differentiation of atypical atrioventricular node re-entrant tachycardia from orthodromic reciprocating tachycardia using a septal accessory pathway by the response to ventricular pacing.
- Moses, K. Weston, et al., A Practical Guide to Cardiac Pacing, 4th Ed., Little and Brown Co., 1995
- Moulton, Kreigh, Electrophysiology Review Course Book 1 & 2, 2002
- Murgatroyd & Krahn, Handbook of Cardiac Electrophysiology, Remedica, 2002
- Murgatroyd, F & Krahn A. (2003, Jan 5) Handbook of Cardiac Electrophysiology: A Practical Guide to Invasive EP Studies and Catheter Ablation.
- Musa, K. (2014, Dec 15) Anatomy of the heart. Retrieved from http://www.slideshare.net/Abomustafa/anatomy-of-the-heart-42723933
- NanoDomino (2014, Feb 14) Domino Heart. Retrieved from https://www.youtube.com/watch?v=hu59C1K5stM
- Nantou, Taiwan, 2010 http://homepage.vghtpe.gov.tw/~jcma/73/9/471.pdf

- Nazarian, S., Kolandaivelu, A., Zvimuan, M., Meininger, G., Kato, R., Susil, R., Roguin, A., Dickfeld, T., Ashikaga, H., Calkins, H., Berger, R., Bluemke, D., Lardo, A., & Halperin, H. (2008, Jun 23) Feasibility of Real-Time Magnetic Resonance Imaging for Catheter Guidance in Electrophysiology Studies. Retrieved from http://circ.ahajournals.org/content/118/3/223
- NIBIB gov (2015, Jun 5) How Ultrasound Works. Retrieved from https://youtu.be/I1Bdp2tMFsY
- NIH. U.S. National Library of Medicine. Genetics Home Reference. Published 2019, Oct 1. Retrieved from https://ghr.nlm.nih.gov/condition/romano-ward-syndrome#resources
- Nogami, A. (2018) European Cardiology Review: Vol. 6, Issue 4. Diagnosis and Ablation of Fascicular Tachycardia.
- Nordkamp, L. (2013, Mar 25) Textbook of Cardiology. LQTS. Retrieved from https://www.textbookofcardiology.org/wiki/LQTS (2019, Oct 3)
- Nordkamp, L. (2014, Mar 26) Textbook of Cardiology. SQTS. Retrieved from https://www.textbookofcardiology.org/wiki/SQTS (2019, Oct 3)
- Opie, Lionel H., Drugs for the Heart, 4th Edition, W. B. Saunders, 2005
- PACES. The Pediatric & Congenital Electrophysiology Society. Cardiac Channelopathies. Retrieved from http://pediatricepsociety.org/Patient-Resources/Cardiac-Channelopathies.aspx (2019, Oct 3)
- Parikh, V. & Kowalski, M. (2015, Dec 31) Journal of Atrial Fibrillation. Comparison of Phrenic Nerve Injury during Atrial Fibrillation Ablation between Different Modalities, Pathophysiology and Management.
- Patel, V. (2017, Jan 4) TheHeart.org Medscape: Digitalis Toxicity Treatment & Management. Retrieved from http://emedicine.medscape.com/article/154336-treatment
- Permanent Pacemaker Implantation. (2016, July 28) Peel-away of Right Ventricular Lead Sheath. Retrieved from https://youtu.be/i9iaVBxAng8
- Popovic, D. (Retrieved July 2018) Noise in ECG and how to deal with it. Retrieved from http://www-classes.usc.edu/engr/bme/620/LectureECGNoise.pdf
- Protonotarios, N., Tsatsopoulou, A. (2006, Mar 13) Orphanet Journal of Rare Diseases. Naxos disease: Cardiocutaneous syndrome due to cell adhesion defect.
- Published by Cardioelectric, 1st Edition, 2012
- Purves, Klein, Leong-Sit, Yee, Skanes, Gula, & Krahn, Cardiac Electrophysiology, A Visual Guide for Nurses, Techs, and Fellows, 2012
- Quallich, S., Goff, R. & Iaizzo, P. Journal of Medical Devices: Vol. 8/Issue 2. High-Speed Visualization of Steam Pops During Radiofrequency Ablation. Retrieved from http://medicaldevices.asmedigitalcollection.asme.org/article.aspx?articleid=1876472
- Rafla, S. (2013, July 12) Technique of Ablation of AVNRT and case presentation. Retrieved from https://www.slideshare.net/SamirRafla/samir-rafla-technique-of-ablation-of-avnrt-and-case-presentation
- Raza, S. (2006, Oct) Radiation Exposure in the Cath Lab – Safety and Precautions. Retrieved from http://www.priory.com/med/radiation.htm

- Reddy, VY., Shah, D., Kautzner, J., Schmidt, B., Sadodi, N., Herrera, C., Jais, P., Hindricks, G., Peichl, P., Yulzari, A., Lambert, H., Neuzil, P., Natale, A. & Kuck, KH. (Nov 2012) Heart Rhythm. The relationship between contact force and clinical outcome during radiofrequency catheter ablation of atrial fibrillation in the TOCCATA study. Retrieved from https://www.ncbi.nlm.nih.gov/pubmed/22820056
- Retrieved from https://www.ncbi.nlm.nih.gov/pmc/articles/PMC1435994/ (2019, Oct 3)
- Reynolds, Terry, RDCS, BS, ULTRASOUND PHYSICS, A Registry Exam Preparation Guide, School of Cardiac Ultrasound, Arizona Heart Institute Foundation, Phoenix, AZ 1996
- Roberts-Thomson, Kurt & Kistler, Peter & M Kalman, Jonathan. (2005). Atrial Tachycardia: Mechanisms, Diagnosis, and Management. Current problems in cardiology. 30. 529-73. 10.1016/j.cpcardiol.2005.06.004. Retrieved from https://www.researchgate.net/publication/7582173_Atrial_Tachycardia_Mechanisms_Diagnosis_and_Management
- Saint Jude Medical, http://professional.sjm.com/
- Saksena, S. (2015, May 1) Interventional Cardiac Electrophysiology: A Multidisciplinary Approach.
- Schneider, Peter, Endovascular Skills, Guidewire and Catheter Skills for Endovascular Surgery, 2nd Edition, Marcel Dekker, Inc., 2003
- Schotten, U., Verheule, S., Kirchhof, P. & Goette, A. (2011, Jan 1) American Physiological Society: Physiological Reviews. Vol. 91, No. 1 Pathophysiological Mechanisms of Atrial Fibrillation: A Translational Appraisal.
- Sheikh, M., Bruhl, S., Foster, W., Grubb, B. & Kanjwal, Y. (Jan 2011) EP Lab Digest, Volume 11, Issue 1. Premature Ventricular Contractions May Not Be All That Benign: The Role of Radiofrequency Ablation.
- Siemens.com AcuNav instruction manual online, //www.medical.siemens.com/siemens/en_US/gg_us_FBAs/files/brochures/AcuNav/Instructional_Guide.pdf
- Smith, S. (2016, June 3) Dr. Smith's ECG Blog: Instructive ECGs in Emergency Medicine Clinical Context. Wide Complex Tachycardia with Fusion and Capture Beats. Not what you think. Retrieved from http://hqmeded-ecg.blogspot.com/2016/06/wide-complex-tachycardia-with-fusion.html
- Sorgente, A., Chierchia, G., Asmundis, C., Sarkozy, A., Capulzini, L., Brugada, P. (2011, July 21) EP Europace. Complications of Atrial Fibrillation Ablation: When Prevention Is Better Than Cure.
- Steinberg J.S, and Suneet, M, Electrophysiology: The Basics: A Companion Guide for the Cardiology Fellow during the EP Rotation, Published by Lippincott, 1st Edition, 2009
- Stevenson, W. & Soejima, K. (2018, Nov 25) Recording Techniques for Clinical Electrophysiology. Medscape. Retrieved from https://www.medscape.com/viewarticle/512810_2
- Tabatabaei, N., & Asirvatham, S. (2009, Jun 1) Circulation: Arrhythmia and Electrophysiology. Vol. 2, No. 3. Supravalvular Arrhythmia: Identifying and Ablating the Substrate.

- Tadvi, N. (2013, Sep 25) Antiarrhythmic drugs. Retrieved from https://www.slideshare.net/nasertadvi/antiarrhythmic-drugs-26524937
- Taiwan Heart Rhythm Society (2013, Apr 11) Electrophysiology Study: Pacing Methods & EP Testing. Retrieved from http://www.slideshare.net/thrs/electrophysiologic-study
- Taiwan Heart Rhythm Society (2013, Apr 11) Intracardiac Electrograms. Retrieved from https://www.slideshare.net/thrs/intracardiac-electrograms
- Tipp, Alice, Basic Pathophysiological Mechanisms of Congestive Heart Failure, McGraw-Hill, 1979 Torres, Basic Medical Techniques and Patient Care for Radiologic Technologists,
- Underhill, S. L., Ed., CARDIAC NURSING, 2nd Ed., J. B. Lippincott Co., 1989 Wiggers diagram:
- Valves of the Heart. Retrieved from http://www.apsubiology.org/anatomy/2020/2020_Exam_Reviews/Exam_1/CH18_Valves_of_the_Heart.htm
- Vitulano, N., Pazzano, V., Pelargonio, G. & Narducci, ML (2014, Sept 19) Dovepress: Medical Devices: Evidence and Research Vol 8. Technology update: intracardiac echocardiography – a review of the literature. Retrieved from https://www.dovepress.com/technology-update-intracardiac-echocardiography-ndash-a-review-of-the--peer-reviewed-fulltext-article-MDER#F2
- Waksman and Ajani, Pharmacology in the Catheterization Laboratory, Wiley-Blackwell, 2010 Watson, Sandy, Ed., Invasive Cardiology, A manual for Cath Lab Personnel, 2nd Ed., Physicians Press, 2005 Wilson, J.H., Cardiac EP Exam Preparation: A review for allied professionals,
- Watson, L. (2009) EP Studies in Bradyarrhythmias. Retrieved from http://slideplayer.com/slide/230395/
- Webber, J., Jang, J., Gustavson, S. & Olin, J. (2007, May 22) Contemporary Management of Postcatheterization Pseudoaneurysms. Retrieved from http://circ.ahajournals.org/content/115/20/2666
- WebMD, LLC. (2018, May 9) Vagal Maneuvers to Slow Heart Rate. Retrieved from http://www.webmd.com/heart-disease/atrial-fibrillation/tc/vagal-maneuvers-for-a-fast-heart-rate-topic-overview
- Wells, P. (2018) Heart Racing: RF vs. Cryoablation. Retrieved from http://www.heartracing.com/patients/rf.vs.cryoablation.asp
- Wikipedia contributors. (2018, Oct 23) Antiarrhythmic Agent. In Wikipedia, The Free Encyclopedia. Retrieved from https://en.wikipedia.org/wiki/Antiarrhythmic_agent
- Wikipedia contributors. (2018, Oct 29) Long QT Syndrome. In Wikipedia, The Free Encyclopedia. Retrieved from https://en.wikipedia.org/wiki/Long_QT_syndrome
- Wikipedia contributors. (2018, Sept 10) Fluoroscopy. In Wikipedia, The Free Encyclopedia. Retrieved from https://en.wikipedia.org/wiki/Fluoroscopy
- Wong, M., Edwards, G., Spence, S., Kalman, J., Kumar, S., Joseph, S. & Morton, J. (2013, Oct 17) Circulation: Arrhythmia and Electrophysiology: Vol. 6, No. 6 Characterization of Catheter – Tissue Contact Force During Epicardial Radiofrequency Ablation in an Ovine Model

- Wu, J., Ding, W., Horie, M. (2016, Jan 27) Journal of Arrhythmia. Molecular pathogenesis of long QT syndrome type 1. Retrieved from https://www.ncbi.nlm.nih.gov/pmc/articles/PMC5063268/ (2019, Oct 3)
- Yaniga, Leslie, RCIS, Cath Lab Pharmacology, Smith Notes, 1998
- Yetkin, U., Ozelci, A., Akyuz, M., Goktogan, T., Yurekli, I. & Gurbuz, A. (2009 Volume 8 Number 2) Surgical Approach To A Giant Post Cardiac Catheterization Pseudoaneurysm After unsuccessful Duplex Ultrasound-Guided Compression. The Internte Journal of Cardiology. Retrieved from http://ispub.com/IJC/8/2/5346
- Yock, Fitzgerald, and Popp, Intravascular Ultrasound, in Scientific American, Science and Medicine, 1995
- Your Pericardium. Retrieved from http://www.cardiachealth.org/your-pericardium
- Zipes, D. & Jalife, J. (2013) Cardiac Electrophysiology: From Cell to Bedside.
- Zipes, D.Z. and Jalife, J., Cardiac Electrophysiology, from Cell to Bedside, published by, Saunders-Elsevier, 5th Edition, 2009
- Петр Иванов (2015, Mar 24) Seldinger Technique. Retrieved from https://www.youtube.com/watch?v=a3pLVr8jShQ&feature=youtu.beguidelines-for-cpr.html

Made in the USA
Las Vegas, NV
27 June 2024

91575322R00234